The Essential Guide to Passing the Board Certified Behavior Analyst® (BCBA) Exam

Rondy Yu, PhD, is an assistant professor of teaching in school psychology and serves as the director of the applied behavior analysis training program at the University of California, Riverside. Dr. Yu is a licensed educational/clinical psychologist, Nationally Certified School Psychologist, and Board Certified Behavior Analyst. He has experience in public schools and nonpublic agencies as a psychologist, behaviorist, clinical supervisor, and researcher. Dr. Yu has presented at professional conferences at the local, national, and international levels on topics related to behavioral consultation, treatment fidelity, and programming for children and adolescents with emotional and behavioral disorders.

Aaron Haddock, PhD, is an associate professor of practice in the Department of Psychology and serves as the director of behavioral health initiatives in the Mosakowski Institute for Public Enterprise at Clark University. Dr. Haddock is a credentialed multiple subject teacher and Nationally Certified School Psychologist. He has experience in school and community settings as a teacher, school psychologist, program evaluator, and consultant. Dr. Haddock's areas of expertise include social–emotional learning, child and adolescent behavioral health, and school-based prevention and intervention.

The Essential Guide to Passing the Board Certified Behavior Analyst® (BCBA) Exam

Rondy Yu, PhD
Aaron Haddock, PhD

 SPRINGER PUBLISHING

Springer Publishing Company, LLC
11 West 42nd Street, New York, NY 10036
www.springerpub.com
connect.springerpub.com/

Acquisitions Editor: Mindy Okura-Marszycki
Compositor: DiacriTech

ISBN: 978-0-8261-8628-7
ebook ISBN: 9780-8261-8629-4
DOI: 10.1891/9780826186294

23 24 25 26 27/ 5 4 3 2 1

The author and the publisher of this Work have made every effort to use sources believed to be reliable to provide information that is accurate and compatible with the standards generally accepted at the time of publication. The author and publisher shall not be liable for any special, consequential, or exemplary damages resulting, in whole or in part, from the readers' use of, or reliance on, the information contained in this book. The publisher has no responsibility for the persistence or accuracy of URLs for external or third-party Internet websites referred to in this publication and does not guarantee that any content on such websites is, or will remain, accurate or appropriate.

Library of Congress Control Number: 2022951052

Contact sales@springerpub.com to receive discount rates on bulk purchases.

Publisher's Note: **New and used products purchased from third-party sellers are not guaranteed for quality, authenticity, or access to any included digital components.**

Printed in the United States of America by Hatteras, Inc.

Tables 1.1–1.4 reprinted with permission. © Behavior Analyst Certification Board®. All rights reserved. Reprinted and/or displayed by permission granted in 2022. The most current version of this document is available at www.BACB.com. Contact the BACB for permission to reprint and/or display this material.

Board Certified Behavior Analyst® is a registered trademark of the Behavior Analyst Certification Board®. Board Certified Behavior Analyst® is used in the title of this publication with limited permission from the Behavior Analyst Certification Board®.

We dedicate this book to the giants upon whose shoulders we stand, and to the current and future generations of behavior analysts striving to make this world a better place for all.

Contents

Contributors

Katina Lambros, PhD, BCBA-D, is an associate professor and director of the school psychology program at San Diego State University. Dr. Lambros is a certified school psychologist and doctoral-level Board Certified Behavior Analyst. She spearheads Project BEAMS (behavioral, emotional, and mental health supports in schools), a large-scale project funded by the Office of Special Education to train school psychologists and special educators to serve diverse students with behavioral, emotional, and mental health challenges in California's public school system. Dr. Lambros's areas of research include school-based mental health and positive behavior supports, evidence-based practices, and culturally responsive services for diverse learners.

Wesley A. Sims, PhD, NCSP, is an assistant professor in school psychology and serves as a core faculty member of the applied behavior analysis training program at the University of California, Riverside. Dr. Sims is a Nationally Certified School Psychologist with training and experience in behavioral assessment and intervention in schools. He is the primary developer of the Direct Behavior Rating-Classroom Management (DBR-CM), a measure of educator classroom management practices using direct behavior rating assessment methodology. Dr. Sims's areas of research include behavioral consultation, classroom management assessment, and implementation science in educational settings.

Preface

▶ OVERALL GOAL OF THE BOOK

Over the past 20 years, the United States witnessed significant growth in behavior analysis—both in terms of the number of behavior analysts in the field and the demand for such professionals serving a range of industries. As the recognition of and need for Board Certified Behavior Analysts® (BCBAs®) continue to rise, so too does the need for high quality training materials—including resources that aim to prepare candidates for the certification exam. The primary goal of this book is to help meet this need.

▶ DISTINGUISHING FEATURES AND LEARNING TOOLS

The BCBA exam is not easy. We know this from the annual pass rates reported by the Behavior Analyst Certification Board® (BACB®). As professionals who care about the preparation of future behavior analysts, we have searched the marketplace for exam prep resources to recommend to students. Unfortunately, we were unable to find a single product that offers all the features we knew could be helpful for candidates in the process of readying themselves for this exam. Rather than wait for a product to come along that would solve our woes, we decided to write this book, which is designed to serve as an effective study guide that explains the newest iteration of the Task List items in a manner that is comprehensive yet concise, engages readers with practice questions designed to enhance learning of the material, provides a full mock exam to simulate the BCBA exam-taking experience, and offers helpful exam prep recommendations (e.g., tips for studying).

▶ INTENDED AUDIENCE

This book is designed for students of behavior analysis and candidates preparing for the BCBA certification exam. However, this book may also be of interest to those preparing for other certifications in behavior analysis (e.g., Board Certified Assistant Behavior Analyst® [BCaBA®]) and educators and field-based supervisors as its content can be extremely useful for teaching. Given the increasing emphasis on evidence-based practice in the field (use of applied behavior analysis in education, healthcare, etc.), this book can prove to be an invaluable resource for many.

▶ CONTENTS

The book begins with a chapter that orients the reader to the BCBA certification process and structure of the exam. Chapter 2 discusses exam preparation, which includes tips for studying, test-taking strategies, and how to use this book. Chapters 3 to 11 cover all essential content areas required for the certification exam, including (a) philosophical underpinnings; (b) concepts and principles; (c) measurement, data display, and interpretation; (d) experimental design; (e) ethics; (f) behavior assessment; (g) behavior-change procedures; (h) selecting and implementing interventions; and (i) personnel supervision and management. Each chapter includes at least one scenario-based practice question accompanied by a breakdown of the process through which we can arrive at the correct solution, as well as a knowledge check consisting of review questions to support content uptake. Chapter 12 offers a full-length practice exam; Chapter 13 presents answers with rationales. Finally, Chapter 14 offers helpful recommendations for those who pass the exam as well as those who have yet to pass the exam.

Dr. Rondy Yu
Dr. Aaron Haddock

Acknowledgments

We would like to thank our colleagues, Dr. Katina Lambros and Dr. Wesley A. Sims, for their contributions to this book. Dr. Lambros gave us thoughtful feedback on the content that helped us to make it better, provided editorial support that enhanced its overall quality, and developed the practice questions found across many of the chapters to engage readers in problem analysis and application of relevant knowledge and skills. Dr. Sims assisted us in the important process of reviewing and developing practice exam questions and their accompanying rationales. We would also like to extend our gratitude to our editorial team at Springer Publishing, including Kirsten Elmer, Mindy Okura-Marszycki, and Rhonda Dearborn, all of whom provided invaluable support throughout the process of getting this book to print. And lastly, we wish to acknowledge our families for inspiring us to do what we do.

About the Book

Chapter 1: The Behavior Analyst Certification Board® (BACB®) is a nonprofit 501(c)(3) corporation that was formed in 1998 to credential behavior analysts. The Board Certified Behavior Analyst® (BCBA®) credential is accredited by the National Commission for Certifying Agencies (NCCA) and functions as a primary certification for the profession in the United States and several other countries, including Canada, Australia, and the United Kingdom. This chapter will provide a general overview of the process for obtaining certification and describe structure of the BCBA exam to give you a sense of what to expect regarding its format and organization.

Chapter 2: Success on standardized tests like the BCBA exam is founded on both mastery of the content and competent test-taking skills. Mastering the content takes planning, time, and consistent and focused study. To facilitate your success in this process and help you get the most out of the time you put into preparing for the exam, this chapter will provide evidence-based recommendations for studying and offer guidance on how to create a study schedule, set goals, and track your progress toward meeting those goals. To help you optimize your performance on the exam, a review is provided featuring relevant test-taking strategies and tips for coping with test anxiety and preparing for exam day. The chapter ends with a brief overview of how to use this book.

Chapter 3: As a discipline, behavior analysis is comprised of the basic science (i.e., experimental analysis of behavior), applied science (i.e., applied behavior analysis), and their philosophy. Behavior analysts must develop an understanding of the philosophical foundations of behavior analysis to understand what they practice and the important concepts that drive how they practice. The purpose of this chapter will be to provide a review of key content related to the philosophical underpinnings of behavior analysis addressed by Task List items A-1 through A-5, including the goals of behavior analysis as a science, the dimensions of applied behavior analysis as defined by Baer et al. (1968), and more.

Chapter 4: Applied behavior analysis can be described as "a science based on the use of learning principles to improve lives" (BACB, 2022). In other words, it is a discipline that focuses on the systematic application of the concepts and principles of behavior analysis to address problems of social significance. Thus, it is critical that behavior analysts develop a solid foundation in their understanding of the concepts and principles of behavior analysis. The purpose of this chapter will be to provide an essential review of Task List items B-1 through B-15, which specifically relate to fundamental concepts and principles for behavior analysts.

Chapter 5: "The systematic measurement of behavior is foundational to the delivery of applied behavior-analytic services" (LeBlanc et al., 2016, p. 77). Behavior analysts frequently engage in the delivery of services to help clients acquire new skills and address problem behavior. To do this effectively, they need to be able to properly measure behavior, graph behavior data, and then interpret the graphed data. The purpose of this chapter will be to provide an essential review of Task List items C-1 through C-11, which specifically relate to the selection and use of measurement systems, various forms of data displays, and interpretation of graphed data.

Chapter 6: It is difficult to overstate the importance of experimentation in the practice of behavior analysis. As noted by Poling and Grosset (1986), "applied behavior analysis relies on experimentation to assess the efficacy of interventions" (p. 7). Through experimentation, which involves the logical configuration of conditions to allow for observation of changes in one physical event to be attributed to that of another, behavior analysts are able to produce evidence of a functional relationship between an intervention and a target response. The purpose of this chapter will be to provide an essential review of Task List items D-1 through D-6, which specifically relate to experimental design.

Chapter 7: "There is nothing more shocking and horrific than the abuse and maltreatment of innocent people who are unable to protect and defend themselves" (Bailey & Burch, 2022, p. 3). To ensure the protection of consumers of behavior analytic services, it is a professional imperative for behavior analysts to practice in a manner that adheres to their profession's Ethics Code. The Code includes an introduction section and six others that include standards related to the various responsibilities of practicing behavior analysts. The purpose of this chapter will be to provide an essential review of Task List items E-1 through E-7, which correspond to sections of the Ethics Code for behavior analysts.

Chapter 8: Behavior analysts are to select, design, and implement assessments before selecting and designing behavior-change interventions (BACB, 2020). This is necessary because assessment is used to capture relevant data that can be used to inform the development of the plan for treatment. It is an essential step of the behavior analytic service delivery process. Various assessment methods can be employed for the purpose of learning about clients' profile of skill strengths and deficits, client preferences, and why problem behavior occurs. The purpose of this chapter will be to provide an essential review of Task List items F-1 through F-9, which specifically relate to behavior assessment.

Chapter 9: Behavior analysts practice applied behavior analysis (ABA), which is a science that uses the behavioral principles derived from decades of experimental analysis to solve problems of behavior that are of social significance. At the core of the responsibilities of a behavior analyst is their role in driving the implementation of behavior-change procedures to improve the lives of others. Thus, it is necessary for practicing behavior analysts to have a strong foundation in the use of behavior-change procedures. The purpose of this chapter will be to provide an essential review of Task List items G-1 through G-22, which cover various behavior-change procedures employed by behavior analysts.

Chapter 10: Behavior analysts must not only be familiar with behavior-change procedures, but also be able to appropriately select and implement them to effectively change socially significant behavior. The research literature supports the practice of using assessment data to strategically match interventions to problems of behavior, as well as the need for implementing interventions with integrity. Through the precise selection and delivery of interventions, behavior analysts can maximize outcomes for their clients. The purpose of this chapter will be to provide an essential review of Task List items H-1 through H-9, which specifically relate to selecting and implementing behavior-change interventions.

Chapter 11: "The field of behavior analysis relies heavily on supervision to shape and maintain the skills of professionals" (Sellers et al., 2016, p. 299). Behavior analysts are frequently engaged in the work of supervising direct support staff to ensure clients receive high quality services. To effectively provide supervision, they must be able to competently train supervisees, support them in their work, and motivate them to perform at their very best. Unlike the last version (i.e., 4th edition) of the Task List, the current iteration (i.e., 5th edition) includes an entire section focused on the development of the skills required for effective supervision. The purpose of this chapter will be to provide an essential review of Task List items I-1 through I-8, which specifically relate to personnel supervision and management.

Chapter 14: Passing the exam and acquiring your board certification is a good start, but it is certainly not the end of your journey to becoming a competent and effective behavior analyst. The field is continuously evolving and demands that behavior analysts keep pace to maintain their competence by actively engaging in professional development activities. This chapter will provide an essential overview of the range of options for continuing your education and further enhancing your professional knowledge and skills. In addition, recommendations are provided for those in the process of seeking a job as a behavior analyst, as well as those who have taken the exam but have yet to pass.

REFERENCES

Baer, D. M., Wolf, M. M., & Risley, T. R. (1968). Some current dimensions of applied behavior analysis. *Journal of Applied Behavior Analysis, 1*(1), 91.

Bailey, J., & Burch, M. (2022). *Ethics for behavior analysts.* Routledge.

Behavior Analyst Certification Board. (2020). *Ethics code for behavior analysts.* Author.

Behavior Analyst Certification Board. (2022). *BACB fact sheet.* Author.

LeBlanc, L. A., Raetz, P. B., Sellers, T. P., & Carr, J. E. (2016). A proposed model for selecting measurement procedures for the assessment and treatment of problem behavior. *Behavior Analysis in Practice, 9*(1), 77–83. https://doi.org/10.1007/s40617-015-0063-2

Poling, A., & Grossett, D. (1986). Basic research designs in applied behavior analysis. In A. Poling & R. W. Fuqua (Eds.), *Research methods in applied behavior analysis* (pp. 7–27). Springer.

Sellers, T. P., Alai-Rosales, S., & MacDonald, R. P. (2016). Taking full responsibility: The ethics of supervision in behavior analytic practice. *Behavior Analysis in Practice, 9*(4), 299–308. https://doi.org/10.1007/s40617-016-0144-x

Pass Guarantee

If you use this resource to prepare for your exam and do not pass, you may return it for a refund of your full purchase price, excluding tax, shipping, and handling. To receive a refund, return your product along with a copy of your exam score report and original receipt showing purchase of new product (not used). Product must be returned and received within 180 days of the original purchase date. Refunds will be issued within 8 weeks from acceptance and approval. One offer per person and address. This offer is valid for U.S. residents only. Void where prohibited. To initiate a refund, please contact Customer Service at csexamprep@springerpub.com.

Overview of the Certification Process

The Behavior Analyst Certification Board (BACB) is a nonprofit 501(c)(3) corporation that was formed in 1998 to credential behavior analysts. The Board Certified Behavior Analyst (BCBA) credential is accredited by the National Commission for Certifying Agencies (NCCA) and functions as a primary certification for the profession in the U.S. and several other countries, including Canada, Australia, and the U.K. This chapter will provide a general overview of the process for obtaining certification and describe structure of the BCBA exam to give you a sense of what to expect regarding its format and organization.

> ## ▶ LEARNING OBJECTIVES
>
> *The purpose of this chapter is to help you:*
> - ■ Review the requirements of the qualifying training components for Board Certified Behavior Analysts® (BCBAs®).
> - ■ Assess your eligibility status for the BCBA exam.
> - ■ Identify the next steps required to submit your initial application for certification.
> - ■ Review the structure and scoring of the exam.

▶ THE BOARD CERTIFIED BEHAVIOR ANALYST CERTIFICATION PROCESS

MEETING DEGREE, COURSEWORK, AND EXPERIENCE REQUIREMENTS

Prior to submitting your application for initial certification, it is necessary that you meet the current eligibility requirements. This includes obtaining a qualifying degree and successfully completing qualifying coursework and supervised experience requirements.

Qualifying Degree

This is a graduate-level degree in a relevant subject from a qualifying institution. In the United States, this means a master's or doctoral degree in behavior analysis, education, or psychology from a college, university, or program that is accredited by the Council for Higher Education.

- ■ If you are unsure of the acceptability of the subject of your degree, further details on this topic can be found at www.bacb.com/acceptable-degree-definitions.
- ■ If you are unsure of the accreditation status of your institution, simply search for it at www.chea.org. If it is listed, it is accredited.
- ■ If, after reviewing these resources, you are still uncertain, the Behavior Analyst Certification Board® (BACB®) offers a degree evaluation service that can be found at www.bacb.com/preliminary-degree-evaluation.

Qualifying Coursework

This is graduate level coursework from a qualifying institution for which you received academic credit. A passing grade ("C" or better; "pass" or equivalent for pass/fail grading) must be earned for each course to be counted. Table 1.1 summarizes the content that the qualifying coursework must cover, along with the minimum hours for each area:

Table 1.1 Required hours of coursework by content area

Content Areas	Required Hours
BACB Ethics Code and Code-Enforcement System; Professionalism	45
Philosophical Underpinnings; Concepts and Principles	90
Measurement, Data Display, and Interpretation; Experimental Design	45
Behavior Assessment	45
Behavior-Change Procedures; Selecting and Implementing Interventions	60
Personnel Supervision and Management	30
Total	315

Note: Content area 1 (BACB Ethics Code . . .) must be taught in one or more "freestanding courses" (i.e., courses with a majority focus on a single content area). For Content area 2 (Philosophical Underpinnings . . .), 45 hours of Concepts and Principles must be taught in a freestanding course. Content area 3 (Measurement . . .) must be taught in one freestanding course.

Copyright © All Rights Reserved. 2022, BACB®. This information was adapted from the *BCBA Handbook*. The latest version of this handbook is available at www.bacb.com.

- If you completed all your coursework through an Association for Behavior Analysis International (ABAI) verified course sequence (VCS) for the BACB, then the qualifying coursework requirement will be met.
- If you are uncertain about the VCS status of your institution, search for it on ABAI's directory of verified programs at https://abainternational.org/vcs/directory.aspx.
- If you completed coursework that covers behavior analytic content outside of a VCS, you can request that the Dean, Chair, or VCS Coordinator at your institution complete a Nonverified Course Content Attestation available at www.bacb.com/wp-content/course-content-attestation and submit the document with your application for certification. You may also want to consider submitting a request for a preliminary review of your coursework by the BACB; the application for this service is available at www.bacb.com/coursework-evaluation-application.

Qualifying Supervised Experience

This is a defined practical supervised experience in behavior analysis. Fulfilling this requirement means you have completed a supervision contract with one or more qualified supervisors and accrued at least the minimum number of supervised experience hours in behavior analytic activities *within 5 consecutive years*. Remember, only hours accrued after you have attended your first class session of your first qualifying course in behavior analysis can be counted to meet this requirement!

A qualified supervisor is (a) an active BCBA, not subject to disciplinary sanction, who has been certified for at least 1 year and meets continuing education requirements for supervision; (b) an active BCBA, not subject to disciplinary sanction, who has been certified for less than 1 year but receives monthly consultation from a qualified supervisor and meets continuing education requirements for supervision; (c) a psychologist certified in Behavioral and Cognitive Psychology by the American Board of Professional Psychology (ABPP) who was tested in behavior analysis; or (d) an authorized instructor of a VCS.

Experience hours are classified as supervised fieldwork (SF) or concentrated supervised fieldwork (CSF). An applicant can accrue experience hours under just one type (e.g., only SF) or both (i.e., SF and CSF). If you submit hours under both, you will need to do a little bit of math—CSF is worth 1.33 times the value of SF (e.g., 1 hour of CSF = 1.33 hours of SF). The requirements for each type of experience are provided in Table 1.2:

Table 1.2 Supervision requirements by experience type

	Supervised Fieldwork	Concentrated Supervised Fieldwork
Fieldwork hours required	2,000	1,500
Fieldwork hours that can be counted in a supervisory period	20 to 130 hours	20 to 130 hours
Required number of contacts with supervisor in a supervisory period	4	6
Required number of times supervisor must observe you with a client in a supervisory period	1	1
Minimum percentage of hours spent in supervision in a supervisory period, with no more than 50% in group supervision	5	10

Note: Supervisory period = 1 calendar month. A minimum of 60% of the hours accrued must have been spent engaged in *unrestricted activities* (what a behavior analyst does, assessment, developing behavior-change programs, etc.); a maximum of 40% of the hours accrued can be from *restricted activities* (i.e., what an interventionist does; delivering instructional procedures).

- You can use the BACB Certificant Registry available at www.bacb.com/find-a-certificant to find/verify the qualifications and status of supervisors.
- Experience requirements may be subject to change, and it's your job to remain current on what they are to ensure that you meet them for certification. Any changes made are published in the BACB newsletters and summarized in a table available at www.bacb.com/upcoming-changes.
- Ensure that you have all required documents. These include a copy of your (a) signed supervision contract, (b) documentation of fieldwork (i.e., detailed record of your qualifying experiences), and (c) completed monthly and final fieldwork verification forms.

OTHER PATHWAYS TO BOARD CERTIFIED BEHAVIOR ANALYST CERTIFICATION

The process described previously is referred to as *Pathway 2* for meeting eligibility requirements by the BACB and serves as the most traveled path to certification. There are, however, three other options (i.e., pathways) that the BACB offers:

Pathway 1

If you obtained a master's or doctoral degree from a training program accredited by ABAI, then you have met the qualifying degree and coursework requirements. Now it's just a matter of also meeting the *qualifying supervised experience* requirements.

Pathway 3

This pathway requires the same degree and supervised experience requirements of *Pathways 1 and 2*. But unlike those other pathways, this one eliminates the need for *qualifying coursework* and instead requires that you, within 5 consecutive years, obtained at least 3 years of full-time work experience as a faculty member at a qualifying institution during which you taught at least five graduate level behavior analytic-focused courses in at least two content areas (i.e., applied behavior analysis, concepts/principles, ethics for behavior analysis, and single-case research). Additionally, at any point in your career, you must have been named as the first, second, or corresponding author of a behavior analytic article involving at least one experimental evaluation that was published in a high quality, peer-reviewed journal (e.g., *Journal of Applied Behavior Analysis*).

Pathway 4

The requirements of this pathway overlap the least with those described for *Pathways 1, 2,* and *3*. This requirement is for those of you who earned a doctoral degree at least 10 years ago from a qualifying institution, and since then accrued at least 10 years of experience practicing behavior analysis under a relevant national or state/provincial credential. To meet the *qualifying supervised experience* requirement of this path, you will also need to have accrued at least 500 hours under a qualified supervisor after you have already accrued at least 10 years of postdoctoral practice experience in the field. At least 5% of the 500 experience hours must be from supervision.

Once you've met the requirements under at least one of the four pathways, the next step is to complete your initial certification application!

SUBMITTING THE CERTIFICATION APPLICATION

Currently, the certification application can be accessed through the BACB Certification Gateway at https://gateway.bacb.com/Account/Login.aspx. Look for the "Certification Applications" tab and follow the on-screen instructions. Once the online application is completed, you will need to pay the application fee and provide the BACB with the supplemental documents listed in Table 1.3.

Table 1.3 Supplemental documents required by certification pathway

Certification Pathway	Supplemental Documentation
1	▪ Official Transcript(s) ▪ Final Experience Verification Form(s) ▪ Nonverified Course Content Attestation (If Applicable)
2	▪ Official Transcript(s) ▪ Final Experience Verification Form(s) ▪ Nonverified Course Content Attestation (If Applicable)
3	▪ Official Transcript(s) ▪ Final Experience Verification Form(s) ▪ Letter From Department Chair re: Faculty Appointment ▪ Syllabi for Relevant Courses Taught ▪ Copy of Published Behavior Analytic Article
4	▪ Official Transcript(s) ▪ Final Experience Verification Form(s) ▪ Curriculum Vitae ▪ Signed Attestation(s) From Current and Former Employers ▪ Proof of Professional Credentials

Note: Supplemental documentation must be submitted within 90 days of the application fee payment.
Copyright © All Rights Reserved. 2022, BACB®. This information was adapted from the *BCBA Handbook*. The latest version of this handbook is available at www.bacb.com.

After you submit your online application, application fee, and supplemental documents for your certification pathway, the BACB will need to review your application and supplemental documents to determine whether you meet the requirements for certification. This process can take up to 45 days—or longer if there are any problems in your application—so be patient. Assuming everything is in order and you do indeed meet eligibility requirements, the next step will be to schedule an appointment to take the BCBA exam!

▶ STRUCTURE OF THE EXAM

The BCBA exam is a computer-based exam administered at Pearson VUE test centers. The questions are presented in multiple-choice format and cover the current Fifth Edition of the Task List items for BCBA. Table 1.4 provides a breakdown of the content areas and number of questions allocated to each on the exam.

Table 1.4 Number of exam items by content area

Content Areas	Number of Questions
Philosophical Underpinnings	6
Concepts and Principles	32
Measurement, Data Display, and Interpretation	21
Experimental Design	12
Ethics	18
Behavior Assessment	18
Behavior-Change Procedures	35
Selecting and Implementing Interventions	16
Personnel Supervision and Management	17
Total	175

During the exam, you will be presented with 185 questions (not 175) because there are 10 extra pilot questions that are not scored. There are four answer options for each question. Some questions may involve opening an "exhibit" or "figure." For a sneak peek at what the test screens will look like and practice navigating through them, Pearson VUE offers a computer-based testing demonstration that can be accessed at https://wsr.pearsonvue.com/demo.

If you have a disability as defined by the Americans with Disabilities Act (ADA), you can submit a request for testing accommodations to the BACB at www.bacb.com/accommodations-documentation. The review process for a request for this can take as long as 2 weeks—or more if the BACB requires additional supporting documentation—so ensure that any such request is submitted at least 15 days before the date of the exam. Possible accommodations can include extra time for completing the exam, access to a scribe/reader, use of a separate testing room, and so on. Pearson VUE test centers are wheelchair accessible, and the text presented on the computer screen during the exam can be enlarged.

SCORING OF THE EXAM

You may be wondering, "How well do I need to do to pass the exam?" Well, the BACB uses the Modified-Angoff method to score the exam. This means that a panel of experts went through the exam questions and, for each one, provided an estimate of the probability that a "minimally competent" examinee will answer correctly. These estimates were then used to determine what the minimum passing score would be.

After you complete the exam, you will receive a scaled score (i.e., a number between 0 and 500 representing the number of questions you answered correctly). A scaled score of 400 or higher is a passing score on the exam!

Figure 1.1 Exam score range.

So now that you know that minimum score is for passing, let's focus on more important matters—like implementing the strategies outlined in the next chapter that will help maximally prepare you for the exam.

▶ CONCLUSION

This chapter focused on orienting you to the certification process. To that end, we provided some background information about the BACB and reviewed the process for obtaining the BCBA certification. Because the process for acquiring certification is rather involved, we included information about meeting degree, coursework, and supervised experience requirements; the multiple pathways to obtaining certification; and preparing and submitting the application. And to give you a general idea of what to expect on the exam, we also described the structure and scoring of the BCBA exam. We hope that, at this point, you have a clear understanding of what the steps are in this process and can plan to move forward in meeting one of the certification pathways.

BIBLIOGRAPHY

Behavior Analyst Certification Board. (2021a). *BACB annual data report*. https://www.bacb.com/bacb-certificant-annual-report-data/

Behavior Analyst Certification Board. (2021b). *BCBA 2022 eligibility requirements*. https://www.bacb.com/bcba-2022-eligibility-guide

Behavior Analyst Certification Board. (2021c). *Information about scoring*. https://www.bacb.com/examination-information/information-about-scoring/

Behavior Analyst Certification Board. (2022). *BCBA handbook*. https://www.bacb.com/bcba-handbook

Clauser, B. E., Margolis, M. J., & Case, S. M. (2006). Testing for licensure and certification in the professions. *Educational Measurement, 4*, 701–731.

Pearson VUE. (2021). *BACB certification testing*. https://home.pearsonvue.com/bacb

Preparing for the Exam

Success on standardized tests like the BCBA exam is founded on both mastery of the content and competent test-taking skills. Mastering the content takes planning, time, and consistent and focused study. To facilitate your success in this process and help you get the most out of the time you put into preparing for the exam, this chapter will provide evidence-based recommendations for studying and offer guidance on how to create a study schedule, set goals, and your progress toward meeting those goals. To help you optimize your performance on the exam, you'll also find a review of relevant test-taking strategies and tips for coping with test anxiety and preparing for exam day. The chapter ends with a brief overview of how to use this book.

> ## ▶ LEARNING OBJECTIVES
>
> *After reading this chapter, you will be able to:*
> - Apply recommended practices for effective studying.
> - Develop a study plan with SMART goals.
> - Evaluate and implement test-taking strategies for multiple-choice questions.
> - Describe the structure and scoring method of the exam.
> - Describe the structure of this book and common notations used.

You've worked hard to meet those Board Certified Behavior Analyst® (BCBA®) eligibility requirements and now have one final task: passing the certification exam. Congratulations! Give yourself a pat on the back and take a moment to let that sink in. BCBAs help people around the world live more fulfilling and successful lives every day, and you're about to join their ranks.

To help you prepare for the exam, this chapter reviews research-backed, time-tested studying tips and test-taking strategies that can improve your performance. The studying tips include recommendations for making the most out of the time you have to study, creating a strategic study plan, setting goals for studying, and monitoring your progress. Test-taking strategies include effective techniques for tackling multiple-choice questions, as well as common mistakes to avoid.

▶ TIPS FOR STUDYING

CULTIVATE A GROWTH MINDSET

B. F. Skinner may have conceptualized thoughts and feelings as behaviors (i.e., "private events"), but he never denied their importance—and neither should you! How you're thinking and feeling about preparing for and taking this exam are critical.

Take a minute to ask yourself . . . are you optimistic, pessimistic, neutral about studying for and taking the exam? Do you expect to do well and pass or are you concerned that you won't? How do you feel about taking high-stakes exams like this? Is it an exciting challenge, a daunting task, or perhaps something in between? What's your previous experience with exams like this? How are those previous test-taking experiences informing your approach to this exam? Do you expect that you'll be able to set aside enough time to study and prepare or are you concerned that other responsibilities or procrastination will get in the way? Does studying for the exam feel like a chore or like an opportunity to develop real mastery of your field?

Let's try this activity: Fill in the following table with your response (in the second column) to each of the six questions posed (in the first column). Using the example responses and their interpretations (in columns 3 and 4), determine whether your responses support a growth mindset. If you identify any negative mindset responses, check out the rightmost column for example statements that reframe negative mindset responses.

Table 2.1 Growth mindset activity

Question to Ask Yourself	Your Response: *Take a Few Moments and Write in Your Answers Here*	Example Responses	Does Your Response Support a Growth Mindset?	Let's Reframe!
How do you feel about taking high-stakes exams like this?		Response A: *I am super nervous. I have heard this is a hard test.*	This is a common response and one that is normal under the circumstances but does not show the potential for growth and improvement.	*Pass rates show this is a challenging exam, but with the right preparation, I have a high chance of passing.* *Test-taking is a learned skill that can improve over time and with the right preparation and study plan. I look forward to this challenge!*
		Response B: *I dread taking these types of exams. For real.*	*No.* An honest response but somewhat pessimistic and "fixed" in nature with no space for future change in outlook.	
		Response C: *I am pretty good at taking high stakes tests and will be ready.*	*Yes.* Sounds like you are up to this challenge. You are all set to put in the work and be ready to pass.	
What's your previous experience with taking exams like this?		Response A: *I tend to stress about exams, but manage to do okay on them.*	*Somewhat.* This response holds some tension about the experience but also offers a semi-positive outcome.	*I embrace the anticipation and nervousness that comes with studying, as I know it is a part of high-stakes testing. Some test anxiety can even improve performance!* *Despite having negative test-taking experiences in the past, I know that with the right preparation and study plan, I can set myself up for a better testing experience.*
		Response B: *I never do well on tests like these—they don't capture all that I know.*	*No.* The word "never" does not leave any wiggle room for a new, improved experience.	
		Response C: *My previous experience has shown that I can do well on exams.*	*Yes.* You are in the right frame of mind, but still must put in the work in order to be ready for this exam!	

(continued)

Table 2.1 Growth mindset activity (*continued*)

Question to Ask Yourself	Your Response: *Take a Few Moments and Write in Your Answers Here*	Example Responses	Does Your Response Support a Growth Mindset?	Let's Reframe!
How are those previous test-taking experiences informing your approach to this exam?		Response A: *I cannot stop thinking about other times I have studied and still done poorly.* Response B: *I know that it is a long shot that I will pass this exam. My colleague took it three times.* Response C: *My previous experiences give me the confidence to believe I can study and will pass this exam.*	*No.* This is a "fixed and narrowly focused" view that you are allowing to extend to all future test-taking experiences. *No.* Just because others have had a particular experience with this exam, does not mean you will have the same one. *Yes.* Your previous experiences are setting the stage for a positive outcome, but you still must execute your study plan to be ready for this exam!	*Previous failures are an opportunity to grow in new ways. My increased study effort will make me a better service provider no matter what.* *Yes, this is a hard test, but my effort and my mindset can really contribute to my performance. LEARNING the material is the true goal.*
Do you expect that you'll be able to set aside enough time to prepare or could other responsibilities or procrastination get in the way?		Response A: *I am just not sure I have the time, but I will plan the best I can.* Response B: *I am very a very busy person. I cannot really envision having enough time to study properly.* Response C: *Yes, I will carefully plan my calendar for the next months to ensure I have enough time.*	*Somewhat.* This honest answer acknowledges the limited time we all have as professionals, but also indicated the need to plan accordingly. *No.* This offers a limited and fixed view of your calendar with little room for expansion and creative scheduling. *Yes.* You are all set; you just need an open calendar and your highlighter!	*Despite being busy, I will find windows of time (e.g., wake up 1 hour earlier, set aside every Saturday morning) to make sure I have study time.* *I am a very creative person, and I can certainly find time in my schedule to do fun things, so I am sure I can find the time I need to study.*

(continued)

Table 2.1 Growth mindset activity (*continued*)

Question to Ask Yourself	Your Response: *Take a Few Moments and Write in Your Answers Here*	Example Responses	Does Your Response Support a Growth Mindset?	Let's Reframe!
Do you expect to do well and pass or are you concerned that you won't?		Response A: *I expect that I might not pass and will have to take it again.* Response B: *I am not sure what to expect, I have heard such varied outcomes about this exam.* Response C: *I expect to do well on this exam.*	*No.* This sets up the expectation of failure right from the beginning. *No.* This view leaves you in a very unsure space with no real direction on how to move forward. *Yes.* Go ahead and put your positive vibes out there! Get started on the execution of your study plan!	*I will have to push through my fear of failure and try some new ways of studying and exam preparation. I expect I will have to put in the time, effort, and energy to adequately prepare for this exam.*
Does studying for the exam feel like a chore or like an opportunity to develop real mastery of your field?		Response A: *Yes, it feels like just another thing on my already full plate.* Response B: *It feels like a lot of work, but hopefully will pay off.* Response C: *Studying for this exam will ensure I am on the cutting edge of my field.*	*No.* This perspective does not allow for the connection to future growth in your work. *Somewhat.* This response acknowledges the work involved in studying, but also some future benefit. *Yes.* Let's get started studying!	*Studying for this exam will better prepare me for the challenging work I will face as a BCBA. I enjoy opportunities to further develop my skills and, with focused effort, I can be prepared for this exam too!*

BCBA, Board Certified Behavior Analyst.

Making note of these thoughts and feelings and, if appropriate, challenging them or reframing them can help set yourself up for success. Cultivating a growth mindset that appreciates how success is a function of hard work, sound strategies, and accurate feedback can be empowering and motivating and enhance your ability to study, learn, and pass the test. When you have a growth mindset, you understand that you'll face setbacks and challenges, but that these are markers of progress and part of a process that will ultimately bring you success.

BEGIN BY TAKING A PRACTICE TEST

At the outset, it can be helpful to take the practice exam located in Chapter 12 to obtain baseline information on your readiness for the exam, identify any areas of weakness that will require additional focus, and get a sense of how the exam is organized and what to expect. Taking practice exams is also a helpful way to frontload the material that you will be learning more about as you make your way through each chapter. They add another learning format and are a great study tool that can be used to enhance the fluency in which you apply what you have learned to various situations. Practice tests require you to process and review data so you can continue to tailor and appropriately sequence your strategic study plan. Lastly, these practice opportunities can reduce anxiety as you become more familiar with the test format. With each administration of a practice exam, make note of the types of questions you struggled with (definition or application) and how long it took you to complete the exam.

DEVELOP AND STICK TO A STUDY SCHEDULE

As the title of this guide makes clear, it's not focused on helping you take the BCBA exam—it's focused on helping you PASS! While we've strived to provide a study guide that is both comprehensive and succinct, there's no getting around the fact that there is a lot of content to master to be ready for the exam. As with any significant undertaking, that requires a solid plan. We recommend you create a study schedule with goals and target completion dates for each goal or section of the study guide.

While it's tempting to plan to study when you can squeeze it in, this rarely works well. There's likely always something else you would prefer to do when you have some time to study—which leads to procrastination. Research on procrastination among college students indicates its prevalence to be somewhere between 25% and 50% of students or even higher. So don't deceive yourself when it comes to delaying studying for the exam. Instead, be proactive and add studying on a consistent basis to your schedule just like any other task you need to complete. When you make regular appointments with yourself to study, you're more likely to do it and this will help you get into a rhythm which, in time, will become a habit.

To help yourself prevent procrastination and get into a rhythm, use self-management techniques to give yourself instant consequences that will thwart the consequences supporting procrastination. For instance, consider giving yourself a reward of some kind after you study as planned. It doesn't have to be huge, just something significant enough to facilitate your motivation. Take a minute now to think about how you might reward yourself each time you stick to your study schedule (e.g., time to watch your favorite show, check social media, or play a video game). Alternatively, you may find that you're more responsive to punishment. If so, consider fining yourself a dollar or two paid to your favorite charity each time you fail to study for the exam when you planned to.

In order to make the most of your study sessions, proactively remove all potential distractions from your environment. Paramount here is to turn off your smartphone, or at the very least turn off all notifications. Research has shown that continuously taking little breaks to respond to texts or check social media negatively impacts studying efficiency and effectiveness. Instead of continually being distracted by your phone, turn it off and then reward yourself with a certain amount of time on your phone after you've successfully completed your study session.

The first step in creating a study schedule is to determine what is realistic given your current responsibilities, commitments, and goals. Determine precisely when you can study each week. Write down the days and times in your calendar. If your schedule seems too full to fit in as many study sessions as you'd like or need, have a critical look at what is getting in the way. Are there activities you could take off your schedule to create more space for studying?

Once you've set a study schedule, do your best to adhere to it. You may find that you need to make adjustments to get it dialed in. That's okay. What's critical is that you're setting aside time on a regular basis to study and getting into a rhythm.

We generally recommend studying for the BCBA exam from 10 to 20 hours a week for 3 to 4 months. The Essential Guide strategic planner aims for users to master one content area each week. You can modify the strategic planner in Table 2.2 to fit your timeframe.

Table 2.2 Strategic planner: Study schedule and SMART goals worksheet

Week 1: __/__/__					
Actions	Score	Completion Goal	Completion Date	Review by Goal	Date Reviewed
Study Task Items ___ - ___	N/A	__/__/__	__/__/__	__/__/__ __/__/__ __/__/__	__/__/__ __/__/__ __/__/__
Practice Test #		__/__/__	__/__/__	__/__/__ __/__/__	__/__/__ __/__/__
Week 2: __/__/__					
Actions	Score	Completion Goal	Completion Date	Review by Goal	Date Reviewed
Study Task Items ___ - ___	N/A	__/__/__	__/__/__	__/__/__ __/__/__ __/__/__	__/__/__ __/__/__ __/__/__
Practice Test #		__/__/__	__/__/__	__/__/__ __/__/__	__/__/__ __/__/__
Week 3: __/__/__					
Actions	Score	Completion Goal	Completion Date	Review by Goal	Date Reviewed
Study Task Items ___ - ___	N/A	__/__/__	__/__/__	__/__/__ __/__/__ __/__/__	__/__/__ __/__/__ __/__/__
Practice Test #		__/__/__	__/__/__	__/__/__ __/__/__	__/__/__ __/__/__
Week 4: __/__/__					
Actions	Score	Completion Goal	Completion Date	Review by Goal	Date Reviewed
Study Task Items ___ - ___	N/A	__/__/__	__/__/__	__/__/__ __/__/__ __/__/__	__/__/__ __/__/__ __/__/__
Practice Test #		__/__/__	__/__/__	__/__/__ __/__/__	__/__/__ __/__/__
Week 5: __/__/__					
Actions	Score	Completion Goal	Completion Date	Review by Goal	Date Reviewed
Study Task Items ___ - ___	N/A	__/__/__	__/__/__	__/__/__ __/__/__ __/__/__	__/__/__ __/__/__ __/__/__
Practice Test #		__/__/__	__/__/__	__/__/__ __/__/__	__/__/__ __/__/__
Week 6: __/__/__					
Actions	Score	Completion Goal	Completion Date	Review by Goal	Date Reviewed
Study Task Items ___ - ___	N/A	__/__/__	__/__/__	__/__/__ __/__/__ __/__/__	__/__/__ __/__/__ __/__/__

(continued)

Table 2.2 Strategic planner: Study schedule and SMART goals worksheet (*continued*)

Actions	Score	Completion Goal	Completion Date	Review by Goal	Date Reviewed
Practice Test #		_/_/_	_/_/_	_/_/_ _/_/_	_/_/_ _/_/_
Week 7: _/_/_					
Actions	Score	Completion Goal	Completion Date	Review by Goal	Date Reviewed
Study Task Items ___ - ___	N/A	_/_/_	_/_/_	_/_/_ _/_/_ _/_/_	_/_/_ _/_/_ _/_/_
Practice Test #		_/_/_	_/_/_	_/_/_ _/_/_	_/_/_ _/_/_
Week 8: _/_/_					
Actions	Score	Completion Goal	Completion Date	Review by Goal	Date Reviewed
Study Task Items ___ - ___	N/A	_/_/_	_/_/_	_/_/_ _/_/_ _/_/_	_/_/_ _/_/_ _/_/_
Practice Test #		_/_/_	_/_/_	_/_/_ _/_/_	_/_/_ _/_/_
Week 9: _/_/_					
Actions	Score	Completion Goal	Completion Date	Review by Goal	Date Reviewed
Study Task Items ___ - ___	N/A	_/_/_	_/_/_	_/_/_ _/_/_ _/_/_	_/_/_ _/_/_ _/_/_
Practice Test #		_/_/_	_/_/_	_/_/_ _/_/_	_/_/_ _/_/_
Week 10: _/_/_					
Actions	Score	Completion Goal	Completion Date	Review by Goal	Date Reviewed
Study Task Items ___ - ___	N/A	_/_/_	_/_/_	_/_/_ _/_/_ _/_/_	_/_/_ _/_/_ _/_/_
Practice Test #		_/_/_	_/_/_	_/_/_ _/_/_	_/_/_ _/_/_
Week 11: _/_/_					
Actions	Score	Completion Goal	Completion Date	Review by Goal	Date Reviewed
Practice Test #	N/A	_/_/_	_/_/_	_/_/_ _/_/_ _/_/_	_/_/_ _/_/_ _/_/_
		_/_/_	_/_/_	_/_/_ _/_/_	_/_/_ _/_/_
Week 12: _/_/_					
Actions	Score	Completion Goal	Completion Date	Review by Goal	Date Reviewed
Study Task Items ___ - ___	N/A	_/_/_	_/_/_	_/_/_ _/_/_ _/_/_	_/_/_ _/_/_ _/_/_

(*continued*)

Table 2.2 Strategic planner: Study schedule and SMART goals worksheet (*continued*)

| Practice Test # | | _/_/_ | _/_/_ | _/_/_
 _/_/_ | _/_/_
 _/_/_ |

Week 13: _/_/_

Actions	Score	Completion Goal	Completion Date	Review by Goal	Date Reviewed
Study Task Items __ - __	N/A	_/_/_	_/_/_	_/_/_ _/_/_ _/_/_	_/_/_ _/_/_ _/_/_
Practice Test #		_/_/_	_/_/_	_/_/_ _/_/_	_/_/_ _/_/_

Week 14: _/_/_

Actions	Score	Completion Goal	Completion Date	Review by Goal	Date Reviewed
Study Task Items __ - __	N/A	_/_/_	_/_/_	_/_/_ _/_/_ _/_/_	_/_/_ _/_/_ _/_/_
Practice Test #		_/_/_	_/_/_	_/_/_ _/_/_	_/_/_ _/_/_

Week 15: _/_/_

Actions	Score	Completion Goal	Completion Date	Review by Goal	Date Reviewed
Study Task Items __ - __	N/A	_/_/_	_/_/_	_/_/_ _/_/_ _/_/_	_/_/_ _/_/_ _/_/_
Practice Test #		_/_/_	_/_/_	_/_/_ _/_/_	_/_/_ _/_/_

Week 16: _/_/_

Actions	Score	Completion Goal	Completion Date	Review by Goal	Date Reviewed
Study Task Items __ - __	N/A	_/_/_	_/_/_	_/_/_ _/_/_ _/_/_	_/_/_ _/_/_ _/_/_
Practice Test #		_/_/_	_/_/_	_/_/_ _/_/_	_/_/_ _/_/_

USE DISTRIBUTED AND INTERLEAVED STUDYING

Spreading out your studying over time is significantly more effective than cramming. Research has documented how engaging with material to be learned multiple times and in different forms over a period of time engenders a distributed-practice effect that greatly enhances long-term retention of information. Moreover, studies have shown that incorporating longer, rather than shorter, lags between revisiting material to be learned is also more effective.

Using a study schedule will enable you to take advantage of the distributed-practice effect and prevent the human tendency to procrastinate and then steadily increase studying as the exam approaches, which is less effective. Instead, you want to study consistently in shorter, intensive study sessions over a longer period of time. It is especially helpful if you're able to study a section and then take some time away from it (e.g., 2 weeks) before reviewing it. This is known as spaced practice, and it's an incredibly effective approach to enhancing your ability to remember information for the test. When you review previously studied material just as you're about to start forgetting it strengthens memory and facilitates your ability to retain the information. This is why it's important to keep track of when you studied what in your study schedule.

Based on when you last studied the material, use your strategic planner to set dates to review the material again at increasingly spaced intervals in time. Specify target completion dates for each section of the study guide in the "Completion Goal" column of your study schedule, then note the date when you finished studying the section in the "Completion Date" column. Based on this date, set a goal to revisit this section of the study guide later (e.g., 2 weeks) and note it in the "Review by Goal" column. When you review the section, note the date in your study schedule in the "Date Reviewed" column. Aim to increase the lags between revisiting each section of the study guide over time.

A related effective technique is to alternate studying different kinds of items or content (i.e., interleaved practice). This is in contrast to focusing on one subtopic at a time (i.e., blocked studying). Given the interrelation between concepts and skills covered in different items within a section, alternating study of the items within a section and across sections will enable you to take advantage of interleaved studying. This is one of the greatest advantages of using a study schedule: It enables you to plan when you'll study certain items as well as when you'll revisit those items for maximum effect.

CREATE SMART GOALS

Creating clear goals that are actionable and effective can help you stick to your study schedule. At first, it can be difficult to know how long it will take you to learn all of the material you need to master to be successful on the exam; however, as you become more familiar with the material, you'll get a better sense of what's reasonable. It's also important to identify content areas that may require more time to achieve competency so that you can allot additional time to master those areas.

In your training as a behavior analyst, you've learned how important it is to set SMART goals for clients. Do the same for yourself. To develop clear and attainable goals, ensure each goal is Specific, Measurable, Achievable, Relevant, and Time-bound.

REINFORCING STUDYING BEHAVIOR

Studying for the BCBA exam affords an excellent opportunity to practice self-management strategies. As we discuss in our review of Task List item G-20, self-management is the personal application of behavior change tactics to produce a desired change in behavior. You can use self-management strategies to develop study habits, achieve study tasks and goals, and prepare for the exam efficiently and effectively. Here are some ways you can incorporate self-management strategies into your approach to preparing for the exam:

- Schedule appointments with yourself to study accompanied by reminders on your phone.
- Dedicate a specific place to studying.
- When the time comes, sit down in your dedicated place and take out your study materials to create motivation to study.
- Remove all items from the environment that could distract you from studying.
- Reward yourself for studying with access to preferred activities and/or items, such as watching TV or using your phone.

Using your study planner as described will facilitate self-monitoring, which is another strategy to support helpful habits and goal acquisition.

▶ GENERAL APPROACH TO PREPARING FOR THE EXAM

Your success on the BCBA exam will be determined by a few factors that we recommend you keep in mind during every study session. While it isn't everything, your mastery of the content assessed by the exam is of paramount importance. While test-taking strategies can help a lot, they can only get you so far. At the end of the day, you're going to have to know your stuff! Think of this as the foundation upon which your success on the exam is built. This study guide will help you ensure your foundation is solid. Spend time reading and reflecting on each of the items in the guide to ensure that you truly understand and can apply all of the concepts and skills covered therein. While you may still occasionally encounter unfamiliar questions, a sound knowledge base will enable you to confidently figure out correct answers.

ACTIVE AND INTENSIVE STUDYING

All of the information you need to know to be successful on the BCBA exam is contained in this study guide. However, as obvious as this may seem, simply reading through it will not prepare you for the exam. You need to study actively and intensively. In this section, we share the most effective study strategies based on psychological and educational research.

As you study, you'll want to keep in mind two different though equally important types of information processing. Surface-level processing emphasizes operation learning and involves memorization and repetition, whereas deep-level processing emphasizes comprehension learning and involves relating what you're learning to the landscape of what you know and critical thinking and application. When actively and intensively studying for the exam, you'll want to aim to engage in both types of information processing.

Summarize It

Research has shown that creating summaries or brief structured outlines that synthesize and rephrase information facilitates focus and boosts learning and retention. While this study guide has condensed everything you need to know to pass the exam, it is still possible to summarize the information further and extract the gist of each section or item. To write a successful summary, identify the main points, key concepts, skills, and supporting details in a brief summary or an at-a-glance guide you can use to review and refresh your memory. Ensure your summary is accurate and captures the key information.

This study guide includes copious tables, figures, and memory aids (i.e., mnemonics) to help synthesize the information and make it easier to comprehend and remember. You can also use this approach as you study! Develop figures, tables, diagrams, concept maps, and mnemonics of your own to actively engage with the material and enhance your ability to remember it on the exam.

Create and Use Flashcards

The use of flashcards has also been shown to be an effective approach to studying. Actively read an item once through identifying the key concepts, skills, and supporting details. Then, when you read it a second time, develop a flashcard either using paper flashcards or a flashcard app for each key concept or skill contained therein. This is an exercise in summarizing what you've read and learned, so be concise (e.g., aim for 15 words or fewer) without sacrificing accuracy. You can then turn your flashcards into your own practice test using a flashcard app.

Employ the SAFMEDS (Say All Fast Minute Every Day Shuffled) approach to learn the content more efficiently and effectively and increase your retention of the information (McDade et al., 1985; Potts et al., 1993). Here's how to do it:

- **Say**—Look at the front of the flashcard and say the answer.
- **All**—Study all of the flashcards in your deck each time.
- **Fast**—Run through the entire deck fast to accelerate learning.
- **Minute**—Practice for 1 minute at a time or an alternate timed unit (e.g., 30 seconds or 2 minutes).
- **Every Day**—Practice with the SAFMEDS procedure every day.
- **Shuffled**—Shuffle the deck between practice sessions.

Test Yourself

Even though we provide you with sample questions for each section and a comprehensive practice test, don't let this deter you from coming up with your own questions and quizzes based on the material. In fact, there's research to suggest that you'll perform optimally if you use this study guide to develop your own study materials and practice tests. After studying a section, write out your own set of exam questions along with complete answers for those questions. If you have a study buddy, quiz each other using your custom questions. Similarly, regularly use active recall as you study. Periodically, put away your study materials and simply talk yourself through or write down what you've been studying.

Teach It to Others

Teach the information to others. If you have a study buddy or study group, arrange to take turns teaching the material to one another. However, if you don't have others to teach it to, pretend you're the instructor and record yourself teaching the material—with or without notes or the study guide. Then watch your recording. If you can provide a clear and understandable description of the concept or skill—complete with your own original examples—it's safe to say you're well on your way to mastering it! If you're not keen on recording yourself, teach the material aloud without recording it.

Use Mental Imagery and Mnemonics

The use of mental imagery is one of the oldest and most well studied learning techniques. It is a powerful technique that has been shown to significantly boost learning and retention. Using mnemonics in the form of an acronym, rhyme, song, phrase, image, or sentence is one of the most popular mental imagery tools used to recall information or an order of operations. For example, many use the phrase "Please excuse my dear aunt Sally." and the acronym PEMDAS to remember the order of math operations or the name ROY G. BIV to recall the spectrum of colors. This study guide includes some mnemonics you can use, but we encourage you to come up with your own as well. The process of developing a mnemonic will increase your ability to remember it and the information it represents. While the use of mnemonics is likely the most familiar, creating simple and clear mental images of information as you study is also a powerfully effective learning technique. For some, creating drawings to represent the information may also prove effective.

Take Practice Tests

A large body of research has shown that regularly taking practice tests is one of the most effective techniques for improving learning and enhancing retention. This is because repeated testing fosters transfer of learning and generates testing effects that change how you encode and mentally organize information in ways that boost retention and test performance.

This study guide includes practice questions at the end of each chapter as well as a full practice exam consisting of 185 questions. Practice testing also includes any approaches you use to quiz yourself, such as using physical or virtual flashcards or covering information and forcing yourself to recall it before looking. After you take a practice test, it's important for you to actively study the questions you missed. Dig into the question and answer to determine why you responded incorrectly. Was it because you didn't possess the knowledge needed to provide a correct response? If so, identify and actively study the content that will enable you to answer this question and similar questions correctly. Was it because you didn't read the question and/or response options carefully enough? If so, note what you could have done differently and aim to avoid this mistake in the future.

Diversify

As outstanding as this study guide is, don't solely rely on it as you prepare for the exam. It can be beneficial to have the information repeated and presented in different terminology and modes. As you begin studying a section of the guide, gather other materials on the topic from classes or books to review as well. Have a look online to see if there are podcasts you can listen to and videos you can watch to experience the information presented in a different mode.

Active and Close Reading

In everyday life, we often read rapidly and skim texts for the gist or general idea. This usually works just fine when reading emails, instructions, news stories, and social media posts, but it doesn't work well when you're studying for or taking an exam. In order to really learn the information presented in this study guide, you'll need to actively engage with the content as you read it and make it meaningful to you. Reading actively will significantly increase your understanding and retention of what you read.

Highlight and Underline

Highlighting and underlining are not the highest utility study techniques, but students are more likely to remember what they highlighted or underlined when studying. In order to select what to highlight or underline, a reader has to consider the text carefully and determine what is most important. Once this has been determined, the isolated and emphasized text stands out and facilitates retention.

Research indicates that the key to using highlighting and underlining effectively is the degree to which this practice is engaged in actively and accurately. Consequently, to be effective, carefully consider what you're reading and only highlight or underline the most important points. If you overdo it or emphasize the wrong things, it will defeat the purpose. Some people prefer to read a printed copy so that they can physically write notes, thoughts, connections, and questions on the text, highlight, and underline; however, for others who are accustomed to reading on a computer, using these same techniques in a digital format also works just fine. Consider which format works best for you and go with it!

Read With Pauses

It's helpful to take periodic breaks to reflect on what you just read, such as at the end of a sentence, paragraph, or table. When you pause, restate or summarize what you just read aloud or in your mind. Some find it helpful to write a short note or bullet points. Next, skim over what you just processed to ensure you got it right and didn't leave out any important details. If you overlooked something, note it and then resume reading. This practice will significantly improve both your retention and understanding of what you've read.

Reread

Rereading is one of the most popular study techniques, and there is research to support its utility for improving learning and information retention. It's also easy to employ—simply read sections of text multiple times. Rereading can be *massed* (i.e., repeatedly reading a section of text without a break) or *spaced* (allowing some time to pass between readings). Since spaced rereading appears to be more effective than massed rereading, it's best to allow a few days to pass before rereading the same material. When it comes to massed rereading, research indicates that it's the second time one reads something that is most helpful, so there's likely little benefit to be had from successively rereading the same material more than twice.

Apply It to Your Experiences

As you read, find ways to apply what you're reviewing or learning to your lived experience. Apply the concepts to your own life and come up with your own examples. The helpful thing about studying for the BCBA exam is that it's all about behavior, which is ubiquitous, so it shouldn't be too difficult to think of numerous examples and applications. You'll want to strive to make connections between what you're reading about and other concepts and skills. This strengthens your overall understanding of the discipline and aids in retention.

Read Like a Detective

Exams call for "close reading." This means paying careful attention to and considering every word of a question and the response options. When reading closely, the reader also carefully attends to syntax or the arrangement of words and phrases and the order in which they appear. You're like a detective, focusing on each detail to accurately determine the precise meaning of each question and response option. Practice this skill as you're reading the guide and taking practice tests until it becomes habitual. The authors have made every effort to be as clear and as succinct as possible, which will require you to practice this form of close reading while working your way through the study guide.

Think Like a Detective

You'll also want to practice slow and careful thinking. Don't rush it. Reading closely will help you slow down and really consider each concept presented in the guide and on practice tests. Again, imagine you're a detective critically and analytically examining each detail of a case. Stay sharp and clear and don't let anything get by you. It's careful attention to detail coupled with lucid, logical thinking that will help you crack it every time!

▶ TEST-TAKING STRATEGIES

If you've made it this far in your education, chances are you've studied for and taken a number of high stakes standardized tests and learned the strategies one should always employ on such tests. In the event these strategies are rusty or unfamiliar, we'll briefly review the most helpful techniques you can use to boost your score.

READ QUESTIONS FULLY AND CAREFULLY

The close reading skills you've practiced while studying will pay off when taking tests—both practice tests and the real thing. This is important because misreading and, as a result, misinterpreting questions is the most common error test-takers make on multiple-choice tests. In our everyday lives, we often skim texts without issue; however, when it comes to tests, carefully reading the complete question before answering is critical. The exam aims to test your knowledge of concepts and skills *and* your ability to comprehend questions about what you know. Use the following approach to avoid this all-too-common mistake:

- Obscure the answers with a piece of paper or your hand before reading the question.
- Read the question carefully, then ask yourself: "What is this question getting at? What is it asking?" Don't make hasty assumptions. Really think about it.
- Be on the lookout for key words and phrases for insight into what the question is about and the body of knowledge you'll need to draw upon to answer it correctly. Carefully attend to adjectives and nouns that describe terms or words you may be less familiar with or not know. Substituting a difficult word with a synonym that you're more familiar with may increase your comprehension of the question. Analyze the prefixes and suffixes of words to assist your understanding and add context.
- Questions often include information that is irrelevant and intended to lead you astray from the correct answer—these are called "distractors." Don't fall for it! Take time to carefully consider and define what the question is asking and the information you need to focus on to answer it correctly.
- Rephrase the question to yourself in a way that makes sense to you. Put it in your own words and, if relevant, come up with an example.
- Consider what you know about the topic the question is probing. Ask yourself: "What are the key ideas or components of this concept or skill? What would I say if I had to briefly explain what this is about?" Write down your thoughts on a piece of paper. This process facilitates access to your long-term memory. You'll likely be surprised to find that you know and/or remember more about a topic than you thought!
- Before you look at the possible answers, formulate a potential response to the question.
- Next, carefully and critically review the possible answers. Determine precisely why each possible answer is correct or incorrect. Eliminate the response options you're certain are wrong. Be suspicious of answer choices with words like *never, always, must,* and *all* as they're usually wrong. If it's a really difficult question and you're struggling to eliminate answers, take a little time to review each answer choice again. On each choice consider whether it offers a satisfactory answer to the question independently of the other choices. Try to narrow it down to two answers.
- Now, revisit the above steps for just these two answers. Ask yourself what you know about this subject.
- Select the best answer from the two choices. If you're unable to discern which of the two is best and are forced to guess, at least you've significantly improved your odds and likely given yourself a 50/50 chance of getting the answer right.

HOW TO SELECT THE CORRECT ANSWER WHEN MULTIPLE ANSWERS SEEM CORRECT

Avoid trying to talk yourself into making an answer true. If a response option does not fully address the question, is only somewhat true, relies on significant assumptions that are not obvious, or true only under certain narrowly defined conditions, it's likely the wrong choice. It's helpful to apply your practical experience when evaluating possible answers, but you should avoid dreaming up obscure scenarios to talk yourself into a certain answer. Most of the time, when test takers think they're dealing with a trick question, they're actually just reading too much into it or have yet to develop an accurate understanding of the question.

THREE TRUTHS AND A LIE

Sometimes questions require test takers to select the response that is *false* or *not correct*. Questions structured in this way can be tricky because they flip the logic typically used for multiple-choice tests.

That is, instead of identifying the most correct response out of a set of incorrect responses, the test taker is tasked with identifying the incorrect response out of a set of correct responses. When you encounter questions organized in this way, recall the old party game Three Truths and a Lie and remember that you've got to figure out which statement is false.

HOW TO INTERPRET UNFAMILIAR QUESTIONS

If you've used this study guide, you'll be prepared to answer all of the questions on the exam. However, you may encounter some questions that, on first blush, seem like you're unprepared to answer. This is because the test makers occasionally present the information in an uncommon or indirect manner that test takers are not used to, or they'll come at a concept from an unfamiliar or uncommon angle. Consequently, you'll need to be prepared to interpret parts of the question in order to answer it correctly. Slow down and work your way through the question piece by piece. Making sense of smaller pieces of the question will gradually build your understanding of the whole question. Stay calm and use the multiple-choice test-taking strategies detailed previously to select the correct answer. *Remember*: On occasion, information presented in previous questions can help you answer subsequent questions. This is yet another reason to read and think carefully about each question!

MAKE PREDICTIONS

We've already discussed the importance of reading slowly and carefully. Another advantage of this technique is that it allows time for your mind to focus on and begin to process the information in the question. This is a great time to predict what the correct answer will be before you look at the answer choices. With your prediction in mind, look over the answer choices provided. If your prediction is among the possible answer choices, it's quite likely that it is the correct answer. You should still read and think critically about the other answer choices before selecting the choice that matches your prediction.

HOLD A KNOCKOUT TOURNAMENT

In a knockout tournament, individuals or teams play against one another and the loser of each match-up is eliminated from the tournament. As you read through the possible answer choices to a question, from first to last, mentally note whether or not an answer strikes you as correct and begin to construct a rank order in your mind of best to worst possible answers. Hold the first answer choice that seems correct in your mind to benchmark the other answer choices against. The answer is the current leader, but it must beat out all the other possible answers to emerge victorious. If it loses to a stronger contender, that answer becomes the new standard to beat. Continue this process until one answer choice is crowned tournament champion!

LOOK OUT FOR FACT TRAPS

A fact trap is an answer choice that is factually accurate, but nevertheless incorrect because it (a) fails to answer the question or (b) fails to answer the question better than another correct answer choice. Sometimes this is because the response contains both correct and incorrect information. Fact traps are some of the most persuasive and tempting wrong answers, so be especially careful of these! To successfully navigate fact traps, continually measure seemingly correct answer choices against what the question is asking. *Remember*: The correct answer is the answer that best answers the question.

DON'T GET TOO FAMILIAR

Test takers often succumb to familiarity traps when they don't understand a question very well and/or they don't know some of the words or concepts included in the question. As a result, the test taker selects an answer choice with a word or concept they do know just because it's familiar—but nevertheless wrong. Instead of immediately selecting the answer choice that is the most familiar, evaluate it critically.

Consider whether or not it is accurate and the best answer to the question. If it's not, eliminate it. You may still not know the answer to the question, but at least you've improved your odds of guessing correctly. See the previous section on *How to Interpret Unfamiliar Questions*.

Occasionally test developers will exactly duplicate a piece of a question in an answer choice. Be careful with answer choices like this! While it could be true, more often than not it's a trap designed to lure you in by its air of familiarity. Correct answers usually summarize, paraphrase, or briefly reference aspects of the question rather than simply repeating it.

ELIMINATE RESPONSES

After carefully considering the question and the answer choices, eliminate answer choices that you're certain are incorrect or extremely unlikely. You should also eliminate responses that are synonymous (e.g., "multi-element design" and "alternating treatments design"); if the two responses are, in effect, the same, one of them can't be correct and the other incorrect, so they both must be incorrect. Simply eliminating answer choices down to two possible answer choices greatly increases your odds of answering the question correctly—even if you have to guess! If, after reviewing all of the answer choices carefully, they all seem wrong, go back over them again and carefully consider each one. Test takers often discover something they missed on a second pass.

BEWARE THE HEDGE

Be on the lookout for hedge terms!

Table 2.3 Hedge terms

not	usually	likely	will often
if	almost	may	sometimes
none	generally	can	often
all	except	mostly	rarely

Test developers often use these to make a question more challenging since, if you fail to attend to the hedge word or phrase, you'll likely select an incorrect answer. Hedge phrases are also used to make statements all-encompassing and without exceptions. Answer choices with decisive words like *always* and *exactly* are often incorrect for this reason.

DON'T OVERTHINK IT

Sometimes test takers read too much into questions when they would be better off accepting the situation presented in a problem at face value. It's best to use your common sense and to refrain from engaging in mental gymnastics to justify an answer choice for a question. If you find yourself performing acrobatic logic, draw on your common sense to bring yourself back down to earth, eliminate the answer choice, and move on. Remind yourself that the test addresses common skills and concepts behaviorists need to know to do their job well—not sit in a cafe theorizing. If your answer is getting too complicated, it's probably because you've overlooked something in the question or haven't thought about it carefully enough.

NEW INFORMATION HAS COME TO LIGHT

Sometimes test developers include new information in an answer choice. This should make you suspicious. Questions typically contain everything you need to know to answer them correctly, though you may need to engage in some additional reasoning. As such, responses that include new information are often incorrect; look askance at them and, if warranted, eliminate.

MIND THE CURVE

Pay close attention when words or phrases are used that indicate changes in thought or meaning. "But" is the reversal word you'll come across most frequently, but stay alert for other reversal words and phrases.

Table 2.4 Reversal words and phrases

however	although
on the other hand	nevertheless
even though	regardless of
in spite of	despite

RESPONSE CHOICE GROUPS

This is a lesser-known test-taking technique, but one that often pays dividends. A response choice group is a set of two or three answer choices that are constructed in a very similar manner, but usually mean nearly the opposite. Sometimes the set of answer choices provided contains two or more answer choices that are opposites or parallels; typically, one of these answers is correct. For example, a set contains a response that states an intervention increases a behavior as well as responses that indicate that an intervention decreases a behavior or a different intervention increases a behavior. When you're presented with a response choice group such as this, the correct answer is usually one of the answers in the group—not an answer choice that does not fit how the response choice group has constructed the choices. Consequently, you can often eliminate answers outside of the response choice group and focus on determining which answer in the group is the correct answer.

GO WITH YOUR FIRST GUESS—IF YOU REALLY HAVE TO GUESS

If you've followed this study guide's test prep plan, it's unlikely that you'll need to guess or go with a hunch on what the correct answer is. Nevertheless, in the event that you find yourself in this situation, you should go with your first hunch as it's most likely to be correct. If you don't have a solid, well-thought-out reason to change answers, it's best to stick with your first guess. That said, if you realize that you misread the question or recall helpful information from a previous question that offers insights into which is the correct answer, by all means change your answer.

CHECK YOUR WORK

We know you've heard this since you were in elementary school, but that doesn't make it any less true or important. If you have time, look back over your test to ensure you've provided an answer to every question and not made any careless mistakes. It can be hard to force yourself to look back over every question one more time when you just want to be finished, but it'll be worth it if you catch mistakes or incorrect answers!

TIME MANAGEMENT

The practice tests in this study guide will help you get a feel for the pace you'll need to keep to successfully finish the test in time. You should work on your timing and endeavor to speed up your pace without sacrificing accuracy. Honing your ability to identify and eliminate incorrect answers is one of the best ways to quicken your pace. *Remember:* There's no advantage to finishing early. Pace yourself and use the time you've been given to read and think carefully.

STAY CALM—COPING WITH TEST ANXIETY

Anxiety is the tense emotional state that occurs when you can't predict the outcome of a situation or guarantee that the outcome will be to your liking. It's no wonder then that tests are one of the most common sources of performance anxiety. Fortunately, there are several strategies you can use to overcome it. Before we consider behavioral and psychological strategies, we should note the importance of simply feeling well prepared and confident. Our aim in this guide is to provide you with a game plan and all of the information you'll need to be successful on the exam. Mastering the content of the exam and feeling like you're ready to ace it will go a long way toward staving off test-taking jitters.

However, even when very well prepared, some test takers continue to experience high levels of stress and performance anxiety. This can tax their cognitive faculties and ability to regulate negative emotions, which in turn impacts their performance. Anxiety can also lead to avoidance behaviors that prevent students from studying and even taking the exam. The good news is that learning and practicing skills to manage worried thoughts and regulate negative emotions significantly improves performance on tests.

Managing Worries

Any time you take a test, there's a chance that you'll fail to perform well. The possibility of failure can generate worried thoughts, which is the cognitive aspect of test anxiety. Sometimes we're aware of our concerns, but more often than not our worries are running in the background, draining our mental energy and impinging on our focus and ability to think.

Get to know your anxiety. How do you experience it? Where do you feel it in your body? Knowing how you experience anxiety will help you recognize these feelings early—before they are overwhelming. Simply acknowledging that you are worried and writing about your concerns can assuage worries and facilitate emotion regulation. Research has shown that thinking and writing about your anxiety before taking tests can reduce the symptoms of anxiety and engender a sense of control that leads to improved performance on exams.

These worries can also stem from the stories we tell ourselves. As human beings, we have an inner world made up of our thoughts and feelings. We all have an inner voice that's talking to us all the time. It's important to pay attention to how you talk to yourself because it influences how you feel and what you do. Self-talk can be helpful and positive or unhelpful and negative. Embracing a narrative that one is not good at tests or fails tests due to an inability to effectively cope with the associated stress and anxiety can become a self-fulfilling prophecy. Instead, talk to yourself like you would to a good friend or someone you love. Say encouraging and comforting things to yourself when you're feeling anxious and stressed. Show yourself compassion and remind yourself that you're not alone.

Regulating Negative Emotions

Since our thoughts and emotions are tightly connected, worried thoughts can generate negative emotions and stress, which register in the body as physiological arousal (e.g., a racing heart, dizziness, sweating, stomachache). For some, these signs of stress are seen as an indication that they're not going to perform well, which feeds into their already worried mind.

A strategy that has been found to counteract this is for the test taker to reframe their physiological arousal as energizing and facilitative of performance rather than as harmful. Rather than interpreting the signs of stress as harbingers of imminent doom, it helps to view them as the body and mind gearing up for a challenge in order to be successful. This is an example of a broader strategy of talking back to one's worries and replacing irrational, worried thoughts with more rational, calming thoughts.

The key is to get ahead of anxiety by proactively doing things that will keep it at a manageable level, like practicing deep breathing and mindfulness and getting regular exercise. Regularly practicing breathing techniques has been shown to lower stress and anxiety and promote a sense of well-being and relaxation. Try this: Take a deep breath through your nose, counting to 3 or 4 in your mind while you're inhaling. Then, exhale more slowly through pressed lips while you count to 5 or 8. Do this for 2 minutes. You can also try holding your breath for a count of 4 or 7 before exhaling.

It's important to remember that worrying isn't necessarily bad. Moderate, manageable levels of anxiety can increase performance because they provide energy to face and overcome challenges. Fear that you might fail a test can be highly motivating and help you stay focused on studying when other activities seem more enjoyable. Anxiety becomes a problem when it gets so high that it feels overwhelming and lowers performance. The key is to manage your level of anxiety and stress so that it facilitates rather than harms your performance.

▶ PRIOR TO THE EXAM

In addition to studying consistently using this study guide, there are a number of things you can do to enhance your performance on test day.

- Take time to plan out your test-taking day. What time will you wake up? Where is the testing location? How will you get there? How much time do you need to get there? What do you need to bring with you?
- Sound sleep is one of the most important things you can do to be at your best on test day. Stick to your study schedule so that you're not up late at night cramming the week before the test. Instead, build in several rest days prior to test day during which you'll allow all of your hard work to settle in.
- Like sleep, hydration is critical. Drink plenty of water while you study, especially in the days leading up to the test. Coupling hydration with sleep will enhance your mental acuity and enable you to perform optimally on the exam.
- Eat a balanced meal of carbohydrates and proteins before you take the test. This will give you endurance and cognitive energy to perform your best.

YOU'VE GOT THIS!

We're here to tell you that you have every reason to be optimistic about your potential for success. Preparing for the exam will have its challenges, but this study guide contains everything you need to be successful.

▶ USING THIS BOOK

The BCBA exam is challenging. Fortunately, you're using the best study guide available to prepare. It explains the Task List items comprehensively but concisely, provides practice opportunities throughout, and includes a full mock exam. The chapters of the study guide cover all essential content areas of the certification exam. Each content area chapter begins with coverage of the relevant Task List items and concludes with practice questions to assess and support content uptake. A brief overview of the chapters to follow is presented in the following.

CHAPTER 3: PHILOSOPHICAL UNDERPINNINGS

The field of applied behavior analysis (ABA) is grounded in a robust philosophical and scientific framework that distinguishes it from other approaches to behavioral research, defines its focus and goals, and informs its approach to analyzing and intervening in behavior. Familiarity with the field's scientific and philosophical foundation facilitates the BCBA's understanding of the interrelations among the discipline's defining elements and its highly specific use of key terms, concepts, and principles. To that end, Chapter 3 offers a clear and concise guide to ABA's conceptual foundations, defining dimensions, and overall aims. This includes helpful explanations of the philosophical assumptions underlying the science and what distinguishes the perspective of radical behaviorism from other approaches to understanding behavior. In this chapter, you'll also learn about ABA's manifestations as both a science and a practice, including how to tell the difference among behaviorism, experimental analysis of behavior, ABA, and practice guided by the science of behavior analysis. It sounds like a lot, but don't worry—you'll find handy mnemonic aids to help you remember the content covered.

CHAPTER 4: CONCEPTS AND PRINCIPLES

As a professional applying science to analyze and intervene in behavior, the behavior analyst must understand, utilize, and be able to clearly communicate a variety of concepts, technical terms, and principles that define behavior and the environmental events that govern it. Chapter 4 covers the fundamental elements of the scientific analysis of behavior, specific concepts derived from ABA, basic skills, and key terminology and principles employed by behavior analysts. This includes a description of what makes respondent and operant behavior functionally distinct, and a clear illustration of how the environment influences each type of behavior in the form of respondent and operant conditioning. This chapter also reviews positive and negative reinforcement and punishment, the various schedules of reinforcement, stimulus control, and other processes central to behavior analysis. Easy-to-remember examples that facilitate conceptual clarity, comprehension, and retention are provided throughout.

CHAPTER 5: MEASUREMENT, DATA DISPLAY, AND INTERPRETATION

In your graduate training, you've learned how to select behaviors for intervention and then develop and deliver interventions that foster quantifiable alterations of and improvements in clients' lives. BCBAs utilize systematic measurement to document behavioral changes, monitor the progress of interventions, and communicate results to key stakeholders. As such, selecting, defining, and measuring behavior and displaying data are critical skills integral to the competent practice of ABA. Chapter 5 provides a clear and concise review of all items in the most current version of the Task List focused on measurement, data display, and interpretation. It provides guidance on developing well-written operational definitions of behavior and distinguishing among different types of behavioral assessment measures. You'll also find reviews of the various dimensions of behavioral measurement (e.g., occurrence, temporal), designing and implementing sampling procedures, evaluating the validity and reliability of measurement procedures, and selecting a measurement system. Chapter 5 closes with a discussion of graphing data and interpreting the graphs.

CHAPTER 6: EXPERIMENTAL DESIGN

As applied behavior scientists, BCBAs design, conduct, and evaluate experiments to analyze the effects of their interventions and determine the factors driving behavior change. Designing single-subject experiments that identify the functions of behavior and document change is a highly valued skill that distinguishes the BCBA from other behavioral health professionals. As such, experimental design was an important component of your training program. Chapter 6 revisits the essential aspects of experimental design covered on the BCBA exam. It reviews how to distinguish among dependent and independent variables and internal and external validity. It also covers the defining features, advantages, and use of single-subject experimental designs. The chapter closes with an in-depth description of the various rationales for conducting comparative, component, and parametric analyses.

CHAPTER 7: ETHICS

Behavior analysts analyze human behavior in order to change it. Reflect on that. The human desire for agency and autonomy is universal, but the behavior analyst applies behavioral science to alter the choices clients are making for themselves. There are profound ethical ramifications and responsibilities any time a person or group exercises their will over another person or group. Recognizing this, the Behavior Analyst Certification Board® (BACB®) requires that BCBAs understand and adhere to the updated Ethics Code for Behavior Analysts (2020) in their practice. Chapter 7 provides a solid review of all standards across the Ethics Code's six sections, including the behavior analyst's responsibilities as a professional in practice to clients and stakeholders, to supervisees and trainees, in public statements, and in research.

CHAPTER 8: BEHAVIOR ASSESSMENT

Systematically assessing clients' behaviors and interpreting the data gathered are integral skills of the BCBA. Chapter 8 reviews all key components of behavior assessment. It revisits the process of reviewing records ; reviews conducting assessments of preference, skill strengths and deficits, and problem behavior; and covers how to determine whether a client needs behavior analytic services and the common functions of problem behavior. Since a socially significant behavior must be identified as a target for change, this chapter provides the critical questions the BCBA uses to determine the social significance of potential target behaviors and to identify socially significant behavior-change goals.

CHAPTER 9: BEHAVIOR-CHANGE PROCEDURES

While a variety of behavioral health professionals aim to facilitate behavior change in clients, the behavioral health field acknowledges the BCBA's expertise when it comes to behavior-change procedures. In your day-to-day practice as a BCBA, the effective and efficient implementation of such procedures will enable clients to acquire new skills, improve their facility with skills, and maintain behavior changes. Given the importance and breadth of this domain, the related Task List is extensive. Chapter 9 provides a helpful review of key behavior-change procedures along with recommendations for increasing their effectiveness. This chapter also covers the primary outcomes promoted by the procedures, including stimulus and response generalization and maintenance. Clear examples that foster understanding and retention are provided throughout.

CHAPTER 10: SELECTING AND IMPLEMENTING INTERVENTIONS

BCBAs carefully attend to the selection and implementation of interventions to increase their effectiveness. This involves a number of related strategies, all covered in Chapter 10. For example, it reviews stating intervention goals in observable and measurable terms and recommending intervention goals and strategies based on client preferences, supporting environments, risks, constraints, and social validity. In addition, Chapter 10 covers the essential factors driving successful intervention implementation, such as planning for unwanted effects, monitoring client progress and treatment integrity, and making data-based decisions about intervention effectiveness and the need for treatment revision and ongoing services. This chapter closes with a helpful discussion of an important factor underlying many behavioral interventions: service providers using teaming strategies to collaborate effectively.

CHAPTER 11: PERSONNEL SUPERVISION AND MANAGEMENT

BCBAs engage in the important work of serving as supervisors of behavioral professionals in the field. As you'll see, this often involves adapting and applying skills utilized with clients to the supervisor–supervisee relationship. For instance, this chapter covers how to establish clear performance expectations for the supervisor and supervisee; select supervision goals based on an assessment of the supervisee's skills; use performance monitoring, feedback, and reinforcement systems; and use function-based strategies to improve personnel performance. Chapter 11 wraps up with a look at evaluating the effects of supervision on a variety of outcomes.

CHAPTERS 12 AND 13: PRACTICE EXAM

Test your knowledge and skills with a full-length practice exam consisting of 185 questions! The answer to each question, along with an explanation, is provided in Chapter 13.

CHAPTER 14: AFTER THE EXAM

In this final chapter, we provide valuable information about the many professional development resources available to behavior analysts. Chapter 14 also includes helpful tips for acquiring your first job as a professional behavior analyst and recommendations for those who have tried but have not yet passed the exam. Regardless of where you stand after taking the exam, there will be content here that is relevant to you!

COMMON NOTATIONS

Throughout the book, notations are used in explanations of various concepts, examples, and so on. The following table can serve as a helpful reference for the notations used and their associated meanings. It is recommended that you familiarize yourself with these commonly used notations (from the behavior analytic literature) and refer back to the table as needed.

Table 2.5 Notations used throughout the book

Notation	Meaning
S	Stimulus
R	Response
US	Unconditioned stimulus
UR	Unconditioned response
CS	Conditioned stimulus
CR	Conditioned response
S^{R+}	Unconditioned positive reinforcer
S^{r+}	Conditioned positive reinforcer
S^{R-}	Unconditioned negative reinforcer
S^{r-}	Conditioned negative reinforcer
S^{P+}	Unconditioned positive punisher
S^{p+}	Conditioned positive punisher
S^{P-}	Unconditioned negative punisher
S^{p-}	Conditioned negative punisher
S^D	Discriminative stimulus ("s-dee")
S^Δ	Stimulus delta ("s-delta")

▶ CONCLUSION

In this chapter, we shared guidance on strategies that will help maximally prepare you for the BCBA exam, including how to master the content tested by the exam and enhance your test-taking skills. Mastering the content on the exam requires a considerable amount of active and intensive studying; thus, this chapter described numerous evidence-based recommendations for studying. Since time management and planning are key when preparing for an exam like this, this chapter shared guidance on setting goals and creating a study schedule coupled with a strategic plan worksheet for planning weekly study sessions and tracking progress on your goals. To help you optimize your performance on the exam, this chapter also taught multiple-choice test-taking strategies and shared tips on coping with test anxiety and preparing for exam day.

 BIBLIOGRAPHY

Bednall, T. C., & Kehoe, E. J. (2011). Effects of self-regulatory instructional aids on self-directed study. *Instructional Science, 39*, 205–226. https://doi.org/10.1007/s11251-009-9125-6

Benjamin, A. S., & Tullis, J. (2010). What makes distributed practice effective? *Cognitive Psychology, 61*, 228–247. https://doi.org/10.1016/j.cogpsych.2010.05.004

Blanchard, J., & Mikkelson, V. (1987). Underlining performance outcomes in expository text. *The Journal of Educational Research, 80*, 197–201. https://doi.org/10.1080/00220671.1987.10885751

Bretzing, B. H., & Kulhavy, R. W. (1979). Notetaking and depth of processing. *Contemporary Educational Psychology, 4*, 145–153. https://doi.org/10.1016/0361-476X(79)90069-9

Bromage, B. K., & Mayer, R. E. (1986). Quantitative and qualitative effects of repetition on learning from technical text. *Journal of Educational Psychology, 78*, 271–278. https://doi.org/10.1037/0022-0663.78.4.271

Brooks, L. W., Dansereau, D. F., Holley, C. D., & Spurlin, J. E. (1983). Generation of descriptive text headings. *Contemporary Educational Psychology, 8*, 103–108. https://doi.org/10.1016/0361-476X(83)90001-2

Butler, A. C. (2010). Repeated testing produces superior transfer of learning relative to repeated studying. *Journal of Experimental Psychology: Learning, Memory, and Cognition, 36*, 1118–1133. https://doi.org/10.1037/a0019902

Cepeda, N. J., Pashler, H., Vul, E., Wixted, J. T., & Rohrer, D. (2006). Distributed practice in verbal recall tasks: A review and quantitative synthesis. *Psychological Bulletin, 132*, 354–380. https://doi.org/10.1037/0033-2909.132.3.354

Delaney, P. F., Verkoeijen, P. P., & Spirgel, A. (2010). Spacing and testing effects: A deeply critical, lengthy, and at times discursive review of the literature. *Psychology of Learning and Motivation, 53*, 63–147. https://doi.org/10.1016/S0079-7421(10)53003-2

Doctorow, M., Wittrock, M. C., & Marks, C. (1978). Generative processes in reading comprehension. *Journal of Educational Psychology, 70*, 109–118. https://doi.org/10.1037/0022-0663.70.2.109

Dunlosky, J., Rawson, K. A., Marsh, E. J., Nathan, M. J., & Willingham, D. T. (2013). Improving students' learning with effective learning techniques: Promising directions from cognitive and educational psychology. *Psychological Science in the Public Interest, 14*, 4–58. https://doi.org/10.1177/1529100612453266

Fritz, C. O., Morris, P. E., Acton, M., Voelkel, A. R., & Etkind, R. (2007). Comparing and combining retrieval practice and the keyword mnemonic for foreign vocabulary learning. *Applied Cognitive Psychology, 21*, 499–526. https://doi.org/10.1002/acp.1287

Hartley, J., Bartlett, S., & Branthwaite, A. (1980). Underlining can make a difference—Sometimes. *The Journal of Educational Research, 73*, 218–224. https://doi.org/10.1080/00220671.1980.10885239

Jamieson, J. P., Mendes, W. B., & Nock, M. K. (2013). Improving acute stress responses: The power of reappraisal. *Current Directions in Psychological Science, 22*, 51–56. https://doi.org/10.1177/0963721412461500

Johnson, L. L. (1988). Effects of underlining textbook sentences on passage and sentence retention. *Literacy Research and Instruction, 28*, 18–32. https://doi.org/10.1080/19388078809557955

Kang, S. H., & Pashler, H. (2012). Learning painting styles: Spacing is advantageous when it promotes discriminative contrast. *Applied Cognitive Psychology, 26*, 97–103. https://doi.org/10.1002/acp.1801

Kiewra, K. A., Mayer, R. E., Christensen, M., Kim, S. I., & Risch, N. (1991). Effects of repetition on recall and note-taking: Strategies for learning from lectures. *Journal of Educational Psychology, 83*, 120–123.

Leutner, D., Leopold, C., & Sumfleth, E. (2009). Cognitive load and science text comprehension: Effects of drawing and mentally imagining text content. *Computers in Human Behavior, 25*, 284–289. https://doi.org/10.1016/j.chb.2008.12.010

Lorch, R. F. (1989). Text-signaling devices and their effects on reading and memory processes. *Educational Psychology Review, 1*, 209–234. https://doi.org/10.1007/BF01320135

Ramirez, G., & Beilock, S. L. (2011). Writing about testing worries boosts exam performance in the classroom. *Science, 331*(6014), 211–213. https://doi.org/10.1126/science.1199427

Rawson, K. A., & Dunlosky, J. (2011). Optimizing schedules of retrieval practice for durable and efficient learning: How much is enough? *Journal of Experimental Psychology: General, 140*, 283–302. https://doi.org/10.1037/a0023956

Rawson, K. A., & Kintsch, W. (2005). Rereading effects depend on time of test. *Journal of Educational Psychology, 97*, 70–80. https://doi.org/10.1037/0022-0663.97.1.70

Roediger, H. L., III., & Butler, A. C. (2011). The critical role of retrieval practice in long-term retention. *Trends in Cognitive Sciences, 15*, 20–27. https://doi.org/10.1016/j.tics.2010.09.003

Roediger, H. L., III., Putnam, A. L., & Smith, M. A. (2011). Ten benefits of testing and their applications to educational practice. *Psychology of Learning and Motivation, 55*, 1–36. https://doi.org/10.1016/B978-0-12-387691-1.00001-6

Rothkopf, E. Z. (1968). Textual constraint as function of repeated inspection. *Journal of Educational Psychology, 59*, 20–25. https://doi.org/10.1037/h0025378

Rozek, C. S., Ramirez, G., Fine, R. D., & Beilock, S. L. (2019). Reducing socioeconomic disparities in the STEM pipeline through student emotion regulation. *Proceedings of the National Academy of Sciences, 116*(5), 1553–1558. https://doi.org/10.1073/pnas.1808589116

Shapiro, A. M., & Waters, D. L. (2005). An investigation of the cognitive processes underlying the keyword method of foreign vocabulary learning. *Language Teaching Research, 9*(2), 129–146. https://doi.org/10.1191/1362168805lr151oa

Taylor, K., & Rohrer, D. (2010). The effects of interleaved practice. *Applied Cognitive Psychology, 24*, 837–848. https://doi.org/10.1002/acp.1598

Thompson, S. V. (1990). Visual imagery: A discussion. *Educational Psychology, 10*(2), 141–182. https://doi.org/10.1080/0144341900100203

Verkoeijen, P. P., Rikers, R. M., & Özsoy, B. (2008). Distributed rereading can hurt the spacing effect in text memory. *Applied Cognitive Psychology, 22*, 685–695. https://doi.org/10.1002/acp.1388

Philosophical Underpinnings

As a discipline, behavior analysis is comprised of the basic science (i.e., experimental analysis of behavior), applied science (i.e., applied behavior analysis), and their philosophy. Behavior analysts must develop an understanding of the philosophical foundations of behavior analysis to understand what they practice and the important concepts that drive how they practice. The purpose of this chapter will be to provide a review of key content related to the philosophical underpinnings of behavior analysis addressed by Task List items A-1 through A-5, including the goals of behavior analysis as a science, the dimensions of applied behavior analysis as defined by Baer et al. (1968), and more.

> ## ▶ LEARNING OBJECTIVES
>
> The following Task List items related to philosophical underpinnings (A-1 through A-5) serve as the learning objectives of this chapter:
>
> A-1 Identify the goals of behavior analysis as a science (i.e., description, prediction, control).
>
> A-2 Explain the philosophical assumptions underlying the science of behavior analysis (e.g., selectionism, determinism, empiricism, parsimony, pragmatism).
>
> A-3 Describe and explain behavior from the perspective of radical behaviorism.
>
> A-4 Distinguish among behaviorism, the experimental analysis of behavior, applied behavior analysis, and professional practice guided by the science of behavior analysis.
>
> A-5 Describe and define the dimensions of applied behavior analysis (Baer et al., 1968).

▶ TASK LIST ITEM A-1

The objective of this Task List item is to identify the goals of behavior analysis as a science (i.e., description, prediction, control).

The goal of our science is to achieve a thorough understanding of socially important behaviors. The knowledge learned from science allows for one or more of three levels of understanding: (a) description, (b) prediction, and (c) control.

DESCRIPTION

Systematic observations enable us to describe events in quantifiable terms that can be examined for possible interactions with other known facts. These descriptions often suggest hypotheses or questions for further research.

■ *Example*: Rate of verbal praise statements used by a classroom teacher.

PREDICTION

This level of understanding (also known as *covariation* or *correlation*) occurs when repeated observations demonstrate that two events systematically covary (i.e., correlate). While correlations do not provide evidence of a causal relationship between variables, they can be used to predict with a certain degree of confidence the relative probability that one event will occur based on the presence or absence of another event.

■ *Example*: When repeated observations demonstrate that there are fewer incidents of problem behavior among students on days when teachers use more praise statements, we can predict with some degree of confidence that one will occur based on the presence or absence of the other.

CONTROL

This level of understanding (also known as *causation*) results from the discovery of functional relations in controlled experiments that demonstrate that a specific change to one event (independent variable [IV]) reliably produces a specific change in another event (dependent variable [DV]). This is considered the highest level of scientific understanding.

■ *Example*: A controlled experiment demonstrates that fewer incidents of problem behavior are only observed on days when teachers use praise statements in the classroom.

MNEMONIC AID

P̲lease (for Prediction) C̲lean (for Control) the D̲ishes (for Description). Please clean the dishes when asked about the goals of behavior analysis as a science!

▶ TASK LIST ITEM A-2

The objective of this Task List item is to explain the philosophical assumptions underlying the science of behavior analysis (e.g., selectionism, determinism, empiricism, parsimony, pragmatism).

We employ the scientific method to understand and intervene in human behavior. As an applied science, applied behavior analysis (ABA) adheres to the attitudes of science, which are a set of presuppositions and values that inform a scientific approach to understanding reality. These shared assumptions are foundational for the development of scientific knowledge.

DETERMINISM

This refers to the assumption that the universe is rational, governed by discoverable laws, and that events are completely determined by previously existing causes. As a result, all behavior possesses an identifiable cause and is thus predictable and to some degree determinable.

REPLICATION

The validity, reliability, and usefulness of scientific findings are increased when experiments are reproduced and the basic pattern of results is replicated numerous times. This attitude of science requires the replication of findings for results to be included in the knowledge base of any field.

PARSIMONY

This is the principle that an explanation of a thing or event ought to be based on the fewest possible assumptions or unobservable constructs. This attitude of science encourages scientists to prefer the simplest, most logical explanation supported by experiments or reason.

EMPIRICISM

This refers to the practice of objective observation of an event of interest. Systematic measurement and accurate quantification are empirical methods used to develop scientific knowledge.

EXPERIMENTATION

This is the chief strategy used to develop scientific knowledge. It is performed to investigate whether a functional relation exists between events. In an experiment, the IV is systematically controlled and manipulated to clarify its effects on the DV. The aim is to determine whether a functional relation exists between the two variables or events, such that one event plays a causal role in the other event.

PHILOSOPHICAL DOUBT

This refers to the attitude of viewing scientific knowledge as tentative and continually developing. Consequently, scientists remain skeptical about the validity and truthfulness of all scientific knowledge and open to modifying their beliefs based on new knowledge and discoveries.

SELECTIONISM

This concept was employed by B. F. Skinner to explain the origin and extinction of behavior. Selectionistic explanations of behavior posit that behavior is selected to continue or to be extinguished based on an individual's experiences and the consequences of their behavior. The environment affects living things through selectionism at the individual level (ontogeny) and the species level (phylogeny).

MNEMONIC AID

The great philosophy professor, DR. PEEPS, can help you remember the philosophical assumptions underlying the science of behavior analysis: Determinism, Replication, Parsimony, Empiricism, Experimentation, Philosophic doubt, Selectionism.

PRACTICE QUESTION

The part of the human brain that processes visual information has evolved over millions of years, from perceiving engraved markings to recognizing repeating patterns and ultimately making sense of letters, which has become known as reading. Daniel has been interested in books since he was a young toddler. His parents read to him frequently and many books were available in his environment. Daniel's development is accelerated, and he is reading three grade levels above his peers.

Choose the set of assumptions that best represent the example in the scenario presented.

A. Determinism and empiricism
B. Replication and experimentation
C. Philosophical doubt and parsimony
D. Phylogeny and ontogeny

Before moving on to the next section for the solution, we recommend that you to provide a brief explanation for the answer option you selected:

_____
_____

When you're ready, move on to the next section for the solution!

Practice Question Breakdown

Step 1: Examine the question

The question calls for the identification of the philosophical assumptions underlying ABA that best describe the evolution of human reading ability over time and, in particular, Daniel's individual reading development since toddlerhood.

Step 2: Analyze the answer options

A. This is a distractor. Determinism refers to the assumption that all behavior is predictable, while empiricism is the objective observation of an event. While these two terms are included among the philosophical assumptions underlying ABA, they are not directly related to the scenario at hand, which is about factors influencing the development of reading ability over time.

B. This is a distractor. Replication refers to the repetition of an experiment under exact or similar conditions, and experimentation is a controlled study performed to determine whether a functional relation exists between variables. The scenario does not mention replication and experimentation, but the evolution of reading ability in humans and Daniel's individual reading trajectory.

C. This is a distractor. Philosophical doubt considers scientific knowledge as tentative, with some skepticism about its absolute validity. Parsimony refers to the simplest scientific explanation. These philosophical assumptions are not directly related to the scenario.

D. As behavior analysts, we must always consider how the environment impacts human beings and other living things. Explanations of behavior that are based on the experiences of the organism refers to selectionism. One type of selectionism, phylogeny is defined as how a group of organisms evolve over time (i.e., humans learning to read was shaped by millions of years of evolution), while ontogeny is focused on the development of an individual organism (i.e., environmental variables related to reading behaviors shaped Daniel's reading ability).

Step 3: Select the best answer

Among the four answer options presented, answer D (phylogeny and ontogeny) appears to be the best answer.

▶ TASK LIST ITEM A-3

The objective of this Task List item is to describe and explain behavior from the perspective of radical behaviorism.

The conceptual system of radical behaviorism was developed by B. F. Skinner. Radical behaviorism seeks to understand behavior in all its forms and collapses the distinction between private events (i.e., thoughts and feelings) and public events (i.e., behavior that is observable and measurable).

It is *radical* in the sense that it includes all behavior, both public and private, and assumes they are influenced by the same kinds of variables and result from an individual's experiences and environments. From the perspective of radical behaviorism, thoughts and feelings do not cause behavior—thoughts and feelings *are* behavior. As such, thoughts and feelings conform to the laws of behavior and can be addressed utilizing the principles of behavior.

From the perspective of radical behaviorism, all human behavior is understandable in terms of how an individual's behavior develops over their lifetime based on their experiences with the environment (ontogeny) and how a species' behavior has evolved over evolutionary time as it slowly makes changes necessary for survival (phylogeny).

Table 3.1 The difference between ontogeny and phylogeny

Ontogeny	Phylogeny
Recounts the developmental history of an individual within their own lifetime	Recounts the evolutionary history of a species
Focuses on the degree to which the behavior can be changed through learning	Describes the history of the behavior and its shaping through past selective pressures

▶ TASK LIST ITEM A-4

The objective of this Task List item is to distinguish among behaviorism, the experimental analysis of behavior (EAB), applied behavior analysis, and professional practice guided by the science of behavior analysis.

BEHAVIORISM

This is the philosophy of the science of behavior and its various forms. It assumes that a science of behavior is possible, and that behavior can be studied and changed in a manner similar to other sciences (e.g., biology). Behaviorism primarily looks to causes in the external environment for explanations of behavior. As an intervention, behaviorism holds that it is often most effective to organize the environment in such a way that certain behaviors are more or less likely.

EXPERIMENTAL ANALYSIS OF BEHAVIOR

This is a natural science approach to research that defines and clarifies the basic processes and principles of behavior. It was founded by B. F. Skinner with the publication of *The Behavior of Organisms* in 1938. Skinner articulated two types of behavior: (a) *respondent behaviors* that are reflexive and elicited by stimuli immediately preceding them and (b) *operant behaviors* that are elicited by the effects of consequences of past behaviors. The operant three-term contingency is the primary unit of analysis. EAB is primarily a laboratory-based experimental approach that established the foundational principles of operant behavior.

APPLIED BEHAVIOR ANALYSIS

This is the science in which behavior analysts apply techniques derived from the principles of behavior to change behavior (e.g., increase behavior, teach and maintain behavior, reduce problem behavior) and positively enhance socially significant areas (e.g., classroom management, generalization and maintenance of learning, communication). ABA utilizes experimentation to clearly identify the variables driving changes in behavior. ABA applies principles derived from EAB to change behavior.

PROFESSIONAL PRACTICE

This is a domain of behavior analysis. It is guided by the science of behavior analysis and involves delivering behavior analytic services to human subjects in diverse settings and environments that is grounded in the principles of behaviorism, research from the EAB, and ABA. The professional practice of behavior analysis is a hybrid discipline informed by various mental health fields, education, communication disorders, physical therapy, and criminal justice.

▶ TASK LIST ITEM A-5

The objective of this Task List item is to describe and define the dimensions of applied behavior analysis (Baer et al., 1968).

ABA is defined by seven core dimensions: (a) applied, (b) behavioral, (c) analytic, (d) technological, (e) conceptually systematic, (f) effective, and (g) generality.

APPLIED

This means that the variable of interest is important to an individual and/or society; that is, changes that improve an individual's quality of life (i.e., socially significant behaviors) are targeted.

BEHAVIORAL

This term means that a study or intervention analyzes observable and measurable behavior in a precise and objective manner.

ANALYTIC

This means that control over a target behavior can be demonstrated (i.e., can be turned on and off), evidencing the existence of a functional relationship between the manipulated event and occurrence/nonoccurrence of the target behavior.

TECHNOLOGICAL

This means that all procedures of an intervention are clearly detailed and described and that data and results of an experiment or study are clearly presented in an understandable and replicable manner.

CONCEPTUALLY SYSTEMATIC

This means that all of the interventions or procedures are grounded in the basic behavioral principles of behavior analysis in a manner that fosters integration and systematic expansion of the procedures.

EFFECTIVE

An intervention is considered effective if it has altered the target behavior to a significant degree, is meaningful or socially important, and promotes long-term positive changes in the client.

GENERALITY

A change in behavior is considered to have this when it holds over time, across different settings, and/or spreads to other relevant and related behaviors.

MNEMONIC AID

G (for Generality) E (for Effective) T (for Technological) A (for Applied) C (for Conceptually systematic) A (for Analytic) B (for Behavioral). GET A CAB. You can also use BAT CAGE or BEG A CAT, whichever you fancy.

▶ CONCLUSION

In this chapter, we reviewed ABA's conceptual foundations, scientific framework, defining dimensions, and overall aims. This included the goals of behavior analysis and its philosophical assumptions. We also described and explained the perspective of radical behaviorism and what distinguishes it from other approaches to understanding behavior. Having a firm grasp of these key concepts will inform how you approach your practice as a Board Certified Behavior Analyst®, hencethis chapter covered ABA's manifestations as both a science and a practice and delved into how to distinguish among behaviorism, EAB, ABA, and practice guided by the science of behavior analysis. To support your acquisition and retention of the content covered in this chapter, we added several mnemonic aids.

1. The knowledge learned from science allows for one or more of three levels of understanding. These include:

    A. Correlation, control, definition
    B. Control, description, prediction
    C. Covariance, prediction, selectionism
    D. Description, probability, replication

2. Which level of scientific understanding occurs when controlled experiments demonstrate that a specific change to an independent variable reliably produces a specific change in a dependent variable?

    A. Control
    B. Definition
    C. Prediction
    D. Replication

3. Which of the following refers to the philosophical assumption that the universe is rational and governed by discoverable laws, and events are completely determined by previously existing causes?

    A. Determinism
    B. Empiricism
    C. Experimentation
    D. Parsimony

4. _____ is a natural science approach to research founded by B. F. Skinner that defines and clarifies the basic processes and principles of behavior.

    A. Applied behavior analysis (ABA)
    B. Experimental analysis of behavior (EAB)
    C. Natural environment training (NET)
    D. Parametric analysis (PA)

5. Applied behavior analysis is defined by _____ core dimensions.

    A. Three
    B. Five
    C. Seven
    D. Nine

6. Which of the following is the core dimension of applied behavior analysis (ABA) that is concerned with the extent to which procedures are described in a manner consistent with basic behavioral principles?

    A. Applied
    B. Conceptually systematic
    C. Effective
    D. Generality

7. When a change in behavior holds over time, across different settings, and/or spreads to other related behaviors, it is said to have achieved:

    A. Applied
    B. Behavioral
    C. Effective
    D. Generality

(See answers next page.)　　**37**

1. B) Control, description, prediction
The goal of science in any field of study is to develop a greater understanding of its subject. The goal of our science is to understand socially important behaviors through varying levels of description, prediction, and control. Thus, efforts are made to describe behavior in measurable terms, demonstrate correlation between events, and identify variables that reliably predict the occurrence of a behavior or event.

2. A) Control
Control, as a level of scientific understanding, is said to occur when controlled experiments demonstrate that a specific change to an independent variable reliably produces a specific change in a dependent variable. Prediction, which refers to another level of scientific understanding, along with the other two answer options function as distractors.

3. A) Determinism
Determinism refers to the philosophical assumption that the universe is rational, governed by discoverable laws, and events are completely determined by previously existing causes. The other answer options (empiricism, experimentation, and parsimony) refer to other philosophical assumptions and function as distractors.

4. B) Experimental analysis of behavior (EAB)
EAB is the natural science approach to research founded by B. F. Skinner that defines and clarifies the basic processes and principles of behavior. ABA, which is the science in which behavior analysts apply techniques derived from the principles of behavior, along with the other two answer options function as distractors.

5. C) Seven
As described by Baer et al. (1968), applied behavior analysis is defined by seven core dimensions, including: applied, behavioral, analytic, technological, conceptually systematic, effective, and generality.

6. B) Conceptually systematic
Applied behavior analysis is conceptually systematic; that is, all of the interventions or procedures are grounded in the basic behavioral principles. The other answer options (applied, effective, and generality) refer to other core principles and function as distractors.

7. D) Generality
Generality refers to a change in behavior that holds over time, across different settings, and/or spreads to other relevant and related behaviors. The other answer options (applied, behavioral, and effective) refer to other core principles and function as distractors.

REFERENCE

Baer, D. M., Wolf, M. M., & Risley, T. R. (1968). Some current dimensions of applied behavior analysis. *Journal of Applied Behavior Analysis, 1*(1), 91.

BIBLIOGRAPHY

Behavior Analyst Certification Board. (2017). *BCBA task list* (5th ed.). http://ies.ed.gov /ncee/wwc/pdf/wwc_scd.pdf

Cooper, J. O., Heron, T. E., & Heward, W. L. (2020). *Applied behavior analysis* (3rd ed.). Pearson Education.

Morris, E. K., Altus, D. E., & Smith, N. G. (2013). A study in the founding of applied behavior analysis through its publications. *The Behavior Analyst, 36*(1), 73–107.

Concepts and Principles

Applied behavior analysis can be described as "a science based on the use of learning principles to improve lives" (Behavior Analyst Certification Board, 2022). In other words, it is a discipline that focuses on the systematic application of the concepts and principles of behavior analysis to address problems of social significance. Thus, it is critical that behavior analysts develop a solid foundation in their understanding of the concepts and principles of behavior analysis. The purpose of this chapter will be to provide an essential review of Task List items B-1 through B-15, which specifically relate to fundamental concepts and principles for behavior analysts.

▶ LEARNING OBJECTIVES

The following Task List items related to concepts and principles (B-1 through B-15) serve as the learning objectives of this chapter:

B-1   Define and provide examples of behavior, response, and response class.

B-2   Define and provide examples of stimulus and stimulus class.

B-3   Define and provide examples of respondent and operant conditioning.

B-4   Define and provide examples of positive and negative reinforcement contingencies.

B-5   Define and provide examples of schedules of reinforcement.

B-6   Define and provide examples of positive and negative punishment contingencies.

B-7   Define and provide examples of automatic- and socially mediated contingencies.

B-8   Define and provide examples of unconditioned, conditioned, and generalized reinforcers and punishers.

B-9   Define and provide examples of operant extinction.

B-10   Define and provide examples of stimulus control.

B-11   Define and provide examples of discrimination, generalization, and maintenance.

B-12   Define and provide examples of motivating operations.

B-13   Define and provide examples of rule-governed and contingency-shaped behavior.

B-14   Define and provide examples of the verbal operants.

B-15   Define and provide examples of derived stimulus relations.

▶ TASK LIST ITEM B-1

The objective of this Task List item is to define and provide examples of behavior, response, and response class.

BEHAVIOR

This is the "activity of living organisms" (Cooper et al., 2020, p. 25) and includes all manner of human actions (e.g., eating, walking, speaking, breathing, crying). More technically, behavior is an organism's activity that results in a measurable change in its environment. The "dead man's test" for behavior is a rather crude but memorable way of clarifying what is and what is not behavior; that is, if a dead person can do it, it is not considered behavior—unless, of course, the dead person is a zombie.

RESPONSE

This refers to a specific instance (i.e., occurrence) of behavior.

- *Example* (reading): When you read the previous sentence (i.e., definition of a response); that was a response.
- *Example* (passing the guac): You pass the guacamole after a friend asks you for it.

RESPONSE CLASS

This is a group of responses defined by (a) form or (b) function.

TOPOGRAPHICAL RESPONSE CLASS

This defines members of its class in terms of their form (i.e., what they look like).

- *Example*: The diagnostic criteria for autism spectrum disorders is an example of a topographical response class system. A set of symptoms (i.e., behaviors) forms the class that results in the diagnosis, but they don't tell you anything about why they occur (i.e., function).

FUNCTIONAL RESPONSE CLASS

This is a group of responses that share a common function. In other words, this refers to two or more behaviors that produce the same outcome in the environment.

- *Example*: A child may receive attention as a result of several responses that vary in form—yelling, crying, smiling, speaking, and so on.

Table 4.1 The difference between functional and topographical response classes

Functional Response Class	Topographical Response Class
Form of the response may vary	Specifies the form
Includes responses whose occurrence depend on particular antecedent and/or consequence stimuli	May include responses that make up only a subset of those from a functional response class

▶ TASK LIST ITEM B-2

The objective of this Task List item is to define and provide examples of stimulus and stimulus class.

STIMULUS

This is an event that affects the behavior of an individual. It involves a change in energy that affects a living organism through one or more of its sense organs. All living organisms monitor and respond to changes in their environments and inside their bodies. Our five senses are examples of *exteroceptors*. Humans also have sense organs that detect changes inside the body (*interoceptors*) and that foster movement and balance (*proprioceptors*).

- *Example*: The sound (stimulus) of the postal delivery truck stopping at your residence may serve as a stimulus that leads you to walk to the door to see if a package is being delivered.

STIMULUS CLASS

This is a cluster of stimuli with elements in common across one or more of the following dimensions: (a) formal, (b) temporal, and (c) functional.

Formal

This refers to their shared physical feature(s). They either look or sound alike.

■ *Example*: A stimulus class that consists of things that are blue in color.

Temporal

This refers to the timing of their occurrence in relation to a behavior of interest. They are antecedents or consequences for a particular response.

■ *Example*: A stimulus class that consists of things that happen right before you check your mobile phone.

Functional

This refers to their common effect on behavior. They serve as discriminative stimuli for a particular response.

■ *Example*: A stimulus class that consists of things that prompt you to check your mobile phone.

ADDITIONAL NOTE(S)

You may also encounter the terms *arbitrary stimulus class* (which are antecedent stimuli that are dissimilar but bring about the same response) and *feature stimulus class* (which are stimuli that have shared physical features or relative relationships).

▶ TASK LIST ITEM B-3

The objective of this Task List item is to define and provide examples of respondent and operant conditioning.

RESPONDENT CONDITIONING

This is a type of learning (also known as *classical, Pavlovian,* or *stimulus-response conditioning*) whereby new stimuli develop the capacity to elicit responses through the pairing process. Respondent conditioning focuses on responses that are inborn, automatic, and involuntary. Pavlov, with whom this type of learning is most associated, focused on the connections between stimuli and responses, which are known as *reflexes*. Unconditioned reflexes are involuntary (i.e., not learned) and involve an unconditioned stimulus (US) evoking an unconditioned response (UCR).

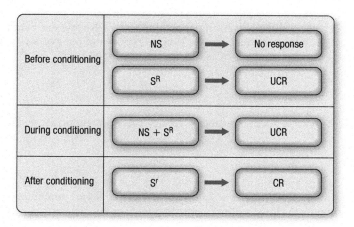

Figure 4.1 Respondent conditioning.
CR, conditioned response; NS, neutral stimulus; S^r, conditioned reinforcer;
S^R, unconditioned reinforcer; UCR, unconditioned response.

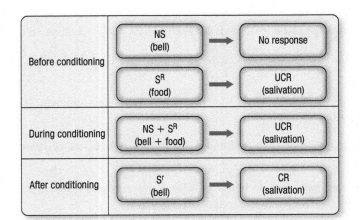

Figure 4.2 Example of respondent conditioning: Pavlov's experiment.
CR, conditioned response; NS, neutral stimulus; S^r, conditioned reinforcer;
S^R, unconditioned reinforcer; UCR, unconditioned response.

In short, respondent conditioning pairs an US with a neutral stimulus (NS) until the NS becomes a conditioned stimulus (CS) that elicits a conditioned response (CR). Thus, antecedents elicit respondent behavior.

- *Example*: Pavlov's famous experiments with dogs demonstrated how meat powder (US), which naturally caused dogs to salivate (UCR) was repeatedly paired with a tone (NS) until the tone elicited salivation (UCR). In this well-known example, the tone was transformed from a NS to a CS, thus establishing a CR.

OPERANT CONDITIONING

This is a type of learning (also known as *instrumental* or *Skinnerian conditioning*) that occurs as a result of rewards and punishments. This concerns operant behavior, which is behavior we have control over. Operant behavior is modified by its history of consequences (i.e., stimulus changes that immediately follow a response). Consequences can be (a) reinforcing, thereby increasing the frequency of a behavior, or (b) punishing, thereby decreasing the frequency of a behavior.

Example (reinforcing consequence): A client is learning to ask for water (the operant behavior) when they are thirsty. When they demonstrate the behavior, water (the reinforcer) is delivered, thereby increasing the future frequency of asking for water when the client is thirsty.

Example (punishing consequence): A client is learning to ask for water (the operant behavior) when they are thirsty. When the client demonstrates the behavior, a vocal reprimand (an aversive stimulus) is delivered, thereby decreasing the future frequency of asking for water behavior.

▶ TASK LIST ITEM B-4

The objective of this Task List item is to define and provide examples of positive and negative reinforcement contingencies.

REINFORCEMENT

This is a basic principle that describes a functional relationship in which a behavior immediately followed by a stimulus change (i.e., consequence) increases the future frequency of the behavior.

Reinforcement can be (a) positive or (b) negative.

Positive Reinforcement

This refers to the presentation (or increase in intensity) of a stimulus immediately subsequent to a behavior that serves to increase the future frequency of the behavior.

Table 4.2 Example of positive reinforcement

R	S^{r+}	Future Frequency of R
Student raises hand	Teacher praises	Increases

R, response; S^{r+}, conditioned positive reinforcer.

Negative Reinforcement

This refers to the removal (or reduction in intensity) of a stimulus immediately subsequent to a behavior that serves to increase the future frequency of the behavior. This stimulus is often referred to as an aversive stimulus whereby removal results in relief.

Table 4.3 Example of negative reinforcement

R	S^{R-}	Future Frequency of R
Closes door when there are loud noises outside	Removal (or reduction) of loud noises	Increases

R, response; S^{R-}, unconditioned negative reinforcer.

MNEMONIC AID

It can be helpful to think of the words *positive* and *negative* in the mathematical sense, where positive = addition (+) and negative = subtraction (−). Positive reinforcement involves the addition of a stimulus, and negative reinforcement involves the subtraction of a stimulus.

▶ TASK LIST ITEM B-5

The objective of this Task List item is to define and provide examples of schedules of reinforcement.

SCHEDULE OF REINFORCEMENT

This is a rule or protocol that specifies the requirements for reinforcement. There are a range of schedules that can be used, each of which differ in terms of the response requirements and environmental arrangements required for reinforcement.

CONTINUOUS REINFORCEMENT SCHEDULE (CRF OR FR1)

This is a schedule that requires the delivery of reinforcement after every occurrence of a target behavior.

Table 4.4 Example of using a continuous reinforcement schedule:
Target behavior = raising hand

Trial	S^D	R	S^{r+}
1	Teacher asks question	Raises hand	Delivered
2	Teacher asks question	Raises hand	Delivered
3	Teacher asks question	Raises hand	Delivered

R, response; S^D, discriminative stimulus; S^{r+}, conditioned positive reinforcer.

INTERMITTENT SCHEDULE OF REINFORCEMENT (INT)

This a schedule that does not involve reinforcing every occurrence of a target behavior. Basic intermittent schedules include (a) fixed ratio (FR) schedules (with the exception of FR1), (b) fixed interval (FI) schedules, (c) variable ratio (VR) schedules, and (d) variable interval (VI) schedules.

Fixed Ratio

This is a schedule that specifies the number of times a target behavior must occur to receive reinforcement. An FR2 schedule means reinforcement is delivered after every two occurrences of the target response, an FR3 means reinforcement is delivered after every three occurrences, and so forth.

Table 4.5 Example of using a FR3 schedule:
Target behavior = raising hand

Trial	S^D	R	S^{r+}
1	Teacher asks question	Raises hand	Not delivered
2	Teacher asks question	Raises hand	Not delivered
3	Teacher asks question	Raises hand	Delivered

FR3, fixed ratio of 3; R, response; S^D, discriminative stimulus; S^{r+}, conditioned positive reinforcer.

Fixed Interval

This is a schedule that specifies the duration that must pass before the first occurrence of a target response will be reinforced. An FI2 (minutes) schedule means reinforcement is delivered for the first occurrence of a target behavior after 2 minutes have elapsed. Once reinforcement is delivered, the time is reset and another 2 minutes must elapse before the next delivery of reinforcement can occur.

Table 4.6 Example of using a FI5 (minutes) schedule:
Target behavior = raising hand

Trial	Time That Must Elapse Before Is S^{r+} Available	R	S^{r+}
1	5 minutes	First raising hand response	Delivered
2	5 minutes	First raising hand response	Delivered
3	5 minutes	First raising hand response	Delivered

FI5, fixed interval of 5; R, response; S^{r+}, conditioned positive reinforcer.

Variable Ratio

This is a schedule that specifies the average number of times a target behavior must occur to receive reinforcement. Thus, the occurrence of reinforcement is less predictable. A VR2 schedule means reinforcement is delivered after an average of every two occurrences of the target response, a VR3 means reinforcement is delivered after an average of every three occurrences, and so forth.

Table 4.7 Example of using a VR2 schedule:
Target behavior = raising hand

Trial	S^D	R	S^{r+}
1	Teacher asks question	Raises hand	Delivered
2	Teacher asks question	Raises hand	Not delivered
3	Teacher asks question	Raises hand	Delivered
4	Teacher asks question	Raises hand	Not delivered
5	Teacher asks question	Raises hand	Not delivered
6	Teacher asks question	Raises hand	Delivered

R, response; S^D, discriminative stimulus; S^{r+}, conditioned positive reinforcer; VR2, variable ratio of 2.

In this example, reinforcement was delivered 3 out of 6 times, which is essentially an average of every two occurrences of the target behavior.

Variable Interval

This is a schedule that specifies the average duration that must pass before the first occurrence of a target response will be reinforced. Thus, the time interval that must elapse before reinforcement is made available is less predictable. An FI2 (minutes) schedule means reinforcement is delivered for the first occurrence of a target behavior after a variable (average) duration of 2 minutes have elapsed. Once reinforcement is delivered, the time is reset and another variable duration of 2 minutes must elapse before the next delivery of reinforcement can occur.

Table 4.8 Example of using a VI5 (minutes) schedule:
Target behavior = raising hand

Trial	Time That Elapses Before Is S^{r+} Available	R	S^{r+}
1	3 minutes	First raising hand response	Delivered
2	5 minutes	First raising hand response	Delivered
3	7 minutes	First raising hand response	Delivered
4	4 minutes	First raising hand response	Delivered
5	5 minutes	First raising hand response	Delivered
6	6 minutes	First raising hand response	Delivered

R, response; S^{r+}, conditioned positive reinforcer; VI5, variable interval of 5.

In this example, the average time elapsed before reinforcement was made available for the first occurrence of the target response is 5 minutes.

There are a number of variations of the basic schedules presented in the preceding examples. These include (a) schedules of differential reinforcement, (b) progressive schedules, and (c) compound schedules.

ADDITIONAL NOTE(S)

The effects of the four basic schedules (i.e., FR, VR, FI, and VI) derived from basic research are well documented. FR schedules produce a break-and-run pattern of responding (i.e., pause [little to no responding] after reinforcement, followed by a transition to a high and constant rate of responding). VR schedules produce a high and constant rate of responding. FI schedules produce a scalloped pattern of responding (i.e., slow at the start, but accelerates toward the end of the interval and typically reaches the highest rate immediately before reinforcement). Lastly, VI schedules produce a constant, low-to-moderate rate of responding.

SCHEDULES OF DIFFERENTIAL REINFORCEMENT

These are schedules in which reinforcement is made contingent upon responses occurring at a predetermined rate of responding. Thus, differential schedules are used to intervene in behavioral problems stemming from the rate at which an individual performs a particular behavior; that is, the person responds too infrequently (i.e., at a lower rate than a predetermined criterion) or too frequently (i.e., at a higher rate than a predetermined criterion).

PROGRESSIVE SCHEDULES

These are schedules in which each successive reinforcement opportunity is thinned regardless of a person's behavior. Schedule requirements can be altered according to a progressive ratio (PR) or a progressive interval (PI) schedule.

COMPOUND SCHEDULES

These are schedules used for investigating a single response in which two or more schedules of reinforcement alternate, appear in succession, or occur at the same time. As such, a compound schedule consists of two or more types of schedules of reinforcement. Compound schedules include (a) concurrent schedules, (b) discriminative schedules, (c) nondiscriminative schedules, and (d) schedules combining the number of responses and time.

Concurrent Schedule of Reinforcement (CONC)

This is a schedule in which two or more separate schedules of reinforcement (e.g., FI and VR), each associated with an independent response (i.e., target behavior), are implemented at the same time.

A concurrent schedule of reinforcement is identifiable by the following criterion: It involves two or more contingencies in effect simultaneously or independently for two or more behaviors.

Discriminative Schedules

These include (a) multiple (MULT) schedules and (b) chained (CHAIN) schedules.

MULTIPLE

This is a schedule where two or more basic schedules of reinforcement are implemented in an alternating and, typically, random order.

CHAINED

This is a schedule that is similar to MULT and typically used to investigate conditioned reinforcement. In a CHAIN, at least two schedules, each accompanied by a distinctive stimulus, must be completed before primary reinforcement occurs. Thus, it makes reinforcement contingent on the client's successful completion of all components in the proper order.

Nondiscriminative Schedules

These include (a) mixed (MIX) schedules and (b) tandem (TAND) schedules.

MIXED

This is a schedule that uses a procedure identical to MULT with the exception that no discriminative stimuli are correlated with the independent schedules. As such, a MIX implements two or more schedules of reinforcement in a random/alternating order without correlated discriminative stimuli.

TANDEM

This is a schedule that uses the same procedure as a CHAIN, but (like the MIX) without any correlated discriminative stimuli.

Schedules Combining the Number of Responses and Time

These include (a) alternative (ALT) schedules and (b) conjunctive (CONJ) schedules.

ALTERNATIVE

This is a schedule in which reinforcement of a response is provided according to either a FI schedule or a FR schedule, whichever is satisfied first.

CONJUNCTIVE

This is a schedule in which reinforcement is given after two or more schedules of reinforcement are completed without respect to the order in which the schedules are completed.

▶ TASK LIST ITEM B-6

The objective of this Task List item is to define and provide examples of positive and negative punishment contingencies.

PUNISHMENT

This is a basic principle that describes a functional relationship in which a behavior immediately followed by a stimulus change (i.e., consequence) decreases the future frequency of the behavior. Punishment can be (a) positive or (b) negative.

POSITIVE PUNISHMENT

This refers to the presentation (or increase in intensity) of a stimulus immediately following a behavior, which decreases the future frequency of the behavior.

Table 4.9 Example of positive punishment

R	S^{P+}	Future Frequency of R
Student yells	Teacher reprimand	Decreases

R, response; S^{P+}, conditioned positive punisher.

NEGATIVE PUNISHMENT

This refers to the removal (or reduction in intensity) of a stimulus immediately following a behavior, which decreases the future frequency of the behavior.

Table 4.10 Example of negative punishment

R	S^{P-}	Future Frequency of R
Student yells	Reduction in length of recess time	Decreases

R, response; S^{P-}, conditioned negative punisher.

MNEMONIC AID

It can be helpful to think of the words *positive* and *negative* in the mathematical sense, where *positive* = addition (+) and *negative* = subtraction (−). Positive punishment involves the addition of a stimulus, and negative punishment involves the subtraction of a stimulus.

▶ TASK LIST ITEM B-7

The objective of this Task List item is to define and provide examples of automatic and socially mediated contingencies.

AUTOMATIC CONTINGENCIES

Also referred to as *direct contingencies*, these refer to environmental contingencies that can affect behavior without the mediation or deliberate actions of another person. As such, these contingencies are considered *nonsocial.* While there are many types of automatic contingencies (e.g., automatic punishment, automatic motivating operation [MO] control, automatic stimulus control), behavior analysts have primarily focused on automatic reinforcement.

Automatic Reinforcement

This occurs when reinforcement is (a) a response product of a behavior or (b) a product of the physical environment resulting from a behavior.

Table 4.11 Example of automatic reinforcement as a response product of a behavior

R	S^{r+}
Singing	Desirable stimulation

R, response; S^{r+}, conditioned positive reinforcer.

Table 4.12 Example of automatic reinforcement as a product of the physical environment resulting from a behavior

R	S^{r+}
Turning on the radio	Desirable stimulation

R, response; S^{r+}, conditioned positive reinforcer.

Socially Mediated Contingencies

Also referred to as *indirect contingencies*, these refer to environmental contingencies that can affect behavior with the mediation or deliberate actions of another person. Behavior analysts have primarily focused on socially mediated reinforcement.

SOCIALLY MEDIATED REINFORCEMENT

This occurs when reinforcement is a product of the actions of another person resulting from a behavior.

Table 4.13 Example of socially mediated reinforcement

R	S^{r+}
Asking for a "cookie"	Someone delivers a cookie

R, response; S^{r+}, conditioned positive reinforcer.

▶ TASK LIST ITEM B-8

The objective of this Task List item is to define and provide examples of unconditioned, conditioned, and generalized reinforcers and punishers.

REINFORCER

This is a stimulus change that increases the future frequency of the behavior that it immediately follows. Reinforcers can be (a) unconditioned, (b) conditioned, or (c) generalized.

Unconditioned Reinforcer

Also known as a *natural* or *primary reinforcer*, this is a stimulus change that increases the future frequency of the behavior that it immediately follows independent of the individual's learning history. It is the product of phylogeny and satisfies the basic life needs of an organism.

- *Examples*: Water, food, oxygen, warmth, sex

Conditioned Reinforcer

Also known as a *learned* or *secondary reinforcer*, this is a stimulus change that increases the future frequency of the behavior that it immediately follows as a result of its previous pairing with one or more other reinforcers. It is the product of ontogeny, varies across individuals, and changes throughout the individual's lifespan.

- *Examples*: Money, grades, praise, tokens

Generalized Reinforcer

This is a conditioned reinforcer that has been paired with many other reinforcers.

- *Example*: Money (because it can be used to gain access to many reinforcing stimuli)

PUNISHER

This is a stimulus change that decreases the future frequency of the behavior that it immediately follows. Punishers can be (a) unconditioned, (b) conditioned, or (c) generalized.

Unconditioned Punisher

Also known as an *unlearned* or *primary punisher*, this is a stimulus change that decreases the future frequency of any behavior that it immediately follows independent of the individual's learning history. It is the product of phylogeny and is naturally undesirable.

- *Examples*: Extreme temperatures, painful stimulation

Conditioned Punisher

Also known as a *learned* or *secondary punisher*, this is a stimulus change that decreases the future frequency of the behavior that it immediately follows as a result of its previous pairing with one or more other punishers. It is the product of ontogeny.

- *Example*: Sight of blood (because it has been previously paired with painful stimulation)

Generalized Punisher

This is a conditioned punisher that has been paired with many other punishers.

- *Example*: Verbal reprimands (because they have been consistently paired with other forms of social disapproval and unconditioned/conditioned punishers)

▶ TASK LIST ITEM B-9

The objective of this Task List item is to define and provide examples of operant extinction (EXT).

OPERANT EXTINCTION

This refers to a reduction in behavior resulting from the discontinuation of reinforcement for it. EXT procedures involve withholding reinforcers that maintain undesirable behavior. In other words, the problem behavior no longer results in reinforcement. As a result, the frequency of its occurrence will decrease in the future.

- *Example*: A client's yelling behavior is maintained by access to toys.

Table 4.14 Problem behavior and
resulting consequence (positive reinforcer)

R	S^{r+}
Yell	Adult delivers toy

R, response; S^{r+}, conditioned positive reinforcer.

Implementation of an EXT procedure will involve withholding toys from the client when they yell, resulting in less yelling in the future.

Table 4.15 Example of using an EXT procedure to
address problem behavior

R	S^{r+}	Future Frequency
Yell	Adult does not deliver toy	↓

EXT, extinction; R, response; S^{r+}, conditioned positive reinforcer.

▶ TASK LIST ITEM B-10

The objective of this Task List item is to define and provide examples of stimulus control.

STIMULUS CONTROL

This refers to the alteration of the frequency, duration, latency, or magnitude of behavior by the presence or absence of an antecedent stimulus. In other words, behavior changes based on whether or not some stimulus is present.

Stimulus control is established when a response is (a) only reinforced when a specific stimulus (discriminative stimulus or S^D) is present and (b) not reinforced when other stimuli (S^Δ) are present.

- *Example*: The doorbell chime acquires stimulus control when opening the door is only reinforced after the doorbell chimes (and not other stimulus events).

Table 4.16 Contingencies for doorbell chime
to acquire stimulus control

S^D	R	S^{r+}
Doorbell chimes	Open door	See friend on doorstep
S^D	**R**	**S^Δ**
Cell phone chimes	Open door	No friend on doorstep
Alarm clock chimes	Open door	No friend on doorstep
Dog barks	Open door	No friend on doorstep

R, response; S^D, discriminative stimulus; S^Δ, stimulus delta; S^{r+}, conditioned positive reinforcer.

▶ TASK LIST ITEM B-11

The objective of this Task List item is to define and provide examples of discrimination, generalization, and maintenance.

Discrimination, generalization, and maintenance are processes central to behavior analysis.

DISCRIMINATION

This refers to the emission of a differential response when presented with two or more stimuli.

Simple Discrimination

This occurs when the client emits a response that is controlled by a single stimulus.

■ *Example*: A client sees a friend at school, Cara, and greets her with, "Hey, Cara!"

Table 4.17 Simple discrimination

S^D	R
Cara	"Hey, Cara!"

R, response; S^D, discriminative stimulus.

Conditional Discrimination

This occurs when the client emits a response that is controlled by a single stimulus when it is in the presence of another stimulus.

■ *Example*: A client sees a friend at school, Cara, and greets her with, "Hey, Cara!" only when it is recess time.

Table 4.18 Conditional discrimination

Conditional Stimulus	S^D	S^r+
Recess time	Cara	"Hey, Cara!"

S^D, discriminative stimulus; S^r+, conditioned positive reinforcer.

GENERALIZATION

This refers to the spreading of the effects of some operation (e.g., reinforcement, punishment, or EXT) on one stimulus to other, different stimuli. When responding is similar in the presence of two different stimuli, the client has generalized between them. Types of generalization include (a) response generalization, (b) stimulus generalization, and (c) setting/situation generalization.

Response Generalization

This occurs when the client emits an untrained response that serves the same function as the trained target behavior. The focus is on function, not form.

■ *Example*: A client learns to greet a friend with, "Hello."

Table 4.19 Learned response

S^D	R
Friend	"Hello"

R, response; S^D, discriminative stimulus.

Then, in the presence of familiar people, the client uses different, untrained responses that serve the same function as "Hello."

Table 4.20 Response generalization

S^D	R
Friend	"Hey"
Another friend	"Good morning"
Therapist	Waves hand

R, response; S^D, discriminative stimulus

Stimulus Generalization

This occurs when the client emits a trained response in the presence of a stimulus that is physically similar to the stimulus that was used to train it.

■ *Example*: A client learns to say "bunny" in the presence of a bunny rabbit.

Table 4.21 Trained response in presence of a specific stimulus

S^D	R
Bunny	"Bunny"

R, response; S^D, discriminative stimulus.

Then, in the presence of other small, furry animals, the client says "bunny."

Table 4.22 Stimulus generalization

S^D	R
Ferret	"Bunny"
Guinea pig	"Bunny"
Squirrel	"Bunny"

R, response; S^D, discriminative stimulus.

Setting/Situation Generalization

This occurs when the client emits a trained response in a setting that is different from where it was trained.

■ *Example*: A client learns to do cartwheels in a gym.

Table 4.23 Trained response in a specific setting

S^D	R
Gym	Cartwheel

R, response; S^D, discriminative stimulus.

Then, the client performs cartwheels in a park.

Table 4.24 Setting/situation generalization

S^D	R
Park	Cartwheel

R, response; S^D, discriminative stimulus.

ADDITIONAL NOTE(S)

It may be helpful to think of discrimination and generalization as two ends of the same spectrum related to stimulus function.

MAINTENANCE

This refers to the extent to which a client continues to perform a behavior when some or all of an intervention that evokes it has been removed.

■ *Example*: An intervention is implemented to teach a client to independently put on their backpack in the morning before leaving home for school, 5 days of the week. After the intervention has been withdrawn, the client has "maintained" the skill by continuing to put on their backpack in the morning before leaving home for school, 5 days of the week.

▶ TASK LIST ITEM B-12

The objective of this Task List item is to define and provide examples of MOs.

MOTIVATING OPERATION

This is an environmental variable that produces two different effects: (a) value altering and (b) behavior altering.

Value Altering

This is a momentary increase or decrease in the reinforcing effects of a stimulus.

If the MO increases the reinforcing effects of a stimulus, it is said to have produced a reinforcer-establishing effect. This type of MO is referred to as an Establishing Operation (EO).

If the MO decreases the reinforcing effects of a stimulus, it is said to have produced a reinforcer-abolishing effect. This type of MO is referred to as an abolishing operation (AO).

Behavior Altering

This is a momentary increase or decrease in the frequency of a behavior that has been reinforced or punished by the stimulus whose value has been changed by the MO.

If the MO increases the frequency of a behavior that has been reinforced by some stimulus, it is said to have produced an evocative effect.

If the MO decreases the frequency of a behavior that has been reinforced by some stimulus, it is said to have produced an abative effect.

■ *Example*: Food deprivation increases the effectiveness of food as a reinforcer (value-altering; reinforcer-establishing effect) and food-seeking behaviors (behavior-altering; evocative effect).

If the MO was food ingestion instead of deprivation, we would see a decrease in the effectiveness of food as a reinforcer (value-altering; reinforcer-abolishing effect) and food-seeking behaviors (behavior-altering; abative effect).

MOs can be conditioned or unconditioned.

UNCONDITIONED MOTIVATING OPERATION

This is an MO that does not require learning to produce value-altering and behavior-altering effects.

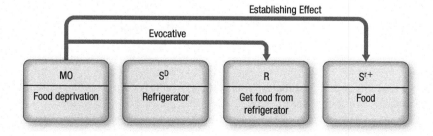

Figure 4.3 Example of value-altering and behavior-altering effects of food deprivation.
MO, Motivating Operation; R, response; S^D, discriminative stimulus; S^{r+}, conditioned positive reinforcer.

Unconditioned Motivating Operation (UMOs) that have reinforcer-establishing and evocative effects include:

- deprivation of food, water, sleep, activity, oxygen, sex
- being too hot or cold
- onset/increase in painful stimulation

UMOs that have reinforcer-abolishing and abative effects include ingestion and engaging in specific activities (e.g., sleep, activity, breathing, sex).

CONDITIONED MOTIVATING OPERATION

Like UMOs, Conditioned Motivating Operations (CMOs) produce value-altering and behavior-altering effects, but unlike UMOs, the value-altering effects of CMOs depend on a learning history. There are three types of CMOs, including: (a) surrogate, (b) reflexive, and (c) transitive.

Surrogate Conditioned Motivating Operation

This is a stimulus that has acquired its effects as an MO as a result of being paired with a UMO.

- *Example*: A person might go to the kitchen where food is kept when they haven't eaten for a period of time. After multiple pairings of food deprivation (UMO) with the kitchen, the kitchen may become a Surrogate Conditioned MO (CMO-S) that establishes food as a reinforcer and evokes food-seeking behaviors.

Reflexive Conditioned Motivating Operation

This is a stimulus that has acquired its effects as an MO as a result of it preceding the onset of unpleasant/painful stimulation. Its own offset functions as a reinforcer.

Transitive Conditioned Motivating Operation

This is a stimulus that establishes or abolishes the reinforcing or punishing value of another stimulus.

- *Example*: Your head hurts. As a Reflexive Conditioned MO (CMO-R), this condition (i.e., your head hurting) is only getting worse, which establishes its own offset as a reinforcer and evokes behavior that has resulted in its offset in the past. As a Transitive Conditioned MO (CMO-T), this condition increases the reinforcing value of aspirin.

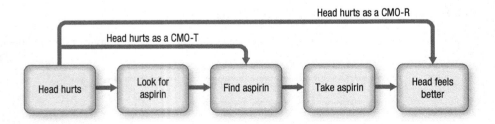

Figure 4.4 Example of painful stimulus (head hurts) as a reflexive conditioned and transitive conditioned motivating operation.
CMO-R, Reflexive Conditioned Motivating Operation CMO-T, Transitive Conditioned Motivating Operation.

▶ TASK LIST ITEM B-13

The objective of this Task List item is to define and provide examples of rule-governed and contingency-shaped behavior.

RULE-GOVERNED BEHAVIOR

This refers to behavior that is under the control of verbal antecedents that are considered rules. There are two types of rules: (a) those in the form of a simple request or instruction and (b) those that describe a behavioral contingency.

Rule-governed behavior is generated through exposure to rules and enables organisms to respond effectively without directly contacting contingencies that would be harmful or inefficient to contact.

For example, a commonly understood rule is that if you touch a stove when it is on you will get burned. This represents an "if/then" rule: If you touch a stove when it is on, then you get burned. An if/then statement is a simple rule that specifies both the antecedent and the behavior(s) that should occur in its presence.

- *Example* (simple request or instruction): "Do not touch that stove when it is on."
- *Example* (describing a contingency): "If you touch that stove when it is on, you will burn your hand."

CONTINGENCY-SHAPED BEHAVIOR

This refers to behavior that is learned through experience with contingencies.

- *Example*: You avoid touching the stove when it is on because you have learned from experience that doing so will burn your hand.

▶ TASK LIST ITEM B-14

The objective of this Task List item is to define and provide examples of the verbal operants.

VERBAL OPERANTS

These are types of expressive language (i.e., verbal behavior), which include the (a) duplic, (b) mand, (c) tact, (d) intraverbal, and (e) codic. Each verbal operant is identified by its source of antecedent control and history of resultant consequence.

Duplic

This type is under the control of a verbal stimulus with point-to-point correspondence (i.e., stimulus parts correspond with response parts), formal similarity (i.e., stimulus and response physically resemble each other), and has a history of generalized reinforcement. There are three types of duplics, including the (a) echoic, (b) mimetic (i.e., motor imitation), and (c) copying text.

- *Example* (echoic): A client hears "Hi" and then says, "Hi."

Table 4.25 Echoic

Verbal S^D	R	Consequence
Hears "Hi"	Says "Hi"	Generalized S^r (e.g., smile, praise)

R, response; S^D, discriminative stimulus; S^r, conditioned reinforcer.

■ *Example* (mimetic): A client sees an adult wave a hand and then waves a hand.

Table 4.26 Mimetic

Verbal S^D	R	Consequence
Sees a hand wave	Waves hand	Generalized S^r

R, response; S^D, discriminative stimulus; S^r, conditioned reinforcer.

■ *Example* (copying text): A client sees "Hi" written on the whiteboard and then writes the word "Hi" on a piece of paper.

Table 4.27 Copying text

Verbal S^D	R	Consequence
Sees "Hi" written on board	Writes "Hi" on paper	Generalized S^r

R, response; S^D, discriminative stimulus; S^r, conditioned reinforcer.

Mand

This type is under the control of a MO and has a history of specific reinforcement.

■ *Example*: A client is thirsty and signs "water."

Table 4.28 Mand

MO	R	Specific Consequence
Deprived of water for a period of time (value of water is high)	Signs "water"	Water

MO, Motivating Operation; R, response.

Tact

This type is under the control of a nonverbal stimulus and has a history of specific reinforcement.

■ *Example*: A client sees a glass of water and then says "water."

Table 4.29 Tact

Nonverbal S^D	R	Consequence
Sees a glass of water	"Water"	Generalized S^r

R, response; S^D, discriminative stimulus; S^r, conditioned reinforcer.

Intraverbal

This type is under the control of a verbal stimulus without point-to-point correspondence and has a history of generalized reinforcement.

■ *Example*: A client hears "How are you?" and responds "I'm fine."

Table 4.30 Intraverbal

Verbal S^D	R	Consequence
Hears "How are you?"	"I'm fine."	Generalized S^r

R, response; S^D, discriminative stimulus; S^r, conditioned reinforcer.

Codic

This type is under the control of a verbal stimulus without point-to-point correspondence but with formal similarity and has a history of generalized reinforcement. There are two types of codics, including (a) textual and (b) dictation.

■ *Example* (textual): A client sees the written word "fine" in a book and then says "fine."

Table 4.31 Textual verbal operant

Verbal S^D	R	Consequence
Sees "fine" in a book	Says "fine"	Generalized S^r

R, response; S^D, discriminative stimulus; S^r, conditioned reinforcer.

■ *Example* (dictation): A client hears the word "fine" and then write the word "fine" on a piece of paper.

Table 4.32 Taking dictation verbal operant

Verbal S^D	R	Consequence
Hears "fine"	Writes "fine" on paper	Generalized S^r

R, response; S^D, discriminative stimulus; S^r, conditioned reinforcer.

▶ TASK LIST ITEM B-15

The objective of this Task List item is to define and provide examples of derived stimulus relations.

DERIVED STIMULUS RELATION

This refers to the emergence of untrained responses indicating a relation (e.g., the same as, opposite of, different from, better than) between two or more stimuli following a history of related instruction or experience.

The properties of equivalence, in which untrained stimulus–stimulus relations result from training of other stimulus–stimulus relations, are derived from the logical relations of (a) reflexivity, (b) symmetry, and (c) transitivity.

Reflexivity

This type of stimulus–stimulus relation is indicated in the selection of a comparison stimulus that matches the sample stimulus (e.g., A = A) without training to do so.

■ *Example*: A client is given the following sample stimulus (i.e., picture):

Figure 4.5 Sample stimulus.

And the following comparison stimuli (i.e., pictures):

Figure 4.6 Comparison stimuli.

Without training, the client makes the following sample stimulus to comparison stimulus match:

Figure 4.7 Demonstration of reflexivity.

Symmetry

This type of stimulus–stimulus relation is indicated in the demonstration of reversibility of a sample stimulus and comparison stimulus (e.g., if A = B, then B = A) without training to do so.

- *Example*: A client is taught the following sample stimulus (i.e., picture) to comparison stimulus (i.e., spoken word) relation:

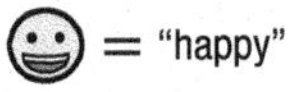

= "happy"

Figure 4.8 Sample stimulus (picture) to comparison stimulus (spoken word).

Without training, the client selects the picture of the happy face when presented with the spoken word "happy."

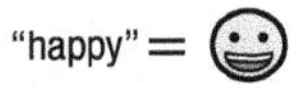

"happy" =

Figure 4.9 Demonstration of symmetry.

Transitivity

This type of stimulus–stimulus relation is indicated in the demonstration of a derived stimulus–stimulus relation following the training of two other stimulus–stimulus relations (e.g., if A = B and B = C, then A = C and C = A).

- *Example*: A client is taught the following relations:

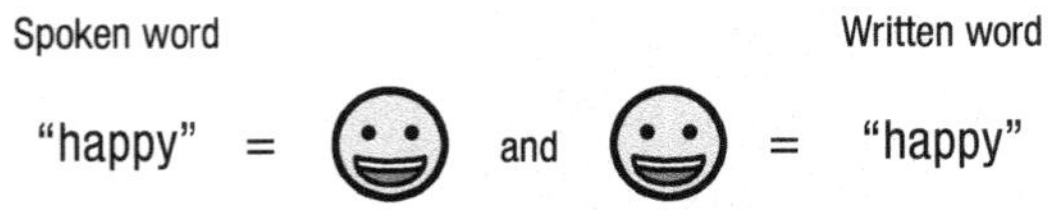

Spoken word   Written word

"happy"   =   and   =   "happy"

Figure 4.10 A (spoken word) = B (picture), and B = C (written word).

- Without training, the following relation emerges:

Spoken word   Written word

"happy"   =   "happy"

Figure 4.11 Demonstration of transitivity.

ADDITIONAL NOTE(S)

There are many different ways in which stimuli can be related. Relations other than *equivalence* can be trained and derived (i.e., nonequivalence relations).

PRACTICE QUESTION

For practice, examine the following question and answer options. After carefully reading it through and conducting your analysis, select the best answer option.

A client, Milo, eats with his hands. After mealtime, his hands are covered with pieces of food. Milo doesn't like this and, in response, wipes his hands on his shirt. Wiping his hands on his shirt effectively removes the pieces of food that were sticking to his hands, which makes Milo more likely to wipe his hands on his shirt in the future. Which of the following provides the best explanation for Milo's increased likelihood of engaging in this behavior (wiping his hands on his shirt) in the future?

A. Negative punishment
B. Negative reinforcement
C. Positive reinforcement
D. Positive punishment

Before moving on to the next section for the solution, we recommend that you to provide a brief explanation for the answer option you selected here:

_____

_____

When you're ready, move on to the next section for the solution!

Practice Question Breakdown

Step 1: Examine the question

The question calls for the identification of the behavior principle that explains Milo's increased likelihood of engaging in a behavior in the future. In the scenario presented, Milo's behavior (wiping his hands on his shirt) resulted in the effective removal of an aversive condition (having his hands covered with pieces of food).

Step 2: Analyze the answer options

A. Negative punishment involves the removal of a stimulus to decrease the likelihood of engaging in a behavior in the future. The question asks for the principle that explains an *increased* likelihood of engaging in a behavior in the future. This answer option is a distractor.
B. Negative reinforcement involves the removal of a stimulus to increase the likelihood of engaging in a behavior in the future. The scenario describes removal of an aversive stimulus condition *and* increased likelihood of engaging in a behavior in the future. This appears to be a promising option!
C. Positive reinforcement involves the presentation of a stimulus to increase the likelihood of engaging in a behavior in the future. However, the scenario involves the *removal* of an aversive stimulus condition. This answer option is a distractor.
D. Positive punishment involves the presentation of a stimulus to decrease the likelihood of engaging in a behavior in the future. The scenario describes the *removal* of an aversive stimulus condition and *increased* likelihood of engaging in a behavior in the future. This answer option is a distractor.

Step 3: Select the best answer

Among the four answer options presented, answer B (negative reinforcement) appears to be the best answer.

▶ CONCLUSION

In this chapter, we reviewed key content for Task List items related to concepts and principles of applied behavior analysis (ABA), including core elements constituting a scientific analysis of behavior and the core principles produced by this analysis. Since the scientific analysis of behavior focuses on controlling variables in the environment, this chapter defined and explicated foundational concepts like behavior, response, response class, stimulus, and stimulus class. The chapter also defined respondent and operant behavior and explained how these two types of behavior are influenced by the environment in respondent and operant conditioning. Building on this foundation, the chapter defined and provided examples of many of the most important concepts and principles in ABA, including reinforcement and punishment; concepts related to the all-important three-term contingency, such as stimulus control; and operant EXT, generalization, maintenance, contingency-shaped behavior, and more.

1. A topographical response class defines members of its class in terms of their:

   A. Form
   B. Function
   C. Rate
   D. Time or place of occurrence

2. A _____ is a group of responses that may vary in form but produce the same effect on the environment.

   A. Behavioral cluster
   B. Functional response class
   C. Response hierarchy
   D. Topographical response class

3. In a stimulus class, stimuli will have elements in common across one or more of the following dimensions except:

   A. Formal
   B. Functional
   C. Spatial
   D. Temporal

4. Respondent conditioning is a type of learning whereby new stimuli develop the capacity to _____ responses through the _____ process.

   A. Elicit; pairing
   B. Elicit; conditioning
   C. Evoke; pairing
   D. Evoke; conditioning

5. Pavlov's famous experiments with dogs demonstrated how meat powder, which naturally caused dogs to salivate, was repeatedly paired with a tone until the tone elicited salivation. In this example, the meat powder served as:

   A. A conditioned stimulus
   B. A neutral stimulus
   C. An unconditioned stimulus
   D. An unconditioned response

6. Operant conditioning focuses on responses that are:

   A. Automatic
   B. Involuntary
   C. Reinforcing
   D. Under our control

1. A) Form
A topographical response class defines members of its class in terms of their form, not function. The other answer options (function, rate, time, or place of occurrence) serve as distractors.

2. B) Functional response class
A functional response class is made up of two or more behaviors that produce the same effect on the environment. The other answer options (behavior cluster, response hierarchy, topographical response class) function as distractors.

3. C) Spatial
In a stimulus class, stimuli will share elements in common across one or more of the following dimensions: formal, temporal, and functional. The remaining answer option (spatial) does not fit into this definition.

4. D) Evoke; conditioning
Respondent conditioning is a type of learning whereby new stimuli develop the capacity to elicit responses through the pairing process. The other answer options (elicit, conditioning; evoke; pairing; evoke, conditioning) does not fit into this definition.

5. C) An unconditioned stimulus
In the example presented, the meat powder served as an unconditioned stimulus that naturally caused Pavlov's dogs to salivate (unconditioned response). The tone is the neutral stimulus that, after pairing with the meat powder, becomes the conditioned stimulus.

6. D) Under our control
Operant conditioning is a type of learning that concerns operant behavior, which is behavior that we have control over. The other answer options (automatic, involuntary, and reinforcing) function as distractors.

7. This refers to the presentation of a stimulus immediately subsequent to a behavior that serves to increase the future frequency of the behavior.

   A. Negative punishment
   B. Negative reinforcement
   C. Positive punishment
   D. Positive reinforcement

8. This refers to the removal of a stimulus immediately subsequent to a behavior that serves to increase the future frequency of the behavior.

   A. Negative punishment
   B. Negative reinforcement
   C. Positive punishment
   D. Positive reinforcement

9. A continuous schedule of reinforcement requires the delivery of reinforcement after _____.

   A. A specified period of time, regardless of whether a target behavior occurred
   B. Each occurrence of a target behavior
   C. Each occurrence of a target behavior following a specified period of time
   D. Every other occurrence of a target behavior

10. Which of the following schedules of reinforcement specifies the average duration that must pass before the first occurrence of a target response will be reinforced?

    A. FI
    B. FR
    C. VI
    D. VR

11. Which of the following schedules of reinforcement specifies a duration that must pass before the first occurrence of a target response will be reinforced?

    A. FI
    B. FR
    C. VI
    D. VR

12. In which of the following types of schedules of reinforcement is each successive reinforcement opportunity thinned regardless of a person's behavior?

    A. Concurrent schedule
    B. Discriminative schedule
    C. Progressive schedule
    D. Nondiscriminative schedule

7. D) Positive reinforcement
Positive reinforcement refers to the presentation of a stimulus immediately subsequent to a behavior that serves to increase the future frequency of the behavior. The other response options (negative punishment, negative reinforcement, positive punishment) function as distractors.

8. B) Negative reinforcement
Negative reinforcement refers to the removal of a stimulus immediately subsequent to a behavior that serves to increase the future frequency of the behavior. The other response options (negative punishment, positive punishment, positive reinforcement) function as distractors.

9. B) Each occurrence of a target behavior
A continuous schedule of reinforcement requires the delivery of reinforcement after each occurrence of a target behavior. The other response options (a specified period of time, regardless of whether a target behavior occurred; each occurrence of a target behavior following a specified period of time; every other occurrence of a target behavior) function as distractors.

10. C) VI
The VI (variable interval) schedule of reinforcement specifies the average duration that must pass before the first occurrence of a target response will be reinforced. The other answer options (FI [fixed interval], FR [fixed ratio], VR [variable ratio]) refer to other schedules of reinforcement and function as distractors.

11. A) FI
The FI (fixed interval) schedule of reinforcement specifies a duration that must pass before the first occurrence of a target response will be reinforced. The other answer options (FR [fixed ratio], VI [variable interval], VR [variable ratio]) refer to other schedules of reinforcement and function as distractors.

12. C) Progressive schedule
Progressive schedule of reinforcement is one in which each successive reinforcement opportunity thinned regardless of an individual's behavior. The other answer options (concurrent schedule, discriminative schedule, nondiscriminative schedule) refer to other schedules of reinforcement and function as distractors.

13. What type of reinforcement is either a response product of a behavior, or a product of the physical environment resulting from a behavior?

  A. Automatic
  B. Positive
  C. Negative
  D. Socially mediated

14. Which of the following best describes socially mediated reinforcement?

  A. It is a product of the actions of another person
  B. It is a product of the actions of another person resulting from a behavior
  C. It is the product of the physical environment resulting from a behavior
  D. It is the response product of a behavior

15. Water and food are examples of:

  A. Arbitrary reinforcers
  B. Conditioned reinforcers
  C. Generalized reinforcers
  D. Unconditioned reinforcers

16. Social praise is an example of:

  A. A conditioned reinforcer
  B. A generalized reinforcer
  C. An arbitrary reinforcer
  D. An unconditioned reinforcer

17. Operant extinction refers to _____ in behavior resulting from the _____ of reinforcement for it.

  A. A reduction; delivery
  B. A reduction; discontinuation
  C. An increase; delivery
  D. An increase; discontinuation

18. Which of the following is established when a response is only reinforced when a specific stimulus is present but not reinforced when other stimuli are present?

  A. Discrimination
  B. Response class
  C. Stimulus class
  D. Stimulus control

19. What type of discrimination occurs when a client emits a response that is controlled by a single stimulus?

  A. Conditional discrimination
  B. Simple discrimination
  C. Simultaneous discrimination
  D. Temporal discrimination

13. A) Automatic
Automatic reinforcement occurs when reinforcement is either a response product of a behavior, or a product of the physical environment resulting from a behavior. The other answer options (positive, negative, socially mediated) refer to other types of reinforcement and function as distractors.

14. B) It is a product of the actions of another person resulting from a behavior
Socially mediated reinforcement is best described as a product of the actions of another person resulting from a behavior. The other answer options (it is a product of the actions of another person, it is the product of the physical environment resulting from a behavior, it is the response product of a behavior) function as distractors.

15. D) Unconditioned reinforcers
Unconditioned reinforcers are the product of phylogeny and satisfies basic life needs, such as water and food. The other answer options (arbitrary reinforcers, conditioned reinforcers, generalized reinforcers) refer to other types of reinforcers and function as distractors.

16. A) A conditioned reinforcer
A generalized reinforcer is a conditioned reinforcer that has been paired with many other reinforcers. Social praise is typically considered an example of this type of reinforcer as it has been paired with many sources of reinforcement. The other answer options (an arbitrary reinforcer, an unconditioned reinforcer, both A and B) function as distractors.

17. B) A reduction; discontinuation
Operant extinction refers to a reduction in behavior resulting from the delivery of reinforcement for it. The other answer options (a reduction, delivery; an increase, delivery; an increase, discontinuation) do not fit this definition and function as distractors.

18. D) Stimulus control
Stimulus control is established when a response is only reinforced when a specific stimulus is present but not reinforced when other stimuli are present. The other answer options (discrimination, response class, stimulus class) refer to other concepts and function as distractors.

19. B) Simple discrimination
Simple discrimination occurs when a client emits a response that is controlled by a single stimulus. The other answer options (conditional discrimination, simultaneous discrimination, temporal discrimination) refer to other types of discrimination and function as distractors.

20. What type of discrimination occurs when a client emits a response that is controlled by a single stimulus when it is in the presence of another stimulus?

   A. Conditional discrimination
   B. Relational discrimination
   C. Simple discrimination
   D. Successive discrimination

21. A client learns to sing a song in a classroom. Then, the client sings the same song at his home. This is an example of:

   A. Overgeneralization
   B. Response generalization
   C. Stimulus generalization
   D. Setting generalization

22. An intervention is implemented to teach a client to perform a skill. After the intervention has been withdrawn, the client continues to perform the skill. This is an example of:

   A. Maintenance
   B. Persistence
   C. Response generalization
   D. Stimulus generalization

23. If a motivating operation momentarily increases the reinforcing effects of a stimulus, it is said to have produced a _____ effect.

   A. Behavior-altering
   B. Reinforcer-abolishing
   C. Reinforcer-establishing
   D. Second-order

24. If a motivating operation increases the frequency of a behavior that has been reinforced by some stimulus, it is said to have produced _____ effect.

   A. An evocative
   B. An abative
   C. A primacy
   D. A reinforcer-establishing

25. Which of the following types of motivating operations does not require learning to produce value-altering and behavior-altering effects?

   A. AO
   B. CMO-R
   C. CMO-S
   D. UMO

26. _____, the condition establishes its own offset as a reinforcer and evokes medicine-seeking behavior which has resulted in relieving stomach pain in the past.

   A. CMO-R
   B. CMO-S
   C. CMO-T
   D. UMO

20. A) Conditional discrimination

Conditional discrimination occurs when a client emits a response that is controlled by a single stimulus when it is in the presence of another stimulus. The other answer options (relational discrimination, simple discrimination, successive discrimination) refer to other types of discrimination and function as distractors.

21. D) Setting generalization

Setting generalization is a type of generalization that occurs when the client emits a trained response in a setting that is different from where it was trained. In the scenario presented, the client learns to sing a song in one environment but then emits the same behavior in a setting that is different from the one in which it was learned. This is an example of setting generalization. The other answer options (overgeneralization, response generalization, stimulus generalization) refer to other types of generalization and function as distractors.

22. A) Maintenance

When an intervention has been implemented to teach a skill and is subsequently withdrawn but the client continues to perform it, the skill is said to have been maintained. This is an example of maintenance. Persistence is not the correct technical term for this concept. The other answer options (persistence, response generalization, stimulus generalization) function as distractors.

23. C) Reinforcer-establishing

A motivating operation produces value-altering and behavior-altering effects. If it momentarily increases the reinforcing effects of a stimulus, it is said to have produced a reinforcer-establishing effect. The other answer options (behavior-altering, reinforcer-abolishing, second-order) serve as distractors.

24. A) An evocative

If a motivating operation increases the frequency of a behavior that has been reinforced by some stimulus, it is said to have produced an evocative (rather than abative) effect. The other answer options (an abative, a primacy, a reinforcer-establishing) serve as distractors.

25. D) UMO

UMOs (unconditioned motivating operations) do not require learning to produce value-altering and behavior-altering effects. The other answer options (AO [abolishing operation], CMO-R [reflexive conditioned motivating operation], CMO-S [surrogate conditioned motivating operation]) refer to other types of motivating operations and function as distractors.

26. A) CMO-R

A CMO-R (reflexive conditioned motivating operation) is a stimulus that acquires its effects as a result of it preceding the onset of unpleasant/painful stimulation. In the example provided, the stomach pain is a CMO-R and its own offset functions as a reinforcer. The other answer options (CMO-S [surrogate conditioned motivating operation], CMO-T [transitive conditioned motivating operation], UMO [unconditioned motivating operation]) are distractors.

27. _____ refers to behavior that is under the control of verbal antecedents that are considered rules, whereas _____ refers to behavior that is learned through experience with contingencies.

   A. Contingency-governed; conditioned responses
   B. Contingency-shaped behavior; rule-governed behavior
   C. Discrete; discriminated
   D. Rule-governed behavior; contingency-shaped behavior

28. Which of the following verbal operants is under the control of a motivating operation and has a history of specific reinforcement?

   A. Codic
   B. Mand
   C. Intraverbal
   D. Tact

29. Which of the following verbal operants is under the control of a nonverbal stimulus and has a history of specific reinforcement?

   A. Duplic
   B. Mand
   C. Intraverbal
   D. Tact

30. Which of the following verbal operants is under the control of a verbal stimulus without point-to-point correspondence and has a history of generalized reinforcement?

   A. Duplic
   B. Mand
   C. Intraverbal
   D. Tact

31. Identify the type of stimulus–stimulus relation that is indicated when the selection of a comparison stimulus matches the sample stimulus without training to do so.

   A. Connectedness
   B. Reflexivity
   C. Symmetry
   D. Transitivity

32. Identify the type of stimulus–stimulus relation that is indicated when a response demonstrates a derived stimulus–stimulus relation following the training of two other stimulus–stimulus relations.

   A. Connectedness
   B. Reflexivity
   C. Symmetry
   D. Transitivity

33. Identify the type of stimulus–stimulus relation that is indicated when a response demonstrates reversibility of a sample stimulus and comparison stimulus without training to do so.

   A. Connectedness
   B. Reflexivity
   C. Symmetry
   D. Transitivity

(See answers next page.)

27. D) Rule-governed behavior; contingency-shaped behavior

Rule-governed behavior refers to behavior that is under the control of verbal antecedents that are considered rules, whereas contingency-shaped behavior refers to behavior that is learned through experience with contingencies. The other answer options (contingency-governed, conditioned responses; contingency-shaped behavior, rule-governed behavior; discrete, discriminated) do not accurately fit into this statement and function as distractors.

28. B) Mand

The mand, commonly referred to as a request, is under the control of a motivating operation and has a history of specific reinforcement. The other answer options (codic, intraverbal, tact) are other types of verbal operants and function as distractors.

29. D) Tact

The tact, often referred to as labeling, is under the control of a nonverbal stimulus and has a history of specific reinforcement. The other answer options (duplic, mand, intraverbal) are other types of verbal operants and function as distractors.

30. C) Intraverbal

The intraverbal is under the control is under the control of a verbal stimulus without point-to-point correspondence and has a history of generalized reinforcement. The other answer options (duplic, mand, tact) are other types of verbal operants and function as distractors.

31. B) Reflexivity

Reflexivity is a type of stimulus–stimulus relation that is indicated when the client selects a comparison stimulus that matches the sample stimulus without having been trained to do so. The other answer options (connectedness, symmetry, transitivity), only two of which are other types of stimulus–stimulus relations, function as distractors.

32. C) Symmetry

Symmetry is a type of stimulus–stimulus relation that is indicated when a client's response demonstrates reversibility of a sample stimulus and comparison stimulus without having been trained to do so (if A = B, then B = A). The other answer options (connectedness, reflexivity, transitivity) function as distractors.

33. D) Transitivity

Transitivity is a type of stimulus–stimulus relation that is indicated when a client's response demonstrates a derived stimulus–stimulus relation following the training of two other stimulus–stimulus relations (if A = B and B = C, then A = C and C = A). The other answer options (connectedness, reflexivity, symmetry) function as distractors.

REFERENCE

Cooper, J. O., Heron, T. E., & Heward, W. L. (2020). *Applied behavior analysis* (3rd ed.). Pearson Education.

BIBLIOGRAPHY

Behavior Analyst Certification Board. (2017). *BCBA task list* (5th ed.). http://ies.ed.gov /ncee/wwc/pdf/wwc_scd.pdf

Behavior Analyst Certification Board. (2022). *BACB fact sheet*. Author.

Johnston, J. M., & Pennypacker, H. S. (1993). *Readings for strategies and tactics of behavioral research*. Lawrence Erlbaum Associates, Inc.

Michael, J. L. (2004). *Concepts and principles of behavior analysis*. Western Michigan University, Association for Behavior Analysis International.

Miltenberger, R. (2008). *Behaviour modification*. Wadsworth Publishing.

Schlinger, H. D., Derenne, A., & Baron, A. (2008). What 50 years of research tell us about pausing under ratio schedules of reinforcement. *The Behavior Analyst, 31*(1), 39–60. https://doi .org/10.1007/BF03392160

Sidman, M. (1994). *Equivalence relations and behavior: A research story*. Authors Cooperative.

Skinner, B. F. (1974). *About behaviorism*. Vintage.

Skinner, B. F. (1957). *Verbal behavior*. Appleton-Century-Crofts.

Measurement, Data Display, and Interpretation

5

"The systematic measurement of behavior is foundational to the delivery of applied behavior-analytic services" (LeBlanc et al., 2016, p. 77). Behavior analysts frequently engage in the delivery of services to help clients acquire new skills and address problem behavior. To do this effectively, they need to be able to properly measure behavior, graph behavior data, and then interpret the graphed data. The purpose of this chapter will be to provide an essential review of Task List items C-1 through C-11, which specifically relate to the selection and use of measurement systems, various forms of data displays, and interpretation of graphed data.

▶ LEARNING OBJECTIVES

The following Task List items related to measurement, data display, and interpretation (C-1 through C-11) serve as the learning objectives of this chapter:

C-1　Establish operational definitions of behavior.

C-2　Distinguish among direct, indirect, and product measures of behavior.

C-3　Measure occurrence (e.g., frequency, rate, percentage).

C-4　Measure temporal dimensions of behavior (e.g., duration, latency, interresponse time).

C-5　Measure form and strength of behavior (e.g., topography, magnitude).

C-6　Measure trials to criterion.

C-7　Design and implement sampling procedures (i.e., interval recording, time sampling).

C-8　Evaluate the validity and reliability of measurement procedures.

C-9　Select a measurement system to obtain representative data given the dimensions of behavior and the logistics of observing and recording.

C-10　Graph data to communicate relevant quantitative relations (e.g., equal-interval graphs, bar graphs, cumulative records).

C-11　Interpret graphed data.

▶ TASK LIST ITEM C-1

The objective of this Task List item is to establish operational definitions of behavior.

Behavior must be defined before it can be measured. Well-written operational definitions of target behaviors allow behavior analysts to gather complete information about their occurrence and nonoccurrence (i.e., measure behavior), precisely apply procedures in a timely manner, and produce an accurate evaluation of intervention effectiveness. For researchers, employing operational definitions allows for others to replicate their work.

OPERATIONAL DEFINITION

This is an objective, clear, and complete description of an observable and measurable target behavior.

Observable
Can be seen or heard.

■ *Examples* (observable behaviors): Asking, hitting, speaking, sitting, touching

Measurable

Can be quantified (i.e., counted or timed).

Write definitions that are (a) objective, (b) clear, and (c) complete.

Objective

Describe behavior in observable terms.

Clear

Unambiguous. Observers should be able to read it and then accurately paraphrase it.

Complete

Establishes which response(s) will count as an instance of the target behavior, and which response(s) do not.

■ *Example* (definition of "on task"): Looking at the teacher/board/seatwork, contributing to the assigned task, and quiet when expected to work independently.
■ *Example* (definition of "talking out"): Any vocalizations that are not initiated by the teacher, are out of turn, and/or are unrelated to academic content.
■ *Example* (definition of "tantrum"): Laying on the floor, crying, yelling, throwing objects, and/or pounding fists on desk. The episode is counted if it lasts 10 seconds or more and is counted as a new incident if separated by 5 minutes or more.

ADDITIONAL NOTE(S)

Operational definitions can include examples and nonexamples that further clarify what is to be counted as an occurrence and what is not, thereby reducing ambiguity and increasing the odds of reliable measurement.

PRACTICE QUESTION

Calvin is a third-grade student in a general education classroom. He is often asked to leave the classroom due to off-task behaviors that interfere with instruction and work completion, as well as instances of disruptive or disrespectful behavior toward his teacher and peers. Calvin's teacher requests a behavior support specialist, who is a contracted Board Certified Behavior Analyst (BCBA), to observe Calvin during his literacy block. Prior to observing Calvin, the behavior support specialist meets with the teacher to narrow down a definition of his problem behavior. Which of the following is an example of an operational definition of Calvin's behavior?

A. The behavior is "disruption," which includes behaviors that interfere with instruction and make the teacher/ staff angry and irritated
B. The behavior is "disrespect," which includes vocalizing or gesturing obscenities at staff, screaming (vocalizations above normal conversational volume) at peers, and screaming "no" when asked by the teacher to begin work
C. The behavior is "off task," which includes not completing assignments he is asked to
D. None of the above

Before moving on to the next section for the solution, we recommend that you to provide a brief explanation for the answer option you selected here:

_____

When you're ready, move on to the next section for the solution!

(continued)

Practice Question Breakdown

Step 1: Examine the question

The question calls for an example of an operational definition of Calvin's off-task and/or disruptive/disrespectful behavior that interferes with his learning. Remember that an operational definition of behavior must be observable, measurable, objective, clear, and complete. Be sure to review the statements presented and evaluate whether they meet all the necessary characteristics of an operational definition.

Step 2: Analyze the answer options

A. This answer does not include specific examples of disruption, which makes it unclear, incomplete, and impossible to measure. It also describes the outcome of a behavior.
B. This definition appears to meet the criteria for an operational definition. It is observable (you can hear vocalizations/screams and observe gestures); measurable (you can tally frequency or document the duration of the behaviors); objective (based on observable behaviors such as vocalizing or gesturing obscenities, screaming = vocalizations above normal conversational volume; screaming "no"); clear and complete (includes information about who the behavior is directed at (staff, peers, teacher); the level of behavior that necessitates an occurrence (screaming = vocalizations above normal conversational volume); and under what conditions the behavior occurs (when asked by the teacher to begin work).
C. This answer does not describe the behavior in observable terms such as walking around the room without permission, and so on, but describes a broad category of possible behaviors with no specificity. This is a distractor.
D. There appears to be at least one response that meets the criteria for an operational definition. This is a distractor.

Step 3: Select the best answer

Among the four answer options presented, answer B (the behavior is "disrespect" . . .) appears to be the best answer.

▶ TASK LIST ITEM C-2

The objective of this Task List item is to distinguish among direct, indirect, and product measures of behavior.

Behavioral assessment involves a variety of measures. These include (a) direct measures, (b) indirect measures, and (c) product measures.

DIRECT MEASURES

This refers to measures that involve the observer recording the target behavior as it occurs.

INDIRECT MEASURES

This refers to measures that do not involve direct observation but require the client or others (e.g., parent, teachers, staff) to recall and report information about the target behavior. These include interviews, checklists, and rating scales.

PRODUCT MEASURES

This refers to measures of behavior through examination of its effects produced on the environment (i.e., permanent product). Measurement takes place after the occurrence of the behavior.

- *Example*: Number of toys placed inside a bin.

MNEMONIC AID

Direct, Indirect, and Product measures. Use DIP in your assessments. It just tastes better.

▶ TASK LIST ITEM C-3

The objective of this Task List item is to measure occurrence (e.g., frequency, rate, percentage).

The occurrence of behavior can be measured in terms of (a) frequency, (b) rate, and (c) percentage. Frequency and rate are measures of the fundamental dimensional quantity of *repeatability*. Percentage is a derivative measure that combines the same dimensional quantities (e.g., count/count).

FREQUENCY

Count of a behavior or behavior class. This is calculated by simply adding up the number of occurrences.

■ *Example*: A target behavior occurred three times.

RATE

Count of behavior or behavior class *per unit of time* (e.g., per minute/hour/day). This is calculated by dividing the number of occurrences by the unit of time in which observations were conducted.

■ *Example*: A target behavior occurred three times per hour.

PERCENTAGE

A ratio expressed as a fraction of 100. This is calculated by multiplying the numeric value (e.g., count of a response divided by the total number of responses or opportunities/intervals in which it could have occurred) by 100.

■ *Example*: A target behavior occurred during 60% of intervals recorded during the observation.

MNEMONIC AID

Please (for Percentage) Remember (for Rate) to Floss (for Frequency). When measuring occurrence of behavior, please remember to floss!

▶ TASK LIST ITEM C-4

The objective of this Task List item is to measure temporal dimensions of behavior (e.g., duration, latency, interresponse time [IRT]).

The temporal dimensions of behavior can be measured in terms of (a) duration, (b) latency, and (c) IRT. Duration is a measure of the fundamental dimensional quantity of *temporal extent*, while latency and IRT are measures of *temporal locus*.

DURATION

The length of time that the behavior occupies; time elapsed between the onset and offset of the behavior.

■ *Example*: The student was seated at their desk for 10 minutes.

LATENCY

The length of time from the onset of a stimulus (e.g., verbal instruction, cue) to the initiation of a behavior.

■ *Example*: The student sat down 10 seconds after the teacher verbally instructed them to.

INTERRESPONSE TIME

The length of time between two responses; time elapsed between the onset of one response to the onset of the next response.

■ *Example*: From the time the student first left his assigned seat to the start of the second time he left his seat, 10 minutes had passed.

▶ TASK LIST ITEM C-5

The objective of this Task List item is to measure form and strength of behavior (e.g., topography, magnitude).

Topography and magnitude are not fundamental dimensional quantities but provide useful information about behavior that allow us to define it and determine its occurrence versus nonoccurrence.

TOPOGRAPHY

Physical form of the behavior; what it looks (or sounds) like. Behaviors with different topographies may or may not serve the same function.

■ *Example*: Pointing to a ball and vocally requesting a ball are two different topographical responses that may serve the same function (i.e., obtaining access to a ball).

MAGNITUDE

Intensity of the behavior; the strength/severity of it. Behaviors must typically meet or surpass some designated threshold in magnitude to be counted.

■ *Example*: Talking with a soft voice and talking with a loud voice are two vocalization responses with different magnitudes. In order for talking to be counted as yelling, it must reach or surpass 75 decibels.

▶ TASK LIST ITEM C-6

The objective of this Task List item is to measure trials to criterion.

Like percentage, *trials to criterion* is a derivative measure. Trials to criterion data can be (a) used to compare two or more treatments, (b) used to assess a learner's increasing ability to acquire new skills, and (c) collected and analyzed as a dependent variable in a research study.

TRIALS TO CRITERION

This is a measure of the number of response opportunities (i.e., trials) required to achieve a predetermined level of performance (i.e., mastery criterion). What the trials look like depend on the target behavior and desired level of performance. Trials to criterion data can be reported in terms of count, rate, duration, or latency.

■ *Example*: The student required 25 trials of adding two single-digit numbers to master the skill.

▶ TASK LIST ITEM C-7

The objective of this Task List item is to design and implement sampling procedures (i.e., interval recording, time sampling).

Interval recording and time sampling refer to a collection of procedures for observing and recording behavior. These include (a) whole interval recording, (b) partial interval recording, and (c) momentary time sampling. For each of these recording procedures, divide the observation period into smaller intervals of equal length. Data obtained from all three procedures are typically *reported as percentages* of the total interval in which the behavior was recorded as having occurred.

WHOLE INTERVAL RECORDING

At the end of each interval, the target behavior is recorded as having occurred if it occurred *throughout the entire interval*. This method usually underestimates the occurrence of the behavior; the longer the interval, the greater the underestimation.

This method is often used to target behaviors that are (a) continuous, (b) high frequency, and (c) to be increased.

PARTIAL INTERVAL RECORDING

At the end of each interval, the target behavior is recorded as having occurred if it occurred at *any time during the interval*. This method usually overestimates the total duration of the behavior; however, the rate of high-frequency behaviors may be underestimated.

This method can be used to target multiple behaviors at the same time. It is often used to target behaviors that are to be decreased.

MOMENTARY TIME SAMPLING

At the end of each interval, the target behavior is recorded as having occurred if it occurred at *only at the end of the interval*. This method may overestimate or underestimate the occurrence of the behavior when intervals exceed 2 minutes.

Unlike whole or partial interval recording, this method does not require the observer's undivided attention to measurement, but much behavior will be missed as a result. The planned activity check (PLACHECK) method is a variation of momentary time sampling that involves recording the count of individuals in a group that are engaged in the target behavior only at the end of the interval.

▶ TASK LIST ITEM C-8

The objective of this Task List item is to evaluate the validity and reliability of measurement procedures. Measurements should be valid, accurate, and reliable.

VALIDITY

This refers to the degree to which *we are measuring what we intend to measure*. Valid measurement requires that (a) a socially significant behavior is directly measured, (b) its relevant dimension (e.g., rate, duration) for answering the question is measured, and (c) the data represent its occurrence under relevant conditions (e.g., time, place) for answering the question.

■ *Example*: To measure the weight of an object, it is placed on a properly tuned weight scale.

RELIABILITY

This refers to the degree to which the measure will *produce consistent results*.

■ *Example*: A properly tuned scale repeatedly reports that an object weighs 10 lbs.

You cannot have a valid measure that lacks reliability. However, it is possible to have a reliable measure that is not valid (e.g., an improperly tuned weight scale may reliably report that a banana weighs 50 lbs, but the measurement would clearly be invalid).

Measurement should also be accurate. *Accuracy* refers to the degree to which the observed value approximates the true value.

Table 5.1 Data outcomes by measurement characteristics

Measurement that is . . .	Results in data that are . . .
Valid, accurate, and reliable	Most useful for guiding practice
Accurate and reliable, but not valid	Not helpful for answering the question
Valid and reliable, but not accurate	Wrong
Valid and accurate, but not reliable	At least sometimes wrong

▶ TASK LIST ITEM C-9

The objective of this Task List item is to select a measurement system to obtain representative data given the dimensions of behavior and the logistics of observing and recording.

There are different features of behavior that can be measured. These are referred to as dimensional quantities, which include: (a) repeatability, (b) temporal extent, and (c) temporal locus.

REPEATABILITY

Behavior can be counted as it repeats across time. Measures based on repeatability include: (a) count, (b) rate, and (c) celeration.

Count
Number of occurrences.

Rate
Number of occurrences over a certain period of time.

Celeration
Rate over a certain period of time. This is a measure of how the rate of a behavior can increase (i.e., accelerate) or decrease (i.e., decelerate) over time.

TEMPORAL EXTENT

Behavior can be timed as it occurs during some amount of time. The measure of duration is based on temporal extent.

Duration
Amount of time elapsed between the onset and offset of a behavior.

TEMPORAL LOCUS

When a behavior happens can be measured as it occurs at a certain point in time with respect to other events. Measures based on temporal locus include (a) latency and (b) IRT.

Latency
Amount of time elapsed between the onset of a stimulus and a response that follows it.

Interresponse Time
Amount of time elapsed between two consecutive occurrences of a behavior.

Methods for measuring behavior include: (a) event recording, (b) timing, and (c) various time sampling procedures.

EVENT RECORDING

This involves recording the number of times that a behavior occurs.

TIMING

This involves recording the passage of time with the use of a timing device (e.g., stopwatch).

TIME SAMPLING

This involves recording the occurrence or nonoccurrence of behavior during intervals of time or at specific points in time. See Task List item C-7 for a summary of time sampling (i.e., interval recording) methods used by behavior analysts.

Table 5.2 Measurement procedure selection

If you want to measure . . .	Then . . .
The number of times a behavior occurs and the behavior can be sufficiently counted	Use event recording.
The number of times a behavior occurs but the behavior is difficult to count	Use time sampling.
How long a behavior lasts	Use duration recording.
How long before the behavior occurs	Use latency recording.

ADDITIONAL NOTE(S)

Consider the following recommendations:

- If the behavior is not observable but produces a physical change in the environment, *permanent product recording* may be used. See Task List item C-2 for a review of product measures.
- Schedule observation sessions to obtain data that are generally representative of the behavior.
- If recording data to determine the effects of an intervention, schedule observations when the behavior is most likely to occur if it is targeted for reduction, but schedule observation when the behavior is least likely to occur if it is targeted for increase.
- Ensure that observers are sufficiently trained. Ongoing training can help to minimize unwanted changes to the way data are collected (i.e., observer drift).
- Monitor observers in the most discreet way possible to minimize measurement errors resulting from their awareness that you are watching them (i.e., observer reactivity).

▶ TASK LIST ITEM C-10

The objective of this Task List item is to graph data to communicate relevant quantitative relations (e.g., equal-interval graphs, bar graphs, cumulative records).

Data are gathered throughout a behavior change program to inform important decisions regarding treatment, including whether to continue or change an intervention. To interpret the data gathered and communicate these results to others, behavior analysts use *graphs* which are visual displays of data. Different types of graphs are used, including (a) equal-interval graphs and (b) semilogarithmic charts.

EQUAL-INTERVAL GRAPHS

This is a graph with both the vertical and horizontal axes divided into equal distances between marks to indicate the addition or subtraction of constant amounts. Equal-interval graphs include: (a) line graphs, (b) bar graphs, (c) cumulative records, and (d) scatterplots.

LINE GRAPHS

This type of graph, based on the Cartesian plane (i.e., two perpendicular number lines), is used to display change over time as a series of connected data points. Each data point represents a relationship between some dimensional quantity of behavior (i.e., dependent variable) and time and/or environmental condition (i.e., independent variable).

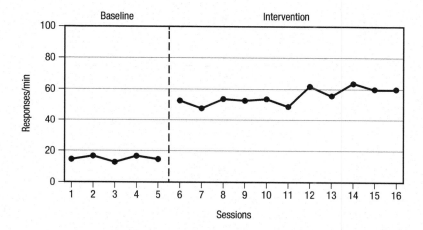

Figure 5.1 Example of a line graph.

BAR GRAPH

This type of graph, also referred to as a histogram, is used to display discrete sets of data (e.g., performance of an individual or group of subjects during different conditions). Unlike the line graph, there are no data points plotted to represent responses over time.

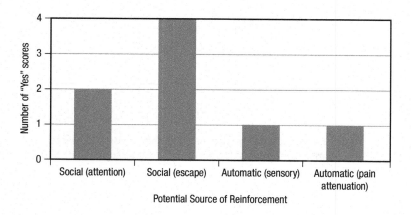

Figure 5.2 Example of a bar graph summarizing the results of a questionnaire.

CUMULATIVE RECORD

This type of graph is used to display the running total of responses over time. The cumulative total is represented on the vertical axis. The data path never descends. A steeper data path indicates a higher response rate.

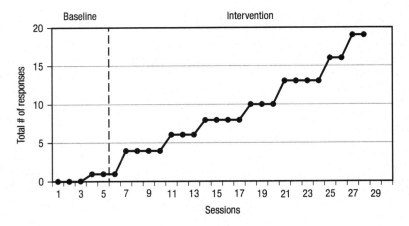

Figure 5.3 Example of a cumulative record.

SCATTERPLOT

This type of graph is used to display the relationship between the variables depicted by the horizontal *x* and vertical *y* axes. The data points do not form a data path, but they can form patterns on the plane that suggest certain relationships.

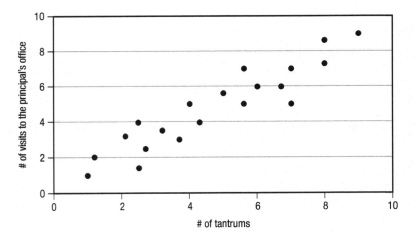

Figure 5.4 Example scatterplot: As *x* (number of visits) increases,
y (number of tantrums) increases (i.e., positive correlation).

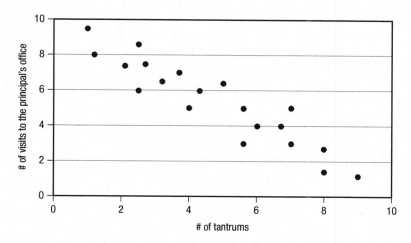

Figure 5.5 Example scatterplot: As *x* decreases, *y* increases (i.e., negative correlation).

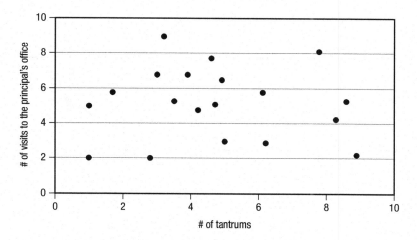

Figure 5.6 Example scatterplot: No clear indication of relationship between *x* and *y* (i.e., no correlation).

Behavior analysts also use scatterplots to show when a target behavior occurs and whether it is associated with certain times.

■ *Example* (scatterplot for timing of behavior): The following graph shows that the behavior is occurring only in the mornings between 9:00 a.m. and 10:00 a.m.

SEMILOGARITHMIC CHART

This type of graph, also referred to as a ratio chart, has a horizontal *x* axis that is divided into equal distances between marks, but the vertical *y* axis uses a logarithmic scale. The Standard Celeration Chart (SCC) is a semilogarithmic chart.

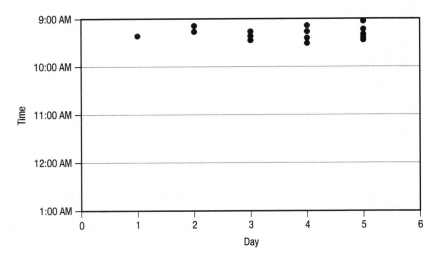

Figure 5.7 Scatterplot for timing of behavior.

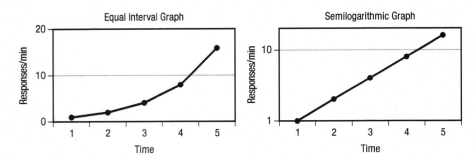

Figure 5.8 The same sample data plotted on an equal interval scale versus logarithmic scale.

STANDARD CELERATION CHART

This type of graph is primarily used to display the fluency and accuracy of a target behavior. The vertical *y* axis uses a logarithmic scale that allows us to record data points representing 0.001 to 1,000 times per minute.

ADDITIONAL NOTE(S)

For those who are interested in learning more about SCCs and how to use them, consider reviewing Calkin's (2005) article on SCCs, Cancio and Maloney's (1994) article on teaching students how to utilize SCCs, and/or White and Neely's (2012) graphic overview of SCC conventions and practices.

▶ TASK LIST ITEM C-11

The objective of this Task List item is to interpret graphed data.

The three basic properties of behavior change over time that are effectively communicated through graphs include (a) level, (b) variability, and (c) trend.

LEVEL

This relates to the position along the vertical y axis where a series of data points converge.

■ *Example*: In the following graph, the data representing the frequency of a particular response occur at a low level in Condition A and at a high level in Condition B.

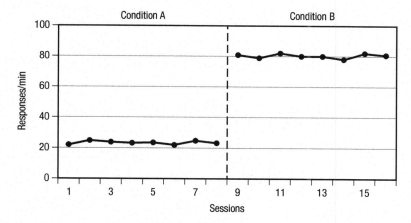

Figure 5.9 Low level of responding in A; High level of responding in B.

A horizontal mean level line can be drawn to summarize the overall level of behavior in a condition if the data points remain fairly stable (i.e., low variability) data paths. If the data points are fairly stable but there are several outliers (i.e., data points that are significantly higher or lower than the others in a series of data points), a median level line can be used instead.

VARIABILITY

This relates to the amount of discrepancy between the values of a series of data points.

■ *Example*: In the following graph, the data representing the frequency of a particular response occur with a low degree of variability in Condition A and with a high degree of variability in Condition B.

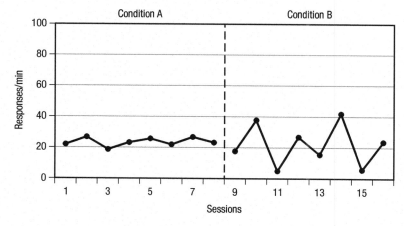

Figure 5.10 Low variability in responding in A;
High variability in responding in B.

Greater variability observed within a condition requires a higher number of data points to establish a predictable pattern in the data, whereas lower variability observed within a condition requires fewer data points to establish a predictable pattern in the data.

TREND

This relates to the direction of a series of data points. The trend is described in terms of direction (i.e., increasing, decreasing, or zero), magnitude, and degree of variability of data points along the data path.

■ *Example*: In the following graph, the data representing the frequency of a particular response occur with an increasing trend in Condition A, decreasing trend in Condition B, and zero trend in Condition C.

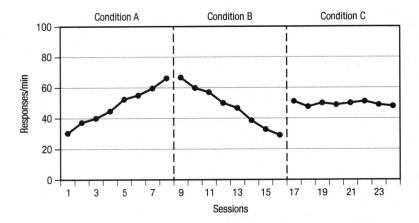

Figure 5.11 Increasing trend in A; Decreasing trend in B; Zero trend in C.

■ In this next graph, the magnitude of the increasing trendline is greater in Condition A than it is in Condition B.

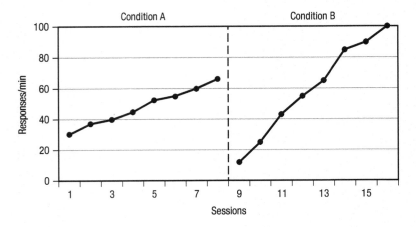

Figure 5.12 Greater magnitude of trendline in A than B.

■ In this next graph, the variability of the data points along the data path is greater in Condition B than it is in Condition A.

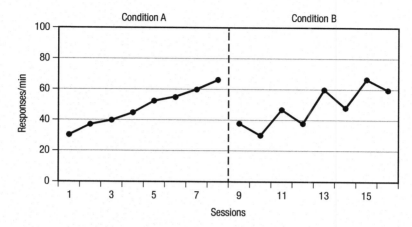

Figure 5.13 Greater variability of responding in B than A.

PRACTICE QUESTION

You are collecting data on an intervention to increase the number of social initiations with a young child having difficulty appropriately interacting with peers. Your single subject data show the following BASELINE pattern (upward trend with moderate variability):

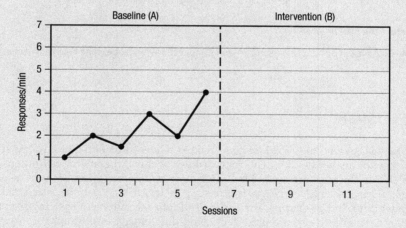

Figure 5.14 Graph of baseline data.

Your next step should be to:
A. Introduce the intervention (IV) to see if it has a positive impact
B. Choose another target behavior
C. Collect additional baseline data to see if stability is achieved
D. None of the above

(*continued*)

Before moving on to the next section for the solution, we recommend that you provide a brief explanation for the answer option you selected here:

_____

_____

When you're ready, move on to the next section for the solution!

Practice Question Breakdown

Step 1: Examine the question

The question asks you to examine the baseline data phase of a graph measuring the number of social initiations for a young child having difficulty appropriately interacting with peers. In the baseline data, you observe an upward trend in baseline, with moderate variability.

Step 2: Analyze the answer options

A. This answer is incorrect as baseline data is already increasing in the absence of intervention implementation, so something else is associated with the increase. Despite the behavior increasing (improving in the case of this targeted DV), this is a commonly misunderstood data pattern and one that is not ideal in that it provides little stability and predictability.

B. This step is not advised because you do not know why the increase is occurring in the number of social initiations, so why introduce or try to measure a different behavior?

C. The best option is to continue to collect baseline data to determine if the behavior stabilizes or becomes more predictable. Remember, greater variability (and/or unexplained trend) observed within a condition requires a higher number of data points to establish a predictable pattern in the data.

D. This answer cannot be correct because answer C offers a reasonable course of action given there is an unexplained trend in the baseline data in the absence of intervention implementation.

Step 3: Select the best answer

Among the four answer options presented, answer C (collect additional baseline data) appears to be the best answer.

▶ CONCLUSION

In this chapter, we covered the Task List items related to measurement, data display, and interpretation in applied behavior analysis (ABA). This included establishing operational definitions of behavior and practices related to the measurement of behavior, such as different approaches to measuring behavior, measurement variables, and different features of behavior that can be measured (e.g., temporal extent, repeatability). In this chapter, we also delved into measurement system selection for obtaining representative data; effectively graphing data using different types of graphs to clearly communicate results to others; and interpreting data according to the three basic properties of behavior change over time. Given behavior analysts' commitment to data-based decision-making and practice, the content covered in this chapter is of paramount importance.

1. Which of the following is not a required characteristic of an operational definition?

   A. Adaptable
   B. Clear
   C. Measurable
   D. Observable

2. A well-written operational definition of a target behavior allows the behavior analyst to do all of the following except:

   A. Gather complete information about its occurrence and nonoccurrence
   B. Establish the reliability of measurement data
   C. Precisely apply procedures in a timely manner
   D. Produce an accurate evaluation of intervention effectiveness

3. What type of measurement involves the observer recording the target behavior as it occurs?

   A. Direct
   B. Indirect
   C. Product
   D. Scatterplot

4. What type of measurement involves the examination of the effects produced on the environment by a behavior?

   A. Direct
   B. Indirect
   C. Product
   D. Scatterplot

5. What type of measurement does not involve direct observation but requires the client or others (e.g., parent, teachers, staff) to recall and report information about the target behavior?

   A. Direct
   B. Indirect
   C. Product
   D. Scatterplot

6. Measures of the fundamental dimensional quantity of repeatability include:

   A. Duration and frequency
   B. Frequency and rate
   C. Interresponse time and latency
   D. Percentage and duration

1. A) Adaptable
Operational definitions are observable, measurable, and clear. They are also objective and complete, but they are not required to be adaptable.

2. B) Establish the reliability of measurement data
A well-written operational definition of a target behavior does not allow behavior analysts to establish the reliability of measurement data. A well-written operation definition does, however, assist behavior analysts in the gathering of information about the occurrence and nonoccurrence of behavior, precisely apply procedures in a timely manner, and produce an accurate evaluation of intervention effectiveness.

3. A) Direct
Direct measurement involves an observer recording the target behavior as it occurs. The other answer options (indirect, product, scatterplot), two of which refer to other types of measures, function as distractors.

4. C) Product
The use of product measures involves the examination of the effects produced on the environment by a behavior. The other answer options (direct, indirect, scatterplot), two of which refer to other types of measures, function as distractors.

5. B) Indirect
Indirect measures, such as interviews and rating scales, do not involve direct observation but require the client or others to recall and report information about the target behavior. The other answer options (direct, product, scatterplot), two of which refer to other types of measures, function as distractors.

6. B) Frequency and rate
Frequency and rate are measures of the fundamental dimensional quantity of repeatability. The other answer options (duration and frequency; interresponse time and latency; percentage and duration) are measures based on other fundamental dimensional quantities and serve as distractors.

7. What derivative measure is calculated by multiplying the numeric value (e.g., count of a response divided by the total number of responses or opportunities/intervals in which it could have occurred) by 100?

   A. Frequency
   B. Latency
   C. Percentage
   D. Rate

8. What measure involves counting occurrences of a behavior or behavior class over the unit of time in which observations were conducted?

   A. Duration
   B. Frequency
   C. Latency
   D. Rate

9. Which of the following is a measure of the length of time from the onset of a stimulus to the initiation of a behavior?

   A. Celeration
   B. Duration
   C. Interresponse time
   D. Latency

10. Which of the following is a measure of the length of time between the onset of a response and the onset of the next response?

    A. Celeration
    B. Duration
    C. Interresponse time
    D. Latency

11. Which of the following best describes the magnitude of a behavior?

    A. Duration of the behavior
    B. Intensity of the behavior
    C. Physical form of the behavior
    D. Rate of the behavior

12. Trials to criterion data can be used for all of the following purposes except:

    A. Analysis of it as a dependent variable in a research study
    B. Assessment of a learner's increasing ability to acquire new skills
    C. Comparison of two or more treatments
    D. Development of a hypothesis regarding the function of a behavior

13. _____ is a measure of the number of response opportunities required to achieve a predetermined level of performance.

    A. Count
    B. Event recording
    C. Percentage
    D. Trials to criterion

7. C) Percentage
Percentage is a derivative measure that is calculated by multiplying the numeric value (e.g., count of a response divided by the total number of responses or opportunities/intervals in which it could have occurred) by 100. The other answer options (frequency, latency, rate) are not derivative measures and function as distractors.

8. D) Rate
Rate involves counting of the behavior or behavior class over the unit of time in which observations were conducted, whether that is by X amount of minutes, hours, and so on. The other answer options (duration, frequency, latency) refer to other dimensional quantities of behavior and function as distractors.

9. D) Latency
Latency is the length of time from the onset of a stimulus to the initiation of a behavior. The other answer options (celeration, duration, interresponse time) refer to other dimensional quantities and function as distractors.

10. C) Interresponse time
Interresponse time is a measure of the length of time between the onset of a response and the onset of the next response. The other answer options (celeration, duration, latency) refer to other dimensional quantities and function as distractors.

11. B) Intensity of the behavior
Magnitude refers to the intensity of the behavior. The other answer options (duration of the behavior, physical form of the behavior, rate of the behavior) do not accurately describe magnitude and serve as distractors.

12. D) Development of a hypothesis regarding the function of a behavior
Trials to criterion data are not used to develop a hypothesis regarding the function of a behavior. However, data can be collected and analyzed as a dependent variable in a research study, used to assess a learner's acquisition of new skills, and used to compare two or more treatments.

13. D) Trials to criterion
Trials to criterion is a measure of the number of response opportunities required to achieve a predetermined level of performance. The other answer options (count, event recording, percentage) refer to other measures and serve as distractors.

14. Trials to criterion data can be reported in terms of:

    A. Count, rate, duration, or latency
    B. Count, rate, latency, or interresponse time
    C. Duration, rate, interresponse time, or magnitude
    D. Frequency, rate, percentage, or latency

15. When implementing this type of sampling procedure, the target behavior is recorded as having occurred at the end of an interval only if it occurred throughout the entire interval.

    A. Momentary time sampling
    B. Partial interval recording
    C. Planned activity check (PLACHECK)
    D. Whole interval recording

16. When implementing this type of sampling procedure, the count of individuals in a group that are engaged in the target behavior at the end of an interval is recorded.

    A. Momentary time sampling
    B. Partial interval recording
    C. Planned activity check (PLACHECK)
    D. Whole interval recording

17. Which sampling procedure usually overestimates the total duration of a targeted behavior, but may underestimate the rate of high-frequency behaviors?

    A. Momentary time sampling
    B. Partial interval recording
    C. Planned activity check (PLACHECK)
    D. Whole interval recording

18. _____ refers to the degree to which we are measuring what we intend to measure, whereas _____ refers to the degree to which the measure will produce consistent results.

    A. Accuracy; repeatability
    B. Accuracy; reliability
    C. Reliability; validity
    D. Validity; reliability

19. What measures are based on the dimensional quantity of temporal locus?

    A. Count and rate
    B. Duration and latency
    C. Latency and interresponse time
    D. Interresponse time and count

20. Which of the following graph types is used to display discrete sets of data?

    A. Bar graph
    B. Equal-interval graph
    C. Line graph
    D. Scatterplot

(See answers next page.)

14. A) Count, rate, duration, or latency
Trials to criterion data can be reported in terms of count, rate, duration, or latency. The other answer options include measurement terms in which trials to criterion data are not reported (e.g., duration, magnitude, percentage) and function as distractors.

15. D) Whole interval recording
When implementing whole interval recording, the target behavior is recorded as having occurred at the end of an interval only if it occurred throughout the entire interval. The other answer options (momentary time sampling, partial interval recording, PLACHECK) refer to other sampling procedures and function as distractors.

16. C) Planned activity check (PLACHECK)
When implementing PLACHECK, the count of individuals in a group that are engaged in the target behavior at the end of an interval is recorded. The other answer options (momentary time sampling, partial interval recording, whole interval recording) refer to other sampling procedures and function as distractors.

17. B) Partial interval recording
Partial interval recording has been identified as a sampling procedure that usually overestimates the total duration of a targeted behavior but may underestimate the rate of high-frequency behaviors. The other answer options (momentary time sampling, PLACHECK, whole interval recording) are measures that have not been found to share these exact same characteristics and function as distractors.

18. D) Validity; reliability
Validity refers to the degree to which we are measuring what we intend to measure, whereas reliability refers to the degree to which the measure will produce consistent results. The other answer options (accuracy, repeatability; accuracy, reliability; reliability, validity) do not accurately fit into the statement and serve as distractors.

19. C) Latency and interresponse time
Latency and interresponse time (IRT) are measures based on the dimensional quantity of temporal locus. The other response options (count and rate; duration and latency; IRT and count) contain measures based on other fundamental dimensional quantities and function as distractors.

20. A) Bar graph
Bar graphs are used to display discrete sets of data. The other answer options (equal-interval graph, line graph, scatterplot) are graphs that are not used to display discrete sets of data and serve as distractors.

21. The _____ is a type of graph that is used to display the running total of responses over time. The data path never descends, and a steeper data path indicates a higher response rate.

   A. Bar graph
   B. Cumulative record
   C. Equal-interval graph
   D. Scatterplot

22. The three basic properties of behavior change over time that are effectively communicated through graphs include all of the following except:

   A. Effect size
   B. Level
   C. Trend
   D. Variability

(See answers next page.)

21. B) Cumulative record

The cumulative record is a type of graph that is used to display the running total of responses over time, with a data path that never descends. The other answer options (bar graph, equal-interval graph, scatterplot) are other types of graphs and function as distractors.

22. A) Effect size

Level, trend, and variability make up the three basic properties of behavior change over time that are effectively communicated through graphs. Effect size is not one of them.

REFERENCES

Calkin, A. B. (2005). Precision teaching: The standard celeration charts. *The Behavior Analyst Today, 6*(4), 207. https://doi.org/10.1037/h0100073

Cancio, E. J., & Maloney, M. (1994). Teaching students how to proficiently utilize the standard celeration chart. *Journal of Precision Teaching, 12*(1), 15–45.

LeBlanc, L. A., Raetz, P. B., Sellers, T. P., & Carr, J. E. (2016). A proposed model for selecting measurement procedures for the assessment and treatment of problem behavior. *Behavior Analysis in Practice, 9*(1), 77–83. https://doi.org/10.1007/s40617-015-0063-2

White, O. R., & Neely, M. D. (2012). *The chart book: An overview of standard celeration chart conventions and practices*. Behavior Research Company.

BIBLIOGRAPHY

Behavior Analyst Certification Board. (2017). *BCBA task list* (5th ed.). http://ies.ed.gov/ncee/wwc/pdf/wwc_scd.pdf

Cooper, J. O., Heron, T. E., & Heward, W. L. (2020). *Applied behavior analysis* (3rd ed.). Pearson Education.

Hawkins, R. P., & Dobes, R. W. (1977). Behavioral definitions in applied behavior analysis: Explicit or implicit?. In B. C. Etzel, J. M. LeBlanc, & D. M. Baer (Eds.), *New developments in behavioral research: Theory, method, and application* (pp. 167–188). Lawrence Erlbaum.

Pennypacker, H. S., Gutierrez, A., & Lidsley, O.R. (2003). *Handbook of the standard celeration chart, deluxe edition*. Cambridge Center for Behavioral Studies.

Experimental Design

It is difficult to overstate the importance of experimentation in the practice of behavior analysis. As noted by Poling and Grosset (1986), "applied behavior analysis relies on experimentation to assess the efficacy of interventions" (p. 7). Through experimentation, which involves the logical configuration of conditions to allow for observation of changes in one physical event to be attributed to that of another, behavior analysts are able to produce evidence of a functional relationship between an intervention and a target response. The purpose of this chapter will be to provide an essential review of Task List items D-1 through D-6, which specifically relate to experimental design.

▶ LEARNING OBJECTIVES

The following Task List items related to experimental design (D-1 through D-6) serve as the learning objectives of this chapter:

D-1 Distinguish between dependent and independent variables.

D-2 Distinguish between internal and external validity.

D-3 Identify the defining features of single-subject experimental designs (e.g., individuals serve as their own controls, repeated measures, prediction, verification, replication).

D-4 Describe the advantages of single-subject experimental designs compared to group designs.

D-5 Use single-subject experimental designs (e.g., reversal, multiple baseline, multielement, changing criterion).

D-6 Describe rationales for conducting comparative, component, and parametric analyses.

▶ TASK LIST ITEM D-1

The objective of this Task List item is to distinguish between dependent variables (DVs) and independent variables (IVs).

DEPENDENT VARIABLE

This is the target behavior; thus, the DV represents some measure of socially significant behavior that an intervention is designed to change. In an experiment, this is measured to ascertain whether systematic manipulations of the IV alter it.

■ *Example*: DV = Student's aggressive behavior.

INDEPENDENT VARIABLE

This is the intervention; thus, the IV represents some treatment variable that is used to intervene on the phenomenon of interest (i.e., target behavior). In an experiment, this is systematically manipulated to determine if alterations to it will produce reliable alterations in the DV.

■ *Example*: IV = Differential reinforcement procedure.

ADDITIONAL NOTE(S)

Any investigation of the "causes" of behavior represents a search for the particular IVs of which behavior is a function.

▶ TASK LIST ITEM D-2

The objective of this Task List item is to distinguish between internal and external validity.

Behavior analysts implementing interventions are concerned with internal and external validity, which are concepts that communicate how trustworthy and meaningful results are.

INTERNAL VALIDITY

This refers to the degree the changes in the DV (i.e., target behavior) can be attributed to the manipulation of the IV (i.e., intervention) and not the result of uncontrolled/extraneous factors. Experiments that reliably demonstrate a cause-and-effect relationship between the IV and DV are said to have a high degree of internal validity.

Internal validity is threatened when there is the possibility that results are affected by uncontrolled/extraneous factors.

EXTERNAL VALIDITY

This refers to the degree to which the results of the intervention (i.e., functional relationship demonstrated in an experiment) can be generalized to other behaviors, environments, and individuals/populations.

External validity is threatened when conditions inherent in the experimental design may limit the generalizability of the results.

Threats to internal and external validity can be reduced through replication. Major threats to internal validity are addressed by behavior analysts using baseline logic (see Task List item D-3) and steady state strategy (i.e., measuring a target behavior repeatedly under each condition and obtaining a stable pattern of responding prior to a condition change).

▶ TASK LIST ITEM D-3

The objective of this Task List item is to identify the defining features of single-subject experimental designs (e.g., individuals serve as their own controls, repeated measures, prediction, verification, replication).

Behavior analysts use single-subject experimental designs (also referred to as single-case, within-subject, intrasubject, and repeated-measures designs) to provide experimental evaluations of intervention effects. In other words, these experimental designs are used to determine whether changes in the IV are driving changes in the DV. See Task List item E-5 for a review of the types of single-subject experimental designs used by behavior analysts.

The defining features of single-subject experimental designs include: (a) the subject is the unit of intervention and data analysis, (b) the subject provides its own control for comparison, and (c) the target behavior is measured repeatedly across different levels or conditions of the intervention.

Note that the subject (sometimes referred to as "the case") may be an individual client or cluster of individuals (e.g., class or school).

THE SUBJECT SERVES AS ITS OWN CONTROL

This means that measurements of the DV between conditions are compared for each subject. In single-subject experimental designs, precise control is maintained of the IV. Thus, the intervention (i.e., IV) is presented, withdrawn, or its value varied to demonstrate the effect it has on the target behavior (i.e., DV) when compared to the subject's own data. To achieve experimental control, a predictable change in the target behavior is demonstrated to be reliable and repeatedly produced by the systematic manipulation of the intervention.

TARGET BEHAVIOR IS MEASURED REPEATEDLY

The target behavior is repeatedly measured. Single-case experimental designs arrange comparisons between control and experimental conditions so that the target behavior is measured multiple times in a condition before contacting the next condition.

Additionally, baseline logic is used.

BASELINE LOGIC

This is a powerful form of experimental reasoning that calls for three elements: (a) prediction, (b) verification, and (c) replication, each of which depends on *steady state strategy*.

Prediction

This is the anticipated outcome of an unknown/future measurement. Sufficient baseline data are needed to allow a behavior analyst to confidently predict a future measurement of the target behavior.

It is recommended that measurement continues until the behavior pattern is clearly stable. If the behavior analyst is unsure about the stability of responding in the baseline condition, then it probably isn't stable enough and additional data should be collected before the intervention is introduced.

Verification

This is the demonstration of a functional relationship between the intervention and target behavior. This would require observing changes in the target behavior associated with the introduction and withdrawal of the intervention, and is accomplished when data convincingly show that baseline responding would remain as is without introduction of the intervention.

Replication

This is the repeating of IV manipulations and obtaining outcomes similar to that of a previous study. Replication provides additional evidence that a particular IV is responsible for change in a DV, and that the behavior change can be reliably made to occur again.

ADDITIONAL NOTE(S)

In single-case experimental studies, basic features also include: (a) details of subject(s)/setting(s) are sufficient to allow for others to replicate it, (b) DVs are operationally defined, (c) implementation fidelity (i.e., whether the IV was presented as intended) is documented, and (d) social significance is established.

▶ TASK LIST ITEM D-4

The objective of this Task List item is to describe the advantages of single-subject experimental designs compared to group designs.

Behavior analysts focus on the direct and repeated measurement of individuals' behaviors. Thus, they use single-subject experimental designs rather than group experimental designs that have historically predominated the social sciences.

GROUP DESIGNS

This type of experimental design, also known as between-groups experimental designs, includes the following features:

- Subjects are randomly selected from a population of interest.
- Subjects are randomly assigned to two or more groups and organized.

■ Groups are organized into a minimum of one treatment group and one control group.
■ Subjects in the treatment group (but not the control group) are exposed to the intervention.
■ Measurements of the DV are conducted for each group; results for each group are combined.
■ Analysis is conducted at the level of the group, not the individual.
■ Conclusions are drawn at the level of the group, not the individual.

SINGLE-SUBJECT EXPERIMENTAL DESIGN

See Task List item D-4 for a review of the features of single-subject experimental designs. The advantages of this type of experimental design are as follows:

■ Subjects serve as their own control.
■ It reveals the performance of individual subjects.
■ Data for subjects are not combined/averaged, which helps to prevent distortion/masking of variability in the data.
■ It enables the demonstration of behavior–environment relations at the level of the individual.
■ It allows for replication of effects within and across individual subjects.

▶ TASK LIST ITEM D-5

The objective of this Task List item is to use single-subject experimental designs (e.g., reversal, multiple baseline, multielement, changing criterion).

AB DESIGN

This is the most basic single-subject design that involves repeated measures taken during a preintervention baseline condition (A) and then again during an intervention condition (B). It is generally only used when other, more powerful designs are untenable.

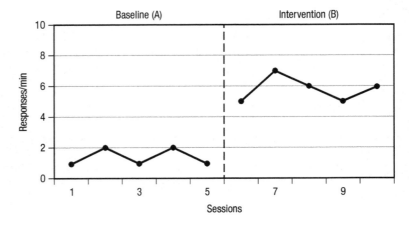

Figure 6.1 Example of a graph of data using an AB design.

ABC DESIGN

This is a variant of the AB design in which a second intervention phase (C) is added following the first intervention phase (B). Consider this an exploratory design.

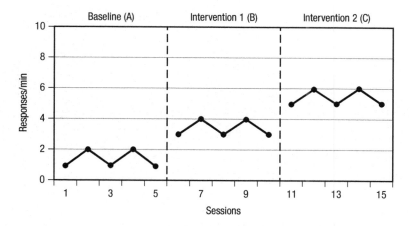

Figure 6.2 Example of a graph of data using an ABC design.

This is an additive design. It doesn't have to end after C. You can also have ABCD, ABCDE, and so on.

REVERSAL DESIGNS

These are designs that demonstrate the effect of an intervention by alternating its presentation and removal over time. Use these when (a) the target behavior is reversible; (b) removal of treatment does not present a concern; and (c) stability, order, and time do not present a concern.

ABA Design

This is the most basic reversal design that involves repeated measures taken during an initial baseline condition (A), then an intervention condition (B), and again after returning to the baseline condition (A).

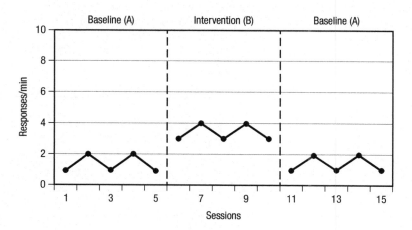

Figure 6.3 Example of a graph of data using an ABA design.

The condition in which there is a return to baseline is also referred to as the *withdrawal phase*.

ABAB Design

This is a type of reversal design that involves an initial baseline phase (A), followed by an intervention phase (B), followed by a withdrawal phase (A), followed by a final intervention phase (B).

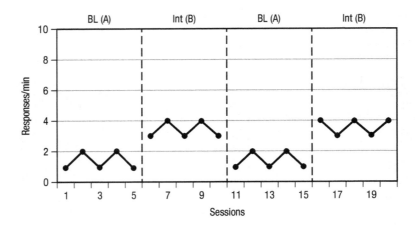

Figure 6.4 Example of a graph of data using an ABAB design.

BL, baseline; Int, intervention.

This is a powerful design that is preferred over the basic ABA design. It is also possible to extend this fundamental reversal design (e.g., ABABA).

Other types of reversal designs include: (a) repeated reversals (e.g., ABABAB); (b) BAB reversal; (c) multiple treatment reversal (e.g., ABCBC); (d) NCR reversal (e.g., A [NCR on FR or VR schedule] B [contingent reinforcement] A [return to NCR]); and (e) DRO/DRI/DRA reversal (e.g., A [DRO] B [contingent reinforcement] A [return to DRO]).

MULTIPLE BASELINE DESIGN

This type of design is commonly used when a reversal is determined to be impractical or unethical. This involves (a) establishing two or more independent baselines and (b) introducing the intervention in a staggered fashion for each baseline. When the behavior for the first baseline is stable, the intervention is then introduced to the second baseline, and so forth. This design can be used to compare responding across different behaviors for a client, a behavior across different clients, or a behavior across different settings.

The more baselines you include in a multiple baseline design, the more convincing your results will be.

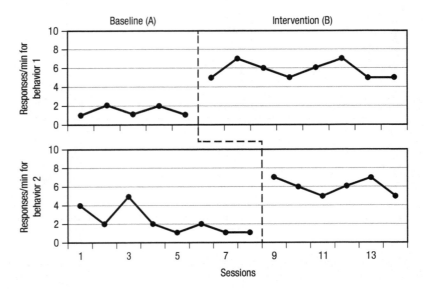

Figure 6.5 Example of a graph of data using multiple baseline design (two baselines representing two different behaviors).

MULTIELEMENT DESIGN

Also commonly referred to as an alternating treatments design, this type of design involves delivering and measuring effects of two or more interventions in a rapid, alternating fashion. This allows behavior analysts to compare the effects of different interventions. It can also be used to compare the effects of an intervention with no intervention (i.e., baseline).

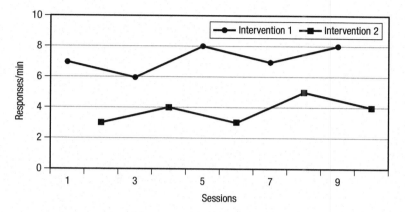

Figure 6.6 Example of a graph of data using a multielement design (two interventions).

CHANGING CRITERION DESIGN

This is a design in which the initial baseline phase is followed by a series of intervention phases with successive/gradual criteria for change. See Task List item D-6 for a review of measuring trials to criterion.

■ *Example* (changing criterion design): In the following graph, a behavior was targeted for decrease. After the initial baseline phase, an intervention phase was introduced with the goal of decreasing the behavior to 6 times per hour. Once reached, the next intervention phase followed with a goal of 3 times per hour.

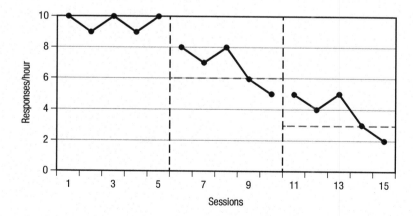

Figure 6.7 Graph of data using a changing criterion design.

▶ TASK LIST ITEM D-6

The objective of this Task List item is to describe rationales for conducting comparative, component, and parametric analyses.

COMPARATIVE ANALYSIS

This type of analysis compares two or more distinct interventions (e.g., multielement experimental designs). Rationales for its use include:

- To evaluate the effects of two or more interventions.
- To answer the question, "Which intervention was most effective?"

COMPONENT ANALYSIS

This type of analysis evaluates the relative contributions of the parts of an intervention. There are two types: (a) *drop-out*, which involves implementing an intervention and then systematically removing parts of it; and (b) *add-in*, which involves systematically assessing parts individually or together before implementing the intervention. Rationales for its use include:

- To evaluate the effects of the individual parts of an intervention.
- To answer the question, "Which part of the intervention was most effective?"

PARAMETRIC ANALYSIS

This type of analysis compares different levels of an intervention. It involves examining the effects generated by manipulating one or more dimensions/levels of the intervention. Rationales for its use include:

- To evaluate the differential effects of a range of values of an intervention on behavior.
- To answer the question, "How much intervention is required to be effective?"
- To answer the question, "How much intervention is most effective?"

PRACTICE QUESTION

A first-grade teacher wants to know how much time is optimal for the instruction of a reading fluency intervention within the scheduled literacy block. She currently instructs this skill for 5 minutes each day. She is investigating the following research question: What effect will incremental increases (5, 10, 15 minutes) in the IV (fluency intervention) have on the DV (fluency probes)? What type of analysis is described?

A. Comparative analysis
B. Competitive analysis
C. Component analysis
D. Parametric analysis

Before moving on to the next section for the solution, we recommend that you provide a brief explanation for the answer option you selected here:

_____

_____

When you're ready, move on to the next section for the solution!

(continued)

Practice Question Breakdown

Step 1: Examine the question

The question calls for you to determine the type of analysis that best describes the research question regarding the optimal number of minutes of a fluency intervention.

Step 2: Analyze the answer options

A. Comparative analysis investigates two or more distinct interventions in relation to a DV. There are not two distinct interventions in the scenario. This answer option is a distractor.
B. This is a type of analysis used in business and does not apply here. This answer option is a distractor.
C. Component analysis examines the individual elements or "parts" from a multicomponent intervention on the DV. There was no mention of multiple components in the fluency intervention. This answer option is a distractor.
D. Parametric analysis examines how behavior changes in relation to variation in the level (or number of minutes) of a reading fluency intervention. This looks like the one!

Step 3: Select the best answer

Among the four answer options presented, answer D (parametric analysis) appears to be the best answer.

▶ CONCLUSION

In this chapter, we reviewed key content for Task List items related to experimental design for behavior analysts. This included the features and advantages of single subject designs, as well as the various types of experimental configurations that allow the behavior analyst to attribute changes in a DV (i.e., behavior of interest) to the actions of an IV (e.g., intervention). In other words, experimentation allows behavior analysts to demonstrate evidence of functional relations. It is through this process that we can evaluate how effective our treatments are in affecting change in behavior. Whether you go on to become a behavior analyst conducting research or delivering behavior analytic services to clients, this content is both relevant and necessary for you.

1. The _____ is the target behavior, whereas the _____ represents some treatment variable.

   A. Dependent variable (DV); independent variable (IV)
   B. Discrete variable; nominal variable
   C. IV; DV
   D. Intervening variable; control variable

2. In an experiment, the _____ variable is measured to ascertain whether systematic manipulations of the treatment variable alter it.

   A. Control
   B. Dependent
   C. Independent
   D. Intervening

3. Which of the following refers to the degree to which results of the intervention can be generalized to other behaviors, environments, and individuals/populations?

   A. Accuracy
   B. External validity
   C. Internal validity
   D. Reliability

4. Which of the following refers to the degree to which the changes in the dependent variable (DV) can be attributed to the manipulation of the independent variable (IV) and not the result of uncontrolled/extraneous factors?

   A. Accuracy
   B. External validity
   C. Internal validity
   D. Reliability

5. The defining features of single-subject experimental designs include all of the following except:

   A. The internal validity of results is accomplished through replication of treatment effects
   B. The subject serves as the unit of intervention and data analysis
   C. The subject provides its own control for comparison
   D. The target behavior is measured repeatedly across different levels or conditions of the intervention

6. Baseline logic is a powerful form of experimental reasoning that calls for prediction, verification, and replication, each of which depends on:

   A. Accuracy of the data
   B. Level and trend of the data path
   C. Steady state strategy
   D. Validity of the results

1. A) Dependent variable (DV); independent variable (IV)

The DV is the target behavior, whereas the IV represents some treatment variable. The other answer options (discrete variable, nominal; IV, DV; intervening variable, control variable) do not accurately fit into the statement and function as distractors.

2. B) Dependent

In an experiment, the dependent variable is measured to ascertain whether systematic manipulations of the treatment variable alter it. The other answer options (control, independent, intervening) refer to other types of variables and serve as distractors.

3. B) External validity

External validity refers to the degree to which results of the intervention can be generalized to other behaviors, environments, and individuals/populations. The other answer options (accuracy, internal validity, reliability) refer to other measurement-related concepts and function as distractors.

4. C) Internal validity

Internal validity refers to the degree to which the changes in the DV can be attributed to the manipulation of the IV and not the result of uncontrolled/extraneous factors. The other answer options (accuracy, external validity, reliability) refer to other concepts and function as distractors.

5. A) The internal validity of results is accomplished through replication of treatment effects

In single-subject experimental designs, the subject serves as the unit of intervention and data analysis, the subject provides its own control for comparison, and the target behavior is measured repeatedly across different levels or conditions of the intervention. It is not the case, however, that the internal validity of results in single-subject designs is accomplished through replication of treatment effects.

6. C) Steady state strategy

Baseline logic is a powerful form of experimental reasoning that calls for prediction, verification, and replication, each of which depends on steady state strategy (i.e., measuring a target behavior repeatedly under each condition and obtaining a stable pattern of responding prior to a condition change). The other answer options (accuracy of the data, level and trend of the data path, validity of the results) do not fit the description and serve as distractors.

7. The demonstration of a functional relationship between the intervention and the target behavior in baseline logic is referred to as:

   A. Prediction
   B. Replication
   C. Validation
   D. Verification

8. Which of the following single-subject experimental designs involves delivering and measuring effects of two or more interventions in a rapid, alternating fashion?

   A. ABC
   B. Changing criterion
   C. Multielement
   D. Multiple baseline

9. Which of the following single-subject experimental designs involves repeated measures taken during a pre-intervention baseline condition and then again during an intervention condition?

   A. AB
   B. ABC
   C. Multiple baseline
   D. Reversal

10. Which of the following single-subject experimental designs involves establishing two or more independent baselines and introducing the intervention in a staggered fashion for each baseline?

    A. ABAB
    B. Changing criterion
    C. Multielement
    D. Multiple baseline

11. In an ABAB design (A = baseline; B = intervention), the withdrawal phase refers to:

    A. The first A condition
    B. The first B condition
    C. The second A condition
    D. The second B condition

12. Identify the type of analysis that compares different levels of an intervention.

    A. Comparative analysis
    B. Component analysis
    C. Functional analysis
    D. Parametric analysis

13. Identify the type of analysis that evaluates the relative contributions of the parts of an intervention.

    A. Comparative analysis
    B. Component analysis
    C. Functional analysis
    D. Parametric analysis

(See answers next page.)

7. D) Verification
Verification involves the demonstration of a functional relationship between the intervention and the target behavior in baseline logic. The other answer options (prediction, replication, validation) do not fit the description and serve as distractors.

8. C) Multielement
The multielement design involves delivering and measuring effects of two or more interventions in a rapid, alternating fashion. The other answer options (ABC, changing criterion, multiple baseline) refer to other types of single-subject experimental designs and function as distractors.

9. A) AB
The AB design is the most basic single-subject design that involves repeated measures taken during a pre-intervention baseline condition and then again during an intervention condition. The other answer options (ABC, multiple baseline, reversal) refer to other types of single-subject experimental designs and function as distractors.

10. D) Multiple baseline
The multiple baseline design involves establishing two or more independent baselines and introducing the intervention in a staggered fashion for each baseline. The other answer options (ABAB, changing criterion, multielement) refer to other types of single-subject experimental designs and function as distractors.

11. C) The second A condition
In an ABAB design (A = baseline; B = intervention), the withdrawal phase refers to the second A condition. The first A condition is the baseline, and both the first and second B conditions present an intervention as opposed to withdrawing an intervention. Thus, the other answer options (the first A condition, the first B condition, the second B condition) serve as distractors.

12. D) Parametric analysis
Parametric analysis can be used to compare different levels of an intervention. The other answer options (comparative analysis, component analysis, functional analysis) refer to other types of analyses and serve as distractors.

13. B) Component analysis
Component analysis can be used to evaluate the relative contributions of the parts of an intervention. The other answer options (comparative analysis, functional analysis, parametric analysis) refer to other types of analyses and serve as distractors.

REFERENCES

Behavior Analyst Certification Board. (2017). *BCBA task list* (5th ed.). https://www.bacb.com/wp-content/bcba-task-list-5th-ed

Cooper, J. O., Heron, T. E., & Heward, W. L. (2020). *Applied behavior analysis* (3rd ed.). Pearson Education.

Hayes, S. C., Rincover, A., & Solnick, J. V. (1980). The technical drift of applied behavior analysis. *Journal of Applied Behavior Analysis, 13*(2), 275–285.

Horner, R. H., Carr, E. G., Halle, J., McGee, G., Odom, S., & Wolery, M. (2005). The use of single-subject research to identify evidence-based practice in special education. *Exceptional Children, 71*(2), 165–179.

Kennedy, C. H. (2005). *Single-case designs for educational research.* Prentice Hall.

Kratochwill, T. R., Hitchcock, J., Horner, R. H., Levin, J. R., Odom, S. L., Rindskopf, D. M., & Shadish, W. R. (2010). *Single-case designs technical documentation.* What Works Clearinghouse. https://files.eric.ed.gov/fulltext/ED510743.pdf

Pennypacker, H. S., & Johnston, J. M. (1980). Strategies and tactics of human behavioral research. *Erlbaum.*

Ward-Horner, J., & Sturmey, P. (2010). Component analyses using single-subject experimental designs: A review. *Journal of Applied Behavior Analysis, 43*(4), 685–704.

BIBLIOGRAPHY

Poling, A., & Grossett, D. (1986). Basic research designs in applied behavior analysis. In A. Poling & R. W. Fuqua (Eds.), *Research methods in applied behavior analysis* (pp. 7–27). Springer.

Ethics

There is nothing more shocking and horrific than the abuse and maltreatment of innocent people who are unable to protect and defend themselves" (p. 3). To ensure the protection of consumers of behavior analytic services, it is a professional imperative for behavior analysts to practice in a manner that adheres to their profession's Code of Ethics. The Code includes an introduction section and six others that include standards related to the various responsibilities of practicing behavior analysts. The purpose of this chapter will be to provide an essential review of Task List items E-1 through E-7, which correspond to sections of the Ethics Code for behavior analysts.

▶ LEARNING OBJECTIVES

The following Task List items related to ethics (E-1 through E-7) serve as the learning objectives of this chapter:

E-1   Introduction.

E-2   Responsibility as a Professional.

E-3   Responsibility in Practice.

E-4   Responsibility to Clients and Stakeholders.

E-5   Responsibility to Supervisees and Trainees.

E-6   Responsibility in Public Statements.

E-7   Responsibility in Research.

In this chapter, please note that "client" refers to someone who receives services directly from a behavior analyst, and "stakeholder" refers to someone who does not receive services directly from a behavior analyst but is nevertheless impacted by those services.

As you review this chapter, focus on the meaning of each standard and what it requires of behavior analysts in practice. You do not need to remember labels (i.e., standard numbers)—no one will ask you, "What exactly does standard 1.06 refer to?" It should be noted that although the standards may seem reasonably straightforward, it is still an imperfect set of rules that can present problems for behavior analysts in practice. This is evident when strict adherence seems contraindicated or even impossible in situations where (a) the context of the dilemma conflicts with the Code, (b) two or more standards conflict with each other, or (c) cultural considerations conflict with the Code. To address some of the most common ethical "dilemmas" or "tensions," extra practice questions are presented to engage you further in the work of applying the standards to various situations that Board Certified Behavior Analyst (BCBAs) may encounter in the field. To learn more about how behavior analysts can address ethical problems, we encourage readers to seek out additional readings about this highly important topic.

▶ TASK LIST ITEM E-1

The introduction section of the Ethics Code describes the (a) scope of the Code (i.e., who it applies to and when), (b) core principles that underlie the standards of the Code, (c) how behavior analysts are to apply the Code, and (d) the Behavior Analyst Certification Board's (BACB's) enforcement of the Code.

SCOPE

The Code applies to behavior analysts (i.e., BCBAs, Board Certified Assistant Behavior Analysts [BCaBAs], and those who have applied for either of these credentials) when they engage in relevant professional activities in the field of behavior analysis, regardless of where or through what mode of delivery it occurs. Although the Code does not apply to behavior analysts' personal behaviors, it is noted that an exception may be made in the event a personal behavior poses a risk to the health and safety of clients, stakeholders, or supervisees.

CORE PRINCIPLES

The four core principles that serve as the framework for standards include: (a) benefit others; (b) treat others with compassion, dignity, and respect; (c) behave with integrity; and (d) ensure competence.

Benefit Others

Engage in behaviors that do no harm and increase benefit to those we serve, including those that:

- Protect the welfare and rights of clients (i.e., your priority) and others you work with.
- Consider both short- and long-term impact of your professional activities.
- Identify and address any conflicts of interest or factors that may negatively impact your ability to do your work as a behavior analyst.
- Collaborate with others in the best interests of clients.

Treat Others With Compassion, Dignity, and Respect

Engage in behaviors that treat others with compassion, dignity, and respect, including those that:

- Treat others equitably, regardless of their demographic attributes (e.g., age, ethnicity, religion).
- Respect others' privacy/confidentiality.
- Promote clients' self-determination (i.e., ability to make choices that pertain to their lives).
- Provide clients and stakeholders with the information necessary to make informed choices about services.

Behave With Integrity

Engage in behaviors that satisfy your responsibility to society, the professional/scientific communities of which you are a part, and the communities you serve. This includes those behaviors that:

- Are honest and dependable.
- Accurately present your work (or that of others).
- Fulfill professional obligations.
- Ensure your accountability as a supervisor who is responsible for the work of their supervisees.
- Meet BACB and other regulatory requirements.
- Create professional environments that uphold the Code.
- Educate others about the Code and how violations can be addressed.

Ensure Competence

Engage in behaviors that ensure your professional competence as a behavior analyst. This includes those behaviors that:

- Ensure you practice what is within your scope of practice.
- Regularly evaluate the boundaries of your competence.
- Engage in professional development (PD) activities to increase your knowledge of best practices in the field.
- Ensure you remain current about potentially risky interventions used in the field.
- Develop your cultural competence.

APPLICATION

Behavior analysts must comply with the Code. Claiming lack of awareness or understanding of the Code (e.g., stating "I didn't know" or "I didn't understand") is not defensible and cannot justify violations of the Code. When addressing violations, document all steps taken to address them. When the professional misconduct of others appears resolvable and does not place anyone at undue risk, the behavior analyst should address concerns directly with the subject (i.e., individual alleged to have violated the Code). This section also (a) emphasizes the importance of behavior analysts' compliance with all laws and requirements relevant to their various professional roles and actively upholding the interests of their clients, and (b) recommends following a systematic approach to ethical decision-making.

ENFORCEMENT

The BACB enforces the Code. Their process for enforcing the Code is described in a separate Code-Enforcement Procedures document available at www.bacb.com/wp-content/BACB_CodeEnforcement_Procedures.

▶ TASK LIST ITEM E-2

Section 1 of the Ethics Code consists of 16 standards (1.01 to 1.16) related to the behavior analyst's "responsibility as a professional."

STANDARD 1.01: BEING TRUTHFUL

Be honest, encourage others to be honest, and immediately correct any inaccurate information presented to required entities (e.g., certification board, funders) and individuals (e.g., clients, stakeholders).

STANDARD 1.02: CONFORMING WITH LEGAL AND PROFESSIONAL REQUIREMENTS

Follow the law and the rules established by the professional community (e.g., certification and state licensing boards).

STANDARD 1.03: ACCOUNTABILITY

Be accountable for your actions and follow through on professional commitments. If this isn't possible, prioritize the welfare of clients and take appropriate steps to address them.

STANDARD 1.04: PRACTICING WITHIN A DEFINED ROLE

Define and document your professional role with relevant parties before providing services.

STANDARD 1.05: PRACTICING WITHIN SCOPE OF COMPETENCE

Practice only what you are competent to practice. Before doing something new (e.g., implementing a new procedure), ensure that either (a) you have received sufficient training and supervision to do it or (b) you are working with a competent professional on the case. If not, make an appropriate referral.

STANDARD 1.06: MAINTAINING COMPETENCE

Engage in PD activities (e.g., reading relevant literature, attending professional training events).

STANDARD 1.07: CULTURAL RESPONSIVENESS AND DIVERSITY

Engage in PD activities to enhance cultural responsiveness. Evaluate your and your supervisees' biases and ability to work with diverse populations.

STANDARD 1.08: NONDISCRIMINATION

Do not discriminate against others. Treat others in an equitable and inclusive manner.

STANDARD 1.09: NONHARASSMENT

Do not harass others.

STANDARD 1.10: AWARENESS OF PERSONAL BIASES AND CHALLENGES

Be aware of personal biases or challenges (e.g., health conditions, relationship problems) that may negatively impact your ability to provide services and take steps to resolve them. Ensure your work is not adversely affected and document actions taken to resolve issues along with their associated outcomes.

STANDARD 1.11: MULTIPLE RELATIONSHIPS

Avoid multiple relationships (e.g., professional, personal, and familial) with clients and colleagues. If they arise, take steps to end them. If they arise and cannot be resolved, take steps to minimize conflicts of interest and plan to eventually end them. Document actions taken to resolve issues along with their associated outcomes.

STANDARD 1.12: GIVING AND RECEIVING GIFTS

Do not give or accept gifts valued more than $10 USD. Inform clients of this at the outset of the professional relationship. While acceptable as an infrequent expression of appreciation, excessive giving/accepting of gifts violates this standard.

STANDARD 1.13: COERCIVE AND EXPLOITATIVE RELATIONSHIPS

Do not abuse your power by coercing or exploiting others (e.g., supervisees).

STANDARD 1.14: ROMANTIC AND SEXUAL RELATIONSHIPS

Do not engage in romantic or sexual relationships with current clients, stakeholders, or supervisees. With former clients/stakeholders, this cannot occur for at least 2 years after the end of the professional relationship; and with supervisees, this cannot occur until the dissolution of the professional relationship has been documented. Also, do not take a supervisee if you have had a romantic/sexual relationship with them within the past 6 months.

STANDARD 1.15: RESPONDING TO REQUESTS

Make efforts to respond to information requests and deadlines from relevant parties (e.g., clients, supervisees) and entities (e.g., certification and state licensing boards). Also follow requirements of the BACB, employers, and governmental entities.

STANDARD 1.16: SELF-REPORTING CRITICAL INFORMATION

Follow self-reporting requirements of relevant entities (e.g., certification and state licensing boards).

PRACTICE QUESTION

Dr. Dalton, BCBA-D, is a supervisor at Healthline Community Agency. She mentions during a break in the employee lunchroom that she is leaving for a short vacation. Dr. Dalton elaborates that she is in a tough predicament as her previously scheduled pet sitter has fallen ill and cannot watch the house or care for her dog. She then casually asks a newly hired supervisee Karen (who loves dogs) if they are available to house/pet sit while she is away. Karen feels bad and knows that Dr. Dalton would have a less stressful trip if someone she trusts cares for her pet. She is a bit conflicted about this because she has plans for the weekend, but eventually says "yes" and rearranges her plans to help Dr. Dalton with her dilemma. Which of the following ethical standards best describes this situation?

A. Practicing within scope of confidence
B. Multiple relationship
C. Coercive/exploitative relationship
D. None of the above

Before moving on to the next section for the solution, we recommend that you provide a brief explanation for the answer option you selected here:

_____

_____

When you're ready, move on to the next section for the solution!

Practice Question Breakdown

Step 1: Examine the question

The question calls for you to examine a supervisor–supervisee situation in which Karen's supervisor is asking her to perform a personal favor outside the duties and role of her job. You are asked which ethical standards best characterize the situation that Karen finds herself in.

Step 2: Analyze the answer options

A. This answer specifically refers to providing professional services that you have been sufficiently trained and supervised to perform. This standard is not directly related to this scenario because Dr. Dalton is asking Karen for a personal favor outside her professional role. This is a distractor.
B. A multiple or dual relationship is when a BCBA has a professional relationship with a client/stakeholder in addition to at least one other form of relationship with that same individual, either before, during, or after the provision of services. Dr. Dalton is neither a client nor a stakeholder in this scenario. A dual relationship has *not yet* occurred between Karen and Dr. Dalton as they have only had a professional relationship thus far. This answer option is a distractor.
C. The scenario seems to be describing the formation of a coercive relationship between Dr. Dalton and Karen. There is a power differential in this supervisor/supervisee relationship, and Karen may feel obligated to assist Dr. Dalton because she has authority over her and evaluates her caseload and work performance. This is the best answer option so far.
D. This is not correct. Answer C offers the best response to the question.

Step 3: Select the best answer

Among the four answer options presented, answer C (coercive/exploitative relationship) appears to be the best answer.

▶ TASK LIST ITEM E-3

Section 2 of the Ethics Code consists of 19 standards (2.01 to 2.19) related to the behavior analyst's "responsibility in practice."

STANDARD 2.01: PROVIDING EFFECTIVE TREATMENT

Prioritize your clients' rights and service needs. Treatment is to be evidence-based, conceptually consistent with behavioral principles, and designed to protect and benefit all parties. You may deliver nonbehavioral services if you have the required training and credentials to do so.

STANDARD 2.02: TIMELINESS

Do your professional work in a timely manner.

STANDARD 2.03: PROTECTING CONFIDENTIAL INFORMATION

Follow confidentiality law/regulations and take steps to protect private information about those with whom you work. This includes information related to services, documentation/data, and verbal/written communications.

STANDARD 2.04: DISCLOSING CONFIDENTIAL INFORMATION

Share confidential information only (a) when you have informed consent, (b) to protect the client or others from harm, (c) to resolve contractual issues, (d) to prevent a crime that can harm someone, or (e) when required by law. When you do this, only share what is needed to resolve the issue.

STANDARD 2.05: DOCUMENTATION PROTECTION AND RETENTION

Follow all requirements for storing, transporting, retaining, and purging documentation related to your professional work.

STANDARD 2.06: ACCURACY IN SERVICE BILLING AND REPORTING

Identify your services accurately and provide this information as required on reports, bills, and receipts. Don't bill for nonbehavioral services under a contract for behavioral services. Any inaccuracies should be reported to all relevant parties and corrected as soon as possible. Document actions taken to resolve issues along with their associated outcomes.

STANDARD 2.07: FEES

Engage in lawful fee practices. Share fee information and do not misrepresent your fees. If you're not responsible for fees, communicate this to the responsible party and resolve any inaccuracies or conflicts. Document actions taken to resolve issues along with their associated outcomes.

STANDARD 2.08: COMMUNICATING ABOUT SERVICES

Use plain language and make sure relevant parties understand. Describe what services are and when they will end before you start. Also describe what assessments and interventions entail before you use them, and then explain what you learn from them when those results are available. If you are asked to provide your credentials and describe your area(s) of competence, do so.

STANDARD 2.09: INVOLVING CLIENTS AND STAKEHOLDERS

Take steps to involve clients/stakeholders throughout the professional relationship (e.g., when selecting goals, planning interventions).

STANDARD 2.10: COLLABORATING WITH COLLEAGUES

Work with other behavior analysts and those in other professions to support clients/stakeholders. Compromise when it's necessary, but always prioritize the client's best interests. Document actions taken to resolve issues along with their associated outcomes.

STANDARD 2.11: OBTAINING INFORMED CONSENT

Explain, obtain, reobtain, and document informed assent/consent from relevant parties (e.g., clients, stakeholders) as required.

STANDARD 2.12: CONSIDERING MEDICAL NEEDS

Do what you can to ensure that medical needs are evaluated and resolved if there is reasonable suspicion that the behavior of interest is impacted by medical/biological factors. Document referrals made and follow up with clients.

STANDARD 2.13: SELECTING, DESIGNING, AND IMPLEMENTING ASSESSMENTS

Before developing a behavior-change program, you must select, design, and use assessments that are (a) consistent with behavioral principles, (b) evidence based, and (c) sensitive to the needs and context of the client/stakeholders. Focus on maximizing benefits and minimizing harm. Provide a written summary of the procedures and results.

STANDARD 2.14: SELECTING, DESIGNING, AND IMPLEMENTING BEHAVIOR-CHANGE INTERVENTIONS

Select, design, and use interventions that are (a) consistent with behavioral principles, (b) evidence based, (c) assessment results based, (d) positive reinforcement focused, and (e) sensitive to the needs and context of the client/stakeholders. Consider relevant risks and benefits and aim to produce outcomes that are more likely to be maintained in the natural environment. Provide a written summary of the procedures.

STANDARD 2.15: MINIMIZING RISK OF BEHAVIOR-CHANGE INTERVENTIONS

When selecting, designing, and using interventions, focus on minimizing harm to clients/stakeholders. Only recommend restrictive/punishment procedures if less restrictive interventions have been ineffective or the risk of harm is greater than the risk associated with the intervention. Closely monitor restrictive/ punishment procedures and change or discontinue quickly if found to be ineffective.

STANDARD 2.16: DESCRIBING BEHAVIOR-CHANGE INTERVENTIONS BEFORE IMPLEMENTATION

Provide a written description of the goals, procedures, and review schedule of an intervention prior to its implementation. Also describe the environmental conditions required for effective implementation to clients/stakeholders. If changes are made to interventions, explain them and obtain informed consent as appropriate.

STANDARD 2.17: COLLECTING AND USING DATA

Select appropriate data collection procedures and ensure that they are conducted correctly. Graph data and use data to inform decisions about continuing or changing/ending services.

STANDARD 2.18: CONTINUAL EVALUATION OF THE BEHAVIOR-CHANGE INTERVENTION

Monitor and assess the implementation and effects of interventions. Make changes when needed to maximize outcomes. If there are concerns related to services provided by another professional, take steps to resolve the issue with the other professional.

STANDARD 2.19: ADDRESSING CONDITIONS INTERFERING WITH SERVICE DELIVERY

Identify and address environmental conditions that may negatively impact your services. Take steps to minimize/remove them by (a) directly doing so, (b) finding ways to modify interventions that do so, and/or (c) recommending help from other professionals. Document actions taken to resolve issues along with their associated outcomes.

PRACTICE QUESTION

You are a BCBA working at a community agency that contracts with a local school district to provide applied behavior analysis (ABA). While supporting a neurodivergent student with focused interests, occasional aggression toward others, and social communication differences, you notice that there are some district/school policies that conflict with your knowledge about evidence-based practice. You observe that members of the school multidisciplinary problem-solving team recommend retention as well as use of zero tolerance and exclusionary discipline as a means of addressing behavioral issues and rule violations. Which of the following ethical standards are involved in this situation?

A. Providing effective treatment
B. Selecting, designing, and implementing behavior-change interventions
C. Minimizing risk of behavior-change interventions
D. All of the above

Before moving on to the next section for the solution, we recommend that you provide a brief explanation for the answer option you selected here:

_____

_____

When you're ready, move on to the next section for the solution!

Practice Question Breakdown

Step 1: Examine the question

The question calls for you to examine the recommended interventions by a multidisciplinary school team that include grade retention as well as use of zero tolerance and exclusionary discipline to address behavioral challenges and rule infractions. In this all-too-common scenario, several ethical standards are intertwined and related to a behavior analyst's responsibility in practice.

Step 2: Analyze the answer options

A. This ethical standard is involved in the scenario. As an ethically minded BCBA, you must provide effective treatment, which includes evidence-based interventions; retention and zero tolerance policies are not currently supported by the empirical literature. Ideally, you want to recommend behavior-change interventions that are consistent with behavioral principles; however, the reality is that schools (and other agencies) sometimes use practices that are not grounded in applied behavioral analysis.
B. This ethical standard is involved in the scenario. As a BCBA, you strive to design, select, and implement behavior-change interventions that facilitate habilitative outcomes, such as inclusion and access to the instructional curriculum, and are responsive to the needs of the clients/stakeholders.
C. This answer is related to the scenario. Chosen interventions must minimize risk that is associated with all interventions, especially those that include restrictive, punitive practices (e.g., retention, zero tolerance policies).
D. The answers refer to standards that all seem to be involved. In choosing the most appropriate intervention for a neurodivergent student (with focused interests, occasional aggression toward others, and social communication differences), you must consider providing effective treatment, carefully select and implement the behavior-change interventions, and minimize the risk of the intervention. As a BCBA, while you may not be able to change prevailing educational policies or practices, continue to advocate for effective treatments and share with colleagues the latest research supporting or discouraging specific practices.

Step 3: Select the best answer

Among the four answer options presented, answer D (all of the above) appears to be the best answer.

▶ TASK LIST ITEM E-4

Section 3 of the Ethics Code consists of 16 standards (3.01 to 3.16) related to the behavior analyst's "responsibility to clients and stakeholders."

STANDARD 3.01: RESPONSIBILITY TO CLIENTS

Act in the best interest of clients and support their rights. Also follow mandated reporting requirements.

STANDARD 3.02: IDENTIFYING STAKEHOLDERS

Identify stakeholders (e.g., parent, teacher) and your obligations to each of them. Document and communicate these obligations to them at the start of the professional relationship.

STANDARD 3.03: ACCEPTING CLIENTS

Only accept clients whose service needs fall within your scope of competence and resources (e.g., capacity, staffing). If instructed to take a client that falls outside of this requirement, take steps to resolve the issue. Document actions taken along with their associated outcomes.

STANDARD 3.04: SERVICE AGREEMENT

Verify that there is a signed service agreement before providing services. This agreement should outline responsibilities of all parties, scope of your services, your obligations to the Code, and procedure for filing a complaint against you. The agreement is updated as needed or required; any updates should be reviewed and signed by the clients/stakeholders.

STANDARD 3.05: FINANCIAL AGREEMENTS

Document financial agreements related to fees and billing practices with clients/stakeholders. Any changes will need to be reviewed with them. Providing pro bono and bartered services require a specific service agreement.

STANDARD 3.06: CONSULTING WITH OTHER PROVIDERS

Arrange for consultations and/or referrals to other providers when it is in the best interest of clients, with consent and following any applicable requirements (e.g., laws, policies).

STANDARD 3.07: THIRD-PARTY CONTRACTS FOR SERVICES

Clarify your obligations to all parties and consider possible conflicts before providing services to a client through a third party (e.g., school). The service contract should outline responsibilities of all parties, scope of your services, how data will be used, your obligations to the Code, and limits to confidentiality. The contract is updated as needed or required; any updates should be reviewed with the relevant parties.

STANDARD 3.08: RESPONSIBILITY TO THE CLIENT WITH THIRD-PARTY CONTRACTS FOR SERVICES

Place the client's welfare above all others. If a third party's request for services violates this Code, take steps to resolve the issues. If the issues cannot be resolved, consider obtaining additional training/consultation, discontinue services following transition procedures, or refer to another behavior analyst. Document actions taken to resolve issues along with their associated outcomes.

STANDARD 3.09: COMMUNICATING WITH STAKEHOLDERS ABOUT THIRD-PARTY CONTRACTED SERVICES

When providing services to someone who cannot legally provide consent for a third party, ensure that the parent or legal guardian of the client is informed of your services and their right to copies of service documentation. Know and comply with informed consent requirements.

STANDARD 3.10: LIMITATIONS OF CONFIDENTIALITY

Inform clients/stakeholders of the limits to confidentiality at the outset of the professional relationship and when it must be broken.

STANDARD 3.11: DOCUMENTING PROFESSIONAL ACTIVITY

Create, maintain, and be accountable for detailed and organized documentation of your work activities to facilitate service delivery, meet applicable requirements, and allow for timely transition of services if needed.

STANDARD 3.12: ADVOCATING FOR APPROPRIATE SERVICES

Advocate for and educate clients/stakeholders about evidence-based assessment and intervention, including the amount required to meet goals.

STANDARD 3.13: REFERRALS

Make referrals based on the needs of clients/stakeholders. Disclose any incentives you receive for referrals and relationships you have with potential providers. Document referrals made, relevant relationships with providers, and incentives received; and follow up with clients/stakeholders.

STANDARD 3.14: FACILITATING CONTINUITY OF SERVICES

Avoid interruption of services. Communicate with all relevant parties and facilitate the continuation of services in a timely manner if interruptions should occur. Include a plan of action for interruptions in service agreements/contracts. Document actions taken along with their associated outcomes.

STANDARD 3.15: APPROPRIATELY DISCONTINUING SERVICES

Specify the conditions for discontinuing services in service agreements/contracts. Discontinuation is considered when (a) the client has met all goals, (b) the client isn't benefiting, (c) you and/or your supervisees are endangered, (d) the client and/or stakeholders ask for termination, (e) stakeholders fail to comply with the intervention after efforts to remove barriers, or (f) funding stops. When discontinuing services, provide the clients/stakeholders with a written plan for it, document acknowledgment of it, and review it. Document all actions taken.

STANDARD 3.16: APPROPRIATELY TRANSITIONING SERVICES

Specify the conditions for transition to another provider in service agreements/contracts. Effectively manage transitions by providing a written plan, reviewing it, and collaborating with other providers to minimize disruptions if needed.

PRACTICE QUESTION

ATTUNE is a community ABA provider for children and adolescents with developmental disabilities. At several clinical team meetings, the BCBA seems distracted (e.g., scrolls through phone, reads other documents, completes paperwork during portions of the team discussion). While presenting on the behavioral-change plan, the BCBA is on point and talks with the family and other team members, but once done speaking, goes back to doing other tasks. Which of the following ethical standards BEST address this scenario?

A. Consulting with other providers
B. Responsibility to clients
C. Limitations to confidentiality
D. Documenting professional activity

Before moving on to the next section for the solution, we recommend that you provide a brief explanation for the answer option you selected here:

_____

_____

When you're ready, move on to the next section for the solution!

Practice Question Breakdown

Step 1: Examine the question

The question calls for you to consider the distracted and off-task behavior of the BCBA while in meetings with the clients/stakeholders to determine the ethical standard that is most relevant to this scenario.

Step 2: Analyze the answer options

A. It might seem like consulting with other providers is relevant to interactions in this multidisciplinary team meeting; however, the BCBA does discuss the behavior-change plan with other providers at particular times in the meeting. This answer does not BEST address the ethical violation. This answer option is a distractor.
B. Professional responsibility to the clients/stakeholders in this meeting seems to be lacking on the part of the BCBA, who is providing direct services. While we are all busy and likely multitasking as part of our job, it is important to act in the best interest of the clients/stakeholders and remain engaged and active in all aspects of the clinical team meeting. This appears to be a promising option!
C. The scenario does not involve issues around the limits of confidentiality in the treatment team meeting. It is likely that prior to this meeting, confidentiality limits were already discussed and agreed to. This answer option is a distractor.
D. Detailed and organized documentation of the BCBA's work activities is not at the heart of this particular scenario. Documenting professional activity covers service provision at a broad level and is not simply focused on one meeting. This answer option is a distractor.

Step 3: Select the best answer

Among the four answer options presented, answer B (responsibility to clients) appears to be the best answer.

▶ TASK LIST ITEM E-5

Section 4 of the Ethics Code consists of 12 standards (4.01 to 4.12) related to the behavior analyst's "responsibility to supervisees and trainees."

STANDARD 4.01: COMPLIANCE WITH SUPERVISION REQUIREMENTS

Know and comply with supervisory requirements of relevant entities (e.g., certification and state licensing boards).

STANDARD 4.02: SUPERVISORY COMPETENCE

Supervise others only after receiving training in effective supervisory practices and in your areas of competence. Continually assess your supervisory practices and improve your skills through PD.

STANDARD 4.03: SUPERVISORY VOLUME

Take only the number of supervisees that will allow you to provide effective supervision. Continually consider relevant factors (e.g., caseload, availability) that affect your effectiveness as a supervisor. When your limit is reached, document this and communicate it to relevant parties (e.g., your employer).

STANDARD 4.04: ACCOUNTABILITY IN SUPERVISION

Be accountable for your supervisory practices and the work activities (e.g., client services, training) of your supervisees.

STANDARD 4.05: MAINTAINING SUPERVISION DOCUMENTATION

Follow all requirements for creating, updating, storing, and purging documentation related to supervisees. Ensure that both you and your supervisees keep complete and accurate documentation. Supervision documentation should be kept for at least 7 years.

STANDARD 4.06: PROVIDING SUPERVISION AND TRAINING

Follow all requirements for supervisory practices and plan to individualize supervision for each supervisee. Use evidence-based procedures that focus on positive reinforcement.

STANDARD 4.07: INCORPORATING AND ADDRESSING DIVERSITY

Cover topics related to diversity in supervision.

STANDARD 4.08: PERFORMANCE MONITORING AND FEEDBACK

Continually document the performance of supervisees and provide timely feedback to improve performance. Document all formal feedback and address any performance problems with an improvement plan.

STANDARD 4.09: DELEGATION OF TASKS

Assign tasks to supervisees that comply with the requirements of relevant entities (e.g., BACB, organization) and they can competently complete.

STANDARD 4.10: EVALUATING EFFECTS OF SUPERVISION AND TRAINING

Continually assess your supervisory practices by gathering feedback from others and monitoring supervisees' outcomes. Document these assessments and use the data to inform your practices.

STANDARD 4.11: FACILITATING CONTINUITY OF SUPERVISION

Avoid interruption of supervision. Communicate with all relevant parties and facilitate the continuation of supervision in a timely manner if interruptions should occur.

STANDARD 4.12: APPROPRIATELY TERMINATING SUPERVISION

When terminating supervision services, communicate with all relevant parties and develop a termination plan that minimizes negative effects for the supervisee. Document actions taken along with their associated outcomes.

PRACTICE QUESTION

You are a new therapist with less than 3 months of experience working in the field, providing in-home services to a 3-year-old client with behavioral challenges. The home environment is less than ideal for providing services—it's crowded and there appears to be multiple safety hazards. Child welfare is involved with the family. You are confined to a very small space to provide services and feel as though you are merely keeping the child from injuring themself rather than working on learning new skills (i.e., you feel more like a babysitter than a therapist). You meet with your BCBA supervisor to ask for assistance. You ask them (a) to attend a home session with you to brainstorm ideas on how to better provide therapy, (b) to hold a clinical team meeting with the family to address safety and space concerns, and/or (c) if this case should be referred to another, more skilled therapist. Your supervisor explains that they are incredibly busy, and unable to accompany you to the home. Also, the agency is short staffed, and you are asked to do the best you can in a difficult situation. Which of the following ethical standards are most related to this scenario?

A. Accountability in supervision
B. Supervisory volume
C. Delegation of tasks
D. All of the above

Before moving on to the next section for the solution, we recommend that you provide a brief explanation for the answer option you selected here:

_____

_____

When you're ready, move on to the next section for the solution!

Practice Question Breakdown

Step 1: Examine the question

The question calls for you to consider interaction between a supervisor and relatively new supervisee, who has requested help with a particularly complex in-home case. The supervisor responds that they are too busy and cannot help because the agency is severely short staffed. You are asked to identify the ethical standard that is most relevant to this scenario.

Step 2: Analyze the answer options

A. This ethical standard is related to the scenario. Ultimately, the BCBA supervisor is responsible for and must be accountable for all work activities of their supervisees.
B. This ethical standard is related to the scenario. In situations where the supervisee feels unsafe and unable to perform job duties, the supervisor should intervene. If unable to do so because of their supervisory volume, then they must address/adjust their caseload such that they are available to provide effective supervision.
C. This ethical standard is related to the scenario. A supervisor must delegate tasks to supervisees that they can competently complete. Ensuring the therapeutic environment is suitable to accomplish this is under the purview of the supervisor.
D. This answer option includes all three relevant and related ethical standards involving accountability in supervision, supervisory volume, and delegation of tasks. Improper and/or inadequate supervision and supervisory delegation is one of the most common ethical violation categories. This is it!

Step 3: Select the best answer

Among the four answer options presented, answer D (all of the above) appears to be the best answer.

▶ TASK LIST ITEM E-6

Section 5 of the Ethics Code consists of 11 standards (5.01 to 5.11) related to the behavior analyst's "responsibility in public statements."

STANDARD 5.01: PROTECTING THE RIGHTS OF CLIENTS, STAKEHOLDERS, SUPERVISEES, AND TRAINEES

Take steps to protect the rights of those with whom you work (e.g., clients, supervisees) when making public statements.

STANDARD 5.02: CONFIDENTIALITY IN PUBLIC STATEMENTS

Protect the confidentiality of clients and supervisees when making public statements, unless disclosure is allowed.

STANDARD 5.03: PUBLIC STATEMENTS BY BEHAVIOR ANALYSTS

Ensure that public statements about your professional activities or those with whom you work are truthful, not misleading, and based on evidence. Do not provide specific advice to address a client's needs in public.

STANDARD 5.04: PUBLIC STATEMENTS BY OTHERS

Be responsible for public statements that promote your work or products, regardless of the source. Take steps to prevent or correct false or misleading statements about the work of products of behavior analysts. Document actions taken to address issues along with their associated outcomes.

STANDARD 5.05: USE OF INTELLECTUAL PROPERTY

Know and comply with intellectual property laws. Obtain permission to use protected works when required and properly cite your sources. Do not unlawfully acquire or disclose proprietary information.

STANDARD 5.06: ADVERTISING NONBEHAVIORAL SERVICES

Do not advertise nonbehavioral services as behavioral. If you provide nonbehavioral services, provide a disclaimer that clearly distinguishes it from those covered by your certification as a behavior analyst. If you work for an organization that violates this standard, take steps to address the problem. Document actions taken to address issues along with their associated outcomes.

STANDARD 5.07: SOLICITING TESTIMONIALS FROM CURRENT CLIENTS FOR ADVERTISING

Do not solicit testimonials from current clients/stakeholders for advertising. Do not use or share any unsolicited reviews on the internet or forums you cannot control. If you work for an organization that violates this standard, take steps to address the problem. Document actions taken to address issues along with their associated outcomes.

STANDARD 5.08: USING TESTIMONIALS FROM FORMER CLIENTS FOR ADVERTISING

When using testimonials from former clients, let them know where/how they will be used and any possible risks and their right to rescind their testimonial at any time. Ensure that you comply with any applicable privacy laws. Testimonials should be identified as solicited or unsolicited, and include a statement that accurately describes your relationship with their authors. If you work for an organization that violates this standard, take steps to address the problem. Document actions taken to address issues along with their associated outcomes.

STANDARD 5.09: USING TESTIMONIALS FOR NONADVERTISING PURPOSES

You can use testimonials from former or current clients/stakeholders if they comply with any applicable laws and are not used for advertising. If you work for an organization that violates this standard, take steps to address the problem. Document actions taken to address issues along with their associated outcomes.

STANDARD 5.10: SOCIAL MEDIA CHANNELS AND WEBSITES

Know about the risks to confidentiality when using social media. Monitor your social media accounts and websites to ensure that only appropriate content is shared. Do not publish digital content of or about clients on personal accounts. If publishing such content on professional accounts, (a) obtain informed consent, (b) include a disclaimer to indicate informed consent was obtained and the content should not be captured/used without permission, (c) publish it in a way that minimizes potential for sharing, and (d) prevent and correct any misuse of the content. Document actions taken to address issues along with their associated outcomes.

STANDARD 5.11: USING DIGITAL CONTENT IN PUBLIC STATEMENTS

Ensure confidentiality and obtain informed consent prior to sharing digital content of or about clients. Only content for the purpose of the public statement should be used, and a disclaimer should be included to indicate informed consent was obtained. If you work for an organization that violates this standard, take steps to address the problem. Document actions taken to address issues along with their associated outcomes.

▶ TASK LIST ITEM E-7

Section 6 of the Ethics Code consists of 11 standards (6.01 to 6.11) related to the behavior analyst's "responsibility in research."

STANDARD 6.01: CONFORMING WITH LAWS AND REGULATIONS IN RESEARCH

Follow all laws and organizational requirements for conducting research.

STANDARD 6.02: RESEARCH REVIEW

Conduct research only after it has been approved by a formal review committee.

STANDARD 6.03: RESEARCH IN SERVICE DELIVERY

When conducting research with clients, follow the standards for service delivery and research. Prioritize the welfare of clients. If services are offered as a part of a study, clarify the nature of the services, obligations, possible risks, and limitations for all involved.

STANDARD 6.04: INFORMED CONSENT IN RESEARCH

Obtain informed consent (or assent) from research participants when required by the review committee and prior to dissemination of data obtained from participants to the scientific community. Inform participants that whether or not they provide consent will not impact services, and that they can withdraw consent at any time.

STANDARD 6.05: CONFIDENTIALITY IN RESEARCH

Prioritize the confidentiality of research participants when possible. Take steps to protect confidential information while conducting and sharing research (e.g., disguising or removing it).

STANDARD 6.06: COMPETENCE IN CONDUCTING RESEARCH

Conduct research independently only when you are competent to do so (i.e., after successfully conducting research under a qualified supervisor in a defined relationship). Before engaging in any activity that you are not trained to conduct, either (a) obtain training and develop the needed competency to do it or (b) collaborate with others who are competent. You are responsible for the ethical conduct of everyone working on the study.

STANDARD 6.07: CONFLICT OF INTEREST IN RESEARCH AND PUBLICATION

Identify, disclose, and work to address any conflicts of interest (e.g., financial, personal) in research, publications, and editorial work.

STANDARD 6.08: APPROPRIATE CREDIT

Give credit to those who contribute to research and ensure that authorship and acknowledgments reflect the relative contributions of all involved.

STANDARD 6.09: PLAGIARISM

Do not take credit for the work of others and present their work as your own. Disclose any instances of publishing previously published work.

STANDARD 6.10: DOCUMENTATION AND DATA RETENTION IN RESEARCH

Know and comply with requirements for storing, transporting, retaining, and purging documentation related to research. Retain data for the longest period of time required. Destroy physical forms of documentation after they have been backed up in digital format or the data have been summarized when allowed by relevant entities.

STANDARD 6.11: ACCURACY AND USE OF DATA

Do not make up data and misrepresent results in research, presentations, and publications. Procedures used and findings should be adequately described. When presenting research, include all data when possible. If this is not possible, explain what was excluded and why. Take steps to correct any errors in published data.

▶ CONCLUSION

In this chapter, we provided a review of the Ethics Code for behavior analysts. This included coverage of the introduction section of the Code, as well as the six sets of standards related to responsibilities in practice, to clients and stakeholders, to supervisees and trainees, in public statements, and in research. Behavior analysts encounter ethical dilemmas regularly in the field; thus, a Code is necessary for ensuring that they practice in a manner that protects and benefits consumers. But please note that although the content presented in this chapter may serve to help familiarize you with what the Code says behavior analysts should and shouldn't do, it must be recognized that the topic of ethics is riddled with complexity and this resource alone is insufficient for interpreting the Code and its application to all events. To expand on your knowledge in this content area, we recommend you seek out additional readings. The reference list for this chapter may be a good place to start.

1. The introduction section of the Ethics Code describes:

    A. The application, core principles, enforcement, and scope of the Code
    B. The application, enforcement, limitations, and standards of the Code
    C. The core principles, rules, scope, and values of the Code
    D. The enforcement, preamble, scope, and standards of the Code

2. The four core principles that serve as the framework for the Ethics Code's standards include all of the following except:

    A. Behave with integrity
    B. Benefit others
    C. Ensure their competence
    D. Respect others' privacy

3. The Code applies to:

    A. BCBAs
    B. BCBAs and BCaBAs
    C. BCBAs, BCaBAs, and applicants for either of these credentials
    D. BCBAs, BCaBAs, RBTs, and applicants for any of these credentials

4. If a behavior analyst were to accept a gift from a client, it cannot be valued at more than _____.

    A. $5 USD
    B. $10 USD
    C. $25 USD
    D. $50 USD

5. A behavior analyst cannot accept as a supervisee an individual with whom they have had a romantic/sexual relationship with within the past _____.

    A. 3 months
    B. 6 months
    C. 12 months
    D. 24 months

6. Multiple relationships with colleagues:

    A. Are acceptable
    B. Are acceptable if there are no present conflicts of interest
    C. Must be reported to the Behavior Analyst Certification Board (BACB)
    D. Should be avoided

7. In which of the following conditions is the disclosure of confidential information not warranted?

    A. When attempting to protect the client or others from harm
    B. When disclosure is required by law
    C. When it is requested for the purpose of resolving a billing issue
    D. When informed consent has been obtained

1. **A) The application, core principles, enforcement, and scope of the Code**
The introduction section of the Ethics Code describes the application, core principles, enforcement, and scope of the Code. The other answer options (application, enforcement, limitations, and standards; core principles, rules, scope, and values; enforcement, preamble, scope, and standards) include other items not described in the introduction section and serve as distractors.

2. **D) Respect others' privacy**
The four core principles that serve as the framework for the Ethics Code's standards include: benefit others; treat other with compassion, dignity, and respect; behave with integrity; and ensure their competence. Although respecting others' privacy is required for treating others with compassion, dignity, and respect, it does not function as a core principle for the Ethics Code's standards.

3. **C) BCBAs, BCaBAs, and applicants for either of these credentials**
The Code clearly states that it applies to not just BCBAs (Board Certified Behavior Analysts), but also BCaBAs (Board Certified Assistant Behavior Analysts) and applicants for either of these credentials. The other answer options (BCBAs; BCBAs and BCaBAs; BCBAs, BCaBAs, RBTs [Registered Behavior Technicians], and applicants for any of these credentials) are either under- or overinclusive and function as distractors.

4. **B) $10 USD**
If a behavior analyst were to accept a gift from a client, it cannot be valued at more than $10 USD. The other answer options ($5 USD, $25 USD, $50 USD) serve as distractors.

5. **B) 6 months**
A behavior analyst cannot accept as a supervisee an individual with whom they have had a romantic/sexual relationship with within the past 6 months. The other answer options (3 months, 12 months, 24 months) serve as distractors.

6. **D) Should be avoided**
Simply put, multiple relationships with colleagues should be avoided. The other answer options (are acceptable, are acceptable if there are no present conflicts of interest, must be reported to the BACB) function as distractors.

7. **C) When it is requested for the purpose of resolving a billing issue**
Confidential information is shared only when you have informed consent, to protect the client or others from harm, to resolve contractual issues, to prevent a crime that can harm someone, or it's required by law. Disclosure is not warranted when it is requested for the purpose of resolving a billing issue.

8. Behavior analysts select, design, and use interventions that are all of the following except:

   A. Assessment results based
   B. Consistent with behavioral principles
   C. Positive and negative reinforcement focused
   D. Sensitive to the needs and context of the clients/stakeholders

9. After the start of services, a behavior analyst decides there is a need for a change to the intervention plan. What should the behavior analyst do to enact the change?

   A. Document the change and explain it to clients/stakeholders
   B. Document the change and proceed to implement it
   C. Explain the change to clients/stakeholders
   D. Explain the change to clients/stakeholders and obtain informed consent as appropriate

10. Restrictive/punishment-based procedures are to be recommended only when:

   A. Less restrictive interventions have been ineffective
   B. The risk of harm is greater than the risk associated with the intervention
   C. The risk of harm is lower than the risk associated with the intervention
   D. Both A and B

11. A behavior analyst is concerned about the services provided by a nonbehavioral professional. They should:

   A. Discontinue services
   B. Refer the client to another professional for relevant services
   C. Report the other professional to the Behavior Analyst Certification Board (BACB)
   D. Take steps to resolve the issue with the other professional

12. A service agreement should address all of the following except:

   A. The behavior analyst's obligation to the Code
   B. The fees schedule
   C. The responsibilities of all parties involved
   D. The scope of the behavior analyst's services

13. The behavior analyst must place the welfare of the _____ above all others.

   A. Client
   B. Funding agency
   C. Organization they represent
   D. Stakeholders

14. When should clients and stakeholders be informed of the limits to confidentiality?

   A. After assessment, but before implementation of the behavior-change program
   B. After confidential information has been disclosed to a third party
   C. At the outset of the professional relationship
   D. When there is a potential need to disclose confidential information to a third-party

8. C) Positive and negative reinforcement focused

Behavior analysts select, design, and use interventions that are assessment results based, consistent with behavioral principles, and sensitive to the needs and context of the clients/stakeholders. However, the Code does not explicitly communicate that they must be positive and negative reinforcement focused.

9. D) Explain the change to clients/stakeholders and obtain informed consent as appropriate

To enact change after the there is an identified need for it after the start of services, the behavior analyst should explain the change to clients/stakeholders and obtain informed consent as appropriate. The other answer options (document the change and explain it to clients/stakeholders, document the change and proceed to implement it, explain the change to clients/stakeholders) describe insufficient plans of action and serve as distractors.

10. D) Both A and B

According to the Code, restrictive/punishment-based procedures are to be recommended only when less restrictive interventions have been tried and found to be ineffective, and the risk of harm is greater than the risk associated with the intervention. It is not the case that they are to be recommended if the risk of harm is lower than the risk associated with the intervention.

11. D) Take steps to resolve the issue with the other professional

When a behavior analyst is concerned about the services provided by a nonbehavioral professional, they should take steps to resolve the issue with the other professional. The other answer options (discontinue services, refer the client to another professional for relevant services, report the other professional to the BACB) do not describe appropriate next steps for addressing the matter and function as distractors.

12. B) The fees schedule

A service agreement should address responsibilities of all parties, scope of your services, your obligations to the Code, and procedure for filing a complaint against you. Although financial agreements related to fees and billing practices need to be documented, it is not required that a fee schedule is included as component of the service agreement.

13. A) Client

Behavior analysts are to place the welfare of the client above all others, including any funding agencies, the organization they represent, and other stakeholders.

14. C) At the outset of the professional relationship

The Code requires that behavior analysts inform clients and stakeholders of the limits to confidentiality at the outset of the professional relationship. The other response options (after assessment, but before implementation of the behavior-change program; after confidential information has been disclosed to a third-party; when there is a potential need to disclose confidential information to a third party) serve as distractors.

15. Which of the following is not a condition for discontinuing services established in a service agreement?

    A. Funding is discontinued for services

    B. Behavioral staff are exposed to harmful conditions that cannot be changed

    C. The client met all their goals

    D. The client only receives some benefit from services

16. Supervision documentation should be kept for at least _____ years.

    A. 3

    B. 5

    C. 7

    D. 10

17. When considering the solicitation of testimonials from clients, which of the following is true?

    A. Behavior analysts may not solicit testimonials from current or former clients

    B. Behavior analysts may solicit testimonials from current clients but not former clients

    C. Behavior analysts may solicit testimonials from current and former clients

    D. Behavior analysts may solicit testimonials from former clients but not current clients

18. Under what circumstances is it permissible for a behavior analyst to publish digital content about their clients on a personal social media account?

    A. A disclaimer is posted to warn against the reusing of any shared content without express permission

    B. Informed consent has been obtained

    C. Informed consent has been obtained and the content is published in a way that reduces the potential for sharing

    D. It is never permissible to publish digital content about clients on a personal social media account

19. Prior to conducting research, a behavior analyst must receive approval from:

    A. A formal research review committee

    B. Their intended participants

    C. Their supervisor

    D. None of the above

15. C) The client met all their goals

Discontinuation is considered if the client is not benefiting from services, but this answer option clearly indicates that there is at least "some" benefit received from services. The other answer options (funding is discontinued for services, behavioral staff are exposed to harmful conditions that cannot changed, the client met all their goals) describe conditions indicated in the Code as those in which discontinuation is considered.

16. C) 7

The Code specifically communicates that supervision documentation should be kept for at least 7 years. The other response options (3, 5, 10) do not accurately fit in this statement and function as distractors.

17. D) Behavior analysts may solicit testimonials from former clients but not current clients

When considering the solicitation of testimonials from clients, behavior analysts may solicit testimonials from former clients but not current clients. The other answer options (behavior analysts may not solicit testimonials from current or former clients, behavior analysts may solicit testimonials from current clients but not former clients, behavior analysts may solicit testimonials from current and former clients) are not true statements and function as distractors.

18. D) It is never permissible to publish digital content about clients on a personal social media account

The Code clearly indicates that it is never permissible to publish digital content about clients on a personal social media account. The other answer options (a disclaimer is posted to warn against the reusing of any shared content without express permission, informed consent has been obtained, informed consent has been obtained and the content is published in a way that reduces the potential for sharing) do not describe circumstances in which it is permissible and serve as distractors.

19. A) A formal research review committee

Prior to conducting research, a behavior analyst must receive approval from a formal research review committee. The other answer options (their intended participants; their supervisor, none of the above) function as distractors.

BIBLIOGRAPHY

Bailey, J., & Burch, M. (2022). *Ethics for behavior analysts*. Routledge.

Behavior Analyst Certification Board. (2017). *BCBA task list* (5th ed.). https://www.bacb.com/wp-content/uploads/2020/08/BCBA-task-list-5th-ed-211019.pdf

Behavior Analyst Certification Board. (2020). *Ethics code for behavior analysts*. Author.

Behavior Analyst Certification Board. (2021). *Code-enforcement procedures*. Author.

Britton, L. N., & Crye, A. A. (2021). Cultivating the ethical repertoires of behavior analysts: Prevention of common violations. *Behavior Analysis in Practice, 14*, 534–548. https://doi.org/10.1007/s40617-020-00540-w

Rosenberg, N. E., & Schwartz, I. S. (2019). Guidance or compliance: What makes an ethical behavior analyst? *Behavior Analysis in Practice, 12*(2), 473–482. https://doi.org/10.1007/s40617-018-00287-5

Behavior Assessment

Behavior analysts are to select, design, and implement assessments before selecting and designing behavior-change interventions (Behavior Analyst Certification Board, 2020). This is necessary because assessment is used to capture relevant data that can be used to inform the development of the plan for treatment. It is an essential step of the behavior analytic service delivery process. Various assessment methods can be employed for the purpose of learning about clients' profile of skill strengths and deficits, client preferences, and why problem behavior occurs. The purpose of this chapter will be to provide an essential review of Task List items F-1 through E-9, which specifically relate to behavior assessment.

> ## ▶ LEARNING OBJECTIVES
>
> The following Task List items related to behavior assessment (F-1 through F-9) serve as the learning objectives of this chapter:
>
> **F-1** Review records and available data (e.g., educational, medical, historical) at the outset of the case.
>
> **F-2** Determine the need for behavior-analytic services.
>
> **F-3** Identify and prioritize socially significant behavior-change goals.
>
> **F-4** Conduct assessments of relevant skill strengths and deficits.
>
> **F-5** Conduct preference assessments.
>
> **F-6** Describe the common functions of problem behavior.
>
> **F-7** Conduct a descriptive assessment of problem behavior.
>
> **F-8** Conduct a functional analysis of problem behavior.
>
> **F-9** Interpret functional assessment data.

▶ TASK LIST ITEM F-1

The objective of this Task List item is to review records and available data (e.g., educational, medical, historical) at the outset of the case.

At the outset of a case and prior to assessment, behavior analysts need to consider the available records and data on what has taken place to identify and address the target behavior.

Some clients may have many types of records available for review while others may have very little available. Possible records may include medical reports, psychological assessment reports, individualized education plans, family service plans, and documents from other allied health providers (e.g., speech therapists, occupational therapists). At the very minimum, behavior analysts should aim to review the following.

RELEVANT EDUCATIONAL DATA

This includes information related to the client's education (e.g., transcripts, academic program, disciplinary file). Educational records may contain documents that evidence the use of behavioral interventions and include functional assessment reports, behavior intervention plans, and progress monitoring data.

RELEVANT MEDICAL DATA

This includes information related to the client's health (e.g., clinical findings, diagnostic test results, care plans, medication). It is important to rule out medical reasons for behavior. If a medical reason is found, treatment of the condition may be necessary prior to the implementation of behavioral interventions.

RELEVANT HISTORICAL DATA

This includes a variety of information from the client's history that may be learned through the review of many different possible types of records available. For behavior analysts, information is reviewed with attention to information that informs them of the nature of the target behavior, its development, and the relevant contingencies at work.

MNEMONIC AID

M (for Medical) E (for Educational) H (for Historical). Sometimes, a review of records can be MEH.

▶ TASK LIST ITEM F-2

The objective of this Task List item is to determine the need for behavior-analytic services.

The decision to recommend behavior-analytic services or not depends on whether such services may help to improve the client's quality of life (i.e., useful and habilitative to maximize reinforcement and minimize punishment for the client and others). At least one socially significant behavior must be identified as a target for change. The identification of potential target behaviors is a product of assessment.

To determine the social significance of a potential target behavior, the following 10 questions are asked: Is the behavior:

- likely to result in reinforcement for the client even after services end?
- required for learning a useful skill?
- something that will increase the client's access to environments where other desirable behaviors can be learned and practiced?
- one that can result in others interacting with the client in a more positive and helpful way?
- a behavioral cusp (i.e., a behavior that can lead to new environments/reinforcers) or pivotal behavior (i.e., a behavior that can lead to new untrained behaviors)?
- age appropriate?
- a problem behavior that can be replaced with an adaptive behavior?
- directly related to the problem/goal?
- really the behavior of interest?
- an actual behavior?

Each answer of "yes" increases the likelihood that a given target behavior can be considered socially significant.

▶ TASK LIST ITEM F-3

The objective of this Task List item is to identify and prioritize socially significant behavior-change goals.

Goal setting involves establishing criteria for behavior change, which occurs after identification of a socially significant target behavior. See Task List items F-2 and H-1 for a review of socially significant behaviors and stating intervention goals, respectively.

If more than one socially significant behavior-change goal is identified, the behavior analyst should consider the order in which goals should be addressed (i.e., *prioritize* goals). To assist in this process, it is important to consider the following questions in review of the target behavior for each goal.

Table 8.1 Questions to consider for prioritizing target behaviors

Question	Note
Does it pose a danger to the client or others?	More danger = higher priority.
How often will the client use it in the natural environment? If it's a problem behavior, how often does it happen?	More often = higher priority.
How long has it been a problem?	Longer = higher priority.
Will changing it result in the client receiving more reinforcement?	More reinforcement = higher priority.
Is it important for the client's future development of other skills or independence?	More important = higher priority.
Will changing it result in fewer negative interactions with others?	Fewer negative interactions = higher priority.
Will changing it result in the client providing more reinforcement to others?	More reinforcement to others = higher priority.
Is its treatment likely to succeed?	More likely to succeed = higher priority.
Is its treatment costly?	High financial cost cannot be an excuse for withholding services. However, the cost of the client's time should be considered. In some cases, a behavior-change program's demand of a client's time may be too much and fail to justify treatment.

Note. A ranking matrix can be used to calculate a numerical score for each target behavior.

▶ TASK LIST ITEM F-4

The objective of this Task List item is to conduct assessments of relevant skill strengths and deficits.

Methods of assessment to discover the skill strengths and deficits of a client may include (a) indirect and (b) direct assessments.

INDIRECT ASSESSMENT

This includes the use of (a) interviews, (b) checklists, and (c) rating scales.

Interview

This involves meeting with significant others (e.g., caregivers, teachers) to obtain relevant information. Behavior analysts conduct interviews that primarily focus on *what* and *when* questions related to the behavior of interest.

Checklist

This is a list of specific behaviors with a description of the conditions under which each behavior will occur.

Rating Scale

This is a list of items (i.e., specific behaviors or statements/questions related to the behavior of interest) that respondents (i.e., significant others) can rate on a numerical or ordinal scale.

ADDITIONAL NOTE(S)

Checklists and rating scales may be used during interviews.

DIRECT ASSESSMENT

This includes the use of (a) standardized tests, (b) criterion-referenced measures, (c) curriculum-based measures, and (d) direct observations.

Standardized Test

An assessment instrument with specific procedures that must be followed for its administration.

Criterion-Referenced Measure

An assessment that measures a client's performance against some predetermined standard.

Curriculum-Based Measure

A type of criterion-referenced measure that is used to measure performance on tasks the client performs as a part of planned instruction (i.e., curriculum).

Direct Observation

This involves directly observing the behavior of interest.

When a client experiences language delays, assessment can be used to determine what the client can and cannot do (e.g., mand, tact). See Task List item B-14 for a review of verbal operants. Data obtained through the use of assessment can help to (a) identify the cause of the delay, (b) compare the client's performance against that of others, and (c) guide intervention planning.

MAND ASSESSMENT

Assessing the mand repertoire involves identifying the evocative effects of motivating operations (MOs) on verbal responses.

TACT ASSESSMENT

Assessing the tact repertoire involves identifying the evocative effects of nonverbal stimuli on verbal responses.

DUPLIC AND CODIC ASSESSMENT

Assessing the duplic and codic repertoire involves identifying the evocative effects of verbal discriminative stimuli (S^Ds) on verbal and nonverbal responses.

LISTENER ASSESSMENT

Assessing the listener repertoire involves measurement of the client's (a) verbal discriminations (i.e., simple verbal discriminations, auditory conditional discriminations, compound verbal discriminations, verbal conditional discriminations, and verbal function-altering effect) and (b) parts of speech (e.g., verbs, adjectives).

INTRAVERBAL ASSESSMENT

Assessing the intraverbal repertoire is arguably the most difficult of the elementary verbal operants. It involves evaluation of verbal discriminations, parts of speech, and evocative effects of MOs and nonverbal S^Ds.

ADDITIONAL NOTE(S)

Autoclitic verbal behavior (i.e., autoclitic mands and tacts) can also be assessed.

PRACTICE QUESTION

Direct observation is the hallmark of behavioral assessment. As a Board Certified Behavior Analyst (BCBA) working in a classroom, you are trying to determine how to gather data about the target behavior (aggression toward peers) of a middle school student. As you develop and refine your direct observation protocol, you realize that there are advantages and disadvantages to every behavioral assessment tool (both direct and indirect). Which of the following are disadvantages associated with direct observation of behavior?

A. Direct observation data can confirm information collected during FBA interviews
B. Temporally distant antecedent events may not be observable during a scheduled observation session
C. Observer drift might impact the data you collect
D. B and C only

Before moving on to the next section for the solution, we recommend that you provide a brief explanation for the answer option you selected here:

_____

_____

When you're ready, move on to the next section for the solution!

Practice Question Breakdown

Step 1: Examine the question

In the scenario, you are choosing a behavioral assessment tool to gather data about the target behavior (aggression toward peers) of a middle school student. Be sure to carefully reread the question whenever you feel an answer does not fit with what you initially read as the question's objective. The question asks you to consider ONLY the disadvantages associated with direct observation of behavior.

Step 2: Analyze the answer options

A. This is actually an advantage of direct observation methods as it is often used to confirm information gathered from other methods (indirect) of behavioral assessment. This answer option is a distractor.
B. This is a disadvantage of direct observation of behavior. Temporally distant antecedent events may not be readily observable during the time you are observing a student, making it harder to determine what sets the occasion for behavior to occur—this is indeed one disadvantage to using direct observation. You must realize that you might miss important information about why a behavior occurs or what is maintaining it if those events do not occur within an observation session.
C. This is a disadvantage of direct observation of behavior. Observer drift, or the tendency for raters to become inconsistent in the application of their observational measurement system, can also be a disadvantage and result in measurement error.
D. This answer includes answers B and C, which are both identified disadvantages of direct observation of behavior. Be sure to remember that all behavioral assessment tools have advantages and disadvantages. To further increase your understanding, try to list three advantages and disadvantages of each method you learn about!

Step 3: Select the best answer

Among the four answer options presented, answer D (B and C only) appears to be the best answer.

▶ TASK LIST ITEM F-5

The objective of this Task List item is to conduct preference assessments.

There are three types of stimulus preference assessments: (a) asking about preferences, (b) free operant observation, and (c) trial-based methods.

ASKING ABOUT PREFERENCES

This involves asking the client what they like. There are multiple approaches to asking about preferences, including the use of (a) open-ended questions, (b) presenting questions in a choice format, and (c) asking the client to rank-order items.

Open-Ended Questions

This involves asking the client questions about preferences that cannot simply be answered with a "yes" or "no."

■ *Example*: "What do you like to do during recess?"

Choice-Formatted Questions

This involves asking the client questions about preferences that are formatted as a choice.

■ *Example*: "Would you rather play hopscotch or tag?"

Rank-Ordering Items

This involves giving the client a list of items or activities and asking the client to put them in order from most to least preferred.

ADDITIONAL NOTE(S)

Questions can be asked orally or in writing, depending on the client. There are also surveys that have been developed to assess client preferences.

FREE-OPERANT OBSERVATION

This involves observing and recording the length of time (i.e., duration) that a client *approaches, contacts*, or *engages* with the stimuli when they are "free" to emit any responses. There are two types of free-operant observation: (a) contrived and (b) naturalistic.

Contrived Free-Operant Observation

This involves prearrangement of the environment to include items/activities that the client may like and can engage with prior to observing.

Naturalistic Free-Operant Observation

This involves no prearrangement of the environment prior to observing. It takes place in the client's natural environment.

ADDITIONAL NOTE(S)

The more a client approaches (i.e., moves toward), contacts (i.e., touches), or engages (i.e., interacts with) a stimulus, the more it is considered a preferred stimulus.

TRIAL-BASED METHODS

This involves presenting a series of trials to the client and recording their responses to determine preferences. There are three types of trial-based methods: (a) single stimulus, (b) paired stimulus, and (c) multiple stimulus.

SINGLE STIMULUS PREFERENCE ASSESSMENT

This method involves presenting target stimuli one at a time in random order. Each item is presented several times, and the client's response to each item (i.e., whether they approach the item, frequency of contact, duration of interaction) is recorded.

PAIRED STIMULUS PREFERENCE ASSESSMENT

This method involves presenting two target stimuli at a time. Each stimulus is randomly paired with all other stimuli, but every possible pair must be presented. The client's selection between the two target stimuli presented at each trial is recorded.

MULTIPLE STIMULUS PREFERENCE ASSESSMENT

This method involves presenting an array of three or more stimuli at a time. There are two variations used: (a) multiple stimulus without replacement (MSWO) and (b) multiple stimulus with replacement (MSW).

Multiple Stimulus Without Replacement Preference Assessment

This method involves removing the item selected by the client from the array, rearranging the remaining unselected items, and then beginning the next trial with a reduced array.

Multiple Stimulus With Replacement Preference Assessment

The method involves keeping the item selected by the client in the array, replacing the remaining unselected items with new items, and then beginning the next trial with the same number of items in the array.

ADDITIONAL NOTE(S)

Trial-based methods, like in free-operant observation, use one or more of the three measures indicative of preference (i.e., approach, contact, and engagement).

▶ TASK LIST ITEM F-6

The objective of this Task List item is to describe the common functions of problem behavior.

FUNCTIONS OF BEHAVIOR

The function(s) of a behavior answers the question, "Why is this behavior occurring?" The answer to this question based on decades of research is, "to get or get out of something." In other words, a function refers to the source of reinforcement for a behavior.

   Common functions of problem behavior include sources of positive and negative reinforcement.

SOURCES OF POSITIVE REINFORCEMENT

These include (a) social positive reinforcement, (b) tangible reinforcement, and (c) automatic reinforcement.

Social Positive Reinforcement

This refers to reinforcing reactions from others (i.e., attention).

■ *Example*: A client engages in yelling behavior that results in and is maintained by surprised facial expressions from peers.

Tangible Reinforcement

This refers to reinforcing materials or other stimuli.

■ *Example*: A client engages in yelling behavior that results in and is maintained by access to cookies.

Automatic Reinforcement

This refers to reinforcement that is directly produced by the behavior (i.e., sensory stimulation).

■ *Example*: A client engages in yelling behavior that results in and is maintained by the physical stimulation it produces in their mouth.

SOURCES OF NEGATIVE REINFORCEMENT

These include (a) social negative reinforcement and (b) automatic negative reinforcement.

Social Negative Reinforcement

This refers to the termination or postponement (i.e., escape) of unwanted interactions with others as well as unpleasant tasks/activities.

■ *Example*: A client engages in yelling behavior that results in and is maintained by the termination of teacher demands to complete unwanted math worksheets.

Automatic Negative Reinforcement

This refers to the termination or postponement (i.e., escape) of aversive stimulation. The behavior directly accomplishes this.

■ *Example*: A client engages in eloping behavior that results in and is maintained by the termination of loud noises in the room.

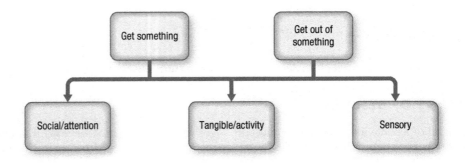

Figure 8.1 The functions of behavior.

▶ TASK LIST ITEM F-7

The objective of this Task List item is to conduct a descriptive assessment of problem behavior.

Descriptive assessment involves observation of the target behavior in relation to other events under naturally occurring conditions. There are three types of descriptive assessment: (a) continuous Antecedent-Behavior-Consequence (ABC) recording, (b) narrative ABC recording, and (c) scatterplot recording.

ABC analyses view behavior as a function of the antecedents that precede it and the consequences that follow it.

CONTINUOUS ANTECEDENT-BEHAVIOR-CONSEQUENCE RECORDING

This involves recording the occurrences of the target behavior and environmental events (i.e., specified antecedents and consequences). Environmental events are recorded when they occur, even when the problem behavior has not.

Table 8.2 Example of a continuous Antecedent-Behavior-Consequence recording form

A	B	C
▨ Teacher instruction ▨ Transition ▨ Unstructured time	▨ Elopement ▨ Tantrum	▨ Access to preferred activity ▨ Peer attention ▨ Task removal ▨ Teacher reprimand
▨ Teacher instruction ▨ Transition ▨ Unstructured time	▨ Elopement ▨ Tantrum	▨ Access to preferred activity ▨ Peer attention ▨ Task removal ▨ Teacher reprimand
▨ Teacher instruction ▨ Transition ▨ Unstructured time	▨ Elopement ▨ Tantrum	▨ Access to preferred activity ▨ Peer attention ▨ Task removal ▨ Teacher reprimand

NARRATIVE ANTECEDENT-BEHAVIOR-CONSEQUENCE RECORDING

This involves recording data only when the target behavior occurs. Unlike continuous ABC recording, environmental events are not specified and are instead open ended. Any events immediately preceding and following the target behavior are recorded.

Table 8.3 Example of a narrative Antecedent-Behavior-Consequence recording form

A	B	C

SCATTERPLOT RECORDING

This involves recording when the target behavior occurs. Specifically, time is divided into shorter intervals (e.g., 15 minutes) and different marks are made on the observation form to indicate the extent to which the behavior occurred for each time interval.

▨ *Example* (scatterplot recording form; chart divided into 1-hour intervals):

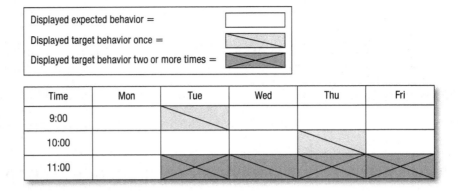

Figure 8.2 Scatterplot recording form (chart divided into 1-hour intervals).

▶ TASK LIST ITEM F-8

The objective of this Task List item is to conduct a functional analysis (FA) of problem behavior.

An FA can be conducted to observe and measure the separate effects of antecedents and consequences on problem behavior. When conducting FAs, analog conditions are used to allow for enhanced control of variables hypothesized to be related to the problem behavior.

The basic FA includes four conditions: (a) contingent attention, (b) contingent escape, (c) alone, and (d) play (i.e., control). The conditions are individually presented and repeated in an alternating sequence. During the presentation of each condition, occurrences of the problem behavior are recorded.

Table 8.4 Example of a functional analysis protocol with four conditions

Condition	Antecedent/ EO	Consequence for Problem Behavior
Attention	Attention withheld	Attention provided
Escape	Task demands presented	Task demands removed
Alone	Nothing; limited stimulation	Problem behavior ignored or redirected
Play/control	Free social attention and access to preferred activities	Problem behavior ignored or redirected

EO, establishing operation.

In addition to the basic FA, there have been several variants developed. These include: (a) brief functional analysis (BFA), (b) trial-based FA (TBFA), (c) latency-based FA (LBFA), (d) FA of precursor behavior, and (e) interview-informed synthesized contingency analysis (IISCA).

BRIEF FUNCTIONAL ANALYSIS

This involves presenting each condition only once or twice, with each session lasting 5 to 10 minutes in length.

TRIAL-BASED FUNCTIONAL ANALYSIS

This involves interspersing a series of trials among regular, naturally occurring activities. Each trial consists of a test and control condition, each lasting 1 minute in length. Sessions are terminated when the problem behavior occurs.

INTERVIEW-INFORMED SYNTHESIZED CONTINGENCY ANALYSIS

This involves presenting synthesized antecedents and consequences (i.e., multiple contingencies) during the test condition to emulate the natural context in which the problem behavior reportedly occurs. In the control condition, noncontingent access to the reinforcers used in the test condition is provided.

LATENCY-BASED FUNCTIONAL ANALYSIS

This involves presenting the establishing operation and then immediately terminating the session when the problem behavior occurs. Unlike the methods previously described that involve recording occurrences of the problem behavior, the LBFA is conducted by recording the time between the onset of the establishing operation (EO) and the first occurrence of the problem behavior.

FUNCTIONAL ANALYSIS OF PRECURSOR BEHAVIOR

This involves presenting the establishing operation and then immediately terminating the session when a precursor behavior (i.e., a behavior that reliably precedes the problem behavior) occurs. The time between the onset of the EO and first occurrence of the precursor behavior is recorded.

▶ TASK LIST ITEM F-9

The objective of this Task List item is to interpret functional assessment data.

Functional-assessment data include information obtained from (a) FA, (b) descriptive assessment, and (c) indirect assessment.

FUNCTIONAL ANALYSIS

Data gathered from an FA can be plotted on a graph for visual inspection.

Table 8.5 Interpretation of data by pattern of responding across conditions

If occurrences of the problem behavior are . . .	Then . . .
Elevated in the contingent attention condition	The data suggest it is maintained by social positive reinforcement
Elevated in the contingent escape condition	The data suggest it is maintained by negative reinforcement
Elevated in the alone condition	The data suggest it is maintained by automatic reinforcement
Low in the play/control condition	That is to be expected
Frequent across all conditions	Responding is undifferentiated and thus results are inconclusive; however, this can also occur when the behavior is maintained by automatic reinforcement
Variable across conditions	Responding is undifferentiated and thus results are inconclusive; however, this can also occur when the behavior is maintained by automatic reinforcement

DESCRIPTIVE ASSESSMENT

Data gathered from ABC recording can be examined for patterns (i.e., specific antecedent and consequence events that occur with the target behavior). Review of ABC recording data may reveal a correlation between specific events and the target behavior, which then allows for the formulation of a possible hypothesis. Behavior analysts may also graph the data obtained from ABC recording for visual inspection.

■ *Example*: The following graphs show the number of times that specific events (i.e., antecedents and consequences) occurred with a target behavior. They suggest the following hypothesis: The target behavior is motivated by task demands and maintained by their removal (i.e., escape, negative reinforcement).

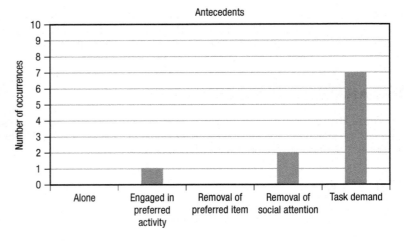

Figure 8.3 Graph of the number of times specific antecedent events occurred with a target behavior.

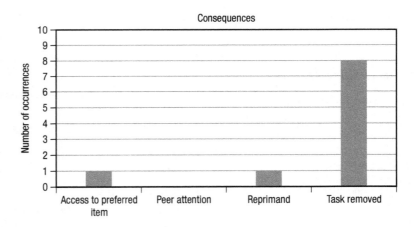

Figure 8.4 Graph of the number of times specific consequent events occurred with a target behavior.

When interpreting scatterplot recording data, behavior analysts conduct a visual examination of the scatterplot to identify specific times when the target behavior occurs. Recurring patterns in data may also be examined in relation to environmental events.

■ *Example* (interpretation of scatterplot data): A target behavior repeatedly occurs across weekdays around noon, a time that is correlated with unstructured time in the lunchroom.

INDIRECT ASSESSMENT

Indirect assessment information gathered from interviews, checklists, and rating scales should be examined for patterns of behavior and environmental events.

Behavior analysts examine the results and consider a possible hypothesis that states: (a) what antecedent(s) may serve to trigger the target behavior, (b) what the target behavior looks like (i.e., topography), and (c) what consequence(s) may serve to maintain the target behavior.

▶ CONCLUSION

In this chapter, we reviewed key content for Task List items related to behavior assessment. This included setting behavior-change goals and the use of various assessment methods to learn about clients' skill strengths and deficits, preferences, and functions of problem behavior. As a data-based practice, applied behavior analysis requires the gathering of relevant information via assessment prior to the development and implementation of an intervention plan. Although the goal is to treat behavior, doing so in a manner that will most efficiently and effectively yield desirable outcomes requires the use of assessment data. By conducting assessment prior to intervention, behavior analysts can use the information collected from the assessment process to identify the intervention strategies most likely to produce the desired change in behavior.

1. At the very minimum, behavior analysts should review relevant _____ data at the outset of a case.

   A. Educational, financial, and medical
   B. Educational, historical, and medical
   C. Personal, correspondence, and medical
   D. Legal, financial, and medical

2. To determine the social significance of a potential target behavior, all of the following questions are asked except:

   A. Is the behavior age appropriate?
   B. Is the behavior directly related to the problem or goal?
   C. Is the behavior likely to generalize across settings?
   D. Is the behavior required for learning a useful skill?

3. Indirect assessment methods include the use of all of the following except:

   A. Checklists
   B. Direct observation
   C. Interviews
   D. Rating scales

4. Which of the following is made up of a list of items (i.e., specific behaviors or statements/questions related to the behavior of interest) that respondents can rate on a numerical or ordinal scale?

   A. Checklist
   B. Interview
   C. Rating scale
   D. Standardized test

5. A _____ is an assessment that measures a client's performance against some predetermined standard.

   A. Competency-based measure
   B. Criterion-reference measure
   C. Rating scale
   D. Standardized test

6. Which of the following is a type of criterion-referenced measure that is used to measure performance on tasks the client performs as a part of planned instruction?

   A. Curriculum-based measure
   B. Direct observation
   C. Standardized test
   D. Trials to criterion

1. B) Educational, historical, and medical
At the very minimum, behavior analysts should review relevant educational, historical, and medical data at the outset of a case. The other answer options (educational, financial, and medical; personal, correspondence, and medical; legal, financial, and medical) contain types of data that do not require review by the behavior analyst at the outset of a case and function as distractors.

2. C) Is the behavior likely to generalize across settings?
Whether the behavior is likely to generalize across settings is not one of the 10 questions for determining the social significance of a potential target behavior. The other answer options (is the behavior age appropriate, is the behavior directly related to the problem or goal, is the behavior required for learning a useful skill) are among the 10 questions asked for determining social significance and serve as distractors.

3. B) Direct observation
Direct observation is a direct assessment method, not an indirect assessment method. The other answer options (checklists, interviews, rating scales) are forms of indirect assessment and serve as distractors.

4. C) Rating scale
Rating scales consist of a list of items (i.e., specific behaviors or statements/questions related to the behavior of interest) that respondents can rate on a numerical or ordinal scale. The other answer options (checklist, interview, standardized test) are other forms of assessment and function as distractors.

5. C) Rating scale
A rating scale is an assessment that measures a client's performance against some predetermined standard. The other answer options (competency-based measure, criterion-reference measure, standardized test) refer to other types of assessment and serve as distractors.

6. A) Curriculum-based measure
A curriculum-based measure is a type of criterion-referenced measure that is used to measure performance on tasks the client performs as a part of planned instruction. The other response options (direct observation, standardized test, trials to criterion) refer to other forms of assessment and function as distractors.

7. Which of the following types of assessment involves the identification of the evocative effects of motivation operations on verbal responses?

   A. Duplic assessment
   B. Intraverbal assessment
   C. Listener assessment
   D. Mand assessment

8. Which of the following preference assessment methods involves observing and recording the length of time that a client approaches, contacts, or engages with the stimuli when they are "free" to emit any responses in an environment that has not been prearranged?

   A. Contrived free-operant observation
   B. Multiple stimulus without replacement (MSWO) observation
   C. Naturalistic free-operant observation
   D. Single stimulus preference assessment

9. The _____ preference assessment method involves presenting an array of three or more stimuli at a time. The item selected by the client is removed from the array, the remaining unselected items are rearranged, and the subsequent trial consists of a reduced array.

   A. Free operant
   B. Paired stimulus
   C. Multiple stimulus with replacement (MSW)
   D. Multiple stimulus without replacement (MSWO)

10. Trial-based methods for assessing client preferences include all of the following except:

   A. Free operant observation
   B. Paired stimulus preference assessment
   C. Multiple stimulus with replacement (MSW) preference assessment
   D. Multiple stimulus without replacement (MSWO) preference assessment

11. Common functions of problem behavior include sources of _____.

   A. Positive and automatic reinforcement
   B. Positive and negative reinforcement
   C. Positive reinforcement
   D. Negative reinforcement

12. Which of the following refers to a source of reinforcement that terminates or postpones unwanted interactions with other people?

   A. Automatic negative reinforcement
   B. Automatic reinforcement
   C. Social negative reinforcement
   D. Social positive reinforcement

7. D) Mand assessment

Mand assessment involves the identification of the evocative effects of motivation operations on verbal responses. The other answer options (duplic assessment, intraverbal assessment, listener assessment) refer to other types of assessment and serve as distractors.

8. C) Naturalistic free-operant observation

Naturalistic free-operant observation is a preference assessment method that involves observing and recording the length of time that a client approaches, contacts, or engages with the stimuli when they are "free" to emit any responses in an environment that has not been prearranged. The other answer options (contrived free-operant observation, MSWO, single stimulus preference assessment) refer to other preference assessment methods and function as distractors.

9. D) Multiple stimulus without replacement (MSWO)

The MSWO preference assessment method involves presenting an array of three or more stimuli at a time, removing the item selected by the client from the array, and then rearranging the remaining items in the array. The other answer options (free operant, paired stimulus, MSW) are other preference assessment methods and function as distractors.

10. A) Free operant observation

Free operant observation is different from trial-based methods of assessing client preference. The other answer options (paired stimulus preference assessment, MSW preference assessment, MSWO preference assessment) are trial-based methods and function as distractors.

11. B) Positive and negative reinforcement

Common functions of problem behavior include sources of positive and negative reinforcement. The other answer options (positive and automatic reinforcement; positive reinforcement; negative reinforcement) function as distractors.

12. C) Social negative reinforcement

Social negative reinforcement refers to a source of reinforcement that terminates or postpones unwanted interactions with other people. The other answer options (automatic negative reinforcement, automatic reinforcement, social positive reinforcement) refer to other sources of reinforcement and serve as distractors.

13. A client engages in singing behavior that results in and is maintained by the auditory stimulation it produces. Which of the following sources of reinforcement best explains the function of the singing behavior?

    A. Automatic reinforcement
    B. Automatic negative reinforcement
    C. Social positive reinforcement
    D. Social negative reinforcement

14. A client engages in yelling behavior that results in and is maintained by the termination of parent demands to eat broccoli. Which of the following sources of reinforcement best explains the function of the yelling behavior?

    A. Automatic reinforcement
    B. Automatic negative reinforcement
    C. Social positive reinforcement
    D. Social negative reinforcement

15. When using _____, the occurrences of the target behavior and environmental events (i.e., specified antecedents and consequences) are recorded. Environmental events are recorded when they occur, even when the problem behavior has not.

    A. Continuous Antecedent-Behavior-Consequence (ABC) recording
    B. Narrative ABC recording
    C. Scatterplot recording
    D. Whole-interval recording

16. When using _____, the target problem behavior is recorded when it occurs on an observation form that divides time into shorter intervals. Different marks are made on the form to indicate the extent to which the behavior occurred for each time interval.

    A. Continuous Antecedent-Behavior-Consequence (ABC) recording
    B. Narrative ABC recording
    C. Scatterplot recording
    D. Whole-interval recording

17. This type of functional analysis (FA) involves presenting each condition only once or twice, with each session lasting 5 to 10 minutes in length.

    A. Brief functional analysis (BFA)
    B. Interview-informed synthesized contingency analysis (IISCA)
    C. Latency-based functional analysis (LBFA)
    D. Trial-based functional analysis (TBFA)

(See answers next page.) **161**

13. A) Automatic reinforcement

If a client engages in singing behavior that results in and is maintained by the auditory stimulation it produces, automatic reinforcement best explains the function of the singing behavior. The other answer options (automatic negative reinforcement, social positive reinforcement, social negative reinforcement) refer to other sources of reinforcement and serve as distractors.

14. D) Social negative reinforcement

In the scenario presented, the client's yelling behavior results in and is maintained by the removal of a demand. Social negative reinforcement, which refers to the termination or postponement of unwanted interactions or tasks, best explains the function of the client's yelling behavior. The other answer options (automatic reinforcement, automatic negative reinforcement, social positive reinforcement) refer to other sources of reinforcement and function as distractors.

15. A) Continuous Antecedent-Behavior-Consequence (ABC) recording

When using continuous ABC recording, the occurrences of the target behavior and environmental events (i.e., specified antecedents and consequences) are recorded. Environmental events are recorded when they occur, even when the problem behavior has not. The other answer options (narrative ABC recording, scatterplot recording, whole-interval recording) refer to other recording procedures and function as distractors.

16. C) Scatterplot recording

When using scatterplot recording, the target problem behavior is recorded when it occurs on an observation form that divides time into shorter intervals. Different marks are made on the form to indicate the extent to which the behavior occurred for each time interval. The other answer options (continuous ABC recording, narrative ABC recording, whole-interval recording) refer to other recording procedures and function as distractors.

17. A) Brief functional analysis (BFA)

The BFA is an FA method that involves presenting each condition only once or twice, with each session lasting 5 to 10 minutes in length. The other answer options (IISCA, LBFA, TBFA) refer to other FA methods and serve as distractors.

18. Which of the following functional analysis (FA) methods involves presenting the establishing operation, immediately terminating the session when the problem behavior occurs, and recording the time between the onset of the establishing operation (EO) and the first occurrence of the problem behavior?

   A. Brief functional analysis (BFA)
   B. FA of precursor behavior
   C. Latency-based functional analysis (LBFA)
   D. Trial-based functional analysis (TBFA)

19. Which of the following types of functional analysis (FA) involves presenting multiple contingencies during the test condition to emulate the natural context in which the problem behavior reportedly occurs?

   A. Brief functional analysis (BFA)
   B. Interview-informed synthesized contingency analysis (IISCA)
   C. Latency-based functional analysis (LBFA)
   D. Trial-based functional analysis (TBFA)

18. C) Latency-based functional analysis (LBFA)

LBFA involves presenting the establishing operation, immediately terminating the session when the problem behavior occurs, and recording the time between the onset of the EO and the first occurrence of the problem behavior. It is sometimes confused with FA of precursor behavior, which involves presenting the EO and then immediately terminating the session when a precursor behavior, rather than the target problem behavior, occurs. The other answer options (BFA, FA of precursor behavior, TBFA) refer to other FA methods that serve as distractors.

19. B) Interview-informed synthesized contingency analysis (IISCA)

The IISCA is a type of FA that involves presenting multiple contingencies during the test condition to emulate the natural context in which the problem behavior reportedly occurs. The other answer options (BFA, LBFA, TBFA) refer to other FA methods and serve as distractors.

BIBLIOGRAPHY

Behavior Analyst Certification Board. (2017). *BCBA task list* (5th ed.). http://ies.ed.gov/ncee/wwc/pdf/wwc_scd.pdf

Behavior Analyst Certification Board. (2020). *Ethics code for behavior analysts*. Author.

Cooper, J. O., Heron, T. E., & Heward, W. L. (2020). *Applied behavior analysis*. Pearson Education.

Hanley, G. P., Jin, C. S., Vanselow, N. R., & Hanratty, L. A. (2014). Producing meaningful improvements in problem behavior of children with autism via synthesized analyses and treatments. *Journal of Applied Behavior Analysis, 47*(1), 16–36. https://doi.org/10.1002/jaba.106

Houten, R. V. (1979). Social validation: The evolution of standards of competency for target behaviors. *Journal of Applied Behavior Analysis, 12*(4), 581–591. https://doi.org/10.1901/jaba.1979.12-581

Iwata, B. A., Dorsey, M. F., Slifer, K. J., Bauman, K. E., & Richman, G. S. (1982). Toward a functional analysis of self-injury. *Analysis and Intervention in Developmental Disabilities, 2*(1), 3–20. https://doi.org/10.1016/0270-4684(82)90003-9

Northup, J., Wacker, D., Sasso, G., Steege, M., Cigrand, K., Cook, J., & DeRaad, A. (1991). A brief functional analysis of aggressive and alternative behavior in an outclinic setting. *Journal of Applied Behavior Analysis, 24*(3), 509–522. https://doi.org/10.1901/jaba.1991.24-509

Sigafoos, J., & Meikle, B. (1996). Functional communication training for the treatment of multiply determined challenging behavior in two boys with autism. *Behavior Modification, 20*(1), 60–84. https://doi.org/10.1177/01454455960201003

Smith, R. G., & Churchill, R. M. (2002). Identification of environmental determinants of behavior disorders through functional analysis of precursor behaviors. *Journal of Applied Behavior Analysis, 35*(2), 125–136. https://doi.org/10.1901/jaba.2002.35-125

Thomason-Sassi, J. L., Iwata, B. A., Neidert, P. L., & Roscoe, E. M. (2011). Response latency as an index of response strength during functional analyses of problem behavior. *Journal of Applied Behavior Analysis, 44*(1), 51–67. https://doi.org/10.1901/jaba.2011.44-51

Behavior-Change Procedures

9

Behavior analysts practice applied behavior analysis (ABA), which is a science that uses the behavioral principles derived from decades of experimental analysis to solve problems of behavior that are of social significance. At the core of the responsibilities of a behavior analyst is their role in driving the implementation of behavior-change procedures to improve the lives of others. Thus, it is necessary for practicing behavior analysts to have a strong foundation in the use of behavior-change procedures. The purpose of this chapter will be to provide an essential review of Task List items G-1 through G-22, which covers various behavior-change procedures employed by behavior analysts.

▶ LEARNING OBJECTIVES

The following Task List items related to behavior-change procedures (G-1 through G-22) serve as the learning objectives of this chapter:

G-1 Use positive and negative reinforcement procedures to strengthen behavior.

G-2 Use interventions based on motivating operations and discriminative stimuli.

G-3 Establish and use conditioned reinforcers.

G-4 Use stimulus and response prompts and fading (e.g., errorless, most-to-least, least-to-most, prompt delay, stimulus fading).

G-5 Use modeling and imitation training.

G-6 Use instructions and rules.

G-7 Use shaping.

G-8 Use chaining.

G-9 Use discrete-trial, free-operant, and naturalistic teaching arrangements.

G-10 Teach simple and conditional discriminations.

G-11 Use Skinner's analysis to teach verbal behavior.

G-12 Use equivalence-based instruction.

G-13 Use the high-probability instructional sequence.

G-14 Use reinforcement procedures to weaken behavior (e.g., differential reinforcement of alternative behavior [DRA], functional communication training [FCT], differential reinforcement of other behavior [DRO], differential reinforcement of low rate behavior [DRL], noncontingent reinforcement [NCR]).

G-15 Use extinction.

G-16 Use positive and negative punishment (e.g., time-out, response cost, overcorrection).

G-17 Use token economies.

G-18 Use group contingencies.

G-19 Use contingency contracting.

G-20 Use self-management strategies.

G-21 Use procedures to promote stimulus and response generalization.

G-22 Use procedures to promote maintenance.

▶ TASK LIST ITEM G-1

The objective of this Task List item is to use positive and negative reinforcement procedures to strengthen behavior.

See Task List item B-4 for a review of positive and negative reinforcement, and Task List item B-5 for a review of schedules of reinforcement that produce different rates of responding.

To strengthen a behavior using positive reinforcement, establish a behavior-consequence contingency in which the consequence is a positive reinforcer.

- *Example*: A socially significant behavior (asking for help) is targeted, and a potential reinforcer (vocal praise) has been identified. To implement positive reinforcement to strengthen this behavior, the following contingency will be established:

Table 9.1 Example of a positive reinforcement contingency

R	C
Says "Help"	Praise

C, consequence; R, response.

To strengthen a behavior using negative reinforcement, establish a behavior-consequence contingency in which the consequence is a negative reinforcer.

- *Example*: A socially significant behavior (asking for help) is targeted, and a potential reinforcer (escape from the task) has been identified. To implement negative reinforcement to strengthen this behavior, the following contingency will be established:

Table 9.2 Example of a negative reinforcement contingency

R	C
Says "Help"	Escape from the task

C, consequence; R, response.

Recommendations for increasing the effectiveness of positive reinforcement procedures are as follows.

SMALL STEPS ENSURE SUCCESS

Set a readily obtainable beginning criterion for reinforcement. Use assessment to determine the client's current ability level. Ensure the client receives reinforcement on their first response. Then, gradually increase the criterion for reinforcement as the client's competence improves.

GIVE THEM WHAT THEY WANT

Use reinforcers of sufficient magnitude that are highly motivating. The quality of the reinforcer may need to be increased to maintain responding on more challenging tasks. Utilize a preference assessment to determine a client's highly preferred stimuli, which may serve as an effective reinforcer.

KEEP YOUR REINFORCERS FRESH

Overusing particular reinforcers can diminish their potency and effectiveness. Reinforcers should be varied to avoid satiation. Making particular reinforcers available less often or available in an unpredictable manner can also increase their effectiveness.

LET 'EM AT IT!

Utilize reinforcement contingencies that grant direct access to the reinforcer to optimize client performance. Research suggests direct reinforcement contingencies are more effective than indirect contingencies.

GIVE IT THE OLD ONE-TWO COMBO

One, reinforce; two, supplement it with a response prompt (e.g., verbal instructions, modeling, and physical guidance) to occasion a correct response. Ka-pow!

REINFORCE EARLY AND OFTEN

In the early stages of learning a new behavior, give the client reinforcement for each occurrence of the target behavior to strengthen the behavior. Then, as the target behavior becomes established, the rate of reinforcement can be thinned such that reinforcement of the target behavior is provided intermittently.

FOCUS ON THE BEHAVIOR YOU WANT TO SEE AND DESCRIBE IT TO THE CLIENT

Providing attention contingently and offering descriptive praise will enhance the effectiveness of positive reinforcement to strengthen behavior. Make it a consistent tool in your intervention toolbelt.

DELAY WILL PAY!

Gradually increase the response-to-reinforcement delay to help your client learn the highly adaptive skill of developing behaviors that yield delayed reinforcement. Delayed consequences promote generalization and maintenance of behavior changes.

FAKE IT 'TIL YOU MAKE IT!

Design interventions that enable your client to gradually move from needing contrived reinforcers (e.g., tokens) to naturally occurring reinforcers (e.g., praise, intrinsic sense of being successful). The goal is to use positive reinforcers that ultimately foster a client's ability to manipulate the environment; it is the ultimate natural reinforcer because it's ubiquitous!

Historically, behavior analysts have placed significantly more emphasis on using positive rather than negative reinforcement to strengthen behavior; however, negative reinforcement can be used to strengthen behavior. In general, the procedures noted earlier for the use of positive reinforcement also apply to effective use of negative reinforcement procedures. To effectively use negative reinforcement to strengthen behavior, ensure:

- The negative reinforcer immediately follows the target behavior.
- The negative reinforcer's magnitude is sufficiently large.
- The target behavior consistently results in escape/postponement of the establishing operation (EO).
- There is no reinforcement available for other competing, nontargeted responses.

▶ TASK LIST ITEM G-2

The objective of this Task List item is to use interventions based on motivating operations (MOs) and discriminative stimuli. For a review of MOs, please refer to Task List item B-12. For a review of discriminative stimuli (S^Ds), please refer to Task List item B-10. Readers may also wish to refer to Task List item G-11, which covers verbal behavior controlled by verbal and nonverbal S^Ds.

Antecedent interventions based on MOs and S^Ds are considered *function-based* interventions. Those based on MOs are *contingency-independent* (i.e., do not rely on differential consequences for the target behavior to create evocative or abative effects), whereas those based on stimulus control are *contingency-dependent* (i.e., rely on differential consequences for the target behavior to create evocative or abative effects).

NONCONTINGENT REINFORCEMENT

This is a contingency-independent antecedent intervention that involves delivering reinforcement on a fixed or variable interval schedule. The increased contact with reinforcement may function as an abolishing operation (AO) and decrease the motivation to engage in reinforcement-seeking behavior. There are three types of noncontingent reinforcement (NCR): (a) with positive reinforcement, (b) with negative reinforcement, and (c) with automatic reinforcement.

Noncontingent Reinforcement With Positive Reinforcement

This involves delivering a positive reinforcer on a fixed or variable interval schedule independent of the client's behavior.

Noncontingent Reinforcement With Negative Reinforcement

This involves delivering a negative reinforcer on a fixed or variable interval schedule independent of the client's behavior.

Noncontingent Reinforcement With Automatic Reinforcement

This involves delivering access to highly preferred objects or activities that the client can manipulate on a fixed or variable interval schedule independent of the client's behavior.

Other empirically supported antecedent interventions based on MOs include (a) the high-probability (high-p) request sequence procedure and (b) functional communication training (FCT).

High-Probability Request Sequence

This is a contingency-independent antecedent intervention that involves presenting a series of simple requests followed by a target request (see Task List item G-13 for more details). The procedure may function as an AO and decrease the motivation to escape from requests.

Functional Communication Training

This is a contingency-independent antecedent intervention that involves the use of *differential reinforcement of alternative behavior* (DRA; see Task List item G-13 for more details) to teach communicative responses that compete with problem behaviors evoked by a MO. Training involves conducting a functional assessment to identify reinforcers maintaining problem behavior, which are then used to teach the communicative behaviors (e.g., vocalizations, signs).

▶ TASK LIST ITEM G-3

The objective of this Task List item is to establish and use conditioned reinforcers.
See Task List item B-8 for a review of conditioned reinforcers.

ESTABLISHING CONDITIONED REINFORCERS

This involves pairing a neutral stimulus (NS) with one or more unconditioned reinforcers (S^Rs) or conditioned reinforcers (S^rs).

USING CONDITIONED REINFORCERS

For a review of using positive and negative reinforcers (which also apply to using conditioned reinforcers), please refer to Task List item G-1.

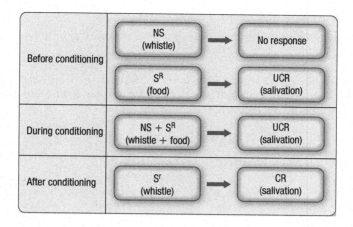

Figure 9.1 Pairing of a neutral stimulus (whistle) with an S^R (food).

CR, conditioned response; NS, neutral stimulus; S^r, conditioned reinforcer; S^R, unconditioned reinforcer; UCR, unconditioned response.

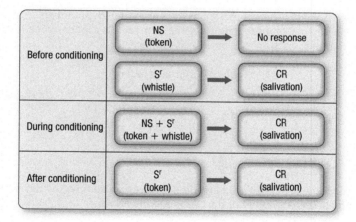

Figure 9.2 Pairing of a neutral stimulus (token) with a S^r (whistle).

CR, conditioned response; NS, neutral stimulus; S^r, conditioned reinforcer.

ADDITIONAL NOTE(S)

S^{r}s that are paired with many other reinforcers become generalized S^{r}s and may become less likely to lose value (i.e., satiate the client).

▶ TASK LIST ITEM G-4

The objective of this Task List item is to use stimulus and response prompts and fading (e.g., errorless, most-to-least, least-to-most, prompt delay, stimulus fading).

STIMULUS PROMPTS

These are antecedent stimuli that operate directly on the antecedent task stimuli (e.g., movement, positioning, redundancy) to assist the client in the emission of a target response. Stimulus prompts include: (a) stimulus shaping and (b) stimulus fading.

Stimulus Shaping

This involves gradually altering the form/topography of a stimulus until it eventually resembles the target criterion.

■ *Example* (Target: Recognizing the word "cat"): In the initial trial, the word "cat" is placed among shapes to allow for easy discrimination. Then, in subsequent trials, letters and words are introduced until the client recognizes all the letters in the word "cat."

Table 9.3 Stimulus shaping

Trial 1	Trial 2	Trial 3	Trial 4
*** cat *** cat *** *** *** *** cat	L cat a cat S b M s cat	Did cat sit cat are Tom how dog cat	sat cat tat cat act nat rat can cat

Stimulus Fading

This involves making some feature of a target stimulus (e.g., color, intensity, size) more salient, and then gradually fading it. Typically, only one feature is altered at a time.

■ *Example* (Target: Recognizing the number 1): In the initial trial, the number 1 is enlarged to allow for easy discrimination. Then, in subsequent trials, the number 1 is gradually made smaller until the client recognizes it among an array of same-sized numbers.

Table 9.4 Stimulus fading

Trial 1	Trial 2	Trial 3	Trial 4
1 2 5	6 8 1	1 9 7	3 1 4

ADDITIONAL NOTE(S)

Stimulus shaping and fading are considered errorless learning procedures as they involve manipulating tasks to reduce/eliminate the possibility of the client making errors.

RESPONSE PROMPTS

These are antecedent stimuli that operate directly on the response (e.g., modeling, physical guidance, verbal instructions) to assist the client in the emission of a target response. Response prompts include: (a) prompt delay, (b) least-to-most, (c) most-to-least, and (d) graduated guidance.

Prompt Delay

This is an errorless teaching strategy that involves fading the prompt using increments of time. Ordinarily, a single prompt type (e.g., verbal prompt) is used throughout instruction. There are two types of prompt delays: (a) constant time delay and (b) progressive time delay.

CONSTANT TIME DELAY

This begins with several rounds of zero-delay instruction (i.e., prompt is delivered at the same time as the S^D). Then, the teacher will add an increment of time (2–4 seconds) after the S^D to allow for the client to respond. This increment of time does not change in subsequent rounds. If the client does not emit the desired response within the set amount of time, the prompt is delivered.

PROGRESSIVE TIME DELAY

This begins with several rounds of zero-delay instruction (i.e., prompt is delivered at the same time as the S^D). Then, the teacher will add an increment of time (1–2 seconds) after the S^D to allow for the client to respond. This increment of time progressively increases by 1 or 2 seconds at a time in subsequent rounds. If the client does not emit the desired response within the set amount of time, the prompt is delivered.

ADDITIONAL NOTE(S)

Simultaneous prompting is another prompting strategy that simply involves the use of zero-delay rounds.

Least-to-Most

This is a prompt system that uses a prompt hierarchy that starts with the least intrusive prompt and systematically graduates to the most intrusive prompt. Using this prompt system begins with the selection of prompts and establishing a hierarchy of least to most intrusive (e.g., gestural, then model, then physical). Once chosen, the teacher determines an increment of time (3–5 seconds) that will occur after the S^D and between prompts to allow for the client to respond with the least intrusive and least amount of prompting possible. If the client does not respond independently within the set amount of time after the S^D is presented, the first prompt in the predetermined prompt hierarchy is used. If the client does not respond within the set amount of time after the first prompt, then the second prompt in the hierarchy is used. This process continues until the client completes the desired response.

Most-to-Least

This is a prompt system that uses a prompt hierarchy that starts with the most intrusive prompt and systematically graduates to the least intrusive prompt as the client responds more independently. The S^D and prompt occur at the same time on each step. A performance criterion must be established for each prompt level; once reached, move to the next (less intrusive) prompt level.

Graduated Guidance

This involves using highly intrusive prompts until the client begins to demonstrate the target response independently. Prompting is gradually faded as the responding becomes more independent. Prompting can also increase if the client does not participate.

ADDITIONAL NOTE(S)

General use guidelines for prompts include: (a) use them judiciously (i.e., fade them quickly but not too quickly), (b) use least-to-most for assessing skills, (c) use most-to-least for teaching new skills, (d) consider returning to a previous prompt level if errors occur, (e) shift from reinforcing prompted to independent responses as soon as possible, and (f) do not assume what works for teaching one skill will also work for another.

▶ TASK LIST ITEM G-5

The objective of this Task List item is to use modeling and imitation training.

The four behavior-environment relations that define modeling and imitation training include: (a) a model stimulus is presented to evoke the imitative response, (b) the imitative response follows immediately (within 3–5 seconds), (c) the model and response look/sound alike, and (d) the model serves as the S^D for the imitative response.

Models can be planned or unplanned.

PLANNED MODELS

These are prearranged antecedent stimuli that show the client exactly what to do.

UNPLANNED MODELS

These are antecedent stimuli that occur in everyday social interactions.

PRETRAINING STEPS

Prior to conducting imitation training, behavior analysts should (a) assess and teach any prerequisite skills, (b) select models, (c) pretest, and (d) sequence models for training.

Assess and Teach Any Prerequisite Skills

Imitation requires that the client attends to the model stimulus. Thus, it is important to evaluate and teach, if necessary, basic attending skills (i.e., staying seated, looking at the teacher/objects).

Select Models

Initial imitation training may begin with approximately 25 models. Begin with one model at a time and advance from simple models (e.g., raising hands, touching nose) to more complex models (i.e., sequences of responses or models involving the manipulation of objects).

Pretest

This is conducted to determine if the client already imitates some models. The procedure for pretesting is as follows: (a) have the client get in a "ready position" (e.g., seated with hands in theirhis/her lap), (b) say the client's name and "do this," (c) present a model, (d) praise imitative responses, and (e) record the response as correct, incorrect, or approximation to the model.

Sequence Models for Training

This involves using the pretest results to arrange the sequence of models for training. Models should be presented in order of easiest to most difficult. Begin with those that the client correctly imitated, followed by those that were approximated, and ending with those that were incorrectly imitated.

CONDUCTING IMITATION TRAINING

This is a four-step process that includes (a) preassessment, (b) training, (c) postassessment, and (d) probes for imitative behavior.

Preassessment

Assess the client's current performance before the training session by presenting the first three models selected for training and presenting them three times each in random order. Those models that the client imitates correctly three times are removed from training.

Training

This involves repeating the presentation of the model that the client most closely approximates of the three models used in the preassessment until the client correctly imitates the model in five consecutive trials (which may require prompting). If prompts are used, gradually fade them as quickly as possible.

Postassessment

Assess the client's ability to perform previously learned imitative responses by presenting five learned models and five in-training models, three times each. Learned models that are correctly imitated in 14 out of 15 trials on three consecutive postassessments should be removed from training.

Probes for Imitative Behavior

Assess for generalized imitation by presenting about five untrained models. This can be conducted at the end of the training session or intermixed with trials.

ADDITIONAL NOTE(S)

When conducting imitation training, keep training sessions short (10–15 minutes), differentially reinforce prompted and independent imitative responses, incorporate tangible reinforcers if needed, and fade verbal and physical prompts as quickly as possible.

▶ TASK LIST ITEM G-6

The objective of this Task List item is to use instructions and rules.

For a review of rules, please refer to Task List item B-13.

Instructions are often viewed as instances of rules, acting as verbal discriminative stimuli that specify responses and contingencies in rule statements. Or, instructions may function as prompts or controlling verbal stimuli. For this item, we treat instructions simply as verbal stimuli specifying responses, and rules as verbal stimuli specifying both responses and contingencies.

Using an instruction involves: (a) getting the client's attention first, and then (b) delivering a verbal stimulus that specifies what the client is to do. Avoid repeating instructions and using unnecessarily long instructional statements. Target one response at a time.

- *Example*: "Client's name" (to get their attention). "Say 'toy.'"

Using a rule involves the previous steps for delivering an instruction and extending it to include a contingency. This can be delivered in the form of an "if/then" statement.

- *Example*: "Client's name" (to get their attention). "If you say 'toy,' then I will give it to you."

Additional recommendations for using instructions and rules include:

- In the event that a client fails to respond to an instruction or rule, use the amount/level of prompting necessary to assist the client in completing the task.
- It is important for clients to receive ample opportunities for practice and reinforcement for following instructions and rules.
- Keep in mind that some clients may require more time to respond than others.
- For some clients, it can be helpful to explain the reasons undergirding particular rules so that the rules do not appear arbitrary.
- Explain the consequences associated with following and not following rules and the reasons behind those consequences.

A contingency contract is a document that clearly identifies the behavior that, when exhibited, grants the client access to or delivery of a specified reward (i.e., a rule). See Task List item G-19 for a review of contingency contracts.

Clients may also be taught how to use self-instruction, which involves using self-statements as controlling responses that guide them through tasks. The following steps are used to teach self-instruction:

- Behavior analyst models the task while talking aloud to themself.
- Client performs the task while the behavior analyst provides verbal instructions and praise.
- Client performs the task while talking aloud to themself, and the behavior analyst quietly gives instructions.
- Client performs the task while quietly speaking the instructions to themself and the behavior analyst moves their lips but makes no sound.
- Client performs the task while mouthing instructions without sound.
- Client performs the task while coaching his/her performance with covert instructions.

▶ TASK LIST ITEM G-7

The objective of this Task List item is to use shaping.

Shaping is the provision of differential reinforcement (DR) for a progression of responses that are more similar to the target response. In other words, shaping is the reinforcement of successive approximations of a terminal behavior.

SHAPING ACROSS RESPONSE TOPOGRAPHIES

Once a target response has been identified, DR is used to (a) reinforce responses that are successively closer to the terminal behavior and (b) not reinforce those responses that are not closer to the terminal behavior. This leads to *response differentiation*.

▪ *Example* (shaping of getting food from the refrigerator behavior):

Table 9.5 What occurred before implementation

EO	S^D	R	S^{R+}
Deprived of food	Refrigerator	Walk to refrigerator	Food given

EO, establishing operation; R, response; S^D, discriminative stimuli; S^{R+}, unconditioned positive reinforcer.

Table 9.6 Step 1

EO	S^D	R	S^{R+}
Deprived of food	Refrigerator	Point to refrigerator	Food given

EO, establishing operation; R, response; S^D, discriminative stimuli; S^{R+}, unconditioned positive reinforcer.

Simply walking to the refrigerator and looking at it is no longer reinforced.

Q1

Table 9.7 Step 2

EO	S^D	R	S^{R+}
Deprived of food	Refrigerator	Touch refrigerator	Food given

EO, establishing operation; R, response; S^D, discriminative stimuli; S^{R+}, unconditioned positive reinforcer.

Simply pointing to the refrigerator is no longer reinforced.

Table 9.8 Step 3

EO	S^D	R	S^{R+}
Deprived of food	Refrigerator	Open refrigerator door	Food given

EO, establishing operation; R, response; S^D, discriminative stimuli; S^{R+}, unconditioned positive reinforcer.

Simply touching the refrigerator is no longer reinforced.

This process continues until the terminal behavior (getting food from the refrigerator) is reached.

SHAPING WITHIN RESPONSE TOPOGRAPHIES

When shaping within response topographies, the topography of behavior remains constant but some other measurable dimension is changed. These other shape-able dimensions include (a) frequency, (b) latency, (c) duration, and (d) magnitude.

▶ TASK LIST ITEM G-8

The objective of this Task List item is to use chaining.

A behavior chain is a sequence of behaviors that results in a terminal outcome. Chaining refers to several methods used to link specific sequences of stimuli and behaviors. Before behaviors can be linked in a chain, behavior analysts must develop a task analysis (TA) that breaks down a complex task into a series of smaller, teachable steps.

ADDITIONAL NOTE(S)

Develop and validate a TA using one of the following methods: (a) observe someone competently performing the task, (b) perform the task yourself, (c) ask for input from an expert, or (d) use a systematic trial-and-error procedure. When determining the number of steps, consider the complexity of each step on the basis of what is manageable for the client.

Table 9.9 Example of a task analysis for morning routine in the classroom

Step	R
1	Take off backpack
2	Open backpack
3	Take out homework
4	Close backpack
5	Place backpack in designated space
6	Give homework to the teacher
7	Sit in designated seat

R, response.

Chaining methods include: (a) forward chaining, (b) total-task chaining, (c) backward chaining, and (d) backward chaining with leap aheads.

FORWARD CHAINING

Teach the client the behaviors identified in the TA in their naturally occurring sequence. Prompt and then fade your prompting to teach first behavior in the chain. When the first behavior is performed independently, use prompting and prompt fading to teach the second behavior in the chain. Continue this process in a forward fashion until the client is able to independently perform the entire chain of behaviors identified in the TA.

■ *Example* (TA for sitting on toilet using forward chaining):

Table 9.10 Example of a task analysis for sitting on toilet using forward chaining

Step	R
1	Grab waist of pants and pull down
2	Grab waist of underwear and pull down
3	Sit down on toilet seat

R, response.

The teaching procedure begins with a focus on step 1. Use prompting and prompt fading to teach step 1. After step 1 is completed, assist the client in completing the remaining steps.

Table 9.11 Working on step 1

Step	R	Status
1	Grab waist of pants and pull down	Working on it (use prompting plus prompt fading); reinforcement provided for this step
2	Grab waist of underwear and pull down	Not mastered; assist client
3	Sit down on toilet seat	Not mastered; assist client

R, response.

After step 1 is mastered (i.e., completed by the client independently), shift focus to step 2.

Table 9.12 Working on step 2

Step	R	Status
1	Grab waist of pants and pull down	Mastered
2	Grab waist of underwear and pull down	Working on it (use prompting plus prompt fading); reinforcement provided for this step
3	Sit down on toilet seat	Not mastered; assist client

R, response.

After both steps 1 and 2 are mastered, shift focus to step 3.

Table 9.13 Working on step 3

Step	R	Status
1	Grab waist of pants and pull down	Mastered
2	Grab waist of underwear and pull down	Mastered
3	Sit down on toilet seat	Working on it (use prompting plus prompt fading); reinforcement provided for this step

R, response.

TOTAL-TASK CHAINING

This is a variation of forward chaining that calls for the provision of training on each behavior in the TA during every training session. Provide the client with assistance using response prompts on any step the client struggles to perform independently. Continue this process until the client competently performs all steps of the TA.

BACKWARD CHAINING

Teach the client the behaviors identified in the TA beginning with the last behavior in the chain. In other words, teach the sequence of behaviors in reverse order. To do so, perform all the behaviors for or with the client *except for the last behavior in the chain*. Prompt and then fade your prompting to teach the final behavior. When the last behavior is performed independently, use prompting and prompt fading to teach the second to last behavior in the chain. Continue this process in a backward fashion until the client is able to independently perform the entire chain of behaviors identified in the TA.

Table 9.14 Example of a task analysis for blowing nose

Step	R
1	Remove one tissue from box
2	Raise tissue to nose
3	Blow into tissue

R, response.

The teaching procedure begins with a focus on step 3. Use prompting and prompt fading to teach step 3. After step 3 is completed, assist the client in completing the remaining steps.

Table 9.15 Working on step 3

Step	R	Status
1	Remove one tissue from box	Not mastered; assist client
2	Raise tissue to nose	Not mastered; assist client
3	Blow into tissue	Working on it (use prompting plus prompt fading); reinforcement provided for this step

R, response.

After step 3 is mastered (i.e., completed by the client independently), shift focus to step 2.

Table 9.16 Working on step 2

Step	R	Status
1	Remove one tissue from box	Not mastered; assist client
2	Raise tissue to nose	Working on it (use prompting plus prompt fading); reinforcement provided for this step
3	Blow into tissue	Mastered

R, response.

After both steps 3 and 2 are mastered, shift focus to step 1.

Table 9.17 Working on step 1

Step	R	Status
1	Remove one tissue from box	Working on it (use prompting plus prompt fading); reinforcement provided for this step
2	Raise tissue to nose	Mastered
3	Blow into tissue	Mastered

R, response.

BACKWARD CHAINING WITH LEAP AHEADS

Follow the same procedures as backward chaining without the requirement that every behavior in the TA is trained. Use of this approach enables the behavior analyst to probe or assess untrained behaviors in the sequence, which can accelerate training of the behavior chain. Backward chaining with leap aheads is helpful when the client already has the prerequisite steps for a final behavior in their behavior chain. For instance, a client may need to learn how to strap the velcro on their shoes (final step). However, the client already knows how to sit down (prior step), put their foot in the shoe (prior step), and take hold of the velcro with their hand (prior step), so these steps do not require teaching.

BEHAVIOR CHAINS WITH A LIMITED HOLD

This involves requiring the client to perform the entire behavior chain or steps within the chain in a given period of time to receive reinforcement.

ADDITIONAL NOTE(S)

The chaining methods described have each been demonstrated to be effective for a wide range of behaviors. To date, there is no clear indication from the research that any one method is more effective than another.

▶ TASK LIST ITEM G-9

The objective of this Task List item is to use discrete-trial, free-operant (FO), and naturalistic teaching arrangements.

DISCRETE-TRIAL TEACHING

This is an instructional procedure that breaks down behavior into discrete steps (i.e., learning trials) with a clear beginning, middle, and end. Trials are repeated with the client receiving reinforcement for correct responding. The components of discrete-trial teaching (DTT) include the (a) antecedent (i.e., discriminative stimulus), (b) behavior, and (c) consequence.

Antecedent (S^D)

This is a brief, clear instruction that alerts the client to the task and fosters the client's ability to connect a specific direction with an appropriate response.

Behavior

This is the client's response to the S^D. The client may respond correctly or incorrectly. Establish clear criteria for a correct response beforehand, and provide prompting as needed. Prompts used should be faded over time.

Consequence

Deliver reinforcement immediately for a correct response. Provide corrective feedback for an incorrect response in a neutral manner.

ADDITIONAL NOTE(S)

There is a brief pause between trials referred to as the *intertrial interval* that lets the client know that the trial has ended, and another is beginning.

Table 9.18 Example of correct responding in a discrete trial

S^D	R	C
Teacher points to a chair as a signal to sit	Client sits	Teacher delivers reinforcer

C, consequence; R, response; S^D, discriminative stimuli.

Table 9.19 Example of incorrect responding in a discrete trial

S^D	R	C
Teacher points to a chair as a signal to sit	Client remains standing	Teacher delivers corrective feedback (i.e., a prompt)

C, consequence; R, response; S^D, discriminative stimuli.

FREE-OPERANT ARRANGEMENT

This is an instructional arrangement that allows for the client to freely emit one or more responses. An S^D is not required but is sometimes present. Reinforcement is not specifically programmed but the client may engage in responses that produce reinforcement continuously or intermittently. Using an FO arrangement involves allowing the client to interact with the environment with naturally occurring MOs. Access to objects may be contingent upon performance of a specific behavior (e.g., saying the name of the object). Interactions with the client around something of interest to them can also serve as teaching moments.

NATURALISTIC TEACHING APPROACHES

There have been a variety of naturalistic teaching approaches (NTAs) developed (e.g., pivotal response training, incidental teaching [IT], natural language paradigm) that use procedures recommended for the programming of generalization to promote the development of clients' verbal behaviors. These procedures tend to be described as loosely structured with no planned order of instruction. Activities are chosen and paced by the client, and loose shaping contingencies are used to reinforce desirable behaviors.

Incidental Teaching

This is one of the many naturalistic teaching methods available. It involves (a) ongoing assessment of the client's interests, (b) restricting access to high interest items/activities, and (c) constructing lessons in a natural context. When a client displays interest (i.e., makes a request) and the teacher determines to use the occasion to teach a verbal behavior, the teacher must (a) make an immediate decision concerning the terminal behavior that the client is to emit; (b) present a cue of attention, followed by a verbal cue if necessary; and then (c) assist the client (with prompts as necessary).

DECIDE ON THE TERMINAL BEHAVIOR

This involves quickly determining the behavior that the client is to emit to terminate the teaching occasion.

PRESENT A CUE OF ATTENTION

This involves physically approaching the client, making eye contact, and presenting a questioning/curious facial expression. If the client fails to respond, present a verbal cue (e.g., "What do you want?").

ASSIST THE CLIENT

When the terminal behavior is emitted, assistance is then provided and the teaching occasion is terminated. However, the client may require prompting (i.e., a request for full, partial, or minimal imitation). If the first attempt to prompt the client fails, they can be prompted a second time. If both the first and second attempts to prompt the client fail, provide assistance anyway.

- *Example* (IT occasion with a cue of attention plus verbal cue and one prompt to fully imitate the terminal behavior):
  Teacher sees a client reaching for a jar of cookies on a high shelf.
  Teacher decides on the terminal behavior of a vocalization of "cookie, please."
  Teacher walks toward the client, makes eye contact, and presents a curious facial expression (i.e., neutral face with eyes wide open).
  Client breaks eye contact and looks toward the jar of cookies.
  Teacher: "What do you want?"
  Client looks toward the teacher and remains silent.
  Teacher: "Say, 'cookie, please.'"
  Client: "Cookie, please."
  Teacher says, "Nice job!" and gets cookie jar for client.

ADDITIONAL NOTE(S)

The IT procedure described is only one of several versions developed. A review of all NTAs falls outside the intended scope of this book, but readers who wish to learn more about NTAs are encouraged to explore the available literature on NTAs.

▶ TASK LIST ITEM G-10

The objective of this Task List item is to teach simple and conditional discriminations.

Nearly all skills require discrimination among stimuli or responding differentially to environmental stimuli (e.g., colors, locations, objects, people, sounds). See Task List item F-4 for a review of intraverbal interventions for simple and conditional verbal discriminations.

Simple discriminations are established by reinforcing certain responses only in the presence of certain antecedents. Thus, teaching a discriminative response involves (a) presentation of a defined antecedent stimulus and (b) delivery of reinforcement if the response is emitted.

- *Example* (naming objects): In the presence of a cookie, the vocal response "cookie" is reinforced and "apple" is not.
- *Example* (following instructions): In the presence of the vocal instruction "sit down," sitting down is reinforced and standing up is not.

Conditional discriminations are established by reinforcing certain responses in the presence of certain antecedents only if they are preceded by certain other stimuli. Thus, teaching a discriminative response involves (a) presentation of a defined antecedent stimulus in the presence of another stimulus, and (b) delivery of reinforcement if the response is emitted.

- *Example* (naming objects): In the presence of a cookie, the vocal response "cookie" is reinforced and "apple" is not, AND in the presence of an apple, the vocal response "apple" is reinforced and "cookie" is not.
- *Example* (following instructions): In the presence of the vocal instruction "sit down," sitting down is reinforced and standing up is not; AND in the presence of the vocal instruction "stand up," standing up is reinforced and sitting down is not.

Conditional discriminations can be taught using matching-to-sample (MTS) procedures. See Task List item G-12 for a review of MTS.

▶ TASK LIST ITEM G-11

The objective of this Task List item is to use Skinner's analysis to teach verbal behavior.

Skinner's analysis offers a framework for language assessment and intervention. Assessment focuses on the identification of a learner's verbal repertoire (e.g., strength of verbal operants, listener skills). Intervention (i.e., teaching of verbal behavior) follows assessment and involves the use of behavior analytic procedures to target impairments. See Task List item B-14 for a review of verbal operants.

DUPLIC AND CODIC ASSESSMENT

This involves identifying the strength of verbal and nonverbal responses under the control of verbal stimuli.

DUPLIC INTERVENTION

This involves teaching motor imitation (i.e., mimetics) and verbal imitation (i.e., echoics).

Teaching Motor Imitation

This can be taught with (a) standard behavior analytic procedures, (b) placement of the imitative behavior within a *mand frame* (i.e., combine motor S^D with an MO and specific reinforcer) during training.

- *Example* (using the mand frame): When there is an MO for cookies, conduct an imitative trial to sign for "cookie" (with physical prompts as necessary), and use a cookie for reinforcement.

Teaching Verbal Imitation

This can be taught with (a) standard behavior analytic procedures, (b) placement of the imitative behavior within a mand frame (i.e., combine verbal S^D with an MO and specific reinforcer), and (c) pairing words with existing reinforcers during training.

- *Example* (using pairing): The teacher says, "cookie" just prior to delivering a cookie.

MAND ASSESSMENT

This involves identifying the strength of MOs' control of verbal responses.

MAND INTERVENTION

For a nonverbal client, it is important to establish an effective response form (i.e., speech, sign language, or picture-selection system). Teaching a client to mand involves using MOs. The teacher can either (a) capture the MO as it occurs naturally, or (b) create the MO by making an environmental change that increases the value of a consequence.

- *Example* (creating the MO): The mand for "open" is targeted. When there is an MO for cookies, the teacher hands the client a container with a cookie inside (that can only be opened with the teacher's assistance).

TACT ASSESSMENT

This involves identifying the strength of nonverbal stimuli's control of verbal responses.

TACT INTERVENTION

This involves prompting the tact response, fading prompts, and reinforcing high quality responses. Specific types of prompts (e.g., "What is this?") can be used to increase the likelihood of tacts. Echoic prompts may also be used to train tacts.

INTRAVERBAL ASSESSMENT

This involves assessing (a) simple verbal discriminations, (b) compound verbal discriminations, (c) verbal conditional discriminations, and (d) delayed intraverbal behavior.

Simple Verbal Discriminations
This can be assessed using simple fill-in-the-blank phrases or Wh questions.

- *Example* (fill-in-the-blank): "1, 2 . . ." is the S^D and "3" is the intraverbal.

- *Example* (WH question): "What is your name?"

Compound Verbal Discriminations
This can be assessed using questions that involve two or more distinct elements.

- *Example*: "What is a green animal?" The question includes two S^Ds: "green" and "animal."

Verbal Conditional Discriminations
This can be assessed using questions that contain contrasting verbal stimuli.

- *Example*: "What can you do with your hands?" with "What can you do with your feet?"

Delayed Intraverbal Behavior
This can be assessed using instructions that require the demonstration of an intraverbal at a later point in time.

- *Example*: "When your mom asks about your day, tell her you played tic-tac-toe."

INTRAVERBAL INTERVENTION

This can involve prompting, fading, and reinforcing specific responses to teach (a) simple verbal discriminations, (b) compound verbal discriminations, (c) verbal conditional discriminations, and (d) delayed intraverbal behavior.

Simple Verbal Discriminations

Training involves establishing verbal responses under simple verbal stimuli (e.g., fill-in-the-blank phrase or WH question).

Compound Verbal Discriminations

Training involves establishing verbal responses under compound verbal stimuli.

Verbal Conditional Discriminations

Training involves establishing conditional discriminations after prerequisite listener and speaker skills have been demonstrated.

Delayed Intraverbal Behavior

Training involves establishing delayed verbal responses to S^Ds that can occur in the future.

LISTENER ASSESSMENT

This involves assessing (a) simple verbal discriminations, (b) auditory conditional discriminations, (c) compound verbal discriminations, (d) verbal conditional discriminations, and (e) delayed listener behavior.

Simple Verbal Discriminations

This involves determining whether verbal stimuli evoke the corresponding nonverbal response.

■ *Example*: A client is told to "sit down." This type of discrimination is made if the client then sits down.

Auditory Conditional Discriminations

This involves presenting a verbal S^D and a nonverbal S^D in an array of stimuli. The client is to scan the array and make a selection response.

■ *Example*: An array of picture cards is placed on a table in front of the client. A nonverbal S^D (picture of a cat) is among the array. A verbal S^D ("Point to the cat") is presented. This type of discrimination is made if the client then points to the picture of a cat.

Compound Verbal Discriminations

This involves presenting combinations of verbal stimuli (after they have been individually tested) to determine whether compounding stimuli will evoke more specific selection responses. Example: The target is for the client to learn to discriminate between pictures of red and green animals and red and green shapes in an array. First, each element is tested individually (e.g., "Which ones are green?" "Which ones are shapes?"). Then, S^Ds with two combined elements are presented (e.g., "Which one is a green animal?"). This type of discrimination is made if the client then points to the picture of a green animal.

Verbal Conditional Discriminations

Assessing verbal conditional discriminations can be rather difficult, but it basically involves sampling increasingly complex combinations of parts of speech.

Delayed Listener Behavior

This can be assessed using verbal instructions that involve a future nonverbal event.

■ *Example*: "When you hear the alarm, go turn off the stove." A verbal function-altering effect has changed the evocative effect of the nonverbal stimulus (alarm) if the client then turns off the stove when they hear the alarm.

LISTENER INTERVENTION

This can involve prompting, fading, and reinforcing specific responses to teach (a) simple verbal discriminations, (b) auditory conditional discriminations, (c) compound verbal discriminations, (d) verbal conditional discriminations, and (e) delayed listener behavior.

Simple Verbal Discriminations

Training involves establishing nonverbal behaviors under the control of verbal stimuli.

Auditory Conditional Discriminations

Training involves asking the client to identify objects, features, and so on by making a selection response. Training begins with simple arrays and items, but systematically progresses to more complex arrays and stimuli.

Compound Verbal Discriminations

Training involves presenting combinations of words that are in the client's listener repertoire. Imitative prompts can be used and faded to establish new compound verbal S^{D}s. As training progresses, new nouns and verbs are systematically added to instruction.

Verbal Conditional Discriminations

The listener responding by function, feature, and class (LRFFC) procedure is used to teach verbal conditional discriminations. Training involves asking the client to identify nonverbal stimuli based on the object's function (e.g., what you can do with it), feature (e.g., some attribute), or class (e.g., category).

Delayed Listener Behavior

Training involves presenting verbal instructions that involve a future nonverbal event. The time between the verbal instructions and the future nonverbal event is gradually increased.

▶ TASK LIST ITEM G-12

The objective of this Task List item is to use equivalence-based instruction (EBI). For a review of equivalence relations, please refer to Task List item B-15.

EQUIVALENCE-BASED INSTRUCTION

The goal of EBI is formation of equivalence classes (i.e., interchangeability between stimuli), which can be taught using a MTS procedure with a minimum of two interrelated conditional discriminations.

MATCHING-TO-SAMPLE

This is a discrete-trial procedure that starts with the client making a response (referred to as the *observing response*) to the sample stimulus (which is the *conditional sample*). The sample stimulus may or may not be removed before presenting the comparison stimuli (which are the *discriminative events*), one of which matches with the conditional sample. When the client selects the comparison stimulus that matches with the sample stimulus, reinforcement is delivered.

■ *Example* (teach A = B): A trial begins with a client making an observing response to the sample stimulus (i.e., listens to the teacher say, "bird"). Then, the following comparison stimuli are presented:

Figure 9.3 Comparison stimuli.

If the client correctly matches the comparison stimulus that matches the sample stimulus (i.e., selects the second stimulus in the array of three comparison stimuli), reinforcement is provided.

Table 9.20 Three-phase matching-to-sample procedure for equivalence-based instruction

Phase 1	Phase 2	Phase 3
Teach A = B	Teach B = C	Test for A = C

▶ TASK LIST ITEM G-13

The objective of this Task List item is to use the high-probability instructional sequence.

The high-p instructional sequence is a contingency-independent antecedent intervention that involves (a) presenting a series of easy-to-follow requests for which the client has a history of compliance (i.e., high-p requests), and (b) presenting the target request (i.e., low-p request) after the client has complied with the high-p requests. Typically, two to five high-p requests precede the presentation of a low-p request.

To effectively implement this procedure, the following guidelines should be followed: (a) present high-p requests that the client is currently able to comply with, (b) present requests in rapid succession, (c) acknowledge compliance with each request, and (d) use high-quality reinforcers.

■ *Example*: A client throws tantrums when they are asked to wash their hands. The teacher uses a high-p to increase the likelihood of compliance with the request without the tantrum.
Teacher: "Give me five!" (high-p request)
Client complies.
Teacher: "Awesome!" (acknowledgment of compliance) "Now touch your nose." (high-p request)
Client complies.
Teacher: "That's great!" (acknowledgment of compliance) "Now make a silly face!" (high-p request)
Client complies.
Teacher: "Okay, nice job!" (acknowledgment of compliance) "Now please go wash your hands." (low-p request)
Client complies.
Teacher delivers high-quality reinforcer for compliance.

ADDITIONAL NOTE(S)

Also consider using variant sequences. In other words, do not always present high-p requests in the same sequence. There is some evidence that this is more effective than using invariant sequences. The ratio of high-p to low-p instructions should be gradually faded to 1:1.

▶ TASK LIST ITEM G-14

The objective of this Task List item is to use reinforcement procedures to weaken behavior (e.g., DRA, FCT, DRO, DRL, NCR).

Reinforcement procedures used for weakening behavior include a variety of DR procedures and NCR.

DIFFERENTIAL REINFORCEMENT OF ALTERNATIVE BEHAVIOR

This procedure involves reinforcing a targeted alternative behavior for the problem behavior and withholding reinforcement for the problem behavior.

- *Example*: A client engages in shouting out behavior after the teacher poses a question to the class, so the teacher (a) delivers reinforcement when the client raises their hand to answer a question, and (b) withholds reinforcement when the client engages in shouting out behavior.

ADDITIONAL NOTE(S)

If either of these procedures uses a negative reinforcer, it is designated as "NR" rather than simply "R" (i.e., differential negative reinforcement of incompatible behavior [DNRI]) and differential negative reinforcement of alternative behavior [DNRA]).

GUIDELINES FOR IMPLEMENTING DIFFERENTIAL REINFORCEMENT OF ALTERNATIVE BEHAVIOR

- Select an alternative behavior that (a) the client can perform, (b) is less effortful than the problem behavior, (c) happens enough to be reinforced, and (d) is likely to be reinforced in the natural environment.
- Identify and then consistently use effective reinforcers.
- Immediately and consistently deliver reinforcement for the alternative behavior until it is well established. Then, gradually thin the schedule of reinforcement.
- Use it with other procedures.

DIFFERENTIAL REINFORCEMENT OF OTHER BEHAVIOR

This procedure involves providing reinforcement when the problem behavior is absent for a predetermined amount of time and withholding reinforcement for the problem behavior. The time interval is reset upon the occurrence of the problem behavior. DRO procedures can use a (a) fixed or (b) variable interval schedule.

- *Example*: A client engages in self-injurious behavior when completing independent seatwork assignments, so the teacher (a) delivers reinforcement when the client does not engage in self-injurious behavior for X amount of time, and (b) withholds reinforcement when the client engages in self-injurious behavior within X amount of time and resets the time interval.

Momentary Differential Reinforcement of Other Behavior

Momentary schedules that are (a) fixed or (b) variable can also be used, which involve delivering reinforcement when the problem behavior is absent at the exact time that the interval ends.

GUIDELINES FOR IMPLEMENTING DIFFERENTIAL REINFORCEMENT OF OTHER BEHAVIOR

- Shorten the interval initially to provide frequent reinforcement.
- Require the absence of the targeted problem behavior *and other problem behaviors* for reinforcement.
- After the problem behavior is brought under control, increase the interval gradually by a constant duration (e.g., 10 seconds), proportionately (e.g., by 10%), or based on the client's performance (e.g., setting the interval as the average interresponse time [IRT] from the last session).
- Introduce this to other activities/times in the day.
- Use it with other procedures.

DIFFERENTIAL REINFORCEMENT OF INCOMPATIBLE BEHAVIOR

This procedure involves reinforcing behaviors that are incompatible with the problem behavior and withholding reinforcement for the problem behavior.

- *Example*: A client engages in out-of-seat behavior, so the teacher (a) delivers reinforcement when the client is seated and (b) withholds reinforcement when the client is out of their seat.

ADDITIONAL NOTE(S)

Differential reinforcement of incompatible behavior (DRI) is considered a type of DRA procedure.

DIFFERENTIAL REINFORCEMENT OF LOW RATE BEHAVIOR

This procedure involves providing reinforcement when the targeted behavior occurs below a predetermined criterion. There are three types of DRL procedures: (a) full session, (b) interval, and (c) spaced-responding.

Full Session
This involves delivering reinforcement when responding for the entire duration of a treatment session is below a predetermined criterion.

- *Example*: A client appropriately raises their hand in class but does this too many times per hour, so the teacher (a) delivers reinforcement when the client only raises their hand X amount of times or less in an hour and (b) withholds reinforcement if the client raises their hand more than X amount of times in an hour.

Interval
This involves delivering reinforcement when responding for an interval of time within a treatment session is below a predetermined criterion.

Spaced-Responding
This involves delivering reinforcement following a behavior that occurs after a predetermined length of time since the last time it occurred (i.e., some IRT duration has been exceeded).

ADDITIONAL NOTE(S)

DRL is typically reserved for socially acceptable behaviors that are occurring too often.

FUNCTIONAL COMMUNICATION TRAINING AND NONCONTINGENT REINFORCEMENT

For a review of FCT and/or NCR, please refer to Task List item G-2.

PRACTICE QUESTION

Differential reinforcement of alternative behavior (DRA) is a procedure that involves reinforcing a targeted alternative behavior for the problem behavior and withholding reinforcement for the problem behavior. When selecting an alternative behavior, which of the following is NOT something you want to do?

A. Select a behavior that the client is unable to perform so you can shape it
B. Select a behavior that happens frequently enough to be reinforced
C. Select a behavior that is less effortful than the problem behavior
D. Select a behavior that is likely to be reinforced in the natural environment

Before moving on to the next section for the solution, we recommend that you provide a brief explanation for the answer option you selected here:

_____

_____

When you're ready, move on to the next section for the solution!

Practice Question Breakdown

Step 1: Examine the question

The question calls for you to examine the guidelines for selecting an alternative behavior within a DRA procedure. More specifically, this question asks which of the posed guidelines is not advisable in a DRA procedure.

Step 2: Analyze the answer options

A. You want to be sure the client can already perform the alternative behavior, otherwise they will likely revert to the more familiar, effective, and efficient problem behavior that already exists in their repertoire. This appears to be a promising option!
B. This answer is advisable when planning for a DRA. You want to be sure the alternative behavior happens frequently enough to be reinforced as reinforcement of a targeted alternative behavior is a significant component of a DRA procedure. This answer option is a distractor.
C. This answer is advisable when planning for a DRA. If possible, you want to select a behavior that is less effortful than the problem behavior, so the likelihood of it increasing with proper reinforcement is high. This answer option is a distractor.
D. This answer is advisable when planning for a DRA. You want to select a behavior that is likely to be reinforced in the natural environment, as natural reinforcement can be more effective at building lasting behaviors. This answer option is a distractor.

Step 3: Select the best answer

Among the four answer options presented, answer A (select a behavior that the client is unable to perform so you can shape it) appears to be the best answer.

▶ TASK LIST ITEM G-15

The objective of this Task List item is to use extinction (EXT).
See Task List item B-9 for a review of EXT.
There are three forms of the EXT procedure: (a) EXT of behavior maintained by positive reinforcement, (b) EXT of behavior maintained by negative reinforcement, and (c) EXT of behavior maintained by automatic reinforcement.

EXTINCTION OF BEHAVIOR MAINTAINED BY POSITIVE REINFORCEMENT

This involves removing the reinforcer for a positively reinforced behavior.

- *Example*: Before EXT is implemented, a client yells to get parents' attention.

Table 9.21 Behavior maintained by positive reinforcement

R	C
Screams	Parents' attention

C, consequence; R, response.

EXT procedure: Parents remove attention provided when the behavior occurs.

Table 9.22 Extinction procedure for behavior maintained by positive reinforcement

R	C
Screams	No parents' attention; behavior is ignored

C, consequence; R, response.

EXTINCTION OF BEHAVIOR MAINTAINED BY NEGATIVE REINFORCEMENT

This involves removing the reinforcer for a negatively reinforced behavior.

- *Example*: Before EXT is implemented, a client screams to avoid bedtime.

Table 9.23 Behavior maintained by negative reinforcement

R	C
Screams	Avoids bedtime

C, consequence; R, response.

EXT procedure: Parents prevent escape from bedtime.

Table 9.24 Extinction procedure for behavior maintained by negative reinforcement

R	C
Screams	Bedtime

C, consequence; R, response.

EXTINCTION MAINTAINED BY AUTOMATIC REINFORCEMENT

This involves removing the reinforcer for an automatically reinforced behavior.

- *Example*: Before EXT is implemented, a client screams for the auditory stimulation it produces.

Table 9.25 Behavior maintained by automatic reinforcement

R	C
Screams	Sensory stimulation produced by the R.

C, consequence; R, response.

EXT procedure: Parents block the sensory stimulation the behavior produces (e.g., has the client wear noise-cancelling headphones).

Table 9.26 Extinction procedure for behavior maintained by automatic reinforcement

R	C
Screams	Sensory stimulation blocked.

C, consequence; R, response.

Recommendations for increasing the effectiveness of EXT procedures are as follows:

- Identify/prevent access to possible reinforcers. Accurate identification and prevention of the consequences maintaining the client's target behavior is the key to implementing EXT effectively.
- Be consistent about preventing reinforcement. Once the reinforcing consequences have been accurately identified, their consistent withholding is critical to the success of EXT.
- Integrate EXT with other interventions. EXT is best coupled with other treatments. It is especially effective when combined with the reinforcement of alternative behaviors.
- Tell clients about the procedure. Informing clients of the EXT procedure being applied frequently fosters a more rapid decrease in the problem behavior being placed on EXT.
- Expect and plan to manage the backlash. Keep in mind that placing a problem behavior on EXT often leads to an increase in behavior that previously occurred infrequently, such as aggressive behavior.
- Increase opportunities for EXT trials. To accelerate the EXT process and improve the efficiency of EXT, prevent problem behaviors from producing reinforcement (i.e., an EXT trial). To accomplish this, set up additional situations that provide opportunities for the problem behavior to occur and implement the EXT procedure.
- Organize and align the client's network of support. For maximum effectiveness, each of the individuals in the client's life should implement the same EXT procedure. Intervention implementation must be comprehensive; if some people reinforce the problem behavior, the extinction procedure will be less effective.
- Avoid accidentally placing desirable behaviors on EXT. Ensure that desirable behaviors continue to be reinforced.
- Keep the EXT procedure in place permanently. In circumstances where permanent implementation of EXT is inconvenient or contraindicated, maintain treatment gains by fading the EXT procedure.
- Don't use EXT if the behavior is likely to be copied or cause harm. EXT is typically used as an intervention for minor behavior problems. In general, best practice is to address behaviors that are harmful to self or others with the most immediately effective and ethical approach possible.

▶ TASK LIST ITEM G-16

The objective of this Task List item is to use positive and negative punishment (e.g., time-out, response cost, overcorrection).

To weaken/decrease a behavior using positive punishment (also known as Type I punishment), establish a behavior-consequence contingency in which the consequence is a positive punisher.

- *Example*: A problem behavior (yelling) is targeted, and a potential punisher (vocal reprimand) has been identified. To implement positive punisher to weaken/decrease this behavior, the following contingency will be established:

Table 9.27 Behavior followed by positive punisher

R	C
Yells	Vocal reprimand

C, consequence; R, response.

Procedures based on positive punishment, include: (a) reprimands, (b) response blocking, (c) contingent exercise, and (d) overcorrection.

REPRIMAND

This involves the use of a verbal expression of disapproval following a target behavior.

RESPONSE BLOCKING

This is a physical intervention that used to interrupt a target behavior at its onset to prevent its completion.

RESPONSE INTERRUPTION AND REDIRECTION (RIRD)

This involves response blocking of stereotypic behavior, followed by redirection to engage in high probability behaviors.

CONTINGENT EXERCISE

This involves requiring a client to perform an aversive activity following a target behavior.

OVERCORRECTION

This involves requiring the client to perform behavior that is clearly connected to remediating the harm or damage stemming from the target behavior. There are two types: (a) positive practice and (b) restitutional overcorrection.

Positive practice
This involves requiring the client to repeatedly perform a correct form of the target behavior or a behavior that contradicts or impedes the target behavior.

Restitutional
This involves requiring the client to fix any damage caused by their behavior and then to guide the client on how to perform actions that further improve the environment.

To weaken/decrease a behavior using negative punishment (also known as Type II punishment), establish a behavior-consequence contingency in which the consequence is a negative punisher.

■ *Example*: A problem behavior (yelling) is targeted, and a potential reinforcer (removal of toy) has been identified. To implement negative punishment to weaken/decrease this behavior, the following contingency will be established:

Table 9.28 Behavior followed by negative punisher

R	C
Yells	Removal of toy

C, con sequence; R, response.

Procedures based on negative punishment, include: (a) response cost and (b) time-out.

RESPONSE COST

There are four key methods for implementing response cost:

Directly Fine the Client a Specific Amount of Reinforcers
■ *Example*: Taking away a specified number of minutes of a preferred activity for each occurrence of a target behavior

Fine the Client a Specific Amount of Available Bonus Reinforcers
■ *Example*: Providing a certain amount of time with a preferred activity that cannot be taken away, along with the possibility of additional "bonus" minutes

Combine Response Cost With Reinforcement
■ *Example*: Offering tokens for on-task behavior in conjunction with removing tokens for off-task behavior

Combine Response Cost With Group Consequences
■ *Example*: Taking away a specific amount of reinforcement from a group when one member of the group engages in a target behavior

ADDITIONAL NOTE(S)

To implement response cost effectively, (a) implement fines as soon as possible after the occurrence of a target behavior; (b) consider what variation of response cost is best to use (i.e., is less aversive, more socially acceptable, and recommended for the type of behavior targeted); (c) make sure you have enough of the reinforcers you will be using; (d) plan for unexpected outcomes (e.g., aggressive or avoidant behavior); (e) save response cost as a last resort; and (f) take data on the effects of response cost.

TIME-OUT

This involves withdrawing opportunities to access positive reinforcement for a certain amount of time and/or contingent on the performance of a particular behavior. There are two types: (a) nonexclusion and (b) exclusion time-out.

Nonexclusion
This type of time-out does not completely remove the client from the physical time-in environment and can take several forms, including: (a) planned ignoring (i.e., withholding social reinforcement) when the client performs the target behavior, (b) removing access to reinforcement when the client performs the target behavior, (c) contingent observation (i.e., repositioning the client so that they can be monitored; access to reinforcement is removed), and (d) placement in select space time-out (i.e., repositioning the client to a space in the time-in setting that is partitioned off; access to reinforcement is removed).

Exclusion
This type of time-out completely removes the client from the physical time-in environment. It involves placing the client in a separate, safe, secure, and supervised time-out space. It is preferred that this space is minimally furnished and located near the time-in setting.

ADDITIONAL NOTE(S)

To implement time-out effectively, (a) create a reinforcing time-in environment, (b) define the behaviors that lead to time-out for all relevant parties, (c) consider nonexclusion procedures first and determine what can be implemented based on physical factors, (d) get permission before using any time-out procedure from the relevant parties, (e) explain the procedure to clients, (f) use time-out each time a target behavior occurs, (g) determine exit criteria (i.e., how a client can be released from time-out), (h) follow legal and ethical requirements regarding the use of time-out, and (i) collect data to evaluate the effectiveness of time-out.

Recommendations for increasing the effectiveness of positive and negative punishment procedures are as follows:

■ Prior to implementation, assess and determine the client's punishers.
■ Use a variety of punishers in a consistent and safe manner.
■ Apply the punisher as early in the behavior chain as possible.

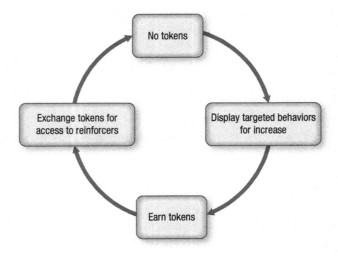

Figure 9.4 Token economy system.

- Deliver the punisher immediately (or as soon as possible) following each occurrence of the target behavior.
- Calibrate the intensity of the punisher such that it is sufficiently intense to be effective, but not unnecessarily intense.
- Initially implement a continuous schedule of punishment, but aim to thin the schedule.
- Utilize mediation with a response-to-punishment delay that more closely approximates how consequences are delivered in the natural environment.
- Implement punishment in conjunction with complementary interventions, such as antecedent interventions, EXT, and DR.
- Be on the lookout for and prepared to address unwanted effects of punishment.
- Collect/review data regularly and make data-based decisions regarding treatment.

▶ TASK LIST ITEM G-17

The objective of this Task List item is to use token economies.

A token economy is a behavior-change system characterized by a set of contingencies that specify how tokens are earned/distributed and exchanged for reinforcers. It has three core components, including (a) a list of target behaviors to be reinforced, (b) a generalized conditioned reinforcer, and (c) a menu of backup reinforcers.

LIST OF TARGET BEHAVIORS

Prior to implementing a token system, identify the behaviors that will be targeted for increase. These should be in concert with the rules of the setting.

GENERALIZED CONDITIONED REINFORCER

This is the token (i.e., object that can be earned) in a token system (e.g., plastic chips, points, stickers). Decide on what this will be and how it will be dispensed prior to implementation. When deciding on the token to use, consider whether the token is safe, durable, portable, and counterfeit proof.

MENU OF BACKUP REINFORCERS

This is a list of items/activities for which clients' can exchange their earned tokens. In addition to listing backup reinforcers, specify the ratio of exchange (i.e., cost; how many tokens are needed for each item/activity). It is recommended that (a) initial cost is low for backup reinforcers, (b) cost and number of backup reinforcers increase when targeted behaviors increase, (c) higher quality backup reinforcers are added as clients earn more tokens, and (d) cost of necessary backup reinforcers increase more than those for unnecessary but high quality backup reinforcers.

ADDITIONAL NOTE(S)

Reinforcement contingencies should not deny clients access to items/activities that deprive them of basic needs and access to personal events.

Token economies can also include a response cost contingency or use a level system.

Response cost

This involves the implementation of a negative punishment procedure in which undesirable behavior results in the loss of tokens.

Level system

This involves establishing a system of levels in which clients ascend or descend based on their performance of specified target behaviors.

Procedures should be written down. It is recommended that the system is tested for a few days to determine whether modifications are necessary before launching it fully.

When implementing the token economy, ensure that (a) staff are adequately trained to implement it and (b) clients are trained on the system.

ADDITIONAL NOTE(S)

When training staff on implementation, it is recommended that the components of the system are systematically taught via direct instruction (i.e., demonstrate it, provide staff opportunities to practice, and offer feedback). Training clients on the system may simply involve providing verbal instructions and then modeling the procedure for (a) token delivery and (b) exchanging tokens for backup reinforcers.

▶ TASK LIST ITEM G-18

The objective of this Task List item is to use group contingencies.

Group contingencies are often used in schools, classrooms, playgrounds, businesses, and the military. Implementation of group contingencies involves making reinforcement for all members dependent on an individual, a set of members drawn from the larger group, or each member of the whole group achieving a performance criterion. This corresponds to three types of group contingencies: (a) dependent, (b) independent, or (c) interdependent.

DEPENDENT GROUP CONTINGENCY

This involves providing reinforcement for all members of a group based on the behavior of one member of the group (or a small group within a larger group).

Table 9.29 Illustration of a dependent group contingency resulting in reinforcement

S^D	R	C
Criterion stated for one client (or small group)	Client (or small group) meets criterion	Reinforcement for the whole group

C, consequence; R, response; S^D, discriminative stimuli.

INDEPENDENT GROUP CONTINGENCY

This involves providing reinforcement for each member of the group based on that member's achievement of a performance criterion that is in place for all members of the group.

TablE 9.30 Illustration of an independent group contingency resulting in reinforcement

S^D	R	C
Criterion stated for the whole group	Some or all members meet criterion	Reinforcement only for members that met criterion

C, consequence; R, response; S^D, discriminative stimuli.

INTERDEPENDENT GROUP CONTINGENCY

This involves providing reinforcement for all members of a group based on each member of the group achieving a performance criterion that is in place for all members of the group.

Table 9.31 Illustration of an interdependent group contingency resulting in reinforcement

S^D	R	C
Criterion stated for the whole group	All members meet criterion	Reinforcement for the whole group

C, consequence; R, response; S^D, discriminative stimuli.

ADDITIONAL NOTE(S)

Group contingencies save time during administration by applying a single consequence to all members. They can also leverage peer influence to achieve the aims of the intervention and foster positive social behaviors within a group.

General recommendations for implementation of group contingencies are as follows:

- Identify the behavior to change and possible collateral behaviors.
- Select the type of group contingency based on programmatic goals and clients whenever possible.
- Use generalized conditioned reinforcers or reinforcer menus whenever possible.
- Ensure that the performance criteria are achievable for clients.
- Monitor the performance of both the group and its individual members.
- Consider combining the group contingency with other procedures (e.g., DRL).

▶ TASK LIST ITEM G-19

The objective of this Task List item is to use contingency contracting.

A contingency contract (a.k.a. *behavioral contract*) is a document that specifies a contingent relationship between the completion of a specific task and access to a specified reinforcer. It should be complete and accurate. Contingency contracts can be implemented in a variety of settings, including in the classroom, home, clinic, and workplace.

Contingency contracts should (a) provide a detailed description of the task and all relevant rules, and (b) describe the reward to be provided upon completion of the specific behavior.

DETAILED DESCRIPTION OF THE TASK AND ALL RELEVANT RULES

This should include

- who will perform the behavior and receive the reinforcer,
- what the person must do to receive the reward,
- when the behavior will be performed, and
- how well the task must be performed for the client to gain access to the reward. Provide enough detail on the specifics of the task so the client or the behaviorist could use it as a checklist.

DETAILED DESCRIPTION OF THE REWARD TO BE PROVIDED UPON COMPLETION OF THE SPECIFIC BEHAVIOR

Specify

- who will determine completion of the task and release the reward,
- what the reward will be,
- when the reward will be provided, and
- how much reward will be given.

Document task completion in a task record or chart that provides a record of the behavior. This will serve as a response prompt for the client and aid with motivation, focus, and compliance. Sometimes it is helpful for the client to mark tasks as they are completed, such as with a check mark or sticker.

Contingency contracts can be developed by the person implementing the contracting or in collaboration with the client, student, or students; collaborative contracting tends to be more effective. For example, teachers often develop behavioral contracts or classroom norms with their students. The class discusses and decides on norms for classroom behavior, reasons for those behaviors, rewards for exhibiting the behaviors, and consequences for not exhibiting the behavior. Once the contract is finalized, all students and the teacher sign the contract, display it prominently in the classroom, and periodically review it.

▶ TASK LIST ITEM G-20

The objective of this Task List item is to use self-management strategies.

Self-management is the personal application of behavior-change tactics to produce a desired change in behavior. Self-management strategies can be used to break or develop habits, achieve tasks or personal goals, and increase efficiency and effectiveness at work, school, or home. There are a variety of approaches to self-management that differ in the degree to which they emphasize antecedents or consequences for the behavior targeted for change.

SELF-MANAGEMENT STRATEGIES

Self-management strategies based on antecedents include: (a) manipulating MOs, (b) using response prompts, (c) performing the first part of a behavior chain, (d) removing necessary materials, (e) limiting stimulus conditions, and (f) using a specific environment for behavior.

Manipulating Motivating Operations

This involves behaving in a way that creates motivation that increases the likelihood of a target behavior.

- *Example*: A client struggling to fall asleep at night refrains from taking a nap during the day.

Using Response Prompts

This involves using stimuli that can later cue a target behavior.

■ *Example*: A client sets a reminder on their phone to cook dinner at 5:00 p.m.

Performing the First Part of a Behavior Chain

This involves performing the initial steps of a chain so that one is later faced with a discriminative stimulus that evokes the target behavior.

■ *Example*: A client places their backpack in front of the door, which later prompts the client to take it on their way out to school.

Removing Necessary Materials

This strategy is used to reduce or eliminate problem behaviors and involves removing items that are necessary for them to occur.

■ *Example*: A client trying to stop drinking alcohol throws out all the alcohol from their home.

Limiting Stimulus Conditions

This strategy is used to reduce or eliminate problem behaviors and involves limiting those stimulus conditions under which they occur.

■ *Example*: A client who continually pulls at their hair limits this behavior to a particular bathroom in their home. The client would go there when they felt the urge to perform the behavior and leave after they finished.

Using a Specific Environment for Behavior

This strategy is used to increase a desired behavior and involves dedicating a specific environment for it.

■ *Example*: A client does their homework at a specific table in their home and refrains from engaging in any other activity there.

ADDITIONAL NOTE(S)

Consider the following when designing a self-management program: (a) establish a goal and define the target behavior; (b) self-monitor (i.e., observe and record the target behavior); (c) engineer contingencies that result in immediate consequences for each occurrence (or nonoccurrence) of the target behavior; (d) publicly make known the goal for behavior change; (e) involve others in the program; and (f) continually monitor and assess the effects of the program, making changes as needed.

SELF-MONITORING

This involves a client observing and recording their own behavior and is often taught in conjunction with self-management strategies. This tactic often produces behavior change due to its obtrusiveness and, as a result, penchant for producing *reactivity* (i.e., an effect on the person's behavior generated by it being closely observed or measured).

ADDITIONAL NOTE(S)

Self-monitoring is often used with goal setting, self-evaluation (i.e., comparing performance with goal), and reinforcement for meeting goals.

Behavior analysts should consider the following recommendations to support clients' use of self-monitoring:

- Provide the necessary materials (e.g., data collection form, tally counter, timer).
- Use auditory, tactile, or visual prompts to cue self-monitoring.
- Have clients self-monitor the dimension of behavior that results directly in progress toward their goals for self-management.
- Encourage frequent self-monitoring, at least initially.
- Reinforce them for accurate self-monitoring.

Other self-management strategies include (a) self-instruction, (b) habit reversal, (c) self-directed systematic desensitization, and (d) massed practice.

SELF-INSTRUCTION

This involves overtly or covertly prompting desired behaviors and guiding oneself through a behavior chain or sequence of tasks.

HABIT REVERSAL

This involves self-monitoring a particular problem behavior and, as early as possible, interrupting the behavior chain by simply engaging in an incompatible behavior.

SELF-DIRECTED SYSTEMATIC DESENSITIZATION

This involves substituting a different behavior that counteracts the target behavior (e.g., doing muscle relaxation exercises when feeling tense). This tactic is often implemented in conjunction with a stimulus hierarchy.

MASSED PRACTICE

This involves forcing oneself to repeatedly engage in the target behavior, which may result in its reduction.

▶ TASK LIST ITEM G-21

The objective of this Task List item is to use procedures to promote stimulus and response generalization.
  When a client generalizes a skill, they (a) exhibit it under different circumstances, settings, or situations (stimulus generalization); and/or (b) use it in an alternative manner that was not trained but is nevertheless functionally equivalent to the target behavior that was trained (response generalization). Thus, behavior analysts strive to promote clients' generalized behavior change across three aspects

- consistency over time,
- appearance across diverse and numerous settings, and
- diffusion to various other behaviors.

ADDITIONAL NOTE(S)

Keep in mind that, while stimulus generalization and response generalization are distinct and can appear in isolation, in practice they often co-occur.
  As a crucial first step, behavior analysts do not simply expect stimulus and response generalization to occur; they systematically plan for it. This planning process involves (a) focusing on target behaviors that will be naturally reinforced by the client's environment; and (b) considering, planning for, and teaching the myriad forms of the target behavior and the varied contexts in which the client is to exhibit it.

General recommendations for teaching relevant stimulus conditions and response requirements include:

- Teach loosely and provide the client with plenty of examples of both stimulus and response.
- Enable the client to experience many different examples in the instructional setting.
- Conduct generalization probes to assess the degree to which the client responds to untaught stimulus and response examples. Discontinue instruction on a class of examples when a probe indicates the client has mastered it.

It may also be helpful to explicitly teach the client which conditions it would be inappropriate for them to exhibit the target behavior using negative teaching examples.

PROCEDURES FOR PROMOTING STIMULUS GENERALIZATION

Creating an Instructional Setting That Resembles the Generalization Setting
- Teach the client to perform the target behavior in the instructional setting in a manner that will enable the client to receive reinforcement in the generalization setting.
- Mix it up when you're teaching so that the client experiences a wide range of possible scenarios in the instructional setting that could occur in the generalization setting. For instance, change the organization of the environment, individuals involved, and materials.
- Once the client is proficiently performing a skill in response to a particular instruction, start varying that instruction to reflect the diverse ways the natural environment may prompt the client to perform the behavior.

Providing Instruction on Enough Stimulus Examples
- Provide the client with instructional examples across four dimensions: what is taught (i.e., the item), the stimulus context, the setting, and the teacher.

Ensuring that the client receives ample reinforcement in the generalization setting
- Use intermittent schedules of reinforcement, delayed rewards, and behavior traps.
- Involve caregivers and significant others in the delivery of reinforcement.

Setting Up a Person or Object to Help Facilitate the Generalization of Skills
- In other words, devise a mediating stimulus.
- Teach the client how to use self-management skills to prompt and maintain targeted behavior changes.

PROCEDURES FOR PROMOTING RESPONSE GENERALIZATION

Providing Instruction on Enough Response Examples
- Provide the client with instruction on a wide variety of examples to assist them in acquiring a "feel" for how the target behavior appears in natural settings and to promote response generalization.

Proactively Instruct Clients on the Utility of Generalizing Skills
- Teach the client that it works well to generalize a target behavior to other settings and then ask/tell them to do it.

Teach Clients to Try Different Approaches and to Use a Trial-and-Error Approach to Problem-Solving
- Reinforce the client when they exhibit response variability and engage in problem-solving.

Also remember to provide praise and show interest and enthusiasm when the client exhibits new or different forms of the target behavior in the same response class.

▶ TASK LIST ITEM G-22

The objective of this Task List item is to use procedures to promote maintenance.

Maintenance refers to the lasting change in behavior or extent to which a client continues to demonstrate a target behavior after some or all of a treatment program has been terminated. Behavior analysts may use the following procedures to promote maintenance:

- Use intermittent schedules of reinforcement to maintain learned behaviors that are appropriate for the setting. See Task List item B-5 for a review of schedules of reinforcement.
- Plan for some part(s) of the initial intervention (e.g., a visual aid) to remain in place.
- Plan for practice. This may involve training relevant individuals to provide the client with opportunities to perform a learned behavior.

▶ CONCLUSION

This chapter covered key content for Task List items related to behavior-change procedures. It is an important chapter because it delineates how behavior analysts competently employ the most frequently used tools in their "intervention toolbox." As such, this chapter offers clear and practical guidance on using behavior-change procedures like positive and negative reinforcement to strengthen behavior; establishing and using conditioned reinforcers; using stimulus and response prompts and fading; using modeling and imitation training; using shaping, chaining, EXT; using a variety of teaching arrangements and approaches to instruction; using procedures to promote stimulus and response generalization and maintenance; and more.

1. Recommendations for increasing the effectiveness of positive reinforcement procedures include all of the following except:

   A. Avoid varying reinforcers to ensure the most effective reinforcers are consistently used

   B. Design interventions that enable the client to gradually move from needing contrived reinforcers to naturally occurring reinforcers

   C. Set a readily obtainable beginning criterion for reinforcement

   D. Use reinforcers of sufficient magnitude that are highly motivating

2. Antecedent interventions based on motivating operations (MOs) are considered _____.

   A. Consequence-based

   B. Contingency-dependent

   C. Contingency-independent

   D. None of the above

3. Which of the following antecedent intervention procedures involves delivering a reinforcement on a fixed or variable interval schedule independent of the client's behavior?

   A. Differential reinforcement of other behavior (DRO)

   B. Functional communication training (FCT)

   C. High-p request sequence

   D. Noncontingent reinforcement (NCR)

4. Which of the following noncontingent reinforcement (NCR) procedures involves delivering access to highly preferred objects or activities that the client can manipulate on a fixed or variable interval schedule independent of the client's behavior?

   A. NCR with automatic reinforcement

   B. NCR with negative reinforcement

   C. NCR with positive reinforcement

   D. None of the above

5. Establishing conditioned reinforcers involves pairing _____ with one or more unconditioned or conditioned reinforcers.

   A. A conditioned stimulus

   B. A discriminative stimulus

   C. A neutral stimulus

   D. An unconditioned stimulus

6. What type of reinforcer results from the pairing of a conditioned reinforcer with many other reinforcers?

   A. Generalized conditioned

   B. Generalized unconditioned

   C. Primary

   D. Secondary

1. **A) Avoid varying reinforcers to ensure the most effective reinforcers are consistently used**

It is recommended that reinforcers are varied, not held constant. The other answer options (design interventions that enable the client to gradually move from needing contrived reinforcers to naturally occurring reinforcers, set a readily obtainable beginning criterion for reinforcement, use reinforcers of sufficient magnitude that are highly motivating) are recommended practices for increasing the effectiveness of positive reinforcement procedures.

2. **C) Contingency-independent**

Antecedent interventions based on MOs are considered contingency-independent, which means they do not rely on differential consequences for the target behavior to create evocative or abative effects. The other answer options (consequence-based, contingency-dependent, none of the above) are not descriptors of antecedent interventions based on MOs and function as distractors.

3. **D) Noncontingent reinforcement (NCR)**

NCR is an antecedent intervention procedure that involves delivering a reinforcement on a fixed or variable interval schedule independent of the client's behavior. The other answer options (DRO, FCT, High-*p* request sequence) refer to other procedures, two of which are also contingency-independent antecedent interventions and serve as distractors.

4. **A) NCR with automatic reinforcement**

NCR with automatic reinforcement involves delivering access to highly preferred objects or activities that the client can manipulate on a fixed or variable interval schedule independent of the client's behavior. The other answer options (NCR with negative reinforcement, NCR with positive reinforcement, none of the above), two of which refer to NCR procedures with other sources of reinforcement, function as distractors.

5. **C) A neutral stimulus**

Establishing conditioned reinforcers involves pairing a neutral stimulus with one or more unconditioned or conditioned reinforcers. The other answer options (a conditioned stimulus, a discriminative stimulus, an unconditioned stimulus) refer to other types of stimuli and serve as distractors.

6. **C) Primary**

A generalized conditioned reinforcer is the result of the pairing of a conditioned reinforcer with many other reinforcers. The other answer options (generalized unconditioned, primary, secondary) refer to other types of reinforcers and function as distractors.

7. Stimulus _____ involves gradually altering the form of a stimulus until it eventually resembles the target criterion.

A. Control
B. Fading
C. Shaping
D. Superimposition

8. Stimulus _____ involves making some feature of a target stimulus (e.g., color, intensity, size) more salient, and then gradually fading it.

A. Control
B. Fading
C. Shaping
D. Superimposition

9. What errorless teaching strategy begins with several rounds of zero-delay instruction and is followed by the addition of an increment of time after the S^D that does not change in subsequent rounds?

A. Assisted time delay
B. Constant time delay
C. Intermittent time delay
D. Progressive time delay

10. _____ involves using highly intrusive prompts until the client begins to demonstrate the target response independently. Prompting is gradually faded as the responding becomes more independent, but it can also increase if the client does not participate.

A. Graduated guidance
B. Least-to-most prompting
C. Most-to-least prompting
D. Prompt delay

11. Which of the following prompt systems uses a prompt hierarchy that starts with the least intrusive prompt and systematically graduates to the most intrusive prompt?

A. Graduated guidance
B. Least-to-most
C. Most-to-least
D. Prompt delay

12. General use guidelines for response prompts include each of the following except:

A. Consider returning to a previous prompt level if errors occur
B. Shift from reinforcing prompted to independent responses as soon as possible
C. Use most-to-least for assessing skills
D. Use response prompts judiciously

(See answers next page.)

7. C) Shaping
Stimulus shaping involves gradually altering the form of a stimulus until it eventually resembles the target criterion. The other answer options (control, fading, superimposition) do not accurately fit into the statement and function as distractors.

8. B) Fading
Stimulus fading involves making some feature of a target stimulus (e.g., color, intensity, size) more salient, and then gradually fading it. The other answer options (control, shaping, superimposition) do not accurately fit into the statement and function as distractors.

9. B) Constant time delay
Constant time delay is an errorless teaching strategy that begins with several rounds of zero-delay instruction and is followed by the addition of an increment of time after the S^D that does not change in subsequent rounds. The other answer options (assisted time delay, intermittent time delay, progressive time delay), only one of which is an errorless teaching strategy described in the professional literature, function as distractors.

10. A) Graduated guidance
Graduated guidance involves using highly intrusive prompts until the client begins to demonstrate the target response independently. Prompting is gradually faded as the responding becomes more independent, but it can also increase if the client does not participate. The other answer options (least-to-most prompting, most-to-least prompting, prompt delay) are other prompt systems and function as distractors.

11. B) Least-to-most
The least-to-most prompt system uses a prompt hierarchy that starts with the least intrusive prompt and systematically graduates to the most intrusive prompt. The other answer options (graduated guidance, most-to-least, prompt delay) are other prompt systems that serve as distractors.

12. B) Shift from reinforcing prompted to independent responses as soon as possible
When using response prompts, behavior analysts should consider returning to a previous prompt level if errors occur, shift from reinforcing prompted to independent responses as soon as possible, and use response prompts judiciously. Using the most-to-least prompt system for assessing skills, however, is not a general use guideline for response prompts.

13. The behavior-environment relations that define modeling and imitation training include all of the following except:

   A. A model stimulus is presented to evoke the imitative response
   B. The imitative response is emitted at any point in time following the model stimulus
   C. The model and imitative response correspond in form
   D. The model serves as the S^D for the imitative response

14. Prior to conducting imitation training, behavior analysts should:

   A. Assess and teach any prerequisite skills, select models, and sequence models for training
   B. Assess and teach any prerequisite skills, select models, pretest, and sequence models for training
   C. Conduct a functional analysis, pretest, probe for imitative behavior, and select models
   D. Probe for imitative behavior, select models, sequence models for training

15. The purpose of the last of the four steps of imitation training (probing for imitative behavior) is:

   A. To assess the client's ability to perform previously learned imitative responses
   B. To assess for generalized imitation
   C. To identify additional imitative responses to target
   D. To identify models for use in the next set of trials

16. A behavior analyst gradually increases the amount of time a client is to remain seated in a chair before the client is allowed to get up from it. This is an example of:

   A. Behavior chaining
   B. Progressive time delay
   C. Shaping across response topographies
   D. Shaping within response topography

17. Before behaviors can be linked in a chain, behavior analysts must develop a _____ that breaks down a complex task into a series of smaller, teachable steps.

   A. Item analysis
   B. Pretest
   C. Task analysis
   D. Task description

18. Which of the following behavior chaining methods begins with teaching the last behavior in the chain?

   A. Backward chaining
   B. Forward chaining
   C. Total-task chaining
   D. None of the above

19. Which of the following behavior chaining methods calls for the provision of training on each behavior in the task analysis during every training session?

   A. Backward chaining
   B. Forward chaining
   C. Total-task chaining
   D. None of the above

13. B) The imitative response is emitted at any point in time following the model stimulus

The imitative response follows the model stimulus immediately, not at just any point in time following the model stimulus. The other response options (a model stimulus is presented to evoke the imitative response, the model and imitative response correspond in form, the model serves as the S^D for the imitative response) accurately describe the behavior-environment relations that define modeling and imitation training.

14. B) Assess and teach any prerequisite skills, select models, pretest, and sequence models for training

Prior to conducting imitation training, behavior analysts should assess and teach any prerequisite skills, select models, pretest, and sequence models for training. The other answer options (assess and teach any prerequisite skills, select models, and sequence models for training; conduct a functional analysis, pretest, probe for imitative behavior, and select models; probe for imitative behavior, select models, sequence models for training) do not accurately include the pretraining steps for imitation training and serve as distractors.

15. B) To assess for generalized imitation

The purpose of the last of the four steps of imitation training (probing for imitative behavior) is to assess for generalized imitation. The other answer options (to assess the client's ability to perform previously learned imitative responses, to identify additional imitative responses to target, to identify models for use in the next set of trials) describe other functions and serve as distractors.

16. D) Shaping within response topography

This is an example of shaping within response topography. In the scenario presented, the behavior being shaped (remaining seated in a chair) remains constant but some other measurable dimension (duration) is changed. The other answer options (behavior chaining, progressive time delay, shaping across response topographies) refer to other procedures and function as distractors.

17. C) Task analysis

Before behaviors can be linked in a chain, behavior analysts must develop a task analysis that breaks down a complex task into a series of smaller, teachable steps. The other answer options (item analysis, pretest, task description) do not accurately fit into the statement and function as distractors.

18. A) Backward chaining

Backward chaining is a behavior chaining method that begins with teaching the last behavior in the chain. The other answer options (forward chaining, total-task chaining, none of the above), two of which refer to behavior chaining methods that begin with the first behavior in the chain, function as distractors.

19. C) Total-task chaining

Total-task chaining is a behavior chaining method that calls for the provision of training on each behavior in the task analysis during every training session. The other answer options (backward chaining, forward chaining, none of the above) serve as distractors.

20. The brief pause between trials in discrete-trial teaching is referred to as the:

   A. Between-trial interval
   B. Intertrial interval
   C. Post-reinforcement pause
   D. Post-trial pause

21. What type of discriminations are established by reinforcing certain responses in the presence of certain antecedents only if they are preceded by certain other stimuli?

   A. Complex
   B. Conditional
   C. Contingent
   D. Simple

22. What type of discriminations are established by reinforcing certain responses only in the presence of certain antecedents?

   A. Complex
   B. Conditional
   C. Contingent
   D. Simple

23. Guidelines for the effective implementation of a high-probability instructional sequence include all of the following except:

   A. Present high-p requests that the client is currently able to comply with
   B. Present each request slowly
   C. Acknowledge compliance with each request
   D. Use high-quality reinforcers

24. Which of the following procedures involves providing reinforcement when the problem behavior is absent for a predetermined amount of time and withholding reinforcement for the problem behavior?

   A. Differential reinforcement of alternative behavior (DRA)
   B. Differential reinforcement of other behavior (DRO)
   C. Differential reinforcement of high rate behavior (DRH)
   D. Differential reinforcement of low rate behavior (DRL)

25. Which of the following procedures involves providing reinforcement when the targeted behavior occurs below a predetermined criterion?

   A. Differential reinforcement of alternative behavior (DRA)
   B. Differential reinforcement of other behavior (DRO)
   C. Differential reinforcement of high rate behavior (DRH)
   D. Differential reinforcement of low rate behavior (DRL)

26. Which of the following procedures involves reinforcing a targeted alternative behavior for the problem behavior and withholding reinforcement for the problem behavior?

   A. Differential reinforcement of alternative behavior (DRA)
   B. Differential reinforcement of other behavior (DRO)
   C. Differential reinforcement of high rate behavior (DRH)
   D. Differential reinforcement of low rate behavior (DRL)

20. B) Intertrial interval

The brief pause between trials in discrete-trial teaching is referred to as the intertrial interval. The other answer options (between-trial interval, post-reinforcement pause, post-trial pause), two of which are not terms used in the professional literature, function as distractors.

21. B) Conditional

Conditional discriminations are established by reinforcing certain responses in the presence of certain antecedents only if they are preceded by certain other stimuli. The other answer options (complex, contingent, simple), one of which is another type of discrimination described in the professional literature, function as distractors.

22. D) Simple

Simple discriminations are established by reinforcing certain responses only in the presence of certain antecedents. The other response options (complex, conditional, contingent) function as distractors.

23. B) Present each request slowly

Requests are to be presented rapidly, not slowly. The other answer options (present high-p requests that the client is currently able to comply with, acknowledge compliance with each request, use high-quality reinforcers) are guidelines to be followed for effectively implementing a high-probability instructional sequence.

24. B) Differential reinforcement of other behavior (DRO)

DRO involves providing reinforcement when the problem behavior is absent for a predetermined amount of time and withholding reinforcement for the problem behavior. The other answer options (DRA, DRH, DRL) refer to other differential reinforcement procedures and function as distractors.

25. D) Differential reinforcement of low rate behavior (DRL)

DRL involves providing reinforcement when the targeted behavior occurs below a predetermined criterion. The other answer options (DRA, DRO, DRH) serve as distractors.

26. A) Differential reinforcement of alternative behavior (DRA)

DRA involves reinforcing a targeted alternative behavior for the problem behavior and withholding reinforcement for the problem behavior. The other answer options (DRO, DRH, DRL) serve as distractors.

27. A client's yelling behavior is reinforced and maintained by the auditory stimulation it produces. An extinction procedure targeting this problem behavior (yelling) would involve:

   A. Blocking the auditory stimulation that the behavior produces
   B. Ignoring the behavior
   C. Placing the client in time-out for no more than 5 minutes each time the behavior occurs
   D. Reprimanding the client when the behavior occurs

28. Which of the following procedures involves requiring a client to perform an aversive activity following a target behavior?

   A. Contingent exercise
   B. Overcorrection
   C. Response blocking
   D. Response interruption and redirection (RIRD)

29. _____ is a procedure that involves response blocking of stereotypic behavior, followed by redirection to engage in high probability behaviors.

   A. Contingent exercise
   B. Overcorrection
   C. Response blocking
   D. Response interruption and redirection (RIRD)

30. The core components of a token economy include all of the following except:

   A. A generalized conditioned reinforcer
   B. A list of target behaviors to be reinforced
   C. A menu of backup reinforcers
   D. A specified fine for each occurrence of a target behavior

31. What type of group contingency calls for the delivery of reinforcement to each member of the group based on that member's achievement of a performance criterion that is in place for all members of the group?

   A. Dependent
   B. Independent
   C. Interdependent
   D. Whole

32. What type of group contingency calls for the delivery of reinforcement to all members of a group based on each member of the group achieving a performance criterion that is in place for all members of the group?

   A. Dependent
   B. Independent
   C. Interdependent
   D. Whole

27. A) Blocking the auditory stimulation that the behavior produces

In the example provided, the problem behavior (yelling) is maintained by the auditory stimulation it produces. In other words, yelling is an automatically reinforced behavior. Thus, implementing an extinction procedure would involve blocking the auditory stimulation that the behavior produces. The other response options (ignoring the behavior, placing the client in time-out for no more than 5 minutes each time the behavior occurs, reprimanding the client when the behavior occurs) are not function-based strategies targeting the removal of the reinforcer for the automatically reinforced behavior and serve as distractors.

28. A) Contingent exercise

Contingent exercise is a punishment-based procedure that involves requiring a client to perform an aversive activity following a target behavior. The other answer options (overcorrection, response blocking, RIRD) are other punishment-based procedures and function as distractors.

29. D) Response interruption and redirection (RIRD)

RIRD is a procedure that involves response blocking of stereotypic behavior, followed by redirection to engage in high probability behaviors. The other answer options (contingent exercise, overcorrection, response blocking) are other punishment-based procedures and function as distractors.

30. D) A specified fine for each occurrence of a target behavior

The core components of a token economy include the use of a generalized conditioned reinforcer, a list of target behaviors to be reinforced, and a menu of backup reinforcers. A specified fine for each occurrence of a target behavior is not required.

31. B) Independent

An independent group contingency calls for the delivery of reinforcement to each member of the group based on that member's achievement of a performance criterion that is in place for all members of the group. The other answer options (dependent, interdependent, whole), two of which refer to other group contingencies, function as distractors.

32. C) Interdependent

An interdependent group contingency calls for the delivery of reinforcement to all members of a group based on each member of the group achieving a performance criterion that is in place for all members of the group. The other answer options (dependent, independent, whole), two of which refer to other group contingencies, function as distractors.

33. A _____ is a document that specifies a contingent relationship between the completion of a specific task and access to a specified reinforcer.

   A. Behavior protocol
   B. Contingency contract
   C. Free-operant arrangement
   D. Token system

34. Which of the following self-management strategies involves forcing oneself to repeatedly engage in a target behavior to reduce its occurrence in the future?

   A. Habit reversal
   B. Massed practice
   C. Self-direct systematic desensitization
   D. Self-instruction

35. Each of the following are considered self-management strategies except:

   A. Manipulating motivating operations
   B. Performing the first part of a behavior chain
   C. Using a specific environment for behavior
   D. Using stimulus prompts

36. Recommended strategies for supporting the maintenance of a learned behavior include all of the following except:

   A. Plan for some part of the initial intervention to teach and reinforce the behavior to remain in place
   B. Plan for practice of the behavior
   C. Proactively instruct the client on the utility of the behavior
   D. Use intermittent schedules of reinforcement that are appropriate for the setting in which the behavior occurs

33. B) Contingency contract

A contingency contract is a document that specifies a contingent relationship between the completion of a specific task and access to a specified reinforcer. The other answer options (behavior protocol, free-operant arrangement, token system) do not accurately fit into this statement and serve as distractors.

34. B) Massed practice

Massed practice is a self-management strategy that involves forcing oneself to repeatedly engage in a target behavior to reduce its occurrence in the future. The other response options (habit reversal, self-direct systematic desensitization, self-instruction) are other self-management strategies and function as distractors.

35. D) Using stimulus prompts

Manipulating motivating operations, performing the first part of a behavior chain, and using a specific environment for behavior are all considered self-management strategies. Using stimulus prompts, however, is not.

36. C) Proactively instruct the client on the utility of the behavior

Proactively instructing clients on the utility of a learned behavior is not among the recommended strategies for supporting the maintenance of a learned behavior. What is recommended includes planning for some part of the initial intervention to teach and reinforce the behavior to remain in place, planning for practice of the behavior, and using intermittent schedules of reinforcement that are appropriate for the setting in which it occurs.

REFERENCES

McDade, C. E., Austin, D. M., & Olander, C. P. (1985). Technological advances in precision teaching: A comparison between computer testing and SAFMEDS. *Journal of Precision Teaching, 6*(3), 49–53.

Potts, L., Eshleman, J. W., & Cooper, J. O. (1993). Ogden R. Lindsley and the historical development of precision teaching. *The Behavior Analyst, 16*, 177–189.

BIBLIOGRAPHY

Baer, D. M., Peterson, R. F., & Sherman, J. A. (1967). The development of imitation by reinforcing behavioral similarity to a model. *Journal of the Experimental Analysis of Behavior, 10*(5), 405–416. https://doi.org/10.1901/jeab.1967.10-405

Baer, D. M., Wolf, M. M., & Risley, T. R. (1968). Some current dimensions of applied behavior analysis. *Journal of Applied Behavior Analysis, 1*, 91–97. https://doi.org/10.1901/jaba.1968.1-91

Behavior Analyst Certification Board. (2017). *BCBA task list* (5th ed.). http://ies.ed.gov/ncee/wwc/pdf/wwc_scd.pdf

Cooper, J. O., Heron, T. E., & Heward, W. L. (2020). *Applied behavior analysis*. Pearson Education.

Davis, C. A., & Reichle, J. (1996). Variant and invariant high-probability requests: Increasing appropriate behaviors in children with emotional-behavioral disorders. *Journal of Applied Behavior Analysis, 29*(4), 471–481. https://doi.org/10.1901/jaba.1996.29-471

Deitz, S. M. (1977). An analysis of programming DRL schedules in educational settings. *Behaviour Research and Therapy, 15*(1), 103–111. https://doi.org/10.1016/0005-7967(77)90093-6

Eikeseth, S., & Smith, D. P. (2013). An analysis of verbal stimulus control in intraverbal behavior: Implications for practice and applied research. *The Analysis of Verbal Behavior, 29*(1), 125–135. https://doi.org/10.1007/bf03393130

Etzel, B. C., & LeBlanc, J. M. (1979). The simplest treatment alternative: The law of parsimony applied to choosing appropriate instructional control and errorless-learning procedures for the difficult-to-teach child. *Journal of Autism and Developmental Disorders, 9*(4), 361–382. https://doi.org/10.1007/BF01531445

Green, G. (2001). Behavior analytic instruction for learners with autism: Advances in stimulus control technology. *Focus on Autism and Other Developmental Disabilities, 16*(2), 72–85. https://doi.org/10.1177/108835760101600203

Hart, B., & Risley, T. R. (1975). Incidental teaching of language in the preschool. *Journal of Applied Behavior Analysis, 8*(4), 411–420. https://doi.org/10.1901/jaba.1975.8-411

Holth, P. (2003). Generalized imitation and generalized matching to sample. *The Behavior Analyst, 26*(1), 155–158. https://doi.org/10.1007/BF03392073

LeBlanc, L. A., Esch, J., Sidener, T. M., & Firth, A. M. (2006). Behavioral language interventions for children with autism: Comparing applied verbal behavior and naturalistic teaching approaches. *The Analysis of Verbal Behavior, 22*(1), 49–60. https://doi.org/10.1007/BF03393026

MacDuff, G. S., Krantz, P. J., & McClannahan, L. E. (2001). Prompts and prompt-fading strategies for people with autism. In C. E. Maurice, G. E. Green, & R. M. Foxx (Eds.), *Making a difference: Behavioral intervention for autism* (pp. 37-50). Pro-Ed.

Meichenbaum, D. H., & Goodman, J. (1971). Training impulsive children to talk to themselves: A means of developing self-control. *Journal of Abnormal Psychology, 77*(2). https://doi.org/10.1037/h0030773

Michael, J. (1993). Establishing operations. *The Behavior Analyst, 16*(2), 191–206. https://doi.org/10.1007/BF03392623

Miltenberger, R. (2015). *Behavior modification: Principles and procedures*. Cengage Learning.

Ribes-Inesta, E. (2000). Instructions, rules, and abstraction: A misconstrued relation. *Behavior and Philosophy, 28*, 41–55.

Sidman, M., Willson-Morris, M., & Kirk, B. (1986). Matching-to-sample procedures and the development of equivalence relations: The role of naming. *Analysis and Intervention in Developmental Disabilities, 6*(1-2), 1–19. https://doi.org/10.1016/0270-4684(86)90003-0

Skinner, B. F. (1957). *Verbal behavior.* Appleton-Century-Crofts.

Smith, T. (2001). Discrete trial training in the treatment of autism. *Focus on Autism and Other Developmental Disabilities, 16*(2), 86–92. https://doi.org/10.1177/108835760101600

Stokes, T. F., & Baer, D. M. (1977). An implicit technology of generalization. *Journal of Applied Behavior Analysis, 10*, 349–367. https://doi.org/10.1901/jaba.1977.10-349

Stokes, T. F., & Osnes, P. G. (1989). An operant pursuit of generalization. *Behavior Therapy, 20*(3), 337–355. https://doi.org/10.1016/S0005-7894(89)80054-1

Striefel, S. (1974). *Behavior modification: Teaching a child to imitate.* Pro-Ed.

Tarbox, J., Zuckerman, C. K., Bishop, M. R., Olive, M. L., & O'Hora, D. P. (2011). Rule-governed behavior: Teaching a preliminary repertoire of rule-following to children with autism. *The Analysis of Verbal Behavior, 27*(1), 125–139. https://doi.org/10.1007/BF03393096

Terrace, H. S. (1963). Errorless discrimination learning in the pigeon: Effects of chlorpromazine and imipramine. *Science, 140*(3564), 318–319. https://doi.org/10.1126/science.140.3564.318

Wolery, M., & Gast, D. L. (1984). Effective and efficient procedures for the transfer of stimulus control. *Topics in Early Childhood Special Education, 4*(3), 52–77. https://doi.org/10.1177/027112148400400305

Selecting and Implementing Interventions

Behavior analysts must not only be familiar with behavior-change procedures, but they must also be able to appropriately select and implement them to effectively change socially significant behavior. The research literature supports the practice of using assessment data to strategically match interventions to problems of behavior, as well as the need for implementing interventions with integrity. Through the precise selection and delivery of interventions, behavior analysts can maximize outcomes for their clients. The purpose of this chapter will be to provide an essential review of Task List items H-1 through H-9, which specifically relate to selecting and implementing behavior-change interventions.

▶ LEARNING OBJECTIVES

The following Task List items related to selecting and implementing interventions (H-1 through H-9) serve as the learning objectives of this chapter:

H-1 State intervention goals in observable and measurable terms.

H-2 Identify potential interventions based on assessment results and the best available scientific evidence.

H-3 Recommend intervention goals and strategies based on such factors as client preferences, supporting environments, risks, constraints, and social validity.

H-4 When a target behavior is to be decreased, select an acceptable alternative behavior to be established or increased.

H-5 Plan for possible unwanted effects when using reinforcement, extinction, and punishment procedures.

H-6 Monitor client progress and treatment integrity.

H-7 Make data-based decisions about the effectiveness of the intervention and the need for treatment revision.

H-8 Make data-based decisions about the need for ongoing services.

H-9 Collaborate with others who support and/or provide services to clients.

▶ TASK LIST ITEM H-1

The objective of this Task List item is to state intervention goals in observable and measurable terms.

Intervention goals must be stated in observable and measurable terms to allow for the accurate measurement of behavior change. To do this, behavior analysts must be able to (a) define target behaviors and (b) set criteria for behavior change.

DEFINING TARGET BEHAVIORS

An intervention goal may target a behavior that is functionally or topographically defined. The definitions should be (a) objective, (b) clear, and (c) complete.

Objective

This means the definition refers to observable aspects of the behavior (and environment, when applicable).

Clear

This means the definition presents with sufficient detail, leaving no room for confusion or doubt.

Complete

This means the definition accurately and concisely describes the target behavior, allowing for discrimination between occurrences and nonoccurrences.

ADDITIONAL NOTE(S)

Function-based definitions describe responses in terms of their effect on the environment (e.g., "any behavior that results in X") whereas topography-based definitions describe responses in terms of their form. Develop function-based definitions whenever possible.

SETTING CRITERIA FOR CHANGE

After a target behavior has been defined, there are two basic approaches to setting socially significant goals: (a) evaluate the performance of those who are highly competent in the behavior of interest and then use the normative data to set performance goals for those that are less competent; and (b) manipulate the behavior of interest so that different performance levels are observed and then determine which specific level produces the best results.

The format of a goal statement can include the following components: (a) condition, (b) name of client, (c) behavior to be increased or decreased, (d) criterion, (e) indication of how it will be measured, and (f) date by which it will be achieved.

- ■ *Example* (goal statement): After recess, when asked to complete independent writing tasks (condition), Sam (name of client) will remain seated at his desk (behavior to be increased) at least 80% of the time (criterion) as measured by interval recording data (indication of how it will be measured) by 6/15/2023 (date by which it will be achieved).

▶ TASK LIST ITEM H-2

The objective of this Task List item is to identify potential interventions based on assessment results and the best available scientific evidence.

The assessment process can provide an individualized client profile that informs intervention planning, including the selection of specific intervention strategies.

ASSESSMENT RESULTS

This refers to information about (a) the client's level of functioning (e.g., performance in communication skills), (b) the client's response to stimuli (i.e., preferences, reinforcers, and punishers), and (c) environmental variables maintaining behavior learned from indirect and/or direct assessment methods used. See Task List item C-2 for a review of direct and indirect measures of behavior. With assessment results in hand, consider antecedent and consequent intervention strategies when the goal is to (a) strengthen, maintain, or teach a new behavior; or (b) weaken a behavior.

When the Goal Is to Strengthen, Maintain, or Teach a New Behavior

Various strategies are employed to strengthen, maintain, or teach a new behavior. See Task List items under Behavior-Change Procedures (G-1 to G-13, and G-17 to G-22) for a review of relevant strategies.

When the Goal Is to Weaken Behavior

Use extinction to decrease the target behavior. This should be combined with reinforcement to strengthen desired/alternative behavior. Instructions/rules and punishment procedures may also be employed. See Task List items under Behavior-Change Procedures (G-2, G-6, and G-14 to G-16) for a review of relevant strategies.

ADDITIONAL NOTE(S)

Selected procedures must be conceptually consistent with behavioral principles.

BEST AVAILABLE SCIENTIFIC EVIDENCE

Refer to the scientific literature and consider its relevance and certainty.

Relevance

This refers to the extent to which the evidence corresponds to the problem in terms of (a) client characteristics, (b) the assessments and procedures used, (c) functions of behavior and expected outcomes, and (d) the context in which intervention is delivered.

Certainty

This refers to the extent to which the evidence supports the use of a procedure and rules out alternative explanations. It is based on two factors: (a) the methodological rigor of the evidence and (b) consistency in replication of outcomes.

Strategies for identifying evidence to guide intervention selection decisions include searching for and reviewing (a) systematic reviews, (b) narrative reviews, (c) best-practice guides, and (d) empirically supported practice guides of potential interventions.

ADDITIONAL NOTE(S)

Sometimes, the available scientific evidence lacks relevance and/or certainty, and behavior analysts will need to make selection decisions based on limited evidence. If this is the case, there will be an increased reliance on progress monitoring to determine whether any intervention is effective for a client. Behavior analysts must also aim to minimize risk of harm to the client, prioritize reinforcement procedures, and consider other relevant factors (e.g., risks, benefits, client preferences, feasibility, cost-effectiveness) when identifying potential interventions.

▶ TASK LIST ITEM H-3

The objective of this Task List item is to recommend intervention goals and strategies based on such factors as client preferences, supporting environments, risks, constraints, and social validity.

Behavior analysts consider client preferences, supporting environments, risks, constraints, and social validity when recommending intervention goals and procedures.

CLIENT PREFERENCES

When appropriate, collaborate with the client and/or caregivers on the selection of intervention goals and procedures. If the procedures are to be delivered by caregivers, take care to recommend those that caregivers can actually implement. In the event a client is unable or unwilling to clarify their preferences, maintain sensitivity to what may be the client's preference and adjust accordingly as indications of their preferences become known.

SUPPORTING ENVIRONMENTS

Select goals and procedures that are appropriate for the level of support available in the environment where treatment is to occur. There are a wide variety of environmental variables to consider, including physical space, materials, staffing, and abilities of individuals implementing the procedures.

RISKS

Take care in selecting goals and procedures that maximize benefits to the client and minimize, if not entirely eliminate, undesirable outcomes.

CONSTRAINTS

When developing intervention goals and procedures, consider factors that may inhibit successful implementation of a treatment program.

SOCIAL VALIDITY

Develop goals and procedures that target socially significant behaviors and are acceptable to clients. Also consider the social value of behavior change.

▶ TASK LIST ITEM H-4

The objective of this Task List item is to, when a target behavior is to be decreased, select an acceptable alternative behavior to be established or increased.

When a problem behavior is targeted for reduction, consider supplementing reduction contingencies with reinforcement contingencies designed to support its decrease.

Select an acceptable alternative behavior that is (a) already in the client's behavioral repertoire, (b) within their current abilities, and (c) less effortful than the problem behavior.

It is also important to consider the maintaining consequences (i.e., function) of the problem behavior. If the function is acceptable as a reinforcer, then an alternative replacement behavior that produces the same consequences may be selected. If the function is unacceptable as a reinforcer, then an alternative behavior that does not serve as a "replacement" (i.e., does not produce the same consequences) may be selected.

- *Example* (function that is typically acceptable as a reinforcer): Social attention from caregivers
- *Example* (function that is unacceptable as a reinforcer): Effects of fire on flammable materials

ADDITIONAL NOTE(S)

If the problem behavior is severe, occurs constantly or frequently, and has a significant impact on the environment, consider an alternative behavior that is incompatible with the problem behavior.

▶ TASK LIST ITEM H-5

The objective of this Task List item is to plan for possible unwanted effects when using reinforcement, extinction, and punishment procedures.

When using reinforcement, extinction, and punishment procedures, behavior analysts must consider and plan for the possibility of unwanted effects.

REINFORCEMENT

Possible unwanted effects resulting from reinforcement-based procedures include:

- suppress the desired response
- not be feasible for a client with little to no learning history with the reinforcement contingency

- increase rate of problem behavior and decrease rate of other desirable behavior
- evoke aggression in others
- result in lower than baseline responding once reinforcement has been removed
- result in too much of the desired behavior

EXTINCTION

Possible unwanted effects resulting from extinction procedures include:

- evoke emotional/aggressive reactions
- initially increase the rate of the problem behavior (i.e., produce an extinction burst)
- initially increase the magnitude of the problem behavior
- result in the reappearance of the problem behavior after it has been reduced/eliminated (i.e., spontaneous recovery)
- result in the reappearance of a previously extinguished problem behavior that was replaced by the targeted problem behavior

PUNISHMENT

Possible unwanted effects resulting from punishment-based procedures include:

- evoke emotional/aggressive reactions
- evoke escape/avoidance
- produce behavioral contrast effects (i.e., change to the response rate of the problem behavior may increase in other contexts)
- involve modeling of undesirable behavior
- be overused as it produces negative reinforcement for the individual using it

PLANNING FOR UNWANTED EFFECTS

General recommendations for planning for the possibility of unwanted effects include:

- Consider the possibility of unwanted effects that may interfere with an individual client's treatment.
- Monitor the target behavior(s) across contexts. If unwanted effects emerge, take appropriate actions to address them.
- Provide relevant individuals across contexts with necessary information/training to support the client's treatment.
- Progress monitor and adjust treatment as needed to minimize/eliminate risk and maximize benefit for the client.

▶ TASK LIST ITEM H-6

The objective of this Task List item is to monitor client progress and treatment integrity.

MONITORING CLIENT PROGRESS

Behavior analysts monitor client progress to track and evaluate responsiveness to intervention as evidenced by behavior change over time. To do this, we can follow an eight-step process that involves (a) clearly operationalizing the behavior; (b) developing a progress monitoring plan; (c) selecting/creating data collection tools (i.e., measurement system); (d) collecting baseline data and defining goals; (e) setting intervention goals; (f) collecting progress monitoring data; (g) analyzing, summarizing, and visually presenting the data; and (h) evaluating and utilizing data for decision-making.

Clearly Operationalize the Behavior

Describe the client's target behavior in observable and measurable terms (e.g., frequency rate, duration, latency, topography), and write definitions that are objective, clear, and complete. Develop an operational definition that enables complete information about the behavior's occurrence and nonoccurrence to be gathered and intervention effectiveness to be accurately evaluated. See Task List item C-1 for a review of establishing operational definitions of behavior.

Develop a Progress Monitoring Plan

Prior to initiating the intervention, decide how client progress in the intervention will be evaluated and make a plan for data collection. Determine the type of data (e.g., frequency or rate, percentage, duration, latency) that will be collected, who will collect it, when and where it will be collected, how often it will be collected, and how often the data will be reviewed. Recall that behavior can be measured in terms of occurrence, time, and form and strength. See Task List items under Measurement, Data Display, and Interpretation (C-3 to C-5) for a review of measuring behavior in terms of occurrence, temporal dimensions, form, and strength.

Select or Create Data Collection Tools

Behavior analysts employ a variety of evidence-based methods for sampling procedures and collecting progress monitoring data, including direct measures, indirect measures, and product measures. See Task List item C-2 for a review of the distinction between these measures, and item C-7 for a review of sampling procedures. Select a progress monitoring tool that is F.R.E.D.

- Flexible, able to assess the behavior across all contexts in which it is exhibited.
- Repeatable, able to be administered repeatedly within a brief time span.
- Efficient for interventionists to use.
- Defensible as it provides a reliable and valid measure of the client's behavior and is sensitive to client responsiveness to intervention.

Collect Baseline Data and Define Goals

Collect baseline data to determine the client's current level of functioning vis-a-vis the target behavior (i.e., rate/frequency or severity of behavior) prior to intervention. Conduct observations of the target behavior at a time and in a setting when the behavior is likely to occur. Observe the client for a minimum of 15 to 20 minutes on, at minimum, three to five instances to ensure the behavioral trend observed is stable. If the data from three observations are similar, use those three data points to describe the level of current performance. Adhere to any guidelines on the number of times baseline data should be collected provided by the particular assessment tool. Graph the client's baseline data to compare with data from subsequent observations.

Set Intervention Goals or Benchmarks

Use baseline data to determine appropriate and measurable goals or benchmarks (e.g., rate of increase or decrease in behavior) for the client. Intervention goals should be based on the client's present level of performance, the targeted level of performance for the client, and the date by which the client is expected to achieve the targeted level of performance. See Task List items H-1 and H-3.

Collect Progress Monitoring Data

Wait to initiate data collection until after the intervention is being fully implemented. Collect progress monitoring data during the intervention phase using the predetermined progress monitoring tool to repeatedly administer probes. Again, observation of behavior should be conducted at a time and in a setting when the behavior is likely to occur. Ensure that sufficient progress monitoring data are collected to develop an accurate and reliable representation of the behavior and the degree to which change is evident. Collect progress monitoring data as frequently as needed to detect and document behavior change.

Analyze, Summarize, Visually Represent the Data

Securely store client progress monitoring data (e.g., in a password-protected spreadsheet) and generate graphs to document and analyze progress monitoring data collection. Visually inspect summarized data and graphs and evaluate the results against the client's rate of progress toward achieving the predetermined goal. See Task List items C-10 for a review of graphing data, and C-11 for a review of interpreting data.

Evaluate and Utilize Data for Decision-Making

First, assess fidelity of implementation of the intervention; if the intervention was not implemented with fidelity, refrain from altering the intervention until intervention is implemented with fidelity. Based on the progress monitoring data collected, determine whether the client is responding to the intervention and adequate progress toward the goal(s) is being made.

- If progress is being made and the gap between the trend line and the goal line is closing, then continue the intervention. Determine how long the client must consistently exhibit the target behavior to begin fading the intervention.
- If insufficient progress is being made, then modify or intensify the intervention and/or assess fidelity of the implementation of the intervention.
- If sufficient progress has been made and the client has reached their goal(s), then fade and discontinue the intervention.

MONITORING TREATMENT INTEGRITY

Behavior analysts monitor treatment integrity to ensure interventions are consistently implemented precisely as designed. Implementing an intervention with treatment integrity carefully avoids administration of extraneous, confounding variables which, in turn, enables one to correctly infer the relationship between an intervention and a client's behavior, whether behavior is changed or unchanged.

Best practices for monitoring and ensuring treatment integrity include:

- To avoid experimenter bias, implement interventions in a manner that does not privilege one treatment condition over another (e.g., the baseline condition over the treatment condition).
- To avoid treatment drift, consistently deliver all elements of the treatment throughout the duration of the intervention.
- Develop a comprehensive, precise, clear, and explicit operational definition of the treatment procedures across the four dimensions of a treatment; that is, operationally define what should be said (verbal dimension) and/or physically done (physical dimension), when (temporal dimension), and where (spatial dimension).
- Simplify the intervention as much as possible to make it easy to implement.
- Standardize the intervention to the greatest degree possible. This could involve creating materials to guide those implementing the intervention (e.g., script of the procedures, a manual, a video) and/or automating the intervention using, for example, a video, app, or learning management system.
- Provide the individual who will be implementing the intervention with sufficient training, modeling, practice, feedback, and supervision in the skills and knowledge they need to competently implement the intervention with integrity.
- Collect, analyze, and review treatment integrity data regularly throughout intervention implementation.

PRACTICE QUESTION

Zaynab, a BCBA, is training Adam, a behavior technician, to implement a new behavior-change procedure for a 6-year-old client in the home setting. Zaynab breaks down the procedure into five discrete steps and, during an observation of Adam in session with the client, records data on the steps Adam did and did not complete successfully. After the observation session, Zaynab provides vocal and written feedback to Adam about his performance. Which of the following best describes the purpose of the data collection procedure Zaynab employed?

A. To assess client progress and performance on the targeted skill
B. To determine the environmental events affecting the behavior technician's performance
C. To evaluate treatment integrity
D. To calculate interobserver agreement

Before moving on to the next section for the solution, we recommend that you provide a brief explanation for the answer option you selected here:

_____

_____

When you're ready, move on to the next section for the solution!

Practice Question Breakdown

Step 1: Examine the question

The question calls for the identification of the purpose of the data collection procedure that Zaynab was described using (breaking down the steps of a procedure to be implemented by a behavior technician, and recording which steps were completed and which were missed).

Step 2: Analyze the answer options

A. Zaynab is recording data on the behavior technician's performance, not the client's performance. This answer option is a distractor.
B. In order for there to be any sort of evaluation of the effects of environmental events on personnel performance, data on these antecedent and consequent events must be gathered. Zaynab only recorded whether the steps of a procedure occurred. This answer option is a distractor.
C. Recording whether the steps of a procedure occurred is a method of collecting treatment integrity data. This information informs behavior analysts about the extent to which a given procedure is implemented as intended. This just might be the answer!
D. Interobserver agreement indicates the level of agreement between two or more independent observers recording the same event. This answer option is a distractor.

Step 3: Select the best answer

Among the four answer options presented, answer C (to evaluate treatment integrity) appears to be the best answer.

▶ TASK LIST ITEM H-7

The objective of this Task List item is to make data-based decisions about the effectiveness of the intervention and the need for treatment revision.

Behavior analysts adhere to the evidence-based practice model of professional decision-making. This means they rely on the "best available evidence" coupled with clinical expertise to determine whether an intervention is effective and if a treatment needs to be revised.

Behavior analysts examine and interpret graphed data when determining the effectiveness of an intervention and need for treatment revision. See Task List item C-11 for a review of graph interpretation.

Table 10.1 Interpretation of graphed data for determining intervention effectiveness

If the trendline shows that the behavior is . . .	Then . . .
Being performed at a level that meets or exceeds the criterion for mastery	Monitor its maintenance and move to the next target.
Improving at the expected rate	Continue as is.
Improving at a lower rate than expected	Modify prompts and/or add instructional time.
Not improving	Check implementation fidelity. If fidelity is adequate, consider breaking the targeted skill down further. If fidelity is inadequate, provide additional coaching/feedback to implementers.
Variable	Check implementation fidelity. If fidelity is adequate, modify the reinforcer and/or schedule or reinforcement. If fidelity is inadequate, provide additional coaching/feedback to implementers.

ADDITIONAL NOTE(S)

If the last 10 data points show little to no improvement, discontinuation of the intervention may be considered.

▶ TASK LIST ITEM H-8

The objective of this Task List item is to make data-based decisions about the need for ongoing services.
Determining a client's need for ongoing services is a broader question than whether or not a particular intervention should be ended and, consequently, involves a multidimensional assessment of needs and progress. Behavior analysts rely on clinical expertise and adhere to relevant ethical guidelines when determining whether services remain clinically or medically necessary. Factors to consider include the client's progress toward treatment goals as evidenced by assessment results and other forms of data collection, and the degree to which the client has made socially significant progress.

PROGRESS ON TREATMENT GOALS

Data-based decisions about the need for ongoing services should carefully consider the client's progress on treatment goals as evidenced by assessment results and ongoing progress monitoring data collection. If these data indicate that the client has mastered their treatment goals and made socially significant progress, they may no longer need ongoing services. A client may also be discharged from services if data indicate that the client is not demonstrating progress toward goals over a specified period of time. Ongoing services also may no longer be needed if appropriate standardized assessments no longer indicate that a client meets diagnostic criteria for the disorder the services are treating.

TRANSITION AND DISCHARGE

Behavior analysts incorporate transition and discharge planning into the overall treatment planning process. It is recommended that (a) all relevant individuals are included in the planning process 3 to 6 months before a change in service, and (b) transition and discharge become a regular, ongoing part of the conversation with the client and their support team. All relevant individuals should understand the behavioral targets that, when achieved, indicate there is no longer a need for ongoing services. As such, termination of services should never come as a surprise to the client or their network of support; rather, services should be gradually stepped down, a process that typically requires at least 6 months and involves the titration of services during which services are gradually decreased over time.

ADDITIONAL NOTE(S)

If it is unclear whether services are appropriate or effective for a client, an expert panel of behavior analysts and other relevant professionals should review the treatment program.

▶ TASK LIST ITEM H-9

The objective of this Task List item is to collaborate with others who support and/or provide services to clients.

Behavior analysts collaborate with others to serve clients. See Task List item E-2 (code 2.10) for a review of the ethical standard on collaborating with colleagues.

COLLABORATIVE TEAMING

Collaborative teaming strategies include: (a) developing and using a shared language, (b) employing the same data-collection process, (c) displaying results in an understandable way, and (d) working together to develop and implement a behavior-change program.

Developing and Using a Shared Language

The guiding question for this strategy is, "How do we talk about behavior?" Steps for implementation are: (a) create a list of common terms related to observation, assessment, and intervention; (b) define them with the team; and (c) use those that are understood by all.

Employing the Same Data-Collection Process

The guiding questions for this strategy are, "What type of data is needed?" "Who will collect it?" and "What resources (e.g., data-collection skills, feasible data-collection system) are needed?" Steps for implementation are: (a) determine method of data collection; (b) identify those responsible for collecting data; and (c) identify resources needed for data collection.

Displaying Results in an Understandable Way

The guiding question for this strategy is, "How will assessment results be shared with the team?" Steps for implementation are: (a) graph data (and/or use tables for descriptive data) and (b) use understandable language when discussing the results.

Working Together to Develop and Implement a Behavior-Change Program

The guiding questions for this strategy are, "What is an acceptable intervention?" "Have all team members been involved in the development of the behavior-change program?" and "Have all team members received the necessary training to implement the program?" Steps for implementation are: (a) identify skills to be taught to the client and (b) identify supports and skills needed for team members to successfully implement the program.

In the event another nonbehavioral provider recommends a nonbehavioral treatment, the behavior analyst must determine whether it poses a risk to the safety of the client.

Safety Risk Is Present

If this is the case, directly address the issue with the nonbehavioral provider. Also, if the behavior analyst is unfamiliar with the nonbehavioral treatment, it is recommended that they learn about it and reassesses the risk to safety.

Safety Risk Is Absent

If this is the case, then consider the underlying behavioral principles of the treatment and ask, "Is success possible?" If the answer is "yes" or "no, but it doesn't interfere with the client's goals," then do not address the treatment as an issue. If the answer is "no, but it does interfere with the client's goals," then consider the use of the Checklist for Analyzing Proposed Treatments (CAPT) to determine if the impact to the client is enough to warrant possible confrontation with the nonbehavioral provider.

ADDITIONAL NOTE(S)

Readers are encouraged to seek out further readings on other skills (e.g., business skills, assertiveness, leadership) that contribute to effective collaboration with others.

▶ CONCLUSION

In this chapter, we focused on Task List items related to selecting and implementing interventions. This includes information on developing observable and measurable intervention goals; using assessment results and science to identify potential interventions; tailoring intervention goals and strategies to clients; selecting alternative behaviors; planning for unwanted effects; progress monitoring; making data-based decisions; and collaborative teaming. This chapter's emphasis on selecting and implementing interventions nicely complements Chapter 9's focus on behavior-change procedures.

1. Definitions of behavior should be:

    A. Accurate, clear, and reliable
    B. Attainable, clear, and complete
    C. Clear, complete, and objective
    D. Clear, objective, and valid

2. A function-based definition of behavior will describe the behavior in terms of its:

    A. Effects on the environment
    B. Magnitude
    C. Physical form
    D. Social significance

3. To define a target behavior in objective terms, the definition must:

    A. Be concise
    B. Be function based
    C. Provide sufficient detail, leaving no room for doubt
    D. Refer to observable aspects of the behavior

4. Which of the following is not a necessary component of a behavior goal statement?

    A. Criterion to be met
    B. Date by which it will be achieved
    C. Nonexample of the target behavior
    D. Target behavior to be increased or decreased

5. To set socially significant behavior change goals:

    A. Evaluate the performance of those who are highly competent in the behavior and then use the normative data to set performance goals
    B. Manipulate the behavior so that different performance levels are observed and then determine which specific level produces the best results
    C. A or B
    D. None of the above

6. When assessing the relevance of the scientific evidence, each of the following are considered in relation to the problem of interest except:

    A. Client characteristics
    B. The assessment procedures used
    C. The context in which intervention is delivered
    D. The forms of behavior and expected outcomes

1. C) Clear, complete, and objective

Definitions of behavior should be objective, clear, and complete. The other answer options (accurate, clear, and reliable; attainable, clear, and complete; clear, objective, and valid) include terms used to describe goals or measurement data and function as distractors.

2. A) Effects on the environment

A function-based definition of behavior will describe the behavior in terms of its effects on the environment. The other answer options (magnitude, physical form, social significance) refer to other ways in which behavior can be described and serves as distractors.

3. D) Refer to observable aspects of the behavior

To define a target behavior in objective terms, the definition must refer to observable aspects of the behavior. The other answer options (be concise; be function based; provide sufficient detail, leaving no room for doubt) describe other attributes and function as distractors.

4. C) Nonexample of the target behavior

The criterion to be met, date by which it will be achieved, and target behavior to be increased or decreased are necessary components of a behavior goal statement. Nonexamples of the target behavior are sometimes included in definitions, but they are not a required component of goal statements.

5. C) A or B

Behavior analysts may evaluate the performance of those who are highly competent in the behavior and then use the normative data to set performance goals, or they can manipulate the behavior so that different performance levels are observed and then determine which specific level produces the best results to set socially significant behavior change goals.

6. D) The forms of behavior and expected outcomes

The relevance of the scientific evidence refers to the extent to which it corresponds to the problem of interest in terms of client characteristics; the assessments and procedures used; functions of behavior and expected outcomes, rather than forms of behavior and expected outcomes; and the context in which intervention is delivered.

7. When assessing the certainty of the scientific evidence, each of the following are considered except:

    A. The consistency in replication of the outcomes
    B. The functions of behavior and expected outcomes
    C. The methodological rigor of the evidence
    D. Both B and C

8. Which of the following is an unwanted effect of punishment?

    A. It may be overused as it produces negative reinforcement for the individual using it
    B. It may initially increase the magnitude of the problem behavior
    C. It may initially increase the rate of the problem behavior
    D. It may result in too much of the desired behavior

9. Which of the following is not an unwanted effect of reinforcement?

    A. It may evoke aggression in others
    B. It may not be feasible for a client with little to no learning history with the reinforcement contingency
    C. It may result in the reappearance of a previously extinguished problem behavior that was replaced by the targeted problem behavior
    D. It may suppress the desired response

10. Which of the following is an unwanted effect of extinction?

    A. It may be overused as it produces negative reinforcement for the individual using it
    B. It may initially increase the magnitude of the problem behavior
    C. It may produce behavioral contrast effects
    D. It may result in too much of the desired behavior

11. Sometimes, the available scientific evidence lacks relevance and/or certainty and behavior analysts will need to make selection decisions based on limited evidence. If this is the case, there will be an increased reliance on _____ to determine whether any intervention is effective for a client.

    A. Caregiver interviews
    B. Positive reinforcement-based procedures
    C. Progress monitoring
    D. Standardized testing

12. When monitoring client progress, the first step in this process is to:

    A. Clearly operationalize the behavior
    B. Collect baseline data and define goals
    C. Develop a progress-monitoring plan
    D. Select or create data-collection tools

13. What step in the process of monitoring client progress involves gathering data to determine the current level of the behavior targeted for change?

    A. Clearly operationalize the behavior
    B. Collect baseline data and define goals
    C. Develop a progress-monitoring plan
    D. Select or create data-collection tools

7. B) The functions of behavior and expected outcomes

The functions of behavior and expected outcomes is considered when assessing the relevance of the scientific evidence. The remaining answer options (the consistency in replication of the outcomes, the methodological rigor of the evidence, both B and C) include considerations for assessing the certainty of the scientific evidence and function as distractors.

8. A) It may be overused as it produces negative reinforcement for the individual using it

The overuse of punishment, because it produces negative reinforcement for the individual using it, is a known and unwanted effect of punishment. The other answer options (it may initially increase the magnitude of the problem behavior, it may initially increase the rate of the problem behavior, it may result in too much of the desired behavior) describe unwanted effects of reinforcement or extinction and function as distractors.

9. C) It may result in the reappearance of a previously extinguished problem behavior that was replaced by the targeted problem behavior

The reappearance of a previously extinguished problem behavior that was replaced by the targeted problem behavior is an unwanted effect of extinction. The other answer options (it may evoke aggression in others, it may not be feasible for a client with little to no learning history with the reinforcement contingency, it may suppress the desired response) are unwanted effects of reinforcement and serve as distractors.

10. B) It may initially increase the magnitude of the problem behavior

An initial increase in the magnitude of the problem behavior is an unwanted effect of extinction. The other answer options (it may be overused as it produces negative reinforcement for the individual using it, it may produce behavioral contrast effects, it may result in too much of the desired behavior) describe unwanted effects of reinforcement or punishment and function as distractors.

11. C) Progress monitoring

Sometimes, the available scientific evidence lacks relevance and/or certainty and behavior analysts will need to make selection decisions based on limited evidence. If this is the case, there will be an increased reliance on progress monitoring to determine whether any intervention is effective for a client. The other answer options (caregiver interviews, positive reinforcement-based procedures, standardized testing) do not accurately fit into the statement and serve as distractors.

12. A) Clearly operationalize the behavior

When monitoring client progress, the first step in this process is to clearly operationalize the behavior. The other answer options (collect baseline data and define goals, develop a progress-monitoring plan, select or create data-collection tools) describe later steps in the process and function as distractors.

13. B) Collect baseline data and define goals

Collecting baseline data and defining goals involve gathering data to determine the current level of the behavior targeted for change. The other answer options (clearly operationalize the behavior, develop a progress-monitoring plan, select or create data-collection tools) refer to other steps in the process for monitoring client progress and serve as distractors.

14. Which of the following is used to inform the development of initial intervention goals?

    A. Baseline data

    B. Intervention fidelity data

    C. Progress monitoring data

    D. None of the above

15. When evaluating progress-monitoring data, it is observed that the gap between the trend line and the goal line is closing. This suggests:

    A. The client is making progress

    B. The client is not making progress

    C. The intervention should be modified

    D. None of the above

16. When evaluating progress-monitoring data, it is observed that the gap between the trend line and the goal line is closing. This suggests:

    A. The intervention should be discontinued

    B. The intervention should be modified

    C. The intervention should continue

    D. None of the above

17. If progress-monitoring data reveal sufficient progress has been made and the client has reached their goal, then:

    A. Assess the fidelity of the intervention's implementation

    B. Continue the intervention to support the maintenance of the behavior change

    C. Fade and discontinue the intervention

    D. Intensify the intervention for further gains

18. Recommended practices for monitoring and ensuring treatment integrity include each of the following except:

    A. Collect, analyze, and review treatment integrity data regularly

    B. Deliver most of the elements of the treatment as consistently as possible throughout the duration of the intervention

    C. Simplify the intervention as much as possible

    D. Provide the implementers of the intervention with sufficient training and support

14. A) Baseline data

Baseline data are used to inform the development of initial intervention goals. The other answer options (intervention fidelity data, progress monitoring data, none of the above), two of which identify types of data gathered during treatment, function as distractors.

15. A) The client is making progress

The closing of the gap between the trend line and the goal line is an indication of progress. The other answer options (the client is not making progress, the intervention should be modified, none of the above) do not provide an accurate interpretation of the described data and serve as distractors.

16. C) The intervention should continue

The closing of the gap between the trend line and the goal line, which offers evidence of progress, indicates that the intervention should continue. The other answer options (the intervention should be discontinued, the intervention should be modified, none of the above) do not describe recommended courses of action and function as distractors.

17. C) Fade and discontinue the intervention

If progress-monitoring data reveal sufficient progress has been made and the client has reached their goal, then the recommended next step is to fade and discontinue the intervention. The other answer options (assess the fidelity of the intervention's implementation, continue the intervention to support the maintenance of the behavior change, intensify the intervention for further gains) do not describe recommended courses of action and function as distractors.

18. B) Deliver most of the elements of the treatment as consistently as possible throughout the duration of the intervention

The aim is to consistently implement all elements of the treatment, rather than just some of them, throughout the time in which it is to be implemented to avoid treatment drift. The other answer options (collect, analyze, and review treatment integrity data regularly; simplify the intervention as much as possible; provide the implementers of the intervention with sufficient training and support) are recommended practices for monitoring and ensuring treatment integrity and serve as distractors.

BIBLIOGRAPHY

Balsam, P. D., & Bondy, A. S. (1983). The negative side effects of reward. *Journal of Applied Behavior Analysis, 16*(3), 283–296. https://doi.org/10.1901/jaba.1983.16-283

Behavior Analyst Certification Board. (2012). *Guidelines, health plan coverage of applied behavior analysis treatment for autism spectrum disorder.* Author.

Behavior Analyst Certification Board. (2017). *BCBA task list* (5th ed.). http://ies.ed.gov/ncee/wwc/pdf/wwc_scd.pdf

Brodhead, M. T. (2015). Maintaining professional relationships in an interdisciplinary setting: Strategies for navigating nonbehavioral treatment recommendations for individuals with autism. *Behavior Analysis in Practice, 8*(1), 70–78. https://doi.org/10.1007/s40617-015-0042-7

Brodhead, M. T., & Truckenmiller, A. (2021). Proof-of-concept evaluation of a decision-making algorithm. *Behavior Analysis: Research and Practice, 21*(1), 84–89.

Christ, T. J., Riley-Tillman, T. C., & Chafouleas, S. M. (2009). Foundation for the development and use of direct behavior rating (DBR) to assess and evaluate student behavior. *Assessment for Effective Intervention, 34*, 201–213. https://doi.org/10.1177/1534508409340390

Cipani, E., & Schock, K. M. (2010). *Functional behavioral assessment, diagnosis, and treatment: A complete system for education and mental health settings.* Springer Publishing Company.

Cooper, J. O., Heron, T. E., & Heward, W. L. (2020). *Applied behavior analysis.* Pearson Education.

Crone, D. A., Hawken, L. S., & Horner, R. H. (2010). *Responding to problem behavior in schools: The behavior education program.* Guilford Press.

Deno, S. L. (1997). Whether thou goest… Perspectives on progress monitoring. *Issues in Educating Students With Disabilities, 16*, 213–235.

Fuchs, L. S., & Fuchs, D. (2001). *What is scientifically-based research on progress monitoring?* National Center on Student Progress Monitoring.

Johnston, J. M. (2006). "Replacing" problem behavior: An analysis of tactical alternatives. *The Behavior Analyst, 29*(1), 1–11. https://doi.org/10.1007/BF03392114

Johnston, J. M., & Pennypacker, H. S. (1993). *Strategies and tactics of behavioral research* (2nd ed.). Erlbaum.

Kipfmiller, K. J., Brodhead, M. T., Wolfe, K., LaLonde, K., Sipila, E. S., Bak, M. S., & Fisher, M. H. (2019). Training front-line employees to conduct visual analysis using a clinical decision-making model. *Journal of Behavioral Education, 28*(3), 301–322. https://doi.org/10.1007/s10864-018-09318-1

Moulton, S., von der Embse, N., Kilgus, S., & Drymond, M. (2019). Building a better behavior progress monitoring tool using maximally efficient items. *School Psychology, 34*(6), 695. https://doi.org/10.1037/spq0000334

Sanetti, L. M. H., Kratochwill, T. R., Collier-Meek, M. A., & Long, A. C. J. (2014). *PRIME: Planning realistic implementation and maintenance by educators.* Neag School of Education, University of Connecticut.

Slocum, T. A., Detrich, R., Wilczynski, S. M., Spencer, T. D., Lewis, T., & Wolfe, K. (2014). The evidence-based practice of applied behavior analysis. *The Behavior Analyst, 37*(1), 41–56. https://doi.org/10.1007/s40614-014-0005-2

Wahman, C. L., Light-Shriner, C. L., & Pizzella, D. M. (2020). Effective teaming to bridge support for children with challenging behavior. *Young Exceptional Children.* Advance online publication.

Wolf, M. M. (1978). Social validity: The case for subjective measurement or how applied behavior analysis is finding its heart. *Journal of Applied Behavior Analysis, 11*(2), 203–214. https://doi.org/10.1901/jaba.1978.11-203

Wolfe, K., McCammon, M. N., LeJeune, L. M., & Holt, A. K. (2021). Training preservice practitioners to make data-based instructional decisions. *Journal of Behavioral Education*, 1–20. https://doi.org/10.1007/s10864-021-09439-0

Personnel Supervision and Management

"The field of behavior analysis relies heavily on supervision to shape and maintain the skills of professionals" (Sellers et al., 2016). Behavior analysts are frequently engaged in the work of supervising direct support staff to ensure clients receive high quality services. To effectively provide supervision, they must be able to competently train supervisees, support them in their work, and motivate them to perform at their very best. Unlike the last version (i.e., 4th edition) of the Task List, the current iteration (i.e., 5th edition) includes an entire section focused on the development of the skills required for effective supervision. The purpose of this chapter will be to provide an essential review of Task List items I-1 through I-8, which specifically relate to personnel supervision and management.

> ## ▶ LEARNING OBJECTIVES
>
> The following Task List items related to supervision and management (I-1 through I-8) will serve as the learning objectives of this chapter:
>
> I-1   State the reasons for using behavior-analytic supervision and the potential risks of ineffective supervision (e.g., poor client outcomes, poor supervisee performance).
>
> I-2   Establish clear performance expectations for the supervisor and supervisee.
>
> I-3   Select supervision goals based on an assessment of the supervisee's skills.
>
> I-4   Train personnel to competently perform assessment and intervention procedures.
>
> I-5   Use performance monitoring, feedback, and reinforcement systems.
>
> I-6   Use a functional assessment approach (e.g., performance diagnostics) to identify variables affecting personnel performance.
>
> I-7   Use function-based strategies to improve personnel performance.
>
> I-8   Evaluate the effects of supervision (e.g., on client outcomes, on supervisee repertoires).

▶ TASK LIST ITEM I-1

The objective of this Task List item is to state the reasons for using behavior-analytic supervision and the potential risks of ineffective supervision (e.g., poor client outcomes, poor supervisee performance).

REASONS FOR USING BEHAVIOR-ANALYTIC SUPERVISION

- It is necessary for the delivery of quality behavior-analytic services.
- It contributes to the professional development of supervisees and supervisors.
- It is supported as best practice by the field's professional literature.
- It is required per the Professional and Ethical Compliance Code for behavior analysts.

POTENTIAL RISKS OF INEFFECTIVE SUPERVISION

- It can degrade the quality of behavior-analytic services.
- Supervisees may develop faulty or inadequate professional skills, resulting in poor performance.

- It can negatively impact client outcomes.
- It can stunt the growth of the field of behavior analysis.
- It can result in actionable violations of the Ethics Code.

▶ TASK LIST ITEM I-2

The objective of this Task List item is to establish clear performance expectations for the supervisor and supervisee.

Performance expectations for the supervisor and supervisee should be clearly communicated at the outset of a supervisory relationship.

When the supervisory relationship is between a qualified supervisor and a trainee acquiring fieldwork experience to meet Behavior Analyst Certification Board (BACB) certification requirements, a *supervision contract* must be established. The supervision contract is a written document that describes the supervisor–supervisee relationship and expectations for both parties.

For supervisors and supervisees, expectations may include but are not limited to:

- reviewing the BACB experience standards
- adhering to the Ethics Code
- participating in supervision activities
- following the supervision schedule
- completing and maintaining required documentation

A strategy for enhancing a supervisee's professional behavior and providing the supervisor with an opportunity to better plan for an upcoming supervision meeting is to have the supervisee provide a draft agenda 24 hours in advance.

---

1. Check-in (5 min)
2. Discuss behavior analytic activities in the past week (10 min)
3. Review progress on assignments and identify any problems along with possible solutions (15 min)
4. Discuss/practice previously reviewed or new competencies from the Task List (15 min)
5. Review feedback on performance (5 min)
6. Complete supervision documentation (5 min)
7. Final questions/comments (5 min)

Figure 11.1 Example of a draft agenda.

The supervisor can also set expectations for note-taking, deadlines for assigned activities, and systems for managing supervision documentation.

PRACTICE QUESTION

You are a new trainee, working at an in-home applied behavior analysis (ABA) agency. As part of this job, you will be acquiring fieldwork experience under the supervision of a Board Certified Behavior Analyst (BCBA) to meet BACB certification requirements. You meet with your new supervisor to establish a supervision contract that outlines the expectations of the professional relationship. What specific expectations are important to include in this written document?

A. Adhering to the Ethics Code
B. Following the supervision schedule
C. Completing and maintaining required documentation
D. All of the above

Before moving on to the next section for the solution, we recommend that you provide a brief explanation for the answer option you selected here:

_____

_____

When you're ready, move on to the next section for the solution!

Practice Question Breakdown

Step 1: Examine the question

The question calls for you to examine a supervision contract that outlines the expectations of the professional relationship between you and your BCBA supervisor. You are asked to identify the specific expectations that should be included in the written document.

Step 2: Analyze the answer options

A. This answer is an important expectation. Reviewing, discussing, and adhering to the Ethics Code for Behavior Analysts are essential to the professional requirements of the job and should be included in all supervision contracts.

B. This answer is an important expectation. Following a set supervision schedule from the initiation of the supervision relationship allocates time for this important activity to occur and should be included in all supervision contracts.

C. This answer is an important expectation. Completing and maintaining required documentation for supervision is not only important to ensure your supervisee is progressing and learning new skills, but also to meet BACB certification requirements.

D. This answer includes all of the answer options, which refer to important expectations that should be written into all supervision contracts. This is it!

Step 3: Select the best answer

Among the four answer options presented, answer D (all of the above) appears to be the best answer.

▶ TASK LIST ITEM I-3

The objective of this Task List item is to select supervision goals based on an assessment of the supervisee's skills.

Assessment of the supervisee's skills should precede the selection of supervision goals.

ASSESSMENT OF THE SUPERVISEE'S SKILLS

Methods for evaluating a supervisee's skills can include (a) self-assessment, (b) quizzes and interviews, and (c) review of permanent products and direct observation.

Self-Assessment

This involves having the supervisee rate their level of competence for each job and/or Task List item skill.

Quizzes and Interviews

Quizzes (i.e., brief tests of knowledge) and interviews (i.e., questions regarding the supervisee's level of competence across skills) can be presented orally or in written form to verify self-reported knowledge-based skills. Quizzes can include activities such as role-plays and in-vivo practice sessions.

Review of Permanent Products and Direct Observation

A review of permanent products (i.e., work samples) and direct observation can be used to verify self-reported performance-based skills. If a supervisee's skills can be sufficiently evaluated through a review of permanent products, direct observation may not be necessary. Direct observation can be used for skills that cannot be evaluated through other means (i.e., quizzes, interviews, or review of permanent products).

ADDITIONAL NOTE(S)

It is recommended that the assessments described previously are introduced in the sequence presented (i.e., self-assessment first, then quizzes/interviews, then observation and review of permanent products).

Several other methods discussed in the literature include: (a) reviewing the syllabi of relevant coursework completed by the supervisee, (b) meeting with the supervisee's previous supervisors to discuss the supervisee's skills, and (c) reviewing the Task List with the supervisee and using the document as a checklist of items mastered or not yet mastered.

SELECTION OF SUPERVISION GOALS

The baseline performance data (i.e., results of the assessment of the supervisee's skills) are used to set achievable goals. See Task List item H-1 for a review of stating goals in observable and measurable terms. Both long-term and short-term goals should be set.

Long-Term Goals

These are goals that are to be met after an extended period of time (e.g., 3 or 4 months). It is recommended that the following are considered when developing long-term goals: (a) the Task List items relevant to the supervisee's role, (b) their performance across those Task List items, and (c) the expected needs of the agency.

Short-Term Goals

These goals, which follow the determination of long-term goals, are to be met with a short period of time (e.g., 1 month). It is recommended that the following are considered when developing short-term goals: (a) the immediate needs of the agency and (b) the supervisee's ability to meet them.

▶ TASK LIST ITEM I-4

The objective of this Task List item is to train personnel to competently perform assessment and intervention procedures.

For a review of assessment and intervention procedures, please refer to Task List items under Behavior Assessment (F-1 to F-9) and Behavior-Change Procedures (G-1 to G-22). Use *behavioral skills training* (BST) to teach personnel to competently perform assessment and intervention procedures.

The six steps to BST include (a) describe the target skill, (b) provide a written description, (c) demonstrate the target skill, (d) require the supervisee to practice the target skill, (e) provide feedback during practice, and (f) repeat the last two steps until mastery is achieved.

DESCRIBE THE TARGET SKILL

This involves explaining why a skill is to be targeted and then behaviorally defining it.

PROVIDE A WRITTEN DESCRIPTION

This involves providing the explanation of why a skill is to be targeted and the behavioral definition of it in written form. It is recommended that the supervisee be given time to ask questions.

DEMONSTRATE THE TARGET SKILL

This can involve role-playing activities, video models, and/or in-situ demonstrations with a client. During role-plays, the supervisor may stop at certain points to describe what is being done and why, or wait until the end of the role-play to provide feedback.

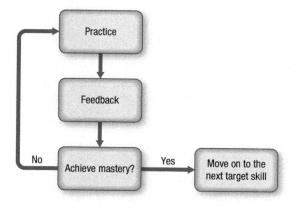

Figure 11.2 Behavioral skills training process.

REQUIRE THE SUPERVISEE TO PRACTICE THE TARGET SKILL

This involves rehearsal of the targeted skill.

PROVIDE FEEDBACK DURING PRACTICE

This involves providing supportive feedback (i.e., describing what was done correctly) and corrective feedback (i.e., specifying what was done incorrectly and providing instruction on how to do it correctly).

REPEAT THE LAST TWO STEPS UNTIL MASTERY IS ACHIEVED

Repeat step 4 (require the supervisee to practice the target skill) and step 5 (provide feedback during practice) until the skill meets the required performance criterion.

▶ TASK LIST ITEM I-5

The objective of this Task List item is to use performance monitoring, feedback, and reinforcement systems.

As supervisors, behavior analysts must (a) monitor the performance of supervisees and (b) provide timely feedback and reinforcement to enhance performance. These practices also help to support procedural integrity.

PERFORMANCE MONITORING

This involves ongoing collection of relevant performance data, including: (a) the number and rate of competencies that a supervisee acquires; (b) the number and rate of errors made in permanent products (e.g., data collection forms, assessment reports, intervention plans); and (c) changes in the use of language (e.g., fluency and accuracy in the use of technical language, ability to explain concepts in nontechnical language).

FEEDBACK AND REINFORCEMENT SYSTEMS

This involves delivering (a) praise or other reinforcers for correct performance and (b) corrective feedback or further instruction when errors are made. When delivering feedback, the following guidelines should be followed:

When delivering praise or other reinforcers:
- Deliver it immediately following the behavior.
- Verbally describe what the supervisee did correctly.

When delivering corrective feedback:
- Find a way to incorporate praise (e.g., "That was a really good attempt").
- Provide instruction that the supervisee can use to improve their performance.
- Focus on one error at a time.
- Empathize and avoid labeling the error as "bad" or "wrong."

ADDITIONAL NOTE(S)

Consider using performance monitoring.

▶ TASK LIST ITEM I-6

The objective of this Task List item is to use a functional-assessment approach (e.g., performance diagnostics) to identify variables affecting personnel performance.

For a review of common functions of behavior and functional assessment, please refer to Task List items under Behavior Assessment (F-6 to F-9). Performance diagnostics (also known as *performance analysis*) uses a functional assessment approach to identify variables affecting personnel performance. The primary model used for performance diagnostics at the individual level is the Antecedent-Behavior-Consequence (ABC) analysis. ABC analysis is recommended when (a) there is a desirable behavior that is not occurring often enough and (b) there is some undesirable behavior that is occurring too often. There are seven steps to conducting performance diagnostics with an ABC analysis:

1. Describe the problem (undesirable behavior).
2. Describe what the person should be doing instead (desirable behavior).
3. Determine how severe the problem is.
4. Complete an ABC analysis for the problem behavior.
5. Complete an ABC analysis for the desirable behavior.
6. Determine the diagnosis (i.e., summarize the antecedent and consequences).
7. Determine the solution (i.e., add positive/immediate/certain consequences and antecedents for desirable behavior).

ADDITIONAL NOTE(S)

The Performance Diagnostic Checklist–Human Services (PDC-HS) has been cited in the behavior analytic literature as a tool that can be used to examine the variables that affect personnel performance in human-service settings.

▶ TASK LIST ITEM I-7

The objective of this Task List item is to use function-based strategies to improve personnel performance.

For a review of using a functional-assessment approach to identify variables affecting personnel performance, please refer to Task List item I-6. Performance diagnostics are conducted to allow behavior analysts to develop function-based strategies for improving personnel performance.

Table 11.1 Possible interventions for problems impacting performance

Problem	Possible Intervention
Lack of training	Use behavioral skills training, improve personnel selection process
Lack of task clarification	Provide task clarification/checklists
Lack of visual aids and verbal/textual reminders	Provide prompts
Poor environment for task	Change task location
Lack of trained staff	Adjust staffing
Materials are disorganized or poorly designed	Organize/redesign materials
Materials are not available	Make materials more accessible
Lack of monitoring by supervisor	Increase presence of supervisor
Lack of feedback	Use performance feedback
Lack of association between accurate task completion and outcomes	Highlight task outcomes
Task is too difficult or requires too much effort	Decrease task difficulty/effort
Task competes with other priorities that take precedence	Decrease aversive task properties

▶ TASK LIST ITEM I-8

The objective of this Task List item is to evaluate the effects of supervision (e.g., on client outcomes, on supervisee repertoires).

Behavior analysts are required to assess the outcomes of their supervision activities. Methods for assessing the effects of supervision include (a) tracking relevant data, (b) requesting feedback, and (c) conducting a survey.

TRACKING RELEVANT DATA

This involves gathering and reviewing relevant performance data, including: (a) the number and rate of competencies that a supervisee acquires, (b) the number and rate of errors made in permanent products, and (c) changes in the use of language.

REQUESTING FEEDBACK

This involves directly asking the supervisee the following questions:

"Are you getting what you need?" and "Am I teaching (knowledge/skill[s]) in the most effective way for you?" Asking these questions can occur regularly as a part of supervision meetings.

CONDUCTING A SURVEY

This involves developing a brief structured survey that the supervisee can complete. Items should address specific areas such as the (a) supervisor's organization, knowledge, and use of feedback/reinforcement, and (b) relevance of knowledge/skills covered. Open-ended questions (e.g., "What would you change about supervision to enhance your learning?") can also be included. This approach may be particularly useful for supervisors who wish to collect feedback from a group of supervisees.

ADDITIONAL NOTE(S)

Supervisors should also collect some sort of data to learn about the effectiveness of the method(s) they choose to evaluate the effects of supervision.

▶ CONCLUSION

In this chapter, we reviewed key content for Task List items related to personnel supervision and management. This included information related to setting performance expectations and goals; using performance monitoring, feedback, and reinforcement systems; using function-based strategies to improve personnel performance; and more. Given the role of behavior analysts as supervisors in the field, it is important that we acquire competencies and engage in practices that bring out the best in those we supervise. It is not an exaggeration to say that the generations of behavior analysts to come will, at least to some extent, be shaped by the supervision practices we adopt today.

1. Which of the following is not considered one of the reasons for using behavior-analytic supervision?

   A. It contributes to the development of supportive workplace friendships
   B. It contributes to the professional development of supervisees and supervisors
   C. It is required per the Ethics Code for Behavior Analysts
   D. It is supported as best practice in the professional literature

2. Potential risks of ineffective supervision include all of the following except:

   A. It can degrade the quality of behavior analytic services
   B. It can negatively impact client outcomes
   C. It can result in actionable violations of the Ethics Code
   D. It can result in supervisor development of inadequate professional skills

3. Performance expectations for the supervisor and supervisee should be clearly communicated _____.

   A. At the outset of a supervisory relationship
   B. During the first performance evaluation
   C. Prior to the first supervision meeting
   D. Prior to the termination of the supervisory relationship

4. When the supervisory relationship is between a qualified supervisor and a trainee acquiring field-work experience to meet Behavior Analyst Certification Board (BACB) certification requirements, a _____ must be established.

   A. Declaration of supervision
   B. Mentorship agreement
   C. Supervision contract
   D. Supervision verification system

5. A supervisor can also set expectations for:

   A. Deadlines for assigned activities
   B. Note-taking
   C. Systems for managing supervision documentation
   D. All of the above

6. Methods for evaluating a supervisee's skills can include:

   A. Self-assessment
   B. Quizzes and interviews
   C. Review of permanent products and direct observation
   D. All of the above

1. A) It contributes to the development of supportive workplace friendships
Contributing to the professional development of supervisees and supervisors, adhering to the requirements of the Code, and engaging in best practice as described in the professional literature are excellent and valid reasons for using behavior-analytic supervision. However, developing workplace friendships is not among the qualifying reasons for providing supervision.

2. D) It can result in supervisor development of inadequate professional skills
Supervisor development of inadequate professional skills is not an identified potential risk of ineffective supervision. The other answer options (it can degrade the quality of behavior analytic services, it can negatively impact client outcomes, it can result in actionable violations of the Ethics Code) are described in the professional literature as potential risks.

3. A) At the outset of a supervisory relationship
Performance expectations for the supervisor and supervisee should be clearly communicated at the outset of a supervisory relationship. The other answer options (during the first performance evaluation, prior to the first supervision meeting, prior to the termination of the supervisory relationship) function as distractors.

4. C) Supervision contract
When the supervisory relationship is between a qualified supervisor and a trainee acquiring fieldwork experience to meet BACB certification requirements, a supervision contract must be established. The other answer options (declaration of supervision, mentorship agreement, supervision verification system) do not accurately fit into the statement and function as distractors.

5. D) All of the above
Deadlines for assigned activities, note-taking, and systems for managing supervision documentation are all items for which supervisors can set expectations.

6. D) All of the above
Self-assessment, quizzes and interviews, and review of permanent products and direct observation are all methods used by behavior analyst supervisors to evaluate the skills of supervisees.

7. When selecting supervision goals, _____ should be used to inform the development of achievable goals.

   A. Baseline performance data
   B. Task List
   C. The supervision contract
   D. None of the above

8. Supervisors should set _____ supervision goals.

   A. Long-term
   B. Long-term and short-term
   C. Interpersonal
   D. Short-term

9. When developing short-term goals, it is recommended that behavior analysts consider:

   A. The Behavior Analyst Certification Board's (BACB's) reporting requirements for supervision hours
   B. The immediate needs of the agency
   C. The supervisee's ability to meet them
   D. Both B and C

10. _____ is an instructional process used to teach personnel to competently perform assessment and intervention procedures.

   A. Analysis, design, development, implementation, and evaluation (ADDIE)
   B. Behavioral skills training (BST)
   C. Competency-based learning (CBL)
   D. Self-directed learning (SDL)

11. Which step of behavior skills training (BST) can involve role-playing activities, video models, and/or in-situ demonstrations with a client?

   A. Describe the target skill
   B. Demonstrate the target skill
   C. Practice the target skill
   D. Provide written description of the target skill

12. When delivering corrective feedback to a supervisee, a behavior analyst should do all of the following except:

   A. Find a way to incorporate praise
   B. Focus on one error at a time
   C. Label the error as "wrong" to ensure the supervisee understands that it is to be avoided in the future
   D. Provide instruction that the supervisee can use to improve their performance

13. The primary model used for performance diagnostics at the individual level is:

   A. Antecedent-Behavior-Consquence (ABC) analysis
   B. Behavioral skills training (BST)
   C. Functional communication training (FCT)
   D. None of the above

7. A) Baseline performance data

When selecting supervision goals, baseline performance data should be used to inform the development of achievable goals. The other answer options (Task List, the supervision contract, none of the above) serve as distractors.

8. B) Long-term and short-term

Just setting either short-term goals or long-term goals is insufficient. Supervisors should set both long-term and short-term goals. The other answer options (long-term, interpersonal, short-term) function as distractors.

9. D) Both B and C

When developing short-term goals, it is recommended that behavior analysts consider the immediate needs of the agency and the supervisee's ability to meet them. The BACB's reporting requirement for supervision hours is not a primary area of consideration when developing short-term goals.

10. B) Behavioral skills training (BST)

BST is an instructional process used to teach personnel to competently perform assessment and intervention procedures. The other answer options (ADDIE, CBL, SDL) are not instructional procedures from the behavior analytic literature and function as distractors.

11. B) Demonstrate the target skill

When implementing BST, the third step (demonstrate the target skill) can involve role-playing activities, video models, and/or in-situ demonstrations with a client. The other answer options (describe the target skill, practice the target skill, provide written description of the target skill) refer to other steps of BST and function as distractors.

12. C) Label the error as "wrong" to ensure the supervisee understands that it is to be avoided in the future

When delivering corrective feedback, a behavior analyst should find a way to incorporate praise, focus on one error at a time, and provide instruction that can be used by the supervisee to improve their performance. They should also empathize and avoid labeling errors as "wrong."

13. A) Antecedent-Behavior-Consquence (ABC) analysis

The primary model used for performance diagnostics at the individual level is ABC analysis. The other answer options (BST, FCT, none of the above) function as distractors.

14. The first step in conducting performance diagnostics with an Antecedent-Behavior-Consequence (ABC) analysis is to:

   A. Describe the desirable behavior
   B. Describe the undesirable behavior
   C. Determine how severe the undesirable behavior is
   D. Determine the diagnosis

15. Performance diagnostics uses a _____ approach to identify variables affecting personnel performance.

   A. Direct assessment
   B. Formative assessment
   C. Functional assessment
   D. Summative assessment

16. Behavior analysts are _____ assess the outcomes of their supervision activities.

   A. Not permitted to
   B. Not required to, but can elect to
   C. Required to
   D. Unable to

17. Methods for assessing the effects of supervision include all of the following except:

   A. Conducting a survey
   B. Interviewing peers
   C. Requesting feedback
   D. Tracking relevant performance data

18. Data that may be tracked by a behavior analyst to assess the effects of their supervision can include:

   A. Changes in the use of language
   B. The number and rate of competencies that a supervisee acquires
   C. The number and rate of errors made in permanent products
   D. All of the above

14. B) Describe the undesirable behavior

The first step in conducting performance diagnostics with an ABC analysis is to describe the undesirable behavior. The other answer options (describe the desirable behavior, determine how severe the undesirable behavior is, determine the diagnosis) describe later steps in the process and function as distractors.

15. C) Functional assessment

Performance diagnostics uses a functional assessment approach to identify variables affecting personnel performance. The other answer options (direct assessment, formative assessment, summative assessment) function as distractors.

16. C) Required to

This is not optional. Behavior analysts are required to assess the outcomes of their supervision activities. The other answer options (not permitted to; not required to, but can elect to; unable to) function as distractors.

17. B) Interviewing peers

Conducting surveys, requesting feedback, and tracking relevant performance data are methods for assessing supervision. Interview peers, however, is not.

18. D) All of the above

Data that may be tracked by a behavior analyst to assess the effects of their supervision can include changes in the use of language, the number and rate of competencies that a supervisee acquires, and the number and rate of errors made in permanent products.

BIBLIOGRAPHY

Austin, J. (2000). Performance analysis and performance diagnostics. In J. E. Carr & J. Austin (Eds.), *Handbook of applied behavior analysis* (pp. 321–349). Context Press.

Behavior Analyst Certification Board. (2017). *BCBA task list* (5th ed.). Author.

Behavior Analyst Certification Board. (n.d.). *Sample supervision contract for BCBA/BCaBA trainees.* Author.

Carr, J. E., Wilder, D. A., Majdalany, L., Mathisen, D., & Strain, L. A. (2013). An assessment-based solution to a human-service employee performance problem. *Behavior Analysis in Practice, 6*(1), 16–32. https://doi.org/10.1007/BF03391789

Daniels, A. C. (2015). *The most powerful leadership tool: Positive reinforcement—5 keys for effective delivery.* http://aubreydaniels.com/positive-reinforcement-most-powerful-leadership-tool

Garza, K. L., McGee, H. M., Schenk, Y. A., & Wiskirchen, R. R. (2018). Some tools for carrying out a proposed process for supervising experience hours for aspiring Board Certified Behavior Analysts®. *Behavior Analysis in Practice, 11*(1), 62–70. https://doi.org/10.1007/s40617-017-0186-8

Miltenberger, R. (2015). *Behavior modification: Principles and procedures.* Cengage Learning.

Parsons, M. B., Rollyson, J. H., & Reid, D. H. (2012). Evidence-based staff training: A guide for practitioners. *Behavior Analysis in Practice, 5*(2), 2–11. https://doi.org/10.1007/BF03391819

Sarokoff, R. A., & Sturmey, P. (2008). The effects of instructions, rehearsal, modeling, and feedback on acquisition and generalization of staff use of discrete trial teaching and student correct responses. *Research in Autism Spectrum Disorders, 2*(1), 125–136. https://doi.org/10.1016/j.rasd.2007.04.002

Sellers, T. P., Alai-Rosales, S., & MacDonald, R. P. (2016). Taking full responsibility: The ethics of supervision in behavior analytic practice. *Behavior Analysis in Practice, 9*(4), 299–308. https://doi.org/10.1007/s40617-016-0144-x

Sellers, T. P., Valentino, A. L., & LeBlanc, L. A. (2016). Recommended practices for individual supervision of aspiring behavior analysts. *Behavior Analysis in Practice, 9*(4), 274–286. https://doi.org/10.1007/s40617-016-0110-7

Turner, L. B., Fischer, A. J., & Luiselli, J. K. (2016). Towards a competency-based, ethical, and socially valid approach to the supervision of applied behavior analytic trainees. *Behavior Analysis in Practice, 9*(4), 287–298. https://doi.org/10.1007/s40617-016-0121-4

Valentino, A. L., LeBlanc, L. A., & Sellers, T. P. (2016). The benefits of group supervision and a recommended structure for implementation. *Behavior Analysis in Practice, 9*(4), 320–328. https://doi.org/10.1007/s40617-016-0138-8

PRACTICE EXAM

You have up to 4 hours to complete this 185-item examination. Read each question carefully and consider all response options. Answers and explanations are provided in the next chapter. *Start the timer and go!*

1. Behavior analysts are required to maintain appropriate professional relationships with clients. Which of the following scenarios presents an ethical problem?

   A. Esther is a behavior analyst who is very well liked by her clients. However, one of the families she works with was offended when they asked her to stay for lunch and she politely declined the invitation

   B. Harold is a behavior analyst who lives next door to a family with a child who struggles with behavior issues. He wants to help but is uncomfortable charging his neighbors for his services, so he instead provides them with free behavioral advice

   C. Kamala is a behavior analyst who has been experiencing some personal problems. When she noticed that they began to impact her performance at work, she contacted her supervisor, requested a leave of absence, and arranged for another behavior analyst to cover her cases

   D. Leonard is a behavior analyst who is very familiar with the research literature on behavior change procedures. However, he only uses very simple language when speaking with clients

2. Which of the following statements is the strongest example of an operational definition of a target behavior?

   A. Hits the table with their hands when they are upset

   B. Hits the table forcefully with their hands when upset, hurting themself as a result

   C. Firmly hits the surface of the table with their hands, producing a highly audible bang

   D. Firmly hits the surface of the table with their hands when upset, producing a highly audible bang that startles others

3. This scientific attitude holds that knowledge is tentative and continually developing. As such, scientists remain skeptical about the validity and truthfulness of all scientific knowledge and open to modifying their beliefs based on new knowledge and discoveries. Which attitude of science does this statement best articulate?

   A. Replication

   B. Philosophical doubt

   C. Empiricism

   D. Parsimony

4. A behavior analyst is considering whether a client needs ongoing services. Best practice is for the behavior analyst to carefully consider all of the following except:

   A. The ethical guidelines addressing termination of services

   B. Assessment results and ongoing progress monitoring data

   C. Their clinical expertise

   D. Insurance reimbursement

5. Supervisors use performance monitoring strategies with supervisees to facilitate performance enhancements and support procedural integrity. One aspect of performance monitoring involves examining the number and rate of errors made in permanent products. Which of the following is the best example of a permanent product?

   A. A skeptical attitude
   B. Awareness of the Ethics Code for Behavior Analysts
   C. A behavior intervention plan
   D. Conceptual understanding client rapport

6. Behavior analysts couple their clinical expertise with this to determine whether an intervention is effective and if a treatment needs to be revised.

   A. The best available evidence
   B. Philosophical doubt
   C. Grounded theory
   D. Experimental analysis of behavior

7. Ms. Keyes is a third-grade teacher who describes one of her students as "highly defiant." When questioned about what this meant, Ms. Keyes reported that the student would throw tantrums, pinch peers, be disrespectful to adults, and occasionally leave the classroom without permission. Which of the following is not an appropriate target for intervention?

   A. Being disrespectful to adults
   B. Leaving the classroom without permission
   C. Pinching peers
   D. Throwing tantrums

8. In this branch of behavior analysis, researchers conduct basic research in laboratory settings to define and clarify the basic processes and principles of behavior. What branch of behavior analysis is this?

   A. Applied Behavior Analysis
   B. Experimental Analysis of Behavior
   C. Behaviorism
   D. Professional practice guided by the science of behavior analysis

9. Board Certified Behavior Analysts (BCBAs) are encouraged to develop definitions of behavior that describe responses in terms of their effect on the environment (e.g., "any behavior that results in X"). This statement best describes which of the following definitions of behavior?

   A. Topography-based definitions
   B. Gestalt-based definitions
   C. Outcome-based definitions
   D. Function-based definitions

10. Ms. King is a sixth-grade teacher who uses a token economy system in her classroom to support her classroom management efforts. When Ms. King catches students following class rules, she gives them "K-bucks." Students can exchange their K-bucks for rewards, including fruit snacks, juice boxes, potato chips, colorful pencils, and erasers. Since the token system was initially implemented, Ms. King has observed an increase in rule-following behavior among her students. In this example, the K-bucks served as:

    A. Conditioned reinforcers
    B. Noncontingent reinforcers
    C. Primary reinforcers
    D. Unconditioned reinforcers

11. Ashley is a graduate student studying behavior analysis. She just started a new fieldwork experience at a local healthcare center serving children with behavior problems. Her supervisor, Sam, is a Board Certified Behavior Analyst (BCBA) who sometimes seems a bit scattered. Sam was scheduled to conduct his first observation of Ashley at her site last week, but he never showed up. The observation was then rescheduled for earlier this week; but just minutes before the start of the session, Ashley received an email from Sam about canceling the session. "I'm stuck in a meeting and probably won't be able to come see you today," he said. "It seems like you're doing fine. If any problems come up, just ask one of the other behavior support staff at the center. I'll get in touch with you later after things quiet down." Ashley is concerned about the supervision she is receiving. What should she do first?

A. Proceed in conducting fieldwork with or without Sam's supervision. If problems arise, there are other staff that can help

B. Document the missed sessions and report Sam to the Behavior Analyst Certification Board (BACB). Sam is not following the board's requirements for providing supervision

C. Find another supervisor. Sam is clearly lacking availability and does not seem able to meet Ashley's supervision needs

D. Contact Sam and be persistent in finding a time to meet. Ashley should express her concern to Sam and ask if it can be immediately resolved

12. Valid measurement requires all of the following except:

A. Data representing the behavior's occurrence under relevant conditions

B. Direct measurement of a socially significant behavior

C. Measurement of a relevant dimension of the behavior

D. Repeated measurement that yields the same results

13. Developed by B. F. Skinner, this conceptual system seeks to understand behavior in all its forms, including internal events. From the perspective of this conceptual system, thoughts and feelings do not cause behavior—thoughts and feelings *are* behavior. Which behavior analysis conceptual system is this?

A. Applied Behavior Analysis

B. Experimental Analysis of Behavior

C. Human Engineering

D. Radical Behaviorism

14. When Shelly wanted attention, she generally screamed at her father until he paid attention to her. Now, her father is ignoring her screams. Which of the following most accurately describes the procedure used in this situation?

A. Extinction of behavior maintained by positive reinforcement

B. Extinction of behavior maintained by negative reinforcement

C. Extinction of behavior maintained by positive punishment

D. Extinction of behavior maintained by automatic reinforcement

15. DaShon is only 2 years old and cannot reach the kitchen counter where a dish of chocolate-covered almonds was placed. After some experimentation, he learned to use the shelves of the cupboard as a ladder to get on top of the kitchen counter and retrieve a chocolate-covered almond from the dish. DaShon never received any training to perform these steps, nor were chocolate-covered almonds ever paired with another reinforcer. What type of reinforcer did the chocolate-covered almonds most likely serve as?

A. Conditioned

B. Generalized

C. Secondary

D. Unconditioned

16. Which of the following refers to the extent to which a learned response continues to be performed after some or all of the intervention that evokes it has been removed?

    A. Response generalization
    B. Response maintenance
    C. Resurgence
    D. Stimulus generalization

17. Liam conducted an observation of a client, Gus. Before the start of the observation, Liam spent time arranging the environment to include different objects and activities that Gus might like, such as puzzles, blocks, and musical games. During the observation, Liam recorded the length of time Gus would approach, contact, or engage with the different objects and activities available. What type of preference assessment did Liam conduct?

    A. Single stimulus
    B. Contrived free-operant observation
    C. Naturalistic free-operant observation
    D. Multiple stimulus without replacement

18. Which of the following is not an element of baseline logic?

    A. Prediction
    B. Replication
    C. Generalization
    D. Verification

19. What type of validity refers to the degree the changes in the dependent variable (i.e., target behavior) can be attributed to the manipulation of the independent variable (i.e., intervention) and not the result of uncontrolled/extraneous factors?

    A. Criterion validity
    B. Internal validity
    C. Construct validity
    D. External validity

20. Donyea's teachers want to work on decreasing the amount of time it takes him to eat his snack. The behavior technician collects baseline data to determine the amount of time Donyea takes to eat his snack. The timer starts after the teacher places the snack on the table in front of Donyea and he begins to eat it. The timer is stopped when he has consumed all edible parts of the snack item. The time elapsed is recorded for each occurrence. The measurement procedure described in this scenario involves the recording of what dimensional quantity of behavior?

    A. Duration
    B. Response latency
    C. Interresponse time
    D. Frequency

21. As supervisors, behavior analysts must monitor the performance of supervisees and provide timely feedback and reinforcement. These practices enhance supervisees' performance and help to:

    A. Support procedural integrity
    B. Support affective commitment
    C. Support resiliency efforts
    D. Support organizational constraints

22. When using reinforcement, extinction, and punishment procedures, behavior analysts must consider and plan for the possibility of unwanted effects. Of these, _____ is associated with the following unwanted effects: emotional/aggressive reactions, an initial increase in the rate of the problem behavior, an initial increase in the magnitude of the problem behavior, the reappearance of the problem behavior after it has been reduced/eliminated, and the reappearance of a previously extinguished problem behavior that was replaced by the targeted problem behavior.

    A. Reinforcement
    B. Punishment
    C. Extinction
    D. None of the above

23. Which of the following best describes what the Ethics Code says about bartering as a substitute for the collection of fees for behavior analytic services?

    A. Bartering with goods (but not services) is prohibited
    B. Bartering of services (but not goods) is prohibited
    C. Bartering may be acceptable when certain conditions are met
    D. Bartering of any kind is prohibited

24. Dylan is not very fond of homework assignments. Instead of completing his homework assignment for the day, Dylan approaches his mother and nicely asks for access to the computer tablet. He wants to play games on it. Which of the following is a response that Dylan's mother can use that exemplifies the Premack principle?

    A. "You cannot play with the tablet yet."
    B. "Since you haven't finished your homework yet, you can't play with the tablet."
    C. "If you promise to finish your homework later, you can play with the tablet now."
    D. "Finish your homework first, then you can play with the tablet."

25. Behavior analysts identify potential interventions based on assessment results and the best available scientific evidence. When evaluating the scientific evidence to guide intervention selection decisions, Board Certified Behavior Analysts (BCBAs) prioritize its:

    A. Relevance and certainty
    B. Scope and parsimony
    C. Testability and rigor
    D. Classification and certainty

26. A group of inmates at a prison frequently engage in aggressive behavior. A Board Certified Behavior Analyst (BCBA) consulting with the prison conducts systematic observations and recommends implementation of a contingency management system. A token economy is designed and implemented in which the inmates earn vouchers for nonaggressive, socially appropriate behavior. Vouchers are lost for any instances of aggressive behavior. Data collected on the intervention indicate that the contingency management system is associated with decreases in aggressive behavior and increases in prosocial behavior. What is the dependent variable in this intervention?

    A. Contingency management system
    B. Token economy
    C. Aggressive behavior
    D. Systematic observations

27. Which of the following is not an advantage of utilizing continuous measurement methods?

    A. They can detect all occurrences of the target behavior during an observation period
    B. They can be highly accurate
    C. They are more sensitive to small improvements in performance not captured by other methods of measurement
    D. They require less attention from the observer, are time-consuming, and require less training for users

28. Ms. Charlotte, a fourth-grade teacher, tells her students that they are to line up by the classroom door to walk to the cafeteria after the lunch bell rings, but only after she calls their name. When the lunch bell rings, students eagerly wait at their desks until they hear Ms. Charlotte call their name before standing up and lining up by the door. In the example, the students are demonstrating:

    A. Conditional discrimination
    B. Compound discrimination
    C. Simple discrimination
    D. Conditional verbal discrimination

29. What type of validity refers to the degree the results of the intervention (i.e., functional relationship demonstrated in an experiment) can be generalized to other behaviors, environments, and individuals/populations?

    A. Criterion validity
    B. Internal validity
    C. Construct validity
    D. External validity

30. One component of a sound definition of a target behavior is that it refers to observable aspects of the behavior (and environment, when applicable). This means the definition is:

    A. Complete
    B. Functional
    C. Objective
    D. Clear

31. Mike, a Board Certified Behavior Analyst (BCBA) in training, asks his mentor for recommendations on how to help his client generalize a skill to different settings and situations. One of his mentor's recommendations is to devise a mediating stimulus. Which of the following best illustrates this recommendation?

    A. Provide the client with instruction on enough stimulus examples
    B. Set up a person or object to help facilitate the client's generalization of skills
    C. Ensure that the client receives ample reinforcement in the generalization setting
    D. Create an instructional setting that resembles the generalization setting

32. A client is taught that the spoken word "bicicleta" is the same as the spoken word "bicycle." The client is also taught that the spoken word "bicycle" is the same as a physical, two-wheeled vehicle. Without any training to do so, the client then calls a physical, two-wheeled vehicle a "bicicleta." What type of derived stimulus relation does this example illustrate?

    A. Reflexivity
    B. Substitution
    C. Symmetry
    D. Transitivity

33. A behavior-support specialist, Jetta, is working with a student who engages in high rates of elop-ing. Jetta develops an operational definition for the student's eloping: any noncontextual, non-functional, and unsanctioned departure from the classroom. Nonexamples include leaving the classroom to use the restroom with teacher permission, leaving the classroom for lunch, and leav-ing the classroom to attend physical education class. To collect data on this behavior, Jetta divides an observation period into 1-minute intervals and documents whether the student is eloping at the end of each interval. What measurement procedure is Jetta using to record how much this behavior is occurring?

A. Event recording
B. Momentary time sampling
C. Partial-interval recording
D. Whole-interval recording

34. Sunni, a trainee acquiring fieldwork experience to meet Behavior Analyst Certification Board (BACB) certification requirements, meets with Erin, a Board Certified Behavior Analyst (BCBA), for behavior analytic supervision. It is their first meeting, so Erin takes the opportunity to review her expectations of Sunni. These include providing a draft agenda 24 hours in advance of supervi-sion meetings, following firm deadlines for assigned activities, taking notes during feedback meet-ings, and sharing personal reflections on work with clients. All of these are reasonable except for the requirement for Sunni to:

A. Provide a draft agenda 24 hours in advance of supervision meetings
B. Follow firm deadlines for assigned activities
C. Take notes during feedback meetings
D. Provide ongoing evaluation of the effects of supervision

35. Chelsea does not particularly enjoy doing household chores (e.g., doing the dishes, folding laun-dry), but she would frequently volunteer to do them because her father would give her a small amount of money for one that she completed. One day, Chelsea's father decides that "doing things to help out around the house should be inherently rewarding" and stops paying Chelsea for com-pleting chores. Subsequently, Chelsea completes fewer chores. This change in behavior is most likely the result of:

A. Extinction
B. Negative punishment
C. Negative reinforcement
D. Positive punishment

36. A 2-year-old named Sully is working with his father to learn new words. Sully's father is using simple discrimination. Select the example that best exemplifies simple discrimination.

A. Sully's father presents him with a blueberry. When Sully says "blueberry," his father deliv-ers reinforcement. Sully's father then presents him with an apple. When Sully says "apple," his father delivers reinforcement; if Sully says "blueberry" when presented with an apple, reinforcement is not delivered
B. Sully's father presents him with a blueberry. When Sully says "blueberry," his father models how to place the blueberry in his mouth, chew the blueberry, and swallow it
C. Sully's father presents him with a blueberry. When Sully says "blueberry," his father delivers reinforcement. When Sully says any word other than blueberry, his father does not deliver reinforcement
D. Sully's father presents him with a bowl of fruit that includes blueberries, strawberries, black-berries, and raspberries. When Sully picks up a berry, his father verbally identifies it by its name

37. Juan, a Board Certified Behavior Analyst (BCBA), is working with a new client, Maria, who is displaying aggressive behavior at home. Juan is developing an operational definition for the aggressive behavior that will be used by Maria's parents to measure its occurrence throughout the day. Which of the following would be considered a strong operational definition for Juan to share with Maria's parents?

    A. Any physical contact between Maria's body and another person's body

    B. Any physical contact between Maria's hands or feet and another person's body

    C. Any physical contact between Maria's body and another person's body with enough force to be audible or leave a mark

    D. Any physical contact between Maria's body and another person's body with enough force to be audible or leave a mark, outside of activities in which such contact would be appropriate

38. Darnell, a behavior analyst, is developing a treatment plan that targets a client's problem behavior for reduction. The targeted behavior is problematic, but it is not severe, does not occur frequently, and does not have a significant impact on the environment. In the treatment plan, Darnell plans to supplement reduction contingencies with reinforcement contingencies. When selecting an acceptable alternative behavior, Darnell should do all of the following except:

    A. Select an alternative behavior that is already in the client's behavioral repertoire

    B. Select an alternative behavior that is incompatible with the problem behavior

    C. Select an alternative behavior that is within the client's current abilities

    D. Select an alternative behavior that is less effortful than the problem behavior

39. Select the type of analysis that compares different levels of an intervention and involves examining the effects generated by manipulating one or more dimensions/levels of the intervention.

    A. Comparative analysis

    B. Add-in component analysis

    C. Parametric analysis

    D. Drop-out component analysis

40. Behavior analysts monitor client progress to track and evaluate responsiveness to interventions as evidenced by behavior change over time. All of the following are key components of monitoring client progress except:

    A. Evaluating and utilizing data for decision-making

    B. Collecting baseline data and defining goals

    C. Clearly operationalizing the target behavior

    D. Experimenting to explain the fundamental principles of behavior

41. Sam is a behavior technician who works with a client, Frank, in a school setting. In the classroom, Sam observes Frank's teacher vocally instruct him to walk to and stand behind the last student in line by the door to go to the library. Instead of walking toward the line, Frank walks in the opposite direction toward the back of the classroom where the computer station is situated. The teacher quickly positions himself between Frank and the computer station and instructs Frank again to line up by the door. Frank proceeds to cry and kick the teacher who then physically prompts Frank to walk over to a designated "cool down" area of the classroom. Examine the Antecedent-Behavior-Consequence (ABC) data recorded by Sam in the following table. What is the most significant limitation of this recorded narrative?

Table 12.1 Antecedent-Behavior-Consequence data

A	B	C
Teacher instructs Frank to walk to and line up behind his classmates by the door	Frank cries and kicks his teacher	Teacher physically prompts Frank to walk over to the "cool down" area

A. Relevant antecedent details were left out
B. The target behavior is not accurately described
C. The function of the behavior is not included
D. It is not positively and objectively worded

42. Darcy is using an instructional arrangement that allows for her client, Freya, to freely emit one or more responses. Darcy allows Freya to interact with the environment with naturally occurring motivating operations. What instructional arrangement is Darcy using with Freya?

A. Naturalistic teaching approaches (NTAs)
B. Free-operant (FO) arrangement
C. Discrete-trial teaching (DTT)
D. Incidental teaching (IT)

43. Louis is an assistant teacher in a special education classroom helping Salman, a fifth grader, learn the multiplication facts. At the end of the school year, Salman is able to correctly solve 50 multiplication facts in 1 minute. Salman will be transitioning to middle school, and his individualized education program (IEP) team wants to ensure Salman retains what he has learned. All of the following procedures will promote maintenance of Salman's learning except:

A. Provide Salman with regular opportunities to practice the multiplication facts
B. Implement the high-probability instructional sequence (high-p) with Salman in sixth grade
C. Affix a small copy of the multiplication facts table to Salman's desk
D. Provide Salman with reinforcement after he correctly answers a certain number of questions during a practice session

44. Simon, a Board Certified Behavior Analyst (BCBA), is taking on a new 7-year-old client who engages in tantrum behavior in school. After collecting preliminary background information and establishing a contract for services, Simon conducts a functional analysis of the tantrum behavior. Results of the functional analysis showed undifferentiated responding, so Simon developed an intervention plan to address multiple functions. After implementing the plan for over a month, the tantrum behavior remained unchanged. Upon further consultation with the client's teacher, Simon learned that there was an untreated medical condition that may be contributing to the occurrence of the tantrum behavior. What activity did Simon most likely neglect to conduct in the assessment process?

    A. Antecedent-Behavior-Consequence (ABC) recording and analysis
    B. Interview with relevant stakeholders
    C. Review of records
    D. Standardized testing

45. Behavior analysts incorporate transition and discharge planning into the overall treatment planning process. As such, termination of services should never come as a surprise to the client or the client's network of support; rather, services should be gradually stepped down. How long does the process of gradually decreasing services over time typically take?

    A. At least 6 months
    B. At least 1 week
    C. At least 12 weeks
    D. At least 1 month

46. When considering observable behavior, topography can best be defined as:

    A. A method for identifying the impact of the behavior on the environment
    B. A set of behaviors that the individual can perform
    C. The physical form of the behavior
    D. The sense organ that is used to identify external stimuli through hearing, vision, taste, smell, and cutaneous touch

47. Tammi is a 7-year-old client who engages in tantrum behavior at school. Her teacher reported that this occurs in the classroom when Tammi is instructed to sit at her desk and engage in a task that involves writing. There are no reports of this problem behavior occurring anywhere else or at any other time. To avoid disrupting other students' engagement with the class activity, Tammi's teacher sends her to the principal's office when she engages in tantrum behavior. This has negatively impacted Tammi's performance marks in class as she has spent little to no time on most writing tasks. Based on this information, what would you hypothesize to be the function of Tammi's tantrum behavior?

    A. Attention
    B. Escape
    C. Sensory
    D. Tangible

48. Of the following, which is not an advantage afforded by single-subject experimental designs for behavior analysts' measurement of individual behavior?

    A. It reveals the performance of individual subjects
    B. It allows for replication of effects within and across individual subjects
    C. Data for subjects are not combined/averaged, which helps to prevent distortion/masking of variability in the data
    D. It provides strong evidence of external validity and the generalization of results to a broader population

49. Terri, a Board Certified Behavior Analyst (BCBA), teaches Heather, a client, how to implement an intervention procedure to decrease her dog's behavior of chewing on her shoes. Terri instructs Heather to physically block her dog every time it tries to get a shoe in its mouth, redirect the dog to a chew toy, and deliver vocal praise and pet her dog when it engages with a chew toy. Heather's dog responds favorably to this intervention when it is in effect. However, when the intervention is removed, the dog returns to chewing on her shoes. When Heather reimplements the intervention, the dog again stops chewing on her shoes. This fact pattern best exemplifies which type of validity?

    A. Internal validity
    B. Face validity
    C. External validity
    D. Content validity

50. Eliot notices that every day around 4:45 p.m. he begins thinking about and planning to have an alcoholic beverage when he gets off work at 5:00 p.m. Eliot wants to develop healthier habits and change this behavior, so he begins self-monitoring his behavior and going directly to the gym to work out after work. Which self-management strategy is Eliot using?

    A. Habit reversal
    B. Self-instruction
    C. Massed practice
    D. Self-directed systematic desensitization

51. Identify the type of experimental design displayed in the following graph

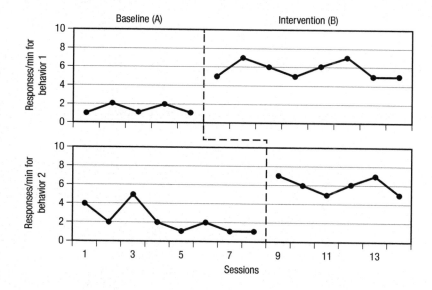

    A. AB design
    B. Changing criterion design
    C. Multielement design
    D. Multiple baseline design

52. Warner is a behavior analyst working in a special education classroom with Derrick, a 12-year-old student with autism spectrum disorder (ASD). Warner determines that attention is the function of Derrick's table-hitting behavior, so he plans to ignore it when it occurs. Warner implements the intervention with Derrick for 5 days, during which time Derrick's table hitting behavior drops from an average of 12 times to an average of three times. The following 5 days, Warner stops implementing the intervention; in this phase, Derrick engaged in table hitting behavior an average of 13 times. Warner then resumes the intervention, and Derrick's table hitting behavior again drops to an average of two times. Identify the element of experimental reasoning this scenario exemplifies.

    A. Prediction
    B. Replication
    C. Generalization
    D. Verification

53. Which of the following schedules of reinforcement produces a slow rate of responding at the beginning of the interval but then accelerates toward the end of the interval, typically reaching its highest rate right before reinforcement?

    A. Fixed interval (FI)
    B. Fixed ratio (FR)
    C. Variable interval (VI)
    D. Variable ratio (VR)

54. A teacher is interested in tracking her students' engagement with class activities. After developing an operational definition of "on-task" behavior, she decides to record the number of students that are on-task at the end of every hour throughout the school day. What type of measurement system is the teacher using?

    A. Event recording
    B. Partial interval recording
    C. Planned activity check (PLACHECK)
    D. Whole interval recording

55. Sometimes clients show a preference for reinforcers that are known to be harmful (e.g., cigarettes). What should behavior analysts do in these situations?

    A. Minimize the use of items as reinforcers when they may be harmful to clients
    B. Plan to use the reinforcers in treatment, even if known to be harmful, when the client has already been accessing it
    C. Use harmful reinforcers only when the behavior-change program is short in duration
    D. Use harmful reinforcers when needed for individual behavior plans

56. A Board Certified Behavior Analyst (BCBA) is planning to implement a 6-week social skills training program for five elementary school students. To evaluate the effectiveness of her efforts, the BCBA develops a plan to monitor each student's social skills performance by asking the students' teachers to provide a daily report on their demonstration of target skills in their classrooms. Data collection is to begin a week before the social skills training program commences and end 2 weeks after the program concludes. Select the visual display format most appropriate for the data to be collected in this scenario.

    A. Cumulative record
    B. Histogram
    C. Line graph
    D. Standard celeration chart

57. A behavior analyst is supporting a client in developing job skills to work as a table busser. When bussing a table, the client is expected to do the following: Wait until everyone at the table has left; place the dish tub in an empty chair at the table; place all dishes, utensils, cups, and napkins in the tub; wipe the table with a cleaning rag; and carry the tub to the dish room. The behavior analyst tracks the number of practice trials it takes for the client to successfully learn to buss a table. What method of measurement is most appropriate for assessing progress toward mastery of this skill?

    A. Rate
    B. Discrete trials
    C. Trials to criterion
    D. Changing criterion design

58. Pedro, a Board Certified Behavior Analyst (BCBA), is preparing to provide behavior analytic supervision to João, a trainee acquiring fieldwork experience to meet BCBA certification requirements. To select supervision goals based on an assessment of João's skills, Pedro performs the following tasks in sequence:

    A. Select long- and short-term supervision goals, review João's permanent products (and conduct direct observations if needed), administer quizzes and interviews to assess his knowledge-based skills, and have João perform a self-assessment
    B. Administer quizzes and interviews to assess his knowledge-based skills, have João perform a self-assessment, review João's permanent products (and conduct direct observations if needed), and select long- and short-term supervision goals
    C. Have João perform a self-assessment, administer quizzes and interviews to assess his knowledge-based skills, review João's permanent products (and conduct direct observations if needed), and select long- and short-term supervision goals
    D. Have João perform a self-assessment, select long- and short-term supervision goals, review João's permanent products (and conduct direct observations if needed), administer quizzes and interviews to assess his knowledge-based skills

59. Erica, a behavior technician, is working with a client, Joseph, on a matching task. She places several objects on a table in front of Joseph, one of which is a crayon. Erica then hands Joseph a crayon that matches the one on the table and says, "Find the match." Joseph initially requires prompting but, after multiple trials, learns to independently and correctly match the crayon in his hand to the crayon on the table. Erica then hands Joseph a different object, which he independently and correctly matches to an identical object on the table. What type of stimulus–stimulus relation is demonstrated in this example?

    A. Congruency
    B. Reflexivity
    C. Symmetry
    D. Transitivity

60. Before, Wally would go down the slide headfirst and usually hurt himself when he landed on his head. Now, Wally only goes down the slide with his feet first. Which of the following is the best descriptor for Wally's sliding-down-feet-first behavior?

    A. Contingency-shaped
    B. Precursor
    C. Rule-governed
    D. Mimetic

61. Jessica is a 22-year-old client with cognitive deficits who engages in severe self-injurious behavior. Recently, the intensity and rate of the behavior has markedly increased. An assessment has not been conducted to identify its function, so the behavior analyst overseeing the case has recommended a functional analysis. However, there is concern among members of Jessica's treatment team that evoking the behavior will endanger Jessica's safety and may result in undesirable long-term effects. What type of functional analysis should the supervising behavior analyst proceed to conduct on Jessica's self-injurious behavior?

   A. Brief functional analysis
   B. Functional analysis of precursor behavior
   C. Indirect assessment of the behavior
   D. Latency-based functional analysis

62. Orion is a 48-year-old who still frequently asks his parents for financial assistance. Though his parents wish he would stop asking for money and achieve financial independence, they nevertheless give him money whenever he asks for it. Which behavior-change procedure are Orion's parents unwittingly implementing with Orion?

   A. Positive punishment
   B. Negative reinforcement
   C. Positive reinforcement
   D. Negative punishment

63. Hanya, a Board Certified Behavior Analyst (BCBA), is working with a client, Kailani, who cries to get her parents' attention. To address this problem behavior, Hanya develops an intervention plan that includes teaching Kailani to say "help" to request adult attention. To strengthen this behavior, Hanya should establish a behavior-consequence contingency in which:

   A. Parent attention is a positive reinforcer
   B. Parent attention is a negative reinforcer
   C. Crying is a positive punisher
   D. Crying is a positive reinforcer

64. The goal of equivalence-based instruction (EBI) is formation of equivalence classes (i.e., interchangeability between stimuli. This can be taught using a discrete-trial procedure that starts with the client making a response to the sample stimulus. When the client selects the comparison stimulus that matches with the sample stimulus, reinforcement is delivered. This is an example of which of the following?

   A. Matching-to-sample (MTS)
   B. High probability instructional sequence (high-p)
   C. Imitation training
   D. Free-operant (FO) arrangement

65. Ms. Jackson asks Amalie to pick up the toys at the end of a free play period and put them away in the current bins. After giving this prompt, she walks away and leaves Amalie alone with the toys. Mrs. Jackson returns after 5 minutes, and all the toys were put away. She provides verbal praise to Amalie for cleaning up the toys and marks the task as complete on Amalie's data sheet. Which of the following most likely represents the type of data collection Ms. Jackson is using?

   A. Duration recording
   B. Latency recording
   C. Momentary time sampling
   D. Permanent product recording

66. Michael is a Board Certified Behavior Analyst (BCBA) who runs a private practice that offers behavioral consultation services to various types of organizations. To promote his practice, Michael created an attractive website with testimonials from former clients who had wonderful things to say about him and his business. The testimonials were identified as solicited, state the relationship with clients, and do not violate any laws. Is this ethical?

    A. Yes, because the Ethics Code does not address the use of testimonials for advertising
    B. Yes, because the testimonials were identified as solicited, state the relationship with clients, and comply with the law
    C. No, because behavior analysts do not solicit or use testimonials about their services
    D. No, because the Ethics Code strictly forbids the use of technology to promote one's business

67. When Griffin is asked to complete independent work in class, he frequently gets out of his seat to blow his nose, sharpen his pencil, use the restroom, throw things in the waste basket, and so on. A behavior technician records the number of times that Griffin gets out of his seat during a 30-minute independent work period. Across three independent work periods, Griffin got out of his seat 7, 6, and 8 times. Based on this information, what is the average rate of Griffin's leaving-his-seat behavior?

    A. 4 times per independent work period
    B. 6 times per independent work period
    C. 7 times per independent work period
    D. 10 times per independent work period

68. _____ is the provision of differential reinforcement for a progression of responses that are more similar to the target response. In other words, it is a process through which reinforcement is delivered for successive approximations of a terminal behavior.

    A. Training
    B. Shaping
    C. Modeling
    D. Chaining

69. A behavior technician, Carl, is working with a 5-year-old client, Renee, to enhance her communication skills. During a lesson, Carl asked Renee a series of simple questions to which she would provide an answer. For example, Carl asked, "What is your name?" to which Renee answered, "Renee." Appropriate responses were reinforced with verbal praise. What verbal operant does the lesson appear to be targeting for instruction?

    A. Codic
    B. Intraverbal
    C. Mand
    D. Tact

70. Behavior certified behavior analysts use this type of supervision:

    A. Behavior analytic
    B. Autocratic pacesetting
    C. General direction
    D. Transformational coaching

71. Examine the following graph of the frequency of three different behaviors across seven sessions. Which of the following descriptions is most accurate for Behavior 3?

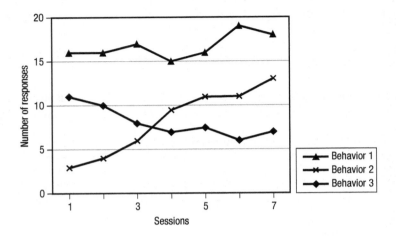

A. High-level responding, low variability, increasing trend
B. Low-level responding, low variability, decreasing trend
C. Mid-level responding, high variability, increasing trend
D. Mid-level responding, low variability, decreasing trend

72. Hillary, a Board Certified Behavior Analyst (BCBA), is about to start her first day on the job at a new behavior analysis service agency. On the morning of her first day, she leaves the house at 8:30 a.m. and runs into traffic on the road. The next day, she leaves half an hour earlier—at 8:00 a.m.—resulting in her avoiding traffic. Subsequently, Hillary leaves for work every weekday morning at 8:00 a.m. In this example, traffic functioned as:

A. A negative punisher for leaving the house at 8:00 a.m.
B. A negative reinforcer for leaving the house at 8:00 a.m.
C. A positive punisher for leaving the house at 8:00 a.m.
D. A positive reinforcer for leaving the house at 8:00 a.m.

73. Mateo is a second-grade student who has trouble making friends at school. One day, Mateo's teacher encourages him to play a game with another student in his class. While initially hesitant, Mateo approaches the other student. During that recess period, they play a ball game together which Mateo seemed to really enjoy. At the start of the next recess period, Mateo approaches the same peer and asks to play a ball game together. Which of the following best explains Mateo's behavior?

A. Automatic reinforcement
B. Graduated guidance
C. Socially mediated reinforcement
D. Tact-to-mand transfer

74. During the day, Simon suddenly develops a headache. The headache becomes increasingly painful as the day goes on, establishing the reinforcing value of pain-relieving medication. In this example, what type of motivating operation (MO) is the headache described as?

    A. Reflexive-conditioned MO (CMO-R)
    B. Surrogate-conditioned MO (CMO-S)
    C. Transitive-conditioned MO (CMO-T)
    D. Unconditioned MO (UMO)

75. Ms. Carson is a seventh-grade science teacher. In her classroom, when she performs a cadence clap, students will stop what they are doing, repeat the cadence clap, and then direct their eyes toward her for instructions. In the absence of her cadence clap, students will simply continue with whatever activity they are engaged with. Which of the following best explains the students' response to Ms. Carson's cadence clap?

    A. Automatic contingency
    B. Reflexivity
    C. Stimulus control
    D. Stimulus equivalence

76. A behavior analyst is working with a 4-year-old client, Emery, who is highly motivated to interact with her parents. Emery will engage in several different responses to get her parents' attention, including grabbing a parent's hand and pulling it toward the living room play area, saying "let's play," climbing tall pieces of furniture (e.g., bookcase and dresser), pushing various items off tables, and crying with tears. These behaviors are best described as:

    A. A functional response class
    B. A stimulus class
    C. A topographical response class
    D. An equivalence class

77. Mia, a Board Certified Behavior Analyst (BCBA), is working with Marley, a young student with an intellectual disability. Before conducting imitation training, Mia evaluates whether Marley is sufficiently able to attend to the model stimulus and discovers that she needs to begin by teaching Marley basic attending skills. Identify the skill that is not essential for Marley to possess in order for Mia to conduct imitation training.

    A. Ability to imitate verbal models
    B. Looking at the teacher
    C. Looking at the objects
    D. Complying with instructions

78. Examine the following graph of the cumulative frequency data collected for a target response over the course of 10 treatment sessions. During which session was the frequency of the target response equal to 2?

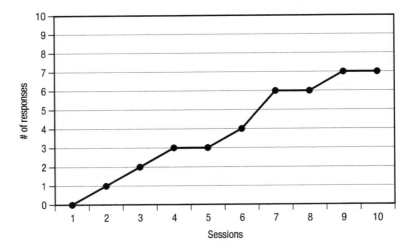

A. Session 3
B. Session 6
C. Session 7
D. Session 9

79. During the first week of school, Ms. Fullalove, a third-grade teacher, holds morning meetings with her students during which they first discuss their hopes and dreams for the year then connect their hopes and dreams with norms for classroom behavior, reasons for those behaviors, and rewards for exhibiting the behaviors and consequences for not exhibiting the behaviors. They then work collaboratively to create a beautiful poster that lists all of the classroom norms they've decided upon. They display the poster prominently on the classroom wall and hold a fun ceremony during which all students and Ms. Fullalove sign it. Ms. Fullalove and her students call this their Caring Community Covenant, but a Board Certified Behavior Analyst (BCBA) would view it as a:

A. Response cost system
B. Contingency contract
C. Positive practice
D. Differential negative reinforcement of incompatible behavior (DRA)

80. A behavior analyst is a member of a multidisciplinary treatment team at a community behavioral health clinic. A client at the clinic is receiving services from the behavior analyst to address self-injurious behavior. The client also receives services from the clinic's psychiatrist and an intern earning his licensed professional counselor (LPC). During a treatment team meeting, the LPC recommends a nonbehavioral treatment that the behavior analyst is unfamiliar with. What is the most pressing question the behavior analyst must answer?

A. Does the treatment interfere with the client's goals?
B. Is the treatment supported by peer-reviewed research?
C. Does the treatment allow for quantitative data collection?
D. Does the treatment pose a risk to the safety of the client?

81. Examine the following graph. What type of experimental design was used?

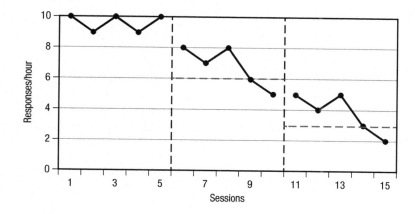

   A. Changing criterion design
   B. Multielement design
   C. Multiple baseline design
   D. AB design

82. Which of the following is an example of an arbitrary stimulus class?

   A. Seeing a bulldog, a chow chow, and a labrador retriever, all of which evoke the response "dog"
   B. Seeing an airplane, a boat, and a bicycle, all of which evoke the word "vehicle"
   C. Pictures of a bulldog, a chow chow, and a labrador retriever, all of which evoke the response "dog"
   D. Pictures of a mandarin orange, a navel orange, and a valencia orange, all of which evoke the word "orange"

83. Bart is a fourth-grade student who has been leaving his assigned seat in the classroom without permission. His teacher, Ms. Andrews, decides to implement a strategy to address his out-of-seat behavior. There is a token system in the classroom that rewards students for desirable behaviors throughout the school day. Each time Bart leaves his seat without permission, Ms. Andrews takes away one of the tokens that Bart has earned. It's not long before Bart's out-of-seat behavior sharply declines. Which of the following best explains the change in target problem behavior?

   A. Negative punishment
   B. Negative reinforcement
   C. Positive punishment
   D. Positive reinforcement

84. Ms. Said is a special education teacher implementing a behavior change system with her students. If the students stop talking when she rings a bell, she gives them points. If the students earn a certain amount of points, they get an extra recess at the end of the day on Friday. If they do not stop talking when she rings a bell, she removes points. Which of the following best describes the behavior change system Ms. Said is implementing?

   A. Token economy with backup reinforcers
   B. Token economy with level system
   C. Token economy with response cost
   D. Token economy with generalized conditioned reinforcer

85. Respondent conditioning involves pairing an unconditioned stimulus with a neutral stimulus until the neutral stimulus becomes a _____ that elicits a _____.

    A. Conditioned stimulus; conditioned response
    B. Conditioned stimulus; unconditioned response
    C. Unconditioned stimulus; conditioned response
    D. Unconditioned stimulus; unconditioned response

86. Lovetta is a Board Certified Behavior Analyst (BCBA) teaching a client to recognize the word "dog." In the initial trial, she places the word "dog" among shapes. Then, in subsequent trials, she introduces letters and words until the client recognizes all the letters in the word "dog." What type of stimulus prompt is Lovetta employing?

    A. Stimulus fading
    B. Least-to-most
    C. Prompt delay
    D. Stimulus shaping

87. Georgia, a Board Certified Behavior Analyst (BCBA), wants to measure how often Mark, a client, displays inappropriate vocalizations during treatment sessions. Which of the following best describes how Georgia can accurately measure the rate of the target behavior?

    A. Record each occurrence of the target behavior, then count the total number of occurrences at the end of the treatment session
    B. Record whether the target behavior occurred or did not occur at the end of 5-minute intervals for the duration of the treatment session
    C. Record each occurrence of the target behavior, then count the total number of occurrences and divide it by the length of the observation period at the end of the treatment session
    D. Record the length of time between the onset and offset of the target behavior, then add up the amount of time across all occurrences at the end of the treatment session

88. Jason is a Board Certified Behavior Analyst (BCBA) who works at an elementary school. One day, a teacher enters his office at the school and says, "Hi, I'm wondering if you might be able to help me. I know you're the behavior specialist here, and I've been struggling with a student in my class. Can you just stop by briefly, have a look at him, and maybe give me some tips for dealing with his behavior? I would really appreciate your support!" What should Jason do?

    A. Agree to conduct the observation
    B. Agree to conduct the observation, but only after obtaining permission from his supervisor
    C. Decline to observe the student
    D. Decline to observe the student, but instead offer to schedule a visit to begin a functional assessment of the problem behavior

89. A behavior analyst is considering terminating services with a client. It is unclear whether services are appropriate or effective for the client. What is the best course of action?

    A. Consult with the client's network of support (e.g., caregiver, teacher, or employer)
    B. Convene an expert panel of behavior analysts and other relevant professionals to review the treatment program
    C. Conduct a systematic interview with the client
    D. Consult the client's insurance company

90. Alejandro, a Board Certified Behavior Analyst (BCBA), is working with Kisa, a 13-year-old student. Alejandro breaks down the behavior he is teaching Kisa into distinct steps (i.e., learning trials) with a clear beginning, middle, and end. As Kisa repeats the trials, she receives reinforcement for correct responding. Identify the instructional procedure Alejandro is using.

    A. Discrete-trial teaching (DTT)
    B. Naturalistic teaching approaches (NTAs)
    C. Incidental teaching (IT)
    D. Free-operant (FO) arrangement

91. Amy, a behavior analyst, is providing behavior analytic supervision to Tyler, who is providing applied behavior analysis (ABA) services to children with autism spectrum disorder (ASD) in a university-based clinic. To monitor Tyler's performance and acquisition of skills, Amy is collecting relevant performance data. Amy should collect all of the following forms of performance data except:

    A. The number and rate of competencies Tyler acquires
    B. The number and rate of errors Tyler makes in permanent products
    C. The impact of the Hawthorne effect on Tyler's performance
    D. Progress in Tyler's fluent and accurate use of technical language

92. Examine the following graph of the results from a functional analysis of Arya's tantrum behavior. Based on this alone, what would you hypothesize to be the function of the tantrum behavior?

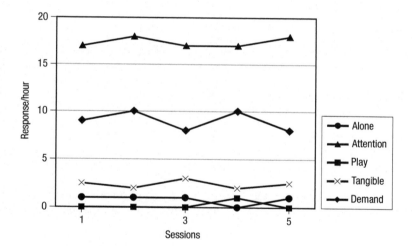

    A. Social positive reinforcement
    B. Social positive reinforcement and social negative reinforcement
    C. Social negative reinforcement and access to tangibles
    D. Inconclusive, the pattern is undifferentiated

93. In the course of developing intervention goals and strategies, a behavior analyst working in a psychiatric treatment facility for adolescent males pays particular attention to the level of support available in the facility (e.g., physical space, staffing), and elements that may inhibit successful implementation of the treatment program. In other words, the behavior analyst is considering which two factors prior to making recommendations?

    A. Risks and social validity
    B. Supporting environments and constraints
    C. Supporting environments and social validity
    D. Social validity and supporting environments

94. Mata is a client learning how to cover his mouth and nose when he sneezes. To teach Mata this behavior, Soren, a Board Certified Behavior Analyst (BCBA), plans a model that includes selecting prearranged stimuli that demonstrates for Mata precisely what he is supposed to do (e.g., lift his arm, bury his nose and mouth in his inner elbow, sneeze). First, Soren assesses and teaches Mata any prerequisite skills, selects models, conducts a pretest, and sequences the models for training. Next, he preassesses Mata's current performance, trains Mata on the model until he does it correctly in five consecutive trials, and then conducts postassessment of Mata's ability to perform the behavior. Which training procedure best describes Soren and Mata's work together?

    A. Shaping
    B. High-p
    C. Modeling and imitation training
    D. Chaining

95. One day at school, Tim drew an obnoxious picture on the whiteboard in his classroom and the entire class laughed. As a result of the attention that he received from the other students, Tim continued to draw obnoxious pictures on the whiteboard at every opportunity throughout the school day for the rest of the week. Tim's behavior is the result of:

    A. Negative punishment
    B. Negative reinforcement
    C. Positive punishment
    D. Positive reinforcement

96. Negative reinforcement involves the _____ of a stimulus immediately following a behavior that serves to _____ the future frequency of the behavior.

    A. Addition; decrease
    B. Addition; increase
    C. Removal; decrease
    D. Removal; increase

97. Benjamin, a behavior technician, is working with a client, Carl, on saying the word "please." When Benjamin says "please," Carl will say the word "please." Contingent on Carl's correct response of saying the word "please," Benjamin will immediately reinforce it with vocal praise. The verbal operant targeted is:

    A. The echoic
    B. The tact
    C. The intraverbal
    D. The mand

98. The Motivation Assessment Scale (MAS), Functional Assessment Screening Tool (FAST), and Questions About Behavioral Functioning (QABF) are considered what type of assessment?

A. Component analysis

B. Direct

C. Indirect

D. Standardized test

99. Gus is a client who engages in physical aggression toward others. During treatment sessions, vocal attempts from staff to redirect Gus when he engages in the problem behavior have been unsuccessful. When staff resorts to using physical restraints to prevent Gus from engaging in physical aggression, he almost immediately relaxes and becomes noticeably calmer; but when he is released from the restraint, Gus will rapidly escalate and engages in the problem behavior again. Given this information, what would you hypothesize to be the function of Gus's aggressive behavior?

A. Attention

B. Escape

C. Sensory

D. Tangible

100. A behavior analyst is consulting with the parents of a 10-year-old boy, Gary, about his extreme resistance to completing homework. When Gary's parents ask him to do his homework, he refuses and, quite often, has a temper tantrum. The behavior analyst meets with Gary and, in the course of their conversation, asks where he likes to do homework, what pen or pencil he likes to use, if he likes to listen to music while doing homework, if he likes to work in bright or soft light, which subjects he likes to work on first, how often he feels he needs a break, and what he likes to do when he takes a break from doing homework. This best exemplifies the consideration of which factor when recommending intervention goals and procedures?

A. Constraints

B. Supporting environments

C. Risks

D. Client preferences

101. Which of the following is a schedule of reinforcement that specifies the average duration that must pass before the first occurrence of a target response will be reinforced?

A. Fixed interval (FI)

B. Fixed ratio (FR)

C. Variable interval (VI)

D. Variable ratio (VR)

102. A behavior analyst, Mieka, is working with a fifth-grade student, Randolph, to improve his initiation of in-class writing activities. Mieka observes Randolph during his English Language Arts (ELA) class and found that, on average, it takes Randolph 104 seconds to begin writing tasks, whereas randomly selected peers take 47 seconds to begin. The measurement starts when the teacher finishes providing instructions for the activity and ends when Randolph uses his writing utensil to write assignment-appropriate information on his paper (e.g., name, date, letters). Which temporal dimension of behavior is measured in this scenario?

A. Duration

B. Interresponse time

C. Latency

D. Whole interval

103. This is a contingency-dependent antecedent intervention that involves presenting a series of simple requests followed by a target request. The procedure may function as an abolishing operation (AO) and decrease the motivation to escape from requests.

    A. Functional communication training
    B. Noncontingent reinforcement with positive reinforcement
    C. Noncontingent reinforcement with negative reinforcement
    D. High-probability request sequence

104. Donald, the chief executive officer of a major corporation, was arrested after he flew into a rage while driving and deliberately forced another driver's car off the road. As a result, Donald was sentenced to attend weekly group therapy meetings for anger management, which he despises and thinks are a waste of time. During each meeting, Donald makes offensive remarks to the other participants and the group leader until he is asked to take a 10-minute break outside to calm down and reconsider his behavior. Once outside, Donald smokes cigarettes and responds to emails on his phone. The group leader notices that, rather than stopping, Donald's aggressive and offensive remarks are beginning earlier in the session and occurring with greater frequency. What is the most likely reason that Donald's aggressive behavior is increasing?

    A. Donald's behavior is reinforced by access to escape from the group
    B. The group leader lacks group management skills
    C. Donald's behavior is reinforced by attention from the other members of the group
    D. The group leader fails to reinforce Donald's participation in the anger management group

105. Examine the following graph of the results from a functional analysis of Walter's scratching behavior. Based on this alone, what would you hypothesize to be the function of the scratching behavior?

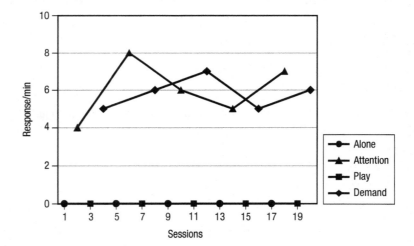

    A. Automatic reinforcement
    B. Automatic reinforcement and social negative reinforcement
    C. Social positive reinforcement and social negative reinforcement
    D. Inconclusive, the pattern is undifferentiated

106. Tamar, a behavior analyst, is initiating a supervisory relationship with a new supervisee. Tamar is aware that supervisors must assess the outcomes of their behavior analytic supervision activities and decides to create an assessment plan that uses recommended methods. Consequently, she considers all of the following methods except:

  A. Covert third-party observation
  B. Tracking relevant data
  C. Requesting feedback
  D. Conducting a survey

107. A behavior analyst is working with a fifth-grade teacher in a general education classroom to gather data on a particular student's frequent question-asking behavior. According to the teacher, the student asks questions constantly throughout the day and sometimes strings questions together so much that it is difficult to identify when an instance of questioning ends and another begins. Based on this information, which of the following measurement procedures should the behavior analyst recommend for collecting data on this student's question-asking behavior?

  A. Frequency recording
  B. Interresponse time recording
  C. Partial interval recording
  D. Whole interval recording

108. Olivia, a Board Certified Behavior Analyst (BCBA), is taking on a new 3-year-old client who engages in food refusal behavior. She has already met with the parents to collect preliminary background information about the client and to review the contract for professional services. After obtaining written consent from the parents to proceed with services, what should Olivia do next?

  A. Conduct a functional analysis
  B. Obtain consent from the 3-year-old client
  C. Refer the client to a healthcare professional
  D. Review records and available data

109. Which of the following is not a defining feature of single-subject experimental designs?

  A. The subject is the unit of intervention and data analysis
  B. Subjects are randomly selected from a population of interest
  C. The subject provides its own control for comparison
  D. The target behavior is measured repeatedly across different levels or conditions of the intervention

110. Corey is a Board Certified Behavior Analyst (BCBA) who is supervising Steven, a graduate student in a behavior analysis training program. Corey discovered that Steven had submitted falsified fieldwork experience verification forms, counting many more hours than he would have been able to complete given his schedule. When Corey confronted Steven about this issue, Steven refused to admit any wrongdoing and claimed that he had indeed complete the hours reported on his experience verification forms. How should Corey proceed?

  A. Ask Steven to make up the extra hours reported. If he agrees, then consider this a lesson learned and the matter closed
  B. Ask Steven to seek out another supervisor. If he agrees, then consider this a lesson learned and the matter closed
  C. Report Steven to his university. He is a graduate student, so this is a university problem
  D. Report Steven to the Behavior Analyst Certification Board. This is a serious breach of the Ethics Code

111. Maggie is a Board Certified Behavior Analyst (BCBA) who has obtained training in supervision. She supervised several graduate students for her agency who complained about her supervision practices. Some of the students reported that Maggie failed to even provide an adequate number of supervisory contacts. As a result, Maggie was eventually reported to the Behavior Analyst Certification Board (BACB) for multiple ethical violations. When questioned about the reported issues, she argued that the training she received did not cover all aspects of her responsibilities as a supervisor. "If my training didn't cover it, how am I supposed to know?" she asked. What would the Ethics Code's position on this matter be?

A. BCBAs are obligated to be familiar with the Ethics Code

B. BCBAs are obligated to be familiar with only those parts of the Ethics Code that are relevant to the work they're doing

C. BCBAs cannot be held liable for their professional conduct if they have not been properly trained

D. BCBAs should immediately take steps to resolve problems when notified that they are out of compliance with the Ethics Code

112. A behavior analyst designs an intervention to be implemented by an elementary school teacher. The intervention plan is presented in clearly articulated, discrete steps. The behavior analyst reviews the steps of the intervention with the teacher, answers any questions, and provides modeling in the specific skills required to implement the intervention as designed. The behavior analyst then periodically visits the teacher's classroom during instruction time to take observational data, noting any deviations from the behavior plan. When the teacher's students go to recess, the behavior analyst meets with the teacher to share feedback based on the observation. Why does the behavior analyst conduct these observations?

A. To assess social validity

B. To monitor treatment integrity

C. To assess social significance

D. To set criteria for behavior change

113. Stewart is a Board Certified Behavior Analyst (BCBA) who is working with a 15-year-old client who engages in several problem behaviors at school. These include shouting at his peers, scribbling in his textbooks, stealing items from his teacher's desk, and leaving the school building without permission. Which of these behaviors should be targeted first?

A. Shouting at peers

B. Scribbling in books

C. Stealing items from teacher's desk

D. Leaving school building without permission

114. A Board Certified Behavior Analyst (BCBA) is the main author of a published study. A researcher contacts the BCBA and asks to see the original data gathered from the study. How should the BCBA respond?

A. Share the data, excluding confidential client information

B. Share the data, including all information on clients

C. Refuse to share the data as they are not required

D. Refer the researcher to the data published in the journal article; the original data do not have to be shared

115. Alex is a behavior analyst who is evaluating the effectiveness of two different instructional procedures for increasing intraverbal behavior. To do this, he measures the number of response opportunities needed to acquire a target behavior for each of the two procedures. The first procedure resulted in acquisition of the target skill after an average of six trials, but the second procedure resulted in acquisition of the target skill after an average of only two trials. What measurement method is Alex using to compare the two instructional procedures?

A. Baseline probe trials

B. Component analysis

C. Task analysis

D. Trials to criterion

116. Ezra is a Board Certified Behavior Analyst (BCBA) who supervises several students enrolled in an applied behavior analysis (ABA) training program at a local university. She has been careful about taking on only the number of supervisees that allows her to be effective as a supervisor and ensures that the training she provides is well within her identified scope of competence. To evaluate the effects of her supervision, what does Ezra need to do?

A. Nothing else as Ezra has already taken the necessary steps for ensuring that she provides high quality supervision

B. Conduct regular meetings with supervisees to discuss supervision and allow opportunities for them to report any concerns

C. Conduct regular evaluations of supervisory performance using feedback from others, clients' outcomes data, and supervisees' outcomes data

D. Examine quarterly and annual evaluation reports from her supervisor to identify areas of concern and set goals for addressing them

117. Mr. Abubakar, an elementary school teacher, is having a difficult time with classroom management during math instruction. He consults with Ms. Crisp, the school's Board Certified Behavior Analyst (BCBA), who conducts several observations during which she records the rate of students' off-task behavior and Mr. Abubakar's use of praise statements. Ms. Crisp analyzes the data and determines that there are far fewer incidents of off-task behavior among students when Mr. Abubakar gives his students more praise statements. Following Ms. Crisp's recommendation, Mr. Abubakar deliberately provides more praise statements during math lessons which appears to improve his students' behavior. The knowledge learned from science allows for one or more of three levels of understanding. At what level is Ms. Crisp and Mr. Abubakar's understanding of these students' behavior during math instruction?

A. Control

B. Prediction and control

C. Description and prediction

D. Description

118. A teacher is implementing a new reward system in her classroom. This system involves having students earn tickets for completing assigned tasks. The students then write their names on the tickets they have earned and place them in a box located on the teacher's desk throughout the week. At the end of the week, the teacher draws a ticket from the box, declares the student whose name is on the ticket as the winner, and gives the winning student a prize. The more tickets the students earn, the greater the chance that one of their tickets will be drawn. What schedule of reinforcement does this system use?

A. Fixed interval (FI)

B. Fixed ratio (FR)

C. Variable interval (VI)

D. Variable ratio (VR)

119. Erin, a Board Certified Behavior Analyst (BCBA), is implementing an antecedent intervention with Shane to increase the likelihood that Shane will comply with requests to wash his hands. This intervention involves delivering several requests that Shane is likely to comply with (e.g., giving a high five, touching his nose, making a silly face) before delivering the request of washing his hands. When Shane complies with the request of washing his hands, a high-quality reinforcer is to be delivered. What type of procedure is Erin using?

    A. Low probability instructional sequence
    B. Noncontingent reinforcement
    C. High-probability instructional sequence
    D. Response blocking

120. To evaluate a client's skillset, a behavior analyst uses a standardized test that requires following specific procedures. What type of assessment is this?

    A. Criterion-referenced
    B. Curriculum-based
    C. Direct
    D. Indirect

121. Mackenzie is a client who has been engaging in problem behavior at school. The Board Certified Behavior Analyst (BCBA) assigned to her case, Eli, conducts an observation of Mackenzie in the school setting and records each occurrence of the target behavior and the environmental events surrounding it. What type of assessment is Eli conducting?

    A. Descriptive
    B. Criterion referenced
    C. Free operant
    D. Indirect

122. Each of the following behaviors can be measured using permanent product recording except:

    A. Completing homework assignment sheets
    B. Making eye contact with peers
    C. Placing toys in toy bins after free play periods
    D. Urinating in diapers

123. A 52-year-old person receiving care in a psychiatric residential treatment facility stands still in silence holding a broom for several hours a day. In a treatment team discussion, a Board Certified Behavior Analyst (BCBA) learns that this person used to sweep the common room while singing every day. One member of the treatment team expresses the view that the person's change in behavior may just be a mystery with no rational explanation or cause. Another team member speculates that the person's change in behavior may be caused by their experience as a young child and repressed emotions that have resurfaced into their consciousness. The BCBA is committed to a scientific approach to understanding and intervening in human behavior. As such, she respectfully shares with the team that all behavior possesses an identifiable cause and, as a result, is to some degree determinable. She then encourages the team to (a) focus on explanations of the person's behavior based on the person's known experiences and the consequences of their behavior; and (b) rule out simple, logical explanations for the person's behavior before entertaining more complex or abstract explanations. In her comments, the BCBA is promoting which three attitudes of science?

    A. Empiricism, parsimony, and philosophical doubt
    B. Determinism, selectionism, and parsimony
    C. Selectionism, determinism, and empiricism
    D. Parsimony, philosophical doubt, and determinism

124. Amy is a Board Certified Behavior Analyst (BCBA) who works at a local clinic for young children with developmental disabilities. Each morning when she arrives at the clinic, she checks her calendar to review the day's planned work activities. On days when she sees an event with the label "supervision meeting" on her calendar, she immediately spends the first 15 minutes of her workday reviewing the discussion points and activities that she will go over with her supervisee at their next meeting. However, when no such event is seen on her calendar, Amy does not spend any time reviewing the discussion points and activities that she will go over with her supervisee at their next meeting. Amy's behavior is likely the result of:

A. Response generalization

B. Socially mediated reinforcement

C. Stimulus control

D. Stimulus generalization

125. What is the Ethics Code's position on the use of punishment procedures?

A. When attempting to decrease behavior, use punishment first to achieve quick results

B. Use reinforcement only. Punishment is bad practice and should never be used

C. Recommend reinforcement rather than punishment whenever possible

D. Use only reinforcement or only punishment

126. Which of the following is an example of an automatically reinforced response?

A. Eating quinoa because you read that it's a healthy thing to do

B. Knocking on a door because you want someone to open it

C. Scratching a spot on your leg because it itches

D. Washing your hands because you were told to

127. Ian is a 3-year-old boy who does not communicate using language very often. He knows many basic words, but he often screams or makes physical gestures to communicate with his parents instead of words—especially when he wants something. Kelly is a Board Certified Behavior Analyst (BCBA) working with Ian and his parents in their home to increase Ian's use of vocal mands. Which procedure is the most appropriate for Kelly to employ?

A. Shaping latency within a response topography

B. Shaping across response topographies

C. Shaping frequency within a response topography

D. Shaping magnitude within a response topography

128. Wanda, a Board Certified Behavior Analyst (BCBA), works in a school with other nonbehavioral professionals. One day, the school counselor tells Wanda that one of her clients was banging her head against a desk during a counseling session. When Wanda asked the counselor what he did about it, the counselor said, "She seemed like she was having a rough day, so I just let her. She needed to release her frustrations out somehow." In a situation such as this, what should a BCBA do?

A. Attempt to resolve the issue directly with the counselor. If it cannot be resolved, report it to the appropriate authority (e.g., administrator, supervisor)

B. File a report with details of the issue to the Behavior Analyst Certification Board (BACB)

C. Avoid conflict with nonbehavioral colleagues. Do not report the incident or attempt to resolve it directly with the counselor

D. Notify the client's parent or legal guardian of the incident

129. Dorria, a behavior technician, is teaching a 4-year-old client, Milo, to say the word "apple." Dorria would emit the vocal response of "apple" as a model, then prompt Milo to replicate the response. Milo's vocal response of "apple" is under the control of Dorria's vocal response of "apple." Milo's vocal response is an example which of the verbal operants?

    A. Codic
    B. Echoic
    C. Mand
    D. Tact

130. Examine the following graph of the results from a functional analysis of Cary's yelling behavior. Based on this alone, what would you hypothesize to be the function of the yelling behavior?

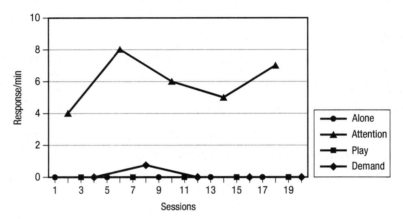

    A. Automatic reinforcement
    B. Social positive reinforcement
    C. Automatic reinforcement and social positive reinforcement
    D. Social negative reinforcement

131. Mr. Caretto, a fourth grade teacher, explains to his students that they will have a pizza party once every student has memorized all of the multiplication facts. What type of group contingency is this?

    A. Dependent group contingency
    B. Intradependent group contingency
    C. Independent group contingency
    D. Interdependent group contingency

132. As supervisors, behavior analysts must provide supervisees with timely feedback and reinforcement to enhance their performance. Dr. Digable, a Board Certified Behavior Analyst (BCBA), conducts observations of her supervisee, Toni, to offer performance feedback. After each observation, Dr. Digable will carefully write up her notes describing what Toni performed correctly, which can take several days, and then praises Toni for it the next time they meet. Despite Dr. Digable's efforts to praise Toni for his good work, she notices that his performance is not improving over time. What might account for this?

    A. Dr. Digable is not delivering feedback in a timely enough manner
    B. Dr. Digable's feedback is unclear
    C. Dr. Digable uses too many technical terms
    D. Dr. Digable focuses on too many errors at a time

133. Diane, a teacher, sees Tony, a client, reaching for a jar of cookies on a high shelf. Diane decides on the terminal behavior of a vocalization of "cookie, please." Diane walks toward Tony, makes eye contact, and presents a curious facial expression (i.e., neutral face with eyes wide open). Tony breaks eye contact and looks toward the jar of cookies. Diane says, "What do you want?" Tony then looks toward Diane and remains silent. Diane says, "Say, 'cookie, please.'" Tony responds, "Cookie, please." Diane says, "Nice job!" and gets the cookie jar for Tony. What type of teaching arrangement is described in the example?

- **A.** Incidental teaching
- **B.** Free-operant arrangement
- **C.** Discrete-trial teaching
- **D.** Mass-trial teaching

134. A floor sign with the words "out of service for maintenance" is positioned directly in front of a restroom entrance. Cooper needs to use the restroom and approaches the entrance but, because he sees the sign, does not go inside. Cooper's behavior is an example of:

- **A.** Contingency-shaped behavior
- **B.** Negative reinforcement
- **C.** Rule-governed behavior
- **D.** Premack principle

135. Danielle has been taught to use a hand signal to communicate to her teacher that she needs to go to the restroom. This usually results in the teacher looking at Danielle and nodding, thereby giving her permission to go to the restroom. Recently, Danielle has started to wave her arms in the air and silently mouth the word "bathroom" when the teacher looks in her direction to ask for permission to go to the restroom. Which of the following best explains this new untrained behavior?

- **A.** Functional response class
- **B.** Response generalization
- **C.** Setting/situation generalization
- **D.** Stimulus generalization

136. Conducting a descriptive assessment of problem behavior can involve any of the following activities except:

- **A.** Administering checklists or rating scales at regular intervals to stakeholders who most frequently observe the problem behavior
- **B.** Continuously recording the occurrence of the problem behavior in relation to environmental events
- **C.** Writing a narrative description of the problem behavior under the conditions in which it occurs
- **D.** Recording when the problem behavior occurs in a scatterplot

137. The format of a goal statement can include several components. Identify the criterion in the following example: After recess, when asked to complete independent writing tasks, Sam will remain seated at his desk at least 80% of the time as measured by interval recording data by 1/1/2024:

- **A.** When asked to complete independent writing tasks
- **B.** Sam will remain seated at his desk
- **C.** At least 80% of the time
- **D.** As measured by interval recording data

138. Before extinction is implemented, a client yells to get the parents' attention. The parents implement an extinction procedure: They remove attention provided when the behavior occurs. Which form of the extinction procedure are the parents implementing?

    A. Extinction of behavior maintained by negative reinforcement
    B. Extinction of behavior maintained by positive reinforcement
    C. Extinction of behavior maintained by differential reinforcement
    D. Extinction of behavior maintained by automatic reinforcement

139. Hector is a graduate student in an applied behavior analysis (ABA) program and works at a preschool for children with disabilities. Several children in the classroom have feeding problems and Hector thinks he may have an intervention idea to help them eat during snack times. Knowing that he will need to complete a research project for graduate school, Hector plans to ask the classroom teacher for permission to conduct a small research project. Once the teacher agrees, he can then begin to take baseline data and implement the snack time intervention. Hector's goal is to have a completed research project ready to submit to his university when it is due. What should Hector do to act in accordance with the Ethics Code?

    A. Proceed as planned as he is not required to obtain approval from the university or school to conduct the study
    B. Obtain the teacher's permission to proceed with data collection and implementation of the intervention
    C. Conduct the project as an employee in the context of his job and have the teacher notify parents of the intervention
    D. Notify his university and obtain approval from the institutional review committee before collecting any data

140. A Board Certified Behavior Analyst (BCBA) for a school is assessing a student's preferences using an interest inventory. After asking the student to identify activities that may serve as reinforcers, the BCBA groups them into different categories: board games, books, and puzzles. The BCBA wants to calculate the total number of activities for each category and graph the results to discuss with the student's teachers. Which of the following data display options is most appropriate for the BCBA to use in this instance?

    A. Bar graph
    B. Cumulative record
    C. Line graph
    D. Semilogarithmic chart

141. You are reviewing classroom observation notes taken by an applied behavior analysis (ABA) student you are supervising. The student notes that the teacher heavily relies on negative punishment procedures for classroom management. If you conducted a follow-up observation, which two negative punishment procedures would you expect to see the teacher implementing?

    A. Response cost and time-out
    B. Reprimands and response cost
    C. Time-out and response blocking
    D. Contingent exercise and overcorrection

142. Martin, a Board Certified Behavior Analyst (BCBA), is teaching a paraprofessional, Sam, in a special education classroom how to competently implement an intervention with integrity. Martin employs behavioral skills training (BST); he describes the target skill, demonstrates it, requires Sam to practice it, provides feedback during practice, and repeats the final two steps (requiring Sam to practice it and providing feedback during practice) until mastery is achieved. Which step of the BST process did Martin miss?

A. Role-play the skill with the client

B. Behaviorally define the target skill

C. Provide a written description of the target skill

D. None of the above; all steps of BST were followed

143. Neena is a Board Certified Behavior Analyst (BCBA) who works in the home setting with an 11-year-old client with autism spectrum disorder (ASD) to reduce incidents of noncompliance and aggression. Prior to the start of services, the client's parents agreed to actively participate in parent training sessions and follow agreed upon intervention procedures. After a couple of months, the parents filed for a divorce and moved to separate homes. Now, the client's father is refusing to follow an established reinforcement procedure and making statements like, "My child needs to do things without a bribe." At the mother's home, she will interrupt therapy and say things like, "My child is going through a lot right now, let's just take it easy and back off." In terms of progress, the client is no longer making any, and parents have stopped showing up to scheduled parent training sessions. What should Neena do next?

A. Continue to work with the client because behavior analysts cannot abandon clients. Neena should make additional attempts to work with the parents

B. Continue to work with the client and leave the parents out of the process. It is likely that the parents' behaviors are a result of the divorce, and the situation may improve over time

C. Call a meeting with her supervisor and the client's parents to discuss how they can solve the issue. If the parents fail to attend, it may be appropriate to begin terminating services

D. Suggest to the parents that she work with the client at school since therapy in the home is not going well and clients have a right to effective treatment

144. A client is taught to select a physical ball when the picture of a ball is presented. The client is then taught to select the picture of a ball when the spoken word "ball" is presented. A relation of symmetry would be demonstrated if a ball is presented and the client:

A. Says "ball"

B. Selects a physical ball

C. Selects a picture of a ball

D. Selects the sample stimulus

145. Alice is a Board Certified Behavior Analyst (BCBA) who is working with a second-grade teacher, Ms. Lee, to enhance her classroom management practices. Alice conducts an observation of Ms. Lee during the school day. At the beginning of the school day, Ms. Lee was observed reviewing a visual schedule posted at the front of the classroom. Then, throughout the day, Ms. Lee intermittently made statements such as "I like how you're following my directions." Ms. Lee also intermittently gave tokens to students when they followed directions and consistently used an egg timer to provide an audible warning prior to every transition. Which of Ms. Lee's observed behaviors belong to the same stimulus class?

A. Giving tokens and providing a transition warning

B. Giving tokens and reviewing visual schedule

C. "I like how you're following my directions" and giving tokens

D. Transition warning and reviewing visual schedule

146. Eddie's dad discovered that he plays video games before completing his homework, so he sat him down for a talk to communicate the expectation that Eddie is to prioritize schoolwork and only play video games after finishing his homework assignments. When Eddie argued, his dad took away his video game controllers for the remainder of the day without hesitation. The next time Eddie's dad has a talk with him about what he is expected to do, Eddie does not argue. What basic principle is likely to be responsible for the change in Eddie's behavior?

    A. Extinction
    B. Negative punishment
    C. Negative reinforcement
    D. Positive punishment

147. As a first-year college student with autism spectrum disorder (ASD), Andy rarely spoke to others and stayed in his dorm room playing video games alone when not in class. He was disengaged from school and lacked friends; as a result, he seriously considered dropping out. In the spring term of that academic year, he worked with a Board Certified Behavior Analyst (BCBA) who implemented an intervention for Andy that involved attendance and engagement in a swing dancing class. Over the course of the intervention, Andy increased the amount of time he spent with others and greatly enhanced his willingness to communicate with others and his conversation skills. Two years later, Andy was involved in several clubs on campus, had numerous friends, was successful in school and work, and was on track to graduate. This is an example of which core dimension of applied behavior analysis?

    A. Technological
    B. Analytic
    C. Replicable
    D. Generality

148. All of the following procedures are used to weaken behavior except:

    A. Differential reinforcement of incompatible behavior (DRI)
    B. High-probability instructional sequence (high-p)
    C. Differential reinforcement of other behavior (DRO)
    D. Differential reinforcement of alternative behavior (DRA)

149. Leslie is an 11-year-old client who engages in physical aggression at school. Her teacher reported that she "scratches, bites, and kicks the other students during recess." When asked what occurs after the problem behavior, the teacher shared that those other students will typically abandon their toys which Leslie then picks up and engages in play with. What is likely to be the function of Leslie's physically aggressive behavior at school during recess?

    A. Access to social reinforcement
    B. Access to tangible reinforcement
    C. Escape from task demands
    D. Sensory reinforcement

150. Nic is a 9-year-old student in the fourth grade who often refuses to complete his academic work, especially in-class math assignments, which he finds very challenging. Frank, a behavior analyst in training, is tasked with developing an intervention to address Nic's work refusal. Which of the following is the most appropriate independent variable for Frank to include in the behavioral intervention for addressing the problem?

    A. Access to a preferred activity after completing a reduced math assignment
    B. Increasing on-task behavior during math instruction
    C. Reducing inattentive behavior
    D. Implementation of the Good Behavior Game

151. Morgan and Pat's 6-year-old child, Noby, refuses to defecate in the toilet. Instead, he puts on a diaper and sits behind the couch when he needs to go. When he's finished, he lets one of his parents know so they can clean him up. After Morgan and Pat offer to buy Noby a new toy every time he goes to the bathroom in the toilet, Noby begins doing so. However, this reward is not sustainable; it's too expensive and Noby's room is now packed with toys. When they stop rewarding him with toys, he resumes defecating in a diaper. Morgan and Pat don't know what to do, so they reach out to a behavior analyst for help. Which is the best strategy for Morgan and Pat to try to solve their problem?

    A. Conduct a functional analysis of Noby's behavior
    B. Teach Noby to let his parents know when he needs to go to the bathroom
    C. Talk with Noby about why he won't use the toilet
    D. Implement an intermittent schedule of reinforcement

152. Anders, a trainee, asks Tiana, a Board Certified Behavior Analyst (BCBA), if she will provide him with behavior analytic supervision. Tiana is quite busy, but she considers Anders's request. All of the following are sound reasons for Tiana to provide Anders with behavior analytic supervision except:

    A. It will contribute to Anders's professional development
    B. It will enable them to further enhance their relationship
    C. It is required per the Professional and Ethical Compliance Code for behavior analysts
    D. It is supported as best practice by the field's professional literature

153. Examine the following graph of the frequency of three different behaviors across seven sessions. Which of the following descriptions is most accurate for Behavior 2?

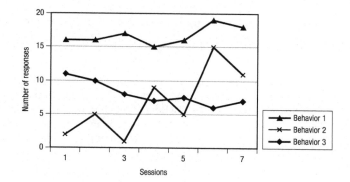

    A. High-level responding, low variability, increasing trend
    B. Mid-level responding, high variability, increasing trend
    C. Mid-level responding, low variability, decreasing trend
    D. Low-level responding, high variability, increasing trend

154. Sheree is struggling to fall asleep at night. Her friend Nicole, a Board Certified Behavior Analyst (BCBA), recommends she manipulate motivating operations to help her fall asleep. Of the following, which is the best example of manipulating motivating operations to facilitate sleep?

    A. Set a reminder to go to bed at 10:00 p.m.
    B. Only sleeping in the bedroom
    C. Removing the television from the bedroom
    D. Refraining from taking a nap during the day

155. Examine the following graph. What type of experimental design was used?.

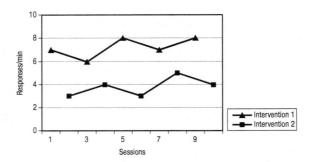

A. AB design
B. Changing-criterion design
C. Multielement design
D. Multiple-baseline design

156. Dr. Sanchez is a Board Certified Behavior Analyst (BCBA) and university professor who teaches courses in behavior analysis. She specializes in classroom management, but the university has asked her to teach a course in the next academic term on behavioral treatment of individuals suffering from traumatic brain injuries. How should Dr. Sanchez respond to this request?

A. Agree to teach the course and read as much as possible on the subject before the next academic term to prepare
B. Agree to teach the course and proceed to plan it out
C. Agree to teach the course and recruit graduate students to help prepare lessons for it
D. Decline to teach the course and perhaps offer to assist in identifying another instructor who is better qualified

157. Martika is a trainee who has recently been hired by a private school to provide a fourth grade student with daily applied behavior analysis (ABA) services. Martika would like to count these hours toward meeting fieldwork requirements for the Board Certified Behavior Analyst (BCBA) certification, so she asks Traci, a BCBA, to provide her with behavior analytic supervision. Traci agrees, and they establish a supervisor–supervisee relationship. Which of these must be clearly communicated at the outset of this new supervisory relationship?

A. Performance expectations for the supervisor and the supervisee in the form of a supervision contract
B. Martika's approach to delivering school-based behavior analytic services
C. When and where supervision meetings will take place
D. Traci's approach to providing Martika with skill-based feedback

158. Rosalie is a Board Certified Behavior Analyst (BCBA) who works at a residential facility for physically disabled clients with severe developmental disabilities. One of her clients, Albert, is 24 years old, nonverbal, and uses a wheelchair. Albert has no prior history of engaging in self-injurious behaviors, but he suddenly begins to engage in multiple episodes of a new behavior: hitting himself in the head with his fists and screaming. Rosalie consults with her supervisor and they both agree there may be a medical cause given the sudden onset of this new behavior. How should Rosalie proceed?

    A. Implement an emergency procedure to maintain Albert's safety and refer him to an appropriate professional for assessment. Programming can be placed on hold
    B. Refer Albert to an appropriate professional for assessment but continue providing his regular program
    C. Conduct a functional assessment to identify the controlling variables
    D. Try some activities that may help Albert calm down, such as seating him in a comfortable lounge chair or playing relaxing music

159. It is recommended that behavior analysts use this strategic approach to improving personnel performance.

    A. Human engineering
    B. Behavioral consultation
    C. Organizational manding
    D. Function-based strategies

160. George, a Board Certified Behavior Analyst (BCBA), is working with Martha. George gets Martha's attention and then says, "If you say 'remote,' then I will give it to you." What is this an example of?

    A. Instruction
    B. Rule
    C. Norm
    D. Command

161. Frank is a behavior analyst at a company that provides applied behavior analysis (ABA) services for youth with autism spectrum disorder (ASD). He has supervised numerous supervisees over the years. The company recently conducted an internal review, which surfaced anonymous feedback from Frank's previous supervisees indicating that he possesses strong ABA skills and knowledge, but that his supervision was not tailored to their specific needs. Of the following practices, which is most likely to enhance Frank's ability to meet his supervisees' unique needs?

    A. Conducting an anonymous and brief structured survey of supervisees
    B. Gathering and reviewing relevant performance data
    C. Directly requesting feedback
    D. Collecting data on the effectiveness of the methods they use to evaluate the effects of supervision

162. A Board Certified Behavior Analyst (BCBA) develops a behavior intervention plan to address a student's disruptive classroom behavior in school. The plan is discussed with the education team during a meeting, and then a typed copy of the plan is shared with the student's teachers via email. After 8 weeks, data collected by the student's teachers indicate the student's disruptive behavior has continued unabated. What should the BCBA recommend that the education team do next?

    A. Intensify the intervention
    B. Continue the intervention
    C. Examine treatment integrity
    D. Modify the intervention

163. During the presentation of a functional analysis condition, the experimenter ignores the client but delivers social positive reinforcement when the client engages in problem behavior. What experimental condition does this describe?

    A. Alone
    B. Contingent attention
    C. Contingent escape
    D. Play

164. Rebecca, a Board Certified Behavior Analyst (BCBA), is reviewing the results of the skill assessments her supervisee, Ian, recently completed in order to set achievable supervision goals. When developing long-term goals for Ian, Rebecca should consider all of the following except:

    A. Task List items relevant to Ian's role
    B. Expected needs of the agency
    C. Immediate needs of the agency
    D. Ian's performance across the Task List items

165. Simon is a very busy and hardworking behavior analyst who receives a lot of email messages from staff and clients. When the number of messages in his inbox at work reaches a certain amount, he spends the next day focused on clearing them out by responding to as many as he can. Otherwise, the amount of email messages he will need to address gets too high and he ends up spending his weekend working on addressing them instead of enjoying his family. In relation to responding to emails in his inbox, the number of messages going above a certain amount is a:

    A. Reflexive-conditioned motivating operation (CMO-R)
    B. Surrogate-conditioned motivating operation (CMO-S)
    C. Transitive-conditioned motivating operation (CMO-T)
    D. Unconditioned motivating operation (UMO)

166. Neil is a Board Certified Behavior Analyst (BCBA) working with Maggie, a 74-year-old who recently experienced a stroke. Neil is teaching Maggie how to put her shoes on using the following steps: (a) Neil models putting on his shoes while talking aloud to himself, (b) Maggie puts on her shoes while Neil provides verbal instructions and praise, (c) Maggie puts on her shoes while talking aloud to herself, and Neil quietly gives instructions, (d) Maggie puts on her shoes while quietly speaking the instructions to herself and Neil moves his lips but makes no sound, (e) Maggie puts on her shoes while mouthing instructions without sound, and (f) Maggie puts on her shoes while coaching her performance with covert instructions. Identify the technique Neil is using to teach Maggie.

    A. Self-management
    B. Self-instruction
    C. Modeling training
    D. Imitation training

167. Clive, a client, is learning how to strap the Velcro on his shoes. He already knows how to sit down, put his foot in the shoe, and take hold of the Velcro with his hand, so these steps do not require teaching. Which of the following is the most appropriate procedure to use?

    A. Backward chaining
    B. Total-task chaining
    C. Backward chaining with leap aheads
    D. Forward chaining

168. In this branch of behavior analysis, behavior analysts systematically apply tactics derived from laboratory-based experimentation and the principles of behavior to positively enhance socially significant behaviors. This applied science utilizes experimentation to clearly identify the environmental variables driving behavior. What branch of behavior analysis is this?

- **A.** Applied Behavior Analysis (ABA)
- **B.** Experimental Analysis of Behavior (EAB)
- **C.** Behaviorism
- **D.** Empiricism

169. Select the example that best exemplifies response generalization.

- **A.** Ten-year-old Shefali regularly brushes her teeth before bed in the bathroom at home. When she goes to 2-week summer camp she continues to brush her teeth before bed in the shared camp bathroom
- **B.** Harold's basketball coach teaches him techniques to jump higher during the winter season. In the spring season, Harold employs those techniques to jump higher when blocking in volleyball
- **C.** Betty, a first-year college student with autism spectrum disorder (ASD), takes a ballroom dancing class with a Board Certified Behavior Analyst (BCBA) during which she learns and practices how to ask people to dance and make small talk. In her second year of college, Betty regularly asks questions in class and responds to professors' questions
- **D.** Friedrich, a 1-year-old Austrian, learns how to make a guttural R sound when learning how to say his name, one of the first words he learns. He later applies this skill when pronouncing other German words with a guttural R sound

170. Julian has been working with a behavior analyst to learn how to appropriately respond to in-class questions, which involves raising his hand, waiting to be called on, and then providing an answer. Observational data suggest Julian frequently displays the desired behavior sequence. However, when called on, he has been yelling his answers to questions which often draws negative attention from others in the classroom. What dimension of the behavior should the behavior analyst target for improvement?

- **A.** Function
- **B.** Latency
- **C.** Magnitude
- **D.** Topography

171. Pat is a dog trainer developing an online course. She wants to teach dog owners how to create a conditioned response using a clicker. Which method should Pat employ to teach her students?

- **A.** Give the dog a treat, then click the clicker. Repeat several times
- **B.** Click the clicker as the dog is given a treat. Repeat several times
- **C.** Click the clicker, then give the dog a treat. Repeat several times
- **D.** Hide a treat and click the clicker when the dog finds it. Repeat several times

172. This approach is used by behavior analysts to identify the variables that affect personnel performance.

- **A.** Adaptive behavior assessment
- **B.** Idiographic assessment
- **C.** Analogue assessment
- **D.** Functional assessment

173. Examine the Antecedent-Behavior-Consequence (ABC) data describing Arya's crying behavior in the table that follows. Based on this alone, what would you hypothesize to be the function of the crying behavior?

Table 12.2 ABC data

A	B	C
Teacher reads to class	Arya cries	Teacher tells Arya to be quiet
Teacher assists another student on worksheet activity	Arya cries	Teacher walks over to Arya and asks, "What's wrong?"
Teacher speaks on the phone	Arya cries	Teacher looks at Arya and whispers, "Hush, Arya! Hush!"
Teacher walks toward another student	Arya cries	Teacher turns toward Arya and asks, "What's wrong, Arya?"
Teacher reviews instructions for class assignment	Arya cries	Teacher tells Arya to stop crying

- A. Access to social reinforcement
- B. Access to tangible reinforcement
- C. Escape from task demands
- D. Sensory reinforcement

174. J.E. is a Board Certified Behavior Analyst (BCBA) teaching a client to recognize the number 7. In the initial trial, the number 7 is enlarged. Then, in subsequent trials, the number 7 is gradually made smaller until the client recognizes it among an array of same-sized numbers. What type of stimulus prompt is J.E. employing?

- A. Stimulus fading
- B. Least-to-most
- C. Prompt delay
- D. Stimulus shaping

175. Velvet, a behavior analyst in training, is preparing to teach a client how to tie his shoes, which involves linking behaviors in a chain. However, to do so, Velvet must first develop which of the following?

- A. Action plan
- B. Treatment plan
- C. Skinner's analysis
- D. Task analysis

176. Heidi is a behavior analyst working with a 6-year-old client, Alvin, who vocally refuses to eat his cereal at breakfast before going to school. In response to Alvin's refusal of cereal during breakfast, his mother immediately removes the cereal and gives him a small bag of his favorite potato chip snack. Heidi advises Alvin's mother to ignore Alvin's vocal refusals during breakfast. After several uncomfortable mornings during which Alvin's refusals were ignored, he ceased to refuse cereal. What procedure did Heidi advise Alvin's mother to use?

- A. Differential reinforcement
- B. Extinction
- C. Premack principle
- D. Shaping

177. Liam arranged six objects on a table in front of a client, Gus. Liam allowed Gus to select a single object from the array and interact with it for 10 seconds, at which point Liam would then remove the object and allow Gus to select another object from those remaining. This process was repeated until no objects were left on the table. What type of preference assessment did Liam conduct?

- **A.** Single stimulus
- **B.** Paired stimulus
- **C.** Multiple stimulus with replacement
- **D.** Multiple stimulus without replacement

178. Which of the following statements is not true about behavior analysts and their responsibility in selecting and designing assessments?

- **A.** They conduct assessments that prioritize reinforcement procedures
- **B.** They conduct assessments that consider the needs, context, and resources of clients and stakeholders
- **C.** They conduct assessments that are conceptually consistent with behavior principles
- **D.** They conduct assessments with a focus on maximizing benefits and minimizing risk of harm to clients and stakeholders

179. Antecedent interventions based on motivating operations (MOs) and discriminative stimuli (S^{D}s) are considered _____. Those based on MOs are _____, whereas those based on stimulus control are _____. Fill in the blanks in the correct order:

- **A.** Contingency-independent; function-based; contingency-dependent
- **B.** Function-based; contingency-independent; contingency-dependent
- **C.** Contingency-dependent; function-based; contingency-independent
- **D.** Function-based; contingency-dependent; contingency-independent

180. In this type of functional assessment, historical data about an organizational setting are gathered and analyzed to inform a consultant's understanding of how the organization operates. These historical data are in the form of organizational artifacts, such as its strategic plan, organizational structure, job descriptions, products and services, culture, employee expectations, performance over time, and personnel.

- **A.** Behavior systems analysis
- **B.** Records review
- **C.** Performance management
- **D.** Informant assessment

181. Toby, a Board Certified Behavior Analyst (BCBA), is working with a 4-year-old client in the home setting. The child's mother, Kirsten, is single. One day, Toby runs into Kirsten in a small café. Kirsten invites Toby to sit with her and so he did. During the chance encounter at the café, Kirsten asked Toby if he would like to join her for a drink after his next session with her child, and he promptly said that he would. Before the next session, Toby notices that he's spending extra time styling his hair and feeling excited about seeing Kirsten. How should Toby proceed?

- **A.** Continue to meet with Kirsten. If they develop a romantic relationship, Toby will just need to be discreet so that there is no impact on services
- **B.** Continue to meet with Kirsten. If they develop a romantic relationship, there is no issue with exploitation as the Ethics Code is only concerned with exploitative relationships between supervisors and supervisees
- **C.** Avoid these social events and end the potential relationship before it starts. If Toby wants to pursue a relationship, he should wait at least 2 years after services have been discontinued
- **D.** Tell his supervisor as soon as possible if he is interested in pursuing a romantic relationship and request to be removed from the case so there would not be any conflict of interest

182. The primary model used for performance diagnostics at the individual level is the Antecedent-Behavior-Consequence (ABC) analysis. There are seven steps to conducting performance diagnostics with an ABC analysis. What is the first step?

    A. Determine how severe the problem is
    B. Describe the problem
    C. Describe what the person should be doing instead
    D. Determine the diagnosis

183. Aziz is a behavior analyst working with a client, Malcolm, who engages in exhibitionistic behavior at the retirement facility where he lives. Aziz conducts a functional analysis of Malcolm's behavior and determines that attention is the function. To address the issue, Aziz develops and implements an intervention with Malcolm that includes a schedule of noncontingent access to attention to decrease Malcolm's motivation to engage in exhibitionistic behavior. After implementing the intervention for 4 weeks, progress monitoring data reveal only a very small reduction in Malcolm's exhibitionistic behavior. As a result, the retirement facility has begun the process of evicting Malcolm. Unfortunately, Aziz's intervention was ineffective because he neglected a critical component of an effective treatment plan. Identify the component Aziz neglected to incorporate.

    A. Aziz neglected to incorporate a skill training component to help Malcolm acquire a functionally equivalent replacement behavior
    B. Aziz neglected to incorporate an extinction procedure that would impede reinforcement for Malcolm's exhibitionistic behavior
    C. Aziz neglected to provide differential reinforcement of other behaviors
    D. Aziz neglected to consult and describe the research on the efficacy of behavioral interventions for exhibitionistic behavior

184. A multidisciplinary school-based treatment team engages Josie, a behavior analyst, to create a behavior intervention plan for Rhiannon, a 12th grade student who has been exhibiting problem behaviors in school. It is very important that all individuals implementing the plan are trained to do so and adhere to the plan as intended. What training method should Josie use to most effectively prepare implementers of the behavior intervention plan?

    A. Behavioral skills training
    B. Record and email a video describing the plan
    C. Create and verbally share a slide deck that provides a summary of the plan
    D. Provide an infographic handout on the plan's essential components

185. A Board Certified Behavior Analyst (BCBA) is working with a 7-year-old child with autism spectrum disorder (ASD) who presents with some motor skills problems and tantrum behavior where she screams and hits her head against hard surfaces. During a treatment team meeting to discuss programming for this client, another professional recommends the use of sensory integration therapy as the primary approach to address the problem behaviors. The BCBA should say:

    A. "I agree, we should implement sensory integration therapy to address the motor skills problems and tantrum behavior."
    B. "It may be helpful to try sensory integration therapy for addressing the motor skills problems. For the tantrums, however, I would suggest that we begin with a functional assessment."
    C. "I completely disagree; this recommendation is not evidence-based."
    D. "Please explain to the team how performing exercises like bouncing on a trampoline can decrease the tantrums."

Practice Exam: Answer Key And Rationales

1. **B) Harold is a behavior analyst who lives next door to a family with a child who struggles with behavior issues. He wants to help but is uncomfortable charging his neighbors for his services, so he instead provides them with free behavioral advice**
   While it is understandable that Harold wants to help his neighbors, the Ethics Code requires that behavior analysts only provide services after having defined and documented their professional role with relevant parties.

2. **C) Firmly hits the surface of the table with his hands, producing a highly audible bang**
   Operational definitions must objectively, clearly, and completely describe an observable and measurable target behavior. Among the options presented, "Firmly hits the surface of the table with his hands, producing a highly audible bang" is the definition that best meets the requirements of a strong operational definition as it describes the topography and magnitude of the behavior.

3. **B) Philosophical doubt**
   Philosophical doubt refers to the attitude of viewing scientific knowledge as tentative and continually developing. Consequently, scientists remain skeptical about the validity and truthfulness of all scientific knowledge and are open to modifying their beliefs based on new knowledge and discoveries.

4. **D) Insurance reimbursement**
   Determining a client's need for ongoing services is a broader question than whether a particular intervention should be ended and, consequently, involves a multidimensional assessment of needs and progress. Behavior analysts rely on clinical expertise and adhere to relevant ethical guidelines when determining whether services remain clinically or medically necessary. Factors to consider include the client's progress toward treatment goals as evidenced by assessment results and other forms of data collection, and the degree to which the client has made socially significant progress.

5. **C) A behavior intervention plan**
   Permanent product measures the effect the behavior produced on the environment. A permanent product is a durable product of a behavior, such as intervention plans, assessment reports, and data collection forms.

6. **A) The best available evidence**
   Behavior analysts adhere to the evidence-based practice model of professional decision-making. This means they rely on the "best available evidence" coupled with clinical expertise to determine whether an intervention is effective and if a treatment needs to be revised. Behavior analysts examine and interpret graphed data when determining the effectiveness of an intervention and need for treatment revision.

7. **A) Being disrespectful to adults**
    When selecting behaviors to target with intervention, it is necessary to focus on those that are observable and measurable. In other words, behaviors targeted for intervention must be observable and measurable in terms of one of the measurable dimensions of behavior (e.g., topography, duration, rate/frequency). "Being disrespectful to adults" is a subjective description of behavior that does not lend itself to observation and valid/reliable measurement.

8. **B) Experimental Analysis of Behavior**
    Experimental Analysis of Behavior (EAB) is the basic research branch of behavior analysis. It takes a natural science approach to research that defines and clarifies the basic processes and principles of behavior. It was founded by B. F. Skinner with the publication of *The Behavior of Organisms* in 1938. Skinner articulated two types of behavior: (a) *respondent behaviors* that are reflexive and elicited by stimuli immediately preceding them, and (b) *operant behaviors* that are elicited by the effects of consequences of past behaviors. The operant three-term contingency is the primary unit of analysis. EAB is primarily a laboratory-based experimental approach that established the foundational principles of operant behavior.

9. **D) Function-based definitions**
    An intervention goal may target a behavior that is functionally or topographically defined. Function-based definitions describe responses in terms of their effect on the environment (e.g., "any behavior that results in X") whereas topography-based definitions describe responses in terms of their form. Whether functionally or topographically defined, definitions should be objective, clear, and complete.

10. **A) Conditioned reinforcers**
    Conditioned reinforcers, also known as learned or secondary reinforcers, are stimuli that have acquired reinforcing properties as a result of having been paired with one or more other reinforcers. In the scenario presented, the tokens (K-bucks) have been paired with multiple reinforcing stimuli (fruit snacks, juice boxes, potato chips, colorful pencils, and erasers).

11. **D) Contact Sam and be persistent in finding a time to meet. Ashley should express her concern to Sam and ask if it can be immediately resolved**
    Behavior analysts should address concerns about the professional misconduct of others directly with them whenever possible. Reporting Sam to the BACB for his actions thus far does not seem warranted. In this situation, reaching out to Sam to problem-solve the issue is an appropriate next step and does not place anyone at undue risk.

12. **D) Repeated measurement that yields the same results**
    Validity refers to the degree to which we are measuring what we intend to measure. Requirements for valid measurement include direct measurement of a socially significant behavior, measurement of its relevant dimension for answering the question, and data representing its occurrence under relevant conditions (e.g., time, place) for answering the question.

13. **D) Radical behaviorism**
    The conceptual system of radical behaviorism was developed by B. F. Skinner. Radical behaviorism seeks to understand behavior in all its forms and collapses the distinction between private events (i.e., thoughts and feelings) and public events (i.e., behavior that is observable and measurable). It is radical in the sense that it includes all behavior, both public and private, and assumes they are influenced by the same kinds of variables and result from an individual's experiences and environments. From the perspective of radical behaviorism, thoughts and feelings do not cause behavior—thoughts and feelings are behavior. As such, thoughts and feelings conform to the laws of behavior and can be addressed utilizing the principles of behavior.

14. **A) Extinction of behavior maintained by positive reinforcement**
In the scenario presented, Shelly engages in a problem behavior (screaming) that is maintained by positive reinforcement (attention from her father). By ignoring the screams, Shelly's father is withholding reinforcement (attention) for the previously reinforced behavior (screaming). This is an example of an extinction procedure for a behavior maintained by positive reinforcement.

15. **D) Unconditioned**
Also known as a primary or natural reinforcer, unconditioned reinforcers are stimuli that increase the future frequency of the behavior that it immediately follows independent of the individual's learning history. These reinforcers satisfy basic life needs (e.g., food) and do not need to be learned. In the scenario presented, the chocolate-covered almonds served as unconditioned reinforcers. DaShon did not need to learn that chocolate-covered almonds were reinforcing.

16. **B) Response maintenance**
Response maintenance refers to extent to which a client continues to perform a behavior when some or all of an intervention that evokes it has been removed.

17. **B) Contrived free-operant observation**
Free-operant observation preference assessments involve observing and recording the duration of engagement with each object/activity available. Free operant observations can be contrived, involving prearrangement of the environment, or naturalistic, involving no prearrangement of the environment. Liam prearranged the environment to include different objects and activities that Gus may like and can engage, so this is an example of a contrived free-operant observation.

18. **C) Generalization**
Baseline logic is a powerful form of experimental reasoning that calls for three elements: prediction (anticipated outcome of an unknown/future measurement), verification (demonstration of a functional relationship between the intervention and target behavior), and replication (repeating of independent variable manipulations and obtaining outcomes similar to that of a previous study).

19. **B) Internal validity**
Internal validity refers to the degree the changes in the dependent variable (DV; i.e., target behavior) can be attributed to the manipulation of the independent variable (IV; i.e., intervention) and not the result of uncontrolled/extraneous factors. Experiments that reliably demonstrate a cause-and-effect relationship between the IV and DV are said to have a high degree of internal validity. Internal validity is threatened when there is the possibility that results are affected by uncontrolled/extraneous factors.

20. **A) Duration**
Duration refers to the amount of time a behavior lasts from start to finish. By starting the timer at the beginning of the behavior, stopping at its end, and then recording the elapsed time for its occurrence, the behavior technician is documenting the duration of the behavior.

21. **A) Support procedural integrity**
When behavior analysts monitor the performance of supervisees and provide timely feedback and reinforcement, it enhances supervisees' performance and supports procedural integrity.

22. **C) Extinction**
Of the procedures listed, the set of unwanted effects presented (i.e., evoke emotional/aggressive reactions, an initial increase in the rate of the problem behavior, an initial increase in the magnitude of the problem behavior, the reappearance of the problem behavior after it has been reduced/

eliminated, and the reappearance of a previously extinguished problem behavior that was replaced by the targeted problem behavior) are uniquely associated with the use of extinction.

23. **C) Bartering may be acceptable when certain conditions are met**
The Ethics Code states that bartered services can be provided but only under a specific service agreement. The barter should be requested by the client, considered customary in the area where services are provided, and fair (i.e., commensurate with the value of the Board Certified Behavior Analyst's [BCBA's] services).

24. **D) "Finish your homework first, then you can play with the tablet."**
The Premack principle involves the use of high-frequency behavior to reinforce low-frequency behavior. Implementation involves offering the client an opportunity to engage in a high-frequency behavior contingent on the occurrence of a low-frequency behavior. Among the response options presented, "Finish your homework first, then you can play with the tablet" is the only one that requires that Dylan performs a target desired behavior (completing his homework assignment) before he is given the chance to engage in something that is reinforcing (playing games on the computer tablet).

25. **A) Relevance and certainty**
Behavior analysts consider the scientific literature's relevance and certainty. Relevance refers to the extent to which the evidence corresponds to the problem in terms of client characteristics, the assessments and procedures used, functions of behavior and expected outcomes, and the context in which intervention is delivered. Certainty refers to the extent to which the evidence supports the use of a procedure and rules out alternative explanations. It is based on two factors, which include the methodological rigor of the evidence and consistency in replication of outcomes.

26. **C) Aggressive behavior**
The dependent variable (DV) represents some measure of socially significant behavior that an intervention is designed to change. In this case, the DV is the inmates' aggressive behavior. In an experiment, the DV is measured to ascertain whether systematic manipulations of the independent variable (IV) alter it.

27. **D) They require less attention from the observer, are time-consuming, and require less training for users**
There are noted advantages to using continuous measurement methods, such as increased accuracy of measurement and sensitivity to small improvements in performance that may be missed by discontinuous methods. However, they are not without limitations. Continuous methods are criticized for being time-consuming, requiring the undivided attention of the observer, and potentially requiring multiple trained personnel for adequate implementation.

28. **A) Conditional discrimination**
Conditional discriminations are established by reinforcing certain responses in the presence of certain antecedents only if they are preceded by certain other stimuli. In this example, students display conditional discrimination when they notice that the lunch bell has rung (preceding stimulus) and then they wait for Ms. Charlotte to call their name (antecedent) to line up to walk to the cafeteria. Allowing students to line up to walk to the cafeteria for demonstrating conditional discrimination and responding correctly reinforces their behavior.

29. **D) External validity**
External validity refers to the degree the results of the intervention (i.e., functional relationship demonstrated in an experiment) can be generalized to other behaviors, environments, and individuals/populations. External validity is threatened when conditions inherent in the experimental design may limit the generalizability of the results.

30. **C) Objective**
Intervention goals must be stated in observable and measurable terms to allow for the accurate measurement of behavior change. To accomplish this, behavior analysts define target behaviors and set criteria for behavior change. Definitions of target behaviors should be objective, clear, and complete. To be objective, the definition must refer to observable aspects of the behavior (and environment, when applicable). To be clear, the definition must present with sufficient detail, leaving no room for confusion or doubt. And to be complete, the definition must accurately and concisely describe the target behavior, allowing for discrimination between occurrences and nonoccurrences.

31. **B) Set up a person or object to help facilitate the client's generalization of skills**
A mediating stimulus is a teaching aide that is used in an instructional setting to teach a skill, and then redeployed in different settings to elicit the same skill. There are many types of resources that can be used as a mediating stimulus, including people (e.g., peers, paraprofessionals) and objects (e.g., visuals, timers).

32. **D) Transitivity**
This is an example of the emergence of a transitive stimulus relation, which is demonstrated when there is a derived stimulus–stimulus relation following the training of two other stimulus–stimulus relations (e.g., if A = B and B = C, then A = C and C = A). In the example presented, the client is taught that the spoken word "bicicleta" (stimulus A) corresponds with the spoken word "bicycle" (stimulus B), and that the spoken word "bicycle" corresponds with the physical bicycle (stimulus C). Then, without training, the client associates the physical bicycle (stimulus C) with the spoken word "bicicleta" (stimulus A).

33. **C) Partial interval recording**
In the scenario presented, the session is broken into smaller time intervals and the behavior is not continuously measured. Jetta is recording whether the eloping behavior occurred only at the end of each interval. Thus, Jetta is using momentary time sampling to record how much the target behavior is occurring. Unlike whole or partial interval recording, this method does not require the observer's undivided attention to measurement, but a significant amount of behavior will be missed as a result.

34. **D) Provide ongoing evaluation of the effects of supervision**
Supervisors can set expectations for the supervisee to develop a draft agenda in advance of the scheduled supervision meeting, follow scheduled deadlines for assigned activities, and take notes during feedback meetings. Additionally, they can set expectations for the supervisee to review BACB experience standards, adhering to the Ethics Code, completing and maintaining required supervision documentation, and so on. However, providing ongoing evaluation of the effects of supervision is an expectation for the supervisor rather than the supervisee.

35. **A) Extinction**
Extinction procedures involve withholding reinforcers that maintain behavior, resulting in the reduction of the behavior. In the scenario presented, Chelsea's behavior (completing chores) resulted in positive reinforcement (money). After her father decides to withhold money for completing chores, a reduction in completion of chores was observed. Thus, the change in Chelsea's behavior is likely the result of extinction.

36. **C) Sully's father presents him with a blueberry. When Sully says "blueberry," his father delivers reinforcement. When Sully says any word other than blueberry, his father does not deliver reinforcement**
This example best exemplifies simple discriminations, which are established by reinforcing certain responses only in the presence of certain antecedents. Thus, teaching a discriminative response involves the presentation of a defined antecedent stimulus (e.g., blueberry), and the delivery of

reinforcement if the response is emitted. Response A is an example of conditional discriminations, which are established by reinforcing certain responses in the presence of certain antecedents only if they are preceded by certain other stimuli.

37. **D) Any physical contact between Maria's body and another person's body with enough force to be audible or leave a mark, outside of activities in which such contact would be appropriate**
Recall that a well-written operational definition allows for a behavior analyst to gather complete information about its occurrence and nonoccurrence, precisely apply procedures in a timely manner, and produce an accurate evaluation of intervention effectiveness. Consequently, it is necessary that the operational definition is an objective, clear, and complete description of an observable and measurable target behavior. Among the options presented, "Any physical contact between Maria's body and another person's body with enough force to be audible or leave a mark, outside of activities in which such contact would be appropriate" is the definition that best meets the requirements of a strong operational definition as it describes the topography and magnitude of Maria's behavior and clarifies which instances of contact should be excluded from measurement.

38. **B) Select an alternative behavior that is incompatible with the problem behavior**
Behavior analysts select acceptable alternative behaviors that are already in the client's behavioral repertoire, within the client's current abilities, and less effortful than the problem behavior. Darnell should only consider selecting an alternative behavior that is incompatible with the problem behavior when the problem behavior is severe, occurs frequently, and has a significant impact on the environment.

39. **C) Parametric analysis**
Parametric analysis compares different levels of an intervention. It involves examining the effects generated by manipulating one or more dimensions/levels of the intervention. Rationales for its use include: (a) to evaluate the differential effects of a range of values of an intervention on behavior, and (b) to answer the questions, "How much intervention is required to be effective?" and "How much intervention is most effective?"

40. **D) Experimenting to explain the fundamental principles of behavior**
Behavior analysts can follow an eight-step process to monitor client progress that involves: clearly operationalizing the behavior; developing a progress monitoring plan; selecting/creating data collection tools (i.e., measurement system); collecting baseline data and defining goals; setting intervention goals; collecting progress monitoring data; analyzing, summarizing, and visually presenting the data; and evaluating and utilizing data for decision-making.

41. **A) Relevant antecedent details were left out**
The narrative recording fails to capture pertinent antecedent details. As described in the scenario, the teacher redirected Frank when he walked toward the back of the classroom, physically standing between Frank and the computer station. This is important information that Sam should have included in the narrative.

42. **B) Free-operant (FO) arrangement**
Darcy is employing FO arrangement with Freya. In an FO arrangement such as this, Darcy would not have specifically programmed reinforcement, but rather allowed Freya to engage in responses that naturally produce reinforcement continuously or intermittently. In an FO arrangement, Darcy might make Freya's access to objects contingent upon performance of a specific behavior (e.g., saying the name of the object), and Darcy would strive to turn interactions with Freya into teaching moments.

43. **B) Implement the high-probability instructional sequence (high-*p*) with Salman in sixth grade**
All of these procedures will help promote maintenance of Salman's learning, except implementing the high-*p* with Salman in sixth grade. The high-*p* is a contingency-independent antecedent intervention to promote compliance for a target behavior. The high-*p* strategy is typically utilized to address problem behaviors, such as refusal to complete academic work or noncompliant behavior. In this instance, the focus is on implementing procedures to promote maintenance of Salman's learning.

44. **C) Review of records**
Behavior analysts should, at the outset of a case, examine the client's records for relevant data. This includes medical information related to the client's health (e.g., clinical findings, diagnostic test results, care plans, medication) to rule out medical reasons for behavior. If a medical reason is found, treatment of the condition may be necessary before implementing behavioral interventions. In this scenario, the behavior analyst did not learn about the medical issue until after the intervention plan was already implemented.

45. **A) At least 6 months**
The process of terminating services typically requires at least 6 months and involves the titration of services during which services are gradually decreased over time.

46. **C) The physical form of the behavior**
Topography refers to the physical characteristics of the behavior. Thus, topography-based definitions of behavior describe instances of the response by the way it looks or sounds.

47. **B) Escape**
In this scenario, there is a demand (i.e., presentation of a task that involves writing). This triggers a behavior (i.e., tantrum) that effectively results in the teacher sending Tammi to the principal's office which effectively removes the aversive written task. This is an example of a problem behavior that is maintained by an escape function (i.e., social negative reinforcement).

48. **D) It provides strong evidence of external validity and the generalization of results to a broader population**
Providing strong evidence of external validity and the generalization of results to a broader population is an advantage afforded by group experimental designs. The advantages of single-subject experimental design include: subjects serve as their own control; it reveals the performance of individual subjects; data for subjects are not combined/averaged, which helps to prevent distortion/masking of variability in the data; it enables the demonstration of behavior–environment relations at the level of the individual; and it allows for replication of effects within and across individual subjects.

49. **A) Internal validity**
In the case example presented, the dog's behavior of chewing on its owner's shoes reliably occurs at a higher rate when the intervention is not in effect but ceases when the intervention is in effect. Experiments that reliably demonstrate a cause-and-effect relationship between changes in a behavior (dependent variable) and the implementation of an intervention (independent variable) and not the result of uncontrolled/extraneous factors are said to have a high degree of internal validity.

50. **A) Habit reversal**
Eliot is using habit reversal, which involves self-monitoring a particular problem behavior and, as early as possible, interrupting the behavior chain by simply engaging in an incompatible behavior. Habit reversal is one approach to personally applying behavior change tactics to produce a desired change in behavior (i.e., self-management).

51. **D) Multiple baseline design**
   The graph presented shows the use of a multiple baseline design. This type of experimental design is commonly used when a reversal is determined to be impractical or unethical. This involves establishing two or more independent baselines and introducing the intervention in a staggered fashion for each baseline. When the behavior for the first baseline is stable, the intervention is then introduced to the second baseline, and so forth. This design can be used to compare responding across different behaviors for a client, a behavior across different clients, or a behavior across different settings.

52. **D) Verification**
   Verification is the demonstration of a functional relationship between the intervention and target behavior. This would require observing changes in the target behavior associated with the introduction and withdrawal of the intervention. It is accomplished when data convincingly show that baseline responding would remain as is without introduction of the intervention.

53. **A) Fixed interval (FI)**
   The FI schedule of reinforcement typically produces a scalloped pattern of responding. This means that responding is slow at the start but then accelerates toward the end of the interval. The highest rate is usually seen just immediately before reinforcement is delivered.

54. **C) Planned activity check (PLACHECK)**
   In the scenario presented, the teacher is using the PLACHECK method. PLACHECK is a variation of momentary time sampling that involves recording the count of individuals in a group that are engaged in the target behavior only at the end of the interval.

55. **A) Minimize the use of items as reinforcers when they may be harmful to clients**
   The general rule is to select and implement behavior-change interventions with a focus on minimizing risk of harm to the client. However, this may not always be possible, and a reinforcer known to be harmful may be selected if it is determined by the treatment team that the benefits of doing so outweigh its risks.

56. **C) Line graph**
   The line graph, which is the most appropriate visual display format for the data collected in the scenario presented, is used to display behavior change over time. The BCBA can plot the students' performance on target skills in response to the social skills training program on a line graph to analyze each student's performance of target skills across time (i.e., level, variability, and trend of their data paths).

57. **C) Trials to criterion**
   As noted in the scenario, the behavior analyst is tracking the number of practice trials it takes for the client to successfully master this specific set of skills to buss a table. Trials to criterion, which can be used to assess progress toward the acquisition of new skills, is a measure of the number of response opportunities (i.e., trials) required to achieve a predetermined level of performance (i.e., mastery criterion).

58. **C) Have João perform a self-assessment, administer quizzes and interviews to assess his knowledge-based skills, review João's permanent products (and conduct direct observations if needed), and select long- and short-term supervision goals**
   Assessment of the supervisee's skills should precede the selection of supervision goals. To assess a supervisee's skills, the recommended process is to start with a supervisee's self-assessment, then administer quizzes/interviews to assess skills, then review permanent products (and conduct direct observations if necessary).

59. **B) Reflexivity**

Reflexivity is indicated when, in this type of stimulus–stimulus relation, the selection of a comparison stimulus matches the sample stimulus (e.g., A = A) without training to do so. In the scenario presented, Erica teaches Joseph to match a crayon (A) to a crayon (A). Joseph is then handed a different object and, without training to do so, matches it to its identical twin on the table. This is an example of reflexivity.

60. **A) Contingency-shaped**

This is an example of contingency-shaped behavior, which is behavior that is learned through experience with contingencies. In the scenario presented, Wally experiences a behavioral contingency (sliding down headfirst = hurt/pain) which has taught him to instead engage in the behavior of going down the slide feet first.

61. **B) Functional analysis of precursor behavior**

Behavior analysts are ethically obligated to consider the safety and welfare of the client when planning for assessment. As noted in the scenario presented, members of the treatment team are concerned about the use of a functional analysis that evokes the problem behavior. To effectively address this concern, the behavior analyst can instead plan for a functional analysis of precursor behavior which involves presenting the establishing operation and then immediately terminating the session when a precursor behavior (i.e., a behavior that reliably precedes the problem behavior) occurs.

62. **C) Positive reinforcement**

Reinforcement is a stimulus change that maintains a behavior or increases the likelihood that the behavior will occur again in the future. Positive reinforcement involves the addition of a stimulus that increases the likelihood that a behavior will occur again in the future. In this scenario, receiving money from his parents serves as a positive reinforcer for Orion's behavior.

63. **A) Parent attention is a positive reinforcer**

To strengthen a behavior using positive reinforcement, a consequence for the desirable behavior should function as a positive reinforcer. In this scenario, access to parent attention is presented as a known positive reinforcer for Kailani. To increase the response of saying "help" to request parent attention, Hanya should help to establish a behavior-consequence contingency in which parent attention is a positive reinforcer.

64. **A) Matching-to-sample (MTS)**

MTS is a discrete-trial procedure that starts with the client making a response (referred to as the observing response) to the sample stimulus (which is the conditional sample). The sample stimulus may or may not be removed before presenting the comparison stimuli (which are the discriminative events), one of which matches with the conditional sample. When the client selects the comparison stimulus that matches with the sample stimulus, reinforcement is delivered.

65. **D) Permanent product recording**

Product measures refers to the measurement of behavior through examination of its effects produced on the environment (i.e., permanent product). This form of measurement takes place after the behavior has occurred. Although Ms. Jackson did not directly observe Amalie's cleaning up behavior, she looked to tangible artifacts that resulted from Amalie's behavior for determining the occurrence of the cleaning up behavior. This scenario accurately describes the use of permanent product recording.

66. **B) Yes, because the testimonials were identified as solicited, state the relationship with clients, and comply with the law**

There is no indication of an ethics violation in this situation. While behavior analysts cannot solicit testimonials from current clients for advertising, they can solicit testimonials from former clients for advertising when certain conditions are met. Testimonials from former clients used to promote a business must be identified as solicited or unsolicited, include a statement of the relationship between the BCBA and the person giving it, and meet legal requirements.

67. **A) 4 times per independent work period**
Rate is the number of responses over the length of time of the observations. To calculate the average rate of Griffin's leaving-his-seat behavior, count the number of times the behavior occurred across the three observation periods (7 + 6 + 8 = 21). Then, divide the total count (21) by the unit of time in which the observations were conducted (per independent work period) (21 ÷ 3 = 7).

68. **B) Shaping**
Shaping is the provision of differential reinforcement for a progression of responses that are more similar to the target response. In other words, shaping is the reinforcement of successive approximations of a terminal behavior.

69. **B) Intraverbal**
The intraverbal is a verbal operant that is under the control of a verbal stimulus without point-to-point correspondence and is maintained by generalized reinforcement. In the example presented, Carl's question ("What is your name?") served as the discriminative stimulus that evoked Renee's verbal response ("Renee"). Renee's appropriate verbal response to Carl's question resulted the delivery of a generalized reinforcer (praise), and there is no point-to-point correspondence between Carl's question and Renee's response.

70. **A) Behavior analytic**
Behavior analysts use behavior analytic supervision because it is necessary for the delivery of quality behavior analytic services, contributes to the professional development of supervisees and supervisors, is supported as best practice by the field's professional literature, and is required per the Ethics Code for Behavior Analysts.

71. **D) Mid-level responding, low variability, decreasing trend**
The graph presented displays the data paths for three different behaviors, all of which can be visually analyzed across the characteristics of level, trend, and variability. Level relates to the position along the vertical y axis where a series of data points converge, variability relates to the amount of discrepancy between the values of a series of data points, and trend relates to the direction of a series of data points. When examining Behavior 3, the path of the data shows mid-level responding with a decreasing trend. Furthermore, the data appear to decrease in a relatively stable, low variability pattern.

72. **B) A negative reinforcer for leaving the house at 8:00 a.m.**
Negative reinforcement refers to the removal or reduction in intensity of a stimulus immediately following a behavior that serves to increase the future frequency of the behavior. Again, it may be helpful to think of "positive" and "negative" in the mathematical sense where "negative" involves the subtraction of a stimulus. In the scenario presented, the removal of aversive stimuli (traffic) followed her leaving-the-house-at-8:00 a.m. behavior. Thus, traffic functioned as a negative reinforcer for leaving the house at 8:00 a.m.

73. **C) Socially mediated reinforcement**
Recall that socially mediated contingencies are environmental contingencies that can affect behavior with the mediation or deliberate actions of another person. Socially mediated reinforcement occurs when reinforcement is a product of the actions of another person resulting from a behavior. In the scenario presented, asking to play a ball game with the same peer indicates that the activity was reinforcing for Mateo. Because this reinforcement was mediated by a peer, this is considered an example of socially mediated reinforcement.

74. C) Transitive-conditioned MO (CMO-T)

A CMO-T is a stimulus that establishes or abolishes the reinforcing or punishing value of another stimulus. In the scenario presented, the stimulus (sudden and painful headache) establishes pain-relieving medication as a conditioned reinforcer. This means the headache was described to function as a CMO-T.

75. C) Stimulus control

Stimulus control refers to the alteration of the frequency, duration, latency, or magnitude of behavior by the presence or absence of an antecedent stimulus. In short, behavior changes based on whether or not a particular stimulus is present. In the scenario presented, the students' response (stopping what they were doing, performing the cadence clap, and then looking at Ms. Carson) only occurred after a specific stimulus (Ms. Carson's cadence clap) was presented.

76. A) A functional response class

A functional response class is a group of responses that share a common function. As indicated in the scenario presented, Emery is highly motivated to interact with her parents and engages in the range of responses listed (grabbing a parent's hand and pulling it toward the living room play area, saying "let's play," climbing tall pieces of furniture, pushing various items off tables, and crying with tears) to get her parents' attention (common function).

77. A) Ability to imitate verbal models

Imitation requires that the client attends to the model stimulus. Thus, it is important for Mia to evaluate and, if necessary, teach Marley basic attending skills (i.e., staying seated, looking at the teacher/objects, complying with instructions) before conducting imitation training. The client's ability to imitate verbal models is not an essential prerequisite skill for imitation training; modeling and imitation training is often utilized to teach nonverbal behaviors.

78. C) Session 7

A cumulative graph is used to display the running total of responses over time. The slope of line represents the response rate: The steeper it is, the higher the response rate. Unlike those between any other two consecutive sessions, the slope of the line between Sessions 6 and 7 is steep and indicates a difference of 2 in the number of responses between them as measured by the markers along the vertical axis. This means that two additional responses occurred during Session 7.

79. B) Contingency contract

Ms. Fullalove is creatively implementing a contingency contract with her students. A contingency contract (a.k.a. behavioral contract) is a document that specifies a contingent relationship between the completion of a specific task and access to a specified reinforcer.

80. D) Does the treatment pose a risk to the safety of the client?

In the event another nonbehavioral provider recommends a nonbehavioral treatment, the behavior analyst must determine whether it poses a risk to the safety of the client. If a safety risk is present, the behavior analyst should directly address the issue with the nonbehavioral provider. If a safety risk is not present, the behavior analyst should consider the underlying behavioral principles of the treatment and ask, "Is success possible?" If the answer is "yes" or "no, but it doesn't interfere with the client's goals," then do not address the treatment as an issue. If the answer is "no, but it does interfere with the client's goals," then consider the use of the Checklist for Analyzing Proposed Treatments (CAPT) to determine if the impact to the client is enough to warrant possible confrontation with the nonbehavioral provider.

81. A) Changing criterion design

The graph presented shows the use of a changing criterion design, which is an experimental design that uses stepwise benchmarks for altering a measurable dimensional quantity (i.e., frequency, duration, latency, magnitude) of a behavior. The initial baseline phase is followed by a series of intervention phases with successive/gradual criteria for change.

82. **B) Seeing an airplane, a boat, and a bicycle, all of which evoke the word "vehicle"**
An arbitrary stimulus class is a cluster of antecedent stimuli that are dissimilar but bring about the same response. While an airplane, a boat, and a bicycle do not have any shared physical features or relative relationships, they still evoke the same response ("vehicle").

83. **A) Negative punishment**
Negative punishment involves the removal of a stimulus immediately following a behavior, which decreases the future frequency of the behavior. In the scenario presented, Ms. Andrews removes a token contingent on the occurrence of Bart's target problem behavior (getting out of his seat without permission) which decreases the future frequency of the target problem behavior.

84. **C) Token economy with response cost**
Ms. Said is implementing a token economy with response cost, which involves the implementation of a negative punishment procedure in which undesirable behavior results in the loss of tokens, as in this case.

85. **A) Conditioned stimulus; conditioned response**
Respondent conditioning is a type of learning whereby new stimuli develop the capacity to elicit responses through the pairing process. It focuses on involuntary responses and involves stimulus–stimulus pairing of an unconditioned stimulus (US) with a neutral stimulus (NS) until the NS becomes a conditioned stimulus (CS) that elicits a conditioned response (CR).

86. **D) Stimulus shaping**
Lovetta is employing stimulus shaping, which involves gradually altering the form/topography of a stimulus until it eventually resembles the target criterion. In this scenario, Lovetta first places the word "dog" among shapes to allow for easy discrimination. She then gradually introduces letters and words to facilitate the client's ability to recognize the letters in the word "dog."

87. **C) Record each occurrence of the target behavior, then count the total number of occurrences and divide it by the length of the observation period at the end of the treatment session**
To measure rate, Georgia needs to collect the count of the target behavior over some unit of time (e.g., per minute, per hour, per day). This is calculated by dividing the number of occurrences of Mark's inappropriate vocalizations by the unit of time in which the observations are conducted.

88. **C) Decline to observe the student**
Behavior analysts are responsible for obtaining informed consent before conducting assessments. In this situation, the student's parents or legal guardian would need to give permission for an observation. Jason should not agree to conduct an observation, informal or not, until informed consent has been obtained.

89. **B) Convene an expert panel of behavior analysts and other relevant professionals to review the treatment program**
If it is unclear whether services are appropriate or effective for a client, an expert panel of behavior analysts and other relevant professionals should review the treatment program.

90. **A) Discrete-trial teaching (DTT)**
Alejandro is using DTT, an instructional procedure that breaks down behavior into discrete steps (i.e., learning trials) with a clear beginning, middle, and end. The components of DTT include the antecedent (i.e., discriminative stimulus), behavior, and consequence.

91. **C) The impact of the Hawthorne effect on Tyler's performance**
Performance monitoring involves ongoing collection of relevant performance data, including the number and rate of competencies that a supervisee acquires, the number and rate of errors made in permanent products (e.g., data collection forms, assessment reports, and intervention plans), and changes in the use of language (e.g., fluency and accuracy in the use of technical language, ability to explain concepts in nontechnical language).

92. **B) Social positive reinforcement and social negative reinforcement**
The graph displays the results of a functional analysis that included five conditions: alone, attention, play, tangible, and demand. The rate of the tantrum behavior is relatively low in the alone, play, and attention conditions. While the data paths for the attention and demand conditions vary in terms of level, they are both elevated and show high levels of responding. Thus, the function of the behavior is likely to be maintained both by social positive reinforcement (i.e., access to attention) and social negative reinforcement (i.e., escape from demand).

93. **B) Supporting environments and constraints**
Behavior analysts consider client preferences, supporting environments, risks, constraints, and social validity when recommending intervention goals and procedures. When considering "supporting environments" (i.e., level of support available where treatment is to occur), there are a wide variety of environmental variables to consider (e.g., physical space, materials, staffing, abilities of individuals implementing the procedures). Constraints refer to factors that may inhibit successful implementation of a treatment program.

94. **C) Modeling and imitation training**
Soren is using modeling and imitation training to teach Mata how to cover his mouth and nose when he sneezes. Soren demonstrates the behavior for Mata and prompts Mata to imitate it. In this way, Mata learns the behavior by virtue of observing and imitating Soren. Note Soren's careful attention to best practice when employing modeling and imitation training.

95. **D) Positive reinforcement**
Positive reinforcement refers to the presentation of a stimulus following a behavior that serves to increase the future frequency of the behavior. In the scenario presented, Tim's behavior (drawing an obnoxious picture on the whiteboard) was followed by his peers' attention (laughter). As a result of the presentation of his peers' attention, the future frequency of the behavior increased.

96. **D) Removal; increase**
Negative reinforcement involves removal, or reduction in intensity, of a stimulus immediately following a behavior that serves to increase the future frequency of the behavior. This stimulus is often referred to as an aversive stimulus whose removal results in relief. In contrast, positive reinforcement involves the presentation of a stimulus immediately following a behavior that serves to increase the future frequency of the behavior.

97. **A) The echoic**
An echoic response corresponds, point-to-point, with a discriminative verbal stimulus. In the scenario presented, there is formal similarity between the behavior technician's vocal response and the client's vocal response ("please"). When Benjamin said "please," it was followed by Carl saying "please." Then, a generalized conditioned reinforcer (praise) was delivered contingent upon Carl's emission of the correct echoic response.

98. **C) Indirect**
The MAS, FAST, and QABF are all examples of rating scales that are used to assess the possible functions of problem behavior. Rating scales, along with interviews and checklists, are types of indirect assessments.

99. **C) Sensory**
As described in the scenario, Gus calms down when he is physically restrained but reengages in the problem behavior when he is released. Vocal attempts from staff to redirect Gus (i.e., attention from others) were unsuccessful. This suggests that the problem behavior is used to obtain access to reinforcing sensory stimulation produced by the physical restraints.

100. **D) Client preferences**
Behavior analysts consider client preferences, supporting environments, risks, constraints, and social validity when recommending intervention goals and procedures. Considering client preferences means collaborating with the client and/or caregivers on the selection of intervention goals and procedures. In this instance, the behavior analyst is interviewing Gary to determine his preferences around doing homework in order to build his preferences into the intervention procedures.

101. **C) Variable interval (VI)**
The VI schedule of reinforcement specifies the average duration that must pass before the first occurrence of a target response will be reinforced. This means that the time interval that must elapse before reinforcement is made available is less predictable than an FI schedule of reinforcement. When reinforcement is delivered, the variable interval is reset.

102. **C) Latency**
Latency measures the time between the presentation of a stimulus and the onset of a targeted response. This scenario describes a measurement of time between the given opportunity to emit writing behavior (i.e., end of teacher's delivery of instructions) and when the targeted response is initiated (i.e., Randolph begins to comply by writing appropriate information on the assignment paper).

103. **D) High-probability request sequence**
The high-probability instructional sequence (high-p) is a contingency-independent antecedent intervention that involves presenting a series of easy-to-follow requests for which the client has a history of compliance (i.e., high-p requests), and presenting the target request (i.e., low-p request) after the client has complied with the high-p requests. Typically, two to five high-p requests precede the presentation of a low-p request. To effectively implement this procedure, the following guidelines should be followed: Present high-p requests that the client is currently able to comply with, present requests in rapid succession, acknowledge compliance with each request, and use high-quality reinforcers. The procedure may function as an AO and decrease the motivation to escape from requests.

104. **A) Donald's behavior is reinforced by access to escape from the group**
Per the scenario, Donald despises the group meetings and thinks they are a waste of time. When he is asked to take a break outside, he escapes from the meeting and is then able to smoke cigarettes and respond to emails on his phone. Given that Donald's aggressive behavior is increasing, it is reasonable to hypothesize that the group leader's current strategy is reinforcing Donald's behavior.

105. **C) Social positive reinforcement and social negative reinforcement**
The graph displays the results of a functional analysis that included four conditions: alone, attention, play, and demand. The rate of the scratching behavior is at zero in the alone and play conditions, but the data paths in both the attention and demand conditions are elevated and show high levels of responding. Thus, the function of the behavior is likely to be maintained both by social positive reinforcement (i.e., access to attention) and social negative reinforcement (i.e., escape from demand).

106. **A) Covert third-party observation**
Covert third-party observation is not a method used for assessing the effects of supervision. To evaluate the effects of supervision activities, supervisors can track relevant performance data of

supervisees (i.e., rate of skill acquisition, rate of errors made in permanent products, and use of language); request feedback from supervisees; and administer brief structured surveys including items related to supervisor performance (e.g., organization, knowledge, use of feedback/ reinforcement).

107. C) Partial interval recording

Based on the information presented in the scenario, partial interval recording is the most appropriate measurement system for collecting data on the student's question-asking behavior. Partial interval recording can be used when the behavior cannot be easily counted (i.e., it is difficult to tell when it begins and ends, or it occurs at too high of a rate) and is often employed to target behaviors that are to be decreased. Also, in a class full of fifth grade students and only one teacher, partial interval recording may be more feasible to implement than some of the other methods available that require more time and attention (e.g., whole interval recording). Using this method, the teacher would record whether the question-asking behavior occurred at any time during the interval or at the end of the interval.

108. D) Review records and available data

Before conducting a formal assessment, Olivia needs to request and review the available records and data on the new client. Records of interest include those that contain educational, medical, and historical information. This is an important task completed at the outset of a case that can serve to provide behavior analysts with relevant background information that may be used to inform decisions related to assessment and treatment.

109. B) Subjects are randomly selected from a population of interest

The defining features of experimental designs include: (a) the subject is the unit of intervention and data analysis, (b) the subject provides their own control for comparison, and (c) the target behavior is measured repeatedly across different levels or conditions of the intervention. Randomly selecting subjects from a population of interest is a feature of group experimental designs.

110. D) Report Steven to the Behavior Analyst Certification Board. This is a serious breach of the Ethics Code

This is a serious violation of the Ethics Code that warrants a report to the Behavior Analyst Certification Board (BACB). Behavior analysts are to be honest and report only accurate information. Even as a student, Corey is obligated to abide by the Ethics Code for Behavior Analysts. With a report from Corey, it is quite likely that Steven will not be able to count his reported fieldwork experience hours.

111. A) BCBAs are obligated to be familiar with the Ethics Code

Saying "I didn't know" does not excuse an ethical violation. As stated in the Ethics Code, behavior analysts are expected to know and comply with the Code. Having a lack of awareness or misunderstanding of the Code is never a justifiable excuse for violating it.

112. B) Monitor treatment integrity

Behavior analysts monitor treatment integrity to ensure interventions are consistently implemented precisely as designed. Implementing an intervention with treatment integrity carefully avoids administration of extraneous, confounding variables which, in turn, enables one to correctly infer the relationship between an intervention and a client's behavior, whether behavior is changed or unchanged.

113. D) Leaving school building without permission

This scenario describes Stewart as a student who engages in four problem behaviors: shouting at his peers, scribbling in his textbooks, stealing items from his teacher's desk, and leaving the school building without permission. When selecting a target behavior to prioritize, it is important to consider whether the behavior poses a danger to the client or to others. The greater the threat, the higher the priority. Among the behaviors listed, leaving the school building without permission is the behavior that poses the greatest threat to the safety of the client and/or others.

114. A) Share the data, excluding confidential client information
Behavior analysts are expected to share their data with other professionals when possible. This practice may allow other researchers to verify our analyses and conclusions. However, the confidentiality of research participants must be protected.

115. D) Trials to criterion
In the scenario presented, Alex is evaluating the effectiveness of two instructional procedures for teaching a target intraverbal behavior. Trials to criterion, a measurement system that can be used to compare two or more treatments, is used to measure the number of response opportunities (i.e., trials) required to achieve a predetermined level of performance (i.e., mastery criterion).

116. C) Conduct regular evaluations of supervisory performance using feedback from others, clients' outcomes data, and supervisees' outcomes data
Ensuring supervisory competence and appropriate supervisory volume is good, but Ezra should not make any assumptions about the effectiveness of her supervisory practices. Behavior analysts are responsible for designing and implementing a system for obtaining and using regular performance feedback data from others (e.g., supervisees, supervisors), clients' outcomes data, and supervisees' outcomes data to inform their supervisory practices.

117. C) Description and prediction
The knowledge learned from science allows for one or more of three levels of understanding: description, prediction, and control. Ms. Crisp's systematic observations of the classroom enabled her to describe classroom events in quantifiable terms and develop a hypothesis about the potential relationship between students' off-task behavior and Mr. Abubakar's use of praise statements. This is an example of knowledge at the description level of understanding. Her repeated observations enabled her to demonstrate that the two events covaried. This correlation between events did not provide evidence of causation between the variables, but did demonstrate with a certain degree of confidence the relative probability that students' on- and off-task behavior occurred based on the presence or absence of Mr. Abubakar's praise statements. This is an example of knowledge at the prediction level of understanding. Since Ms. Crisp did not conduct a controlled experiment, she did not achieve knowledge of the relation between the two variables at the control level of understanding, which is the highest level of scientific understanding.

118. D) Variable ratio (VR)
Recall that the VR schedule specifies the average number of times a target behavior must occur to receive reinforcement. In other words, reinforcement is delivered after a variable number of responses have occurred. Thus, the occurrence of reinforcement is less predictable. In the scenario presented, reinforcement does not occur after a fixed or variable length of time. Students need to demonstrate a target behavior (complete an assigned task) for tickets to place in the box, and having one's name drawn from the box and receiving a reward may or may not occur for any particular student at the end of each week. This is an example of a system that uses a variable ratio schedule of reinforcement.

119. C) High-probability instructional sequence
Erin is using high-probability instructional sequence (high-*p*), which is a contingency-independent antecedent intervention that involves presenting a series of easy-to-follow requests for which the client has a history of compliance (i.e., high-*p* requests), and presenting the target request (i.e., low-*p* request) after the client has complied with the high-*p* requests. Typically, two to five high-*p* requests precede the presentation of a low-*p* request.

120. **C) Direct**

Direct assessment methods include the use of standardized tests, criterion-referenced measures, curriculum-based measures, and direct observations. In the scenario presented, the behavior analyst is using a standardized test, which is a direct assessment instrument with specific procedures that must be followed for its administration.

121. **A) Descriptive**

Descriptive assessment methods, which have been applied to evaluate potential consequences of problem behavior, involve direct observation of the target behavior in relation to other events under naturally occurring conditions. Eli used Antecedent-Behavior-Consequence (ABC) recording, a type of descriptive assessment, to record the occurrences of the target behavior and the environmental events surrounding it (i.e., antecedents and consequences).

122. **B) Making eye contact with peers**

Permanent product recording can be used when the behavior of interest produces effects on the environment that can be measured after its occurrence. Completed homework assignment sheets, toy-filled bins, and wet diapers are examples of permanent products that lend themselves to measurement. Eye contact, however, does not consistently produce effects on the environment that can be measured after its occurrence.

123. **B) Determinism, selectionism, and parsimony**

When explaining that all behavior possesses an identifiable cause and is to some degree determinable, the BCBA advocates for determinism. Determinism is the assumption that the universe is rational, governed by discoverable laws, and that events are completely determined by previously existing causes. Relatedly, she espouses selectionism when encouraging the team to focus on explanations of the person's behavior based on the person's known experiences and the consequences of their behavior. The BCBA advocates for the principle of parsimony when she encourages the team to rule out simple, logical explanations for the person's behavior before entertaining more complex or abstract explanations. As an applied scientist committed to employing the scientific method to understand and intervene in human behavior, the BCBA is certainly committed to the other four attitudes of science (i.e., experimentation, replication, empiricism, and philosophical doubt). However, she does not explicitly advocate for those attitudes in the team meeting.

124. **C) Stimulus control**

Stimulus control refers to behavior change based on whether or not some stimulus is present. In the scenario presented, Amy's response (reviewing discussion points and activities for 15 minutes) only occurs when a particular stimulus (event labeled "supervision meeting") is seen on her calendar. When the event is not seen on her calendar, the response does not occur. This is an example of a behavior that is controlled by a stimulus (i.e., stimulus control).

125. **C) Recommend reinforcement rather than punishment whenever possible**

The Code requires behavior-change interventions prioritize reinforcement-based procedures. However, behavior analysts may recommend and use punishment-based procedures if other (i.e., reinforcement-based) procedures have been tried but failed to produce the desired results, or the intervention team determines that potential benefits of using a punishment-based procedure outweighs the risk of harm to the client.

126. **C) Scratching a spot on your leg because it itches**

Automatic reinforcement occurs when reinforcement is either a response product of a behavior or a product of the physical environment resulting from a behavior. Scratching a spot on your leg because it itches is an example of this as negative reinforcement (relief from itching) is a product of the behavior (scratching).

127. **C) Shaping frequency within a response topography**
When shaping within response topographies, the topography of behavior remains constant, but some other measurable dimension is changed. In this example, Kelly is intervening to increase Ian's use of vocal mands. Shaping frequency within a response topography is most appropriate.

128. **A) Attempt to resolve the issue directly with the counselor. If it cannot be resolved, report it to the appropriate authority (e.g., administrator, supervisor)**
When a behavior analyst experiences a problem with a nonbehavioral professional, they are obligated to attempt to resolve it. In the event Wanda is unable to resolve this problem with the counselor, the next step is to report it to the appropriate authority.

129. **B) Echoic**
An echoic is a verbal operant that is under the control of a vocal-verbal stimulus, with which it shares point-to-point correspondence (i.e., stimulus parts correspond with response parts) and formal similarity (i.e., stimulus and response physically resemble each other). In the scenario presented, Dorria's vocal response of "apple" (vocal-verbal stimulus) evokes Milo's vocal response of "apple." Milo's response is an echoic.

130. **B) Social positive reinforcement**
The graph displays the results of a functional analysis that included four conditions: alone, attention, play, and demand. The rate of yelling behavior is significantly higher in the attention condition when compared to all others. Thus, it is most likely that the function of the yelling behavior is access to social attention.

131. **D) Interdependent group contingency**
Mr. Caretto is implementing an interdependent group contingency, which involves providing reinforcement for all members of a group, in this case his students, based on each member of the group achieving a performance criterion that is in place for all members of the group (i.e., memorization of all multiplication facts).

132. **A) Dr. Digable is not delivering feedback in a timely enough manner**
Dr. Digable is providing praise several days after Toni has performed the desired behaviors that she intended to promote. When delivering praise or other reinforcers, deliver it immediately following the behavior and verbally describe what the supervisee did correctly.

133. **A) Incidental teaching**
Diane is using an incidental teaching arrangement with Tony, which is one of the many naturalistic teaching approaches (NTAs) available. Incidental teaching involves ongoing assessment of the client's interests, restricting access to high interest items/activities, and constructing lessons in a natural context. When a client displays interest (i.e., makes a request; in this case, Tony is interested in having a cookie) and the teacher determines to use the occasion to teach a verbal behavior, the teacher must make an immediate decision concerning the terminal behavior that the client is to emit, present a cue of attention (followed by a verbal cue if necessary), and then assist the client (with prompts as necessary).

134. **C) Rule-governed behavior**
This is an example of rule-governed behavior, which is behavior that is under the control of verbal antecedents that are considered rules. There are two types of rules: those in the form of a simple request or instruction, and those that describe a behavioral contingency. In the scenario presented, the verbal antecedent ("out of service for maintenance" text on the sign) served as a simple instruction that enabled Cooper to respond effectively without directly contacting any contingencies that would be harmful or inefficient to contact.

135. **B) Response generalization**

Response generalization occurs when the client emits an untrained response that serves the same function as the trained target behavior. In the scenario presented, Danielle was taught a response for obtaining permission to access the restroom but then began to emit an untrained response (waving her arms in the air and silently mouthing the word "bathroom") that serves the same function.

136. **A) Administering checklists or rating scales at regular intervals to stakeholders who most frequently observe the problem behavior**

Descriptive assessment involves observation of the target behavior in relation to environmental events and includes continuous Antecedent-Behavior-Consequence (ABC) recording, narrative ABC recording, and scatterplot recording. Administering checklists or rating scales at regular intervals to stakeholders is an indirect assessment activity that can provide progress monitoring data.

137. **C) At least 80% of the time**

The format of a goal statement can include the following components: condition, name of client, behavior to be increased or decreased, criterion, indication of how it will be measured, and date by which it will be achieved. The criterion defines how much, how often, and to what standard the behavior must occur in order to demonstrate that the goal has been reached. In the example presented, "at least 80% of the time" sets the criterion in the goal statement.

138. **B) Extinction of behavior maintained by positive reinforcement**

In the example presented, the client yells for positive reinforcement (parents' attention). The procedure described involves removing the reinforcer for the positively reinforced behavior. Thus, this is an example of extinction of behavior maintained by positive reinforcement.

139. **D) Notify his university and obtain approval from the institutional review committee before collecting any data**

It's not enough to obtain permission only from the context in which Hector would like to conduct his study. If this is a potential research project to be submitted to the university, Hector should notify relevant parties at his university (e.g., his faculty advisor), write a research proposal describing what the study will involve, and obtain approval from the university's institutional review board before proceeding. We do not conduct research until after it has been approved by a formal research review committee.

140. **A) Bar graph**

In the scenario presented, the BCBA wants to display the number of activities that the student reported a preference for in each of the three activity categories. These categories are considered discrete variables (i.e., variables that are quantified by counting). There is no measure of performance over time. The most appropriate data display format for summarizing discrete data would be the bar graph (also known as the histogram).

141. **A) Response cost and time-out**

Procedures based on negative punishment are used to weaken responses by establishing contingencies in which targeted responses are immediately followed by the removal of reinforcing stimulus events. Among the answer options presented, "Response cost and time-out" is the only answer that includes two negative punishment procedures. Response cost involves fining the client a specific amount of reinforcement, and time-out involves the withdrawal of opportunities to access reinforcement. The other answer options each include at least one positive punishment procedure.

142. **C) Provide a written description of the target skill**

The six steps to BST are describe the target skill, provide a written description, demonstrate the target skill, require the supervisee to practice the target skill, provide feedback during practice, and repeat step 4 (require the supervisee to practice the target skill) and step 5 (provide feedback during practice) until mastery is achieved. Martin did not provide an explanation of why a skill is to be targeted and the behavioral definition of it in written form. Ideally, a written description would be provided, and the supervisee would be given time to ask questions about it.

143. **C) Call a meeting with her supervisor and the client's parents to discuss how they can solve the issue. If parents fail to attend, it may be appropriate to begin terminating services**
If parents fail to comply with the program despite appropriate efforts to address barriers, then there is sufficient reason to move forward in discontinuing services. Note that the client is also no longer benefiting from services, which is also in and of itself sufficient for discontinuing services. Additionally, the family can be referred to other appropriate professionals (e.g., BCBAs or counselors).

144. **C) Selects a picture of a ball**
In the scenario presented, the client observed a sample stimulus, the picture of a ball (A), and learned to match the comparison stimulus, a physical ball (B), to it. In other words, the client learned an A = B relation. Symmetry is indicated in the demonstration of reversibility of a sample stimulus and comparison stimulus. This means that a relation of symmetry would be demonstrated if the client was to perform the task in reverse; by observing a physical ball (B) and then selecting the picture of a ball (A), thus indicating the emergence of the B = A relation.

145. **C) "I like how you're following my directions" and giving tokens**
A stimulus class is a group of stimuli with elements in common across formal, temporal, and/or functional dimensions. While the form of making the statement, "I like how you're following my directions" differs from that of giving a token, they are both consequences for desired behavior (i.e., following directions) and the most likely pair of stimuli to serve the same function (e.g., reinforcing following directions).

146. **B) Negative punishment**
This is an example of negative punishment and its effect on behavior. Negative punishment involves the removal of a stimulus immediately following a behavior, which decreases the future frequency of the behavior. In the scenario presented, Eddie's dad removes his video game controllers (i.e., his ability to play video games) immediately following Eddie's arguing behavior. This, in turn, decreases the future frequency of arguing behavior.

147. **D) Generality**
The seven dimensions of applied behavior analysis (ABA) identified by Baer et al. (1968) are applied, behavioral, analytic, technological, conceptually systematic, effective, and generality. A change in behavior is considered to possess generality when it holds over time, across different settings, and/or spreads to other relevant and related behaviors. In the case example presented, Andy's social communication skills spread beyond the swing class environment and was evidenced to be durable over time.

148. **B) High-probability instructional sequence (high-p)**
Reinforcement procedures used for weakening behavior include a variety of differential reinforcement (DR) procedures and noncontingent reinforcement (NCR). The high-probability instructional sequence (high-p) is a contingency-independent antecedent intervention that involves: (a) presenting a series of easy-to-follow requests for which the client has a history of compliance (i.e., high-p requests), and (b) presenting the target request (i.e., low-p request) after the client has complied with the high-p requests. High-p is not a DR or NCR.

149. **B) Access to tangible reinforcement**
In the scenario presented, Leslie's peers relinquish objects in response to her physically aggressive behavior toward them. When these objects are relinquished, Leslie then has access to and

will engage in play with them. Thus, the likely function of Leslie's physically aggressive behavior toward other students at school during recess is socially mediated access to tangible reinforcement.

150. **A) Access to a preferred activity after completing a reduced math assignment**
The independent variable (IV) is the intervention. The IV represents the treatment variable that is used to intervene on the phenomenon of interest (i.e., target behavior). In an experiment, the IV is systematically manipulated to determine if alterations to it will produce reliable alterations in the dependent variable (DV). In this case, the most appropriate IV is providing Nic with access to a preferred activity to reinforce his completion of in-class math assignments (the DV).

151. **D) Implement an intermittent schedule of reinforcement**
The continuous nature of Morgan and Pat's reinforcement schedule makes it unsustainable. They should try using an intermittent schedule of reinforcement instead. For example, they could implement a fixed ratio schedule that provides reinforcement after Noby uses the toilet three times and then gradually increase the ratio over time.

152. **B) It will enable them to further enhance their relationship**
Enabling Tiana to further enhance her relationship with Anders is not a good reason for agreeing to provide supervision. This reason may also be indicative of a slippery slope toward committing an ethics violation if it results in a romantic (i.e., dual) relationship. The reasons for providing supervision are that it is necessary for the delivery of quality behavior analytic services, contributes to the professional development of supervisees and supervisors, is supported as best practice by the field's professional literature, and is required per the Professional and Ethical Compliance Code for behavior analysts.

153. **B) Mid-level responding, high variability, increasing trend**
The graph presented displays the data paths for three different behaviors, all of which can be visually analyzed across the characteristics of level, trend, and variability. Level relates to the position along the vertical y axis where a series of data points converge, variability relates to the amount of discrepancy between the values of a series of data points, and trend relates to the direction of a series of data points. When examining Behavior 2, the path of the data shows mid-level responding with an increasing trend. Furthermore, the data appear to increase in a relatively unstable, high variability pattern.

154. **D) Refraining from taking a nap during the day**
Refraining from taking a nap during the day is the best example of manipulating motivating operations, which involves behaving in a way (e.g., not taking a nap) that creates motivation that increases the likelihood of a target behavior (e.g., falling asleep at night). Setting a reminder to go to bed at 10:00 p.m. is an example of using response prompts (i.e., using stimuli that can later cue a target behavior). Only sleeping in the bedroom is an example of using a specific environment for behavior. Removing the television from the bedroom is an example of removing necessary materials, in this case a device that prevents Sheree from going to sleep.

155. **C) Multielement design**
The graph presented shows the use of a multielement design. Also commonly referred to as an alternating treatments design, this type of experimental design involves delivering and measuring effects of two or more interventions in a rapid, alternating fashion. This allows behavior analysts to compare the effects of different interventions. It can also be used to compare the effects of an intervention with no intervention (i.e., baseline).

156. **D) Decline to teach the course and perhaps offer to assist in identifying another instructor who is better qualified**
Behavior analysts need to recognize the importance of operating within boundaries of competence. Dr. Sanchez is not sufficiently equipped to teach the course. Thus, declining to teach the course is the most appropriate response, even if the university believes that she can do it.

157. **A) Performance expectations for the supervisor and the supervisee in the form of a supervision contract**
Performance expectations for the supervisor and supervisee should be clearly communicated at the outset of a supervisory relationship. When the supervisory relationship is between a qualified supervisor and a trainee acquiring fieldwork experience to meet Behavior Analyst Certification Board (BACB) requirements for the BCBA certification, a supervision contract must be established. The supervision contract is a written document that describes the supervisor–supervisee relationship and expectations for both parties.

158. **A) Implement an emergency procedure to maintain his safety and refer him to an appropriate professional for assessment. Programming can be placed on hold**
The behavior analysts in this situation determined that there is a reasonable likelihood that the new behavior is influenced by medical or biological variables. Given this, a referral to an appropriate professional is necessary for ensuring that the client's medical needs are assessed and addressed. In the meantime, it is imperative that appropriate measures are in place to ensure the safety of the client. Programming can be placed on hold until after results of the assessment are obtained.

159. **D) Function-based strategies**
Behavior analysts use function-based strategies to improve personnel performance. To accomplish this, behavior analysts use performance diagnostics to examine relevant antecedents, behaviors, and consequences in the environment to identify possible reasons (i.e., functions) for performance deficits.

160. **B) Rule**
Using a rule involves the steps for delivering an instruction and extending it to include a contingency. This can be delivered in the form of an "if/then" statement. If George was using an instruction, he would have simply said, "Say 'remote.'"

161. **C) Directly requesting feedback**
Directly requesting feedback from supervisees is the method that is most likely to enhance a supervisor's ability to tailor supervision to meet the specific needs of individual supervisees. Requesting feedback involves directly asking the supervisee the following questions: "Are you getting what you need?" and "Am I teaching [knowledge/skill(s)] in the most effective way for you?" Asking these questions can occur regularly as a part of supervision meetings.

162. **C) Examine treatment integrity**
Before making changes to the intervention, treatment integrity should be assessed. If the intervention plan was not implemented with integrity (i.e., as planned), lack of effectiveness may not be attributable to the design of the plan. Promoting integrity can be particularly challenging in situations involving multiple implementers of the intervention plan. Behavior analysts are to provide implementers with sufficient training and support to competently implement the intervention plan with integrity. Collecting and analyzing treatment integrity data regularly throughout implementation are important for supporting efforts to maintain adherence to the plan and maximize intervention outcomes.

163. **B) Contingent attention**
In the attention condition of a functional analysis, an experimenter withholds social positive reinforcement (i.e., attention) but will deliver it when the client engages in problem behavior. The purpose of this arrangement is to determine whether the problem behavior is maintained by access to social attention. Differentially higher levels of the problem behavior during the contingent attention condition when compared to the control condition would suggest that it is maintained by social positive reinforcement.

164. **C) Immediate needs of the agency**
When developing long-term goals for supervisees, supervisors need to consider the Task List items relevant to the supervisee's role, their performance across those Task List items, and the expected needs of the agency. Immediate needs, while important, are more relevant when developing short-term goals rather than long-term goals.

165. **A) Reflexive-conditioned motivating operation (CMO-R)**
A CMO-R is a stimulus that has acquired its effects as an motivating operation (MO) as a result of it preceding the onset of a situation that is either painful/worsening or improving. In this situation, the stimulus (number of email messages going above a certain amount) acquired its effects as a motivating operation as a result of it preceding the onset of a painful/worsening situation (spending the weekend working on answering email messages), and its own offset functions as a reinforcer. Thus, in relation to completing reports, the number of reports going above a certain amount is a CMO-R.

166. **B) Self-instruction**
Self-instruction involves using self-statements as controlling responses that guide a client through a task. In this question, Neil models for Maggie how to use verbal self-instructions (i.e., talking aloud to himself) to coach herself through the steps of putting on her shoes. The use of self-statements as controlling responses distinguishes this technique from self-management and modeling and imitation training.

167. **C) Backward chaining with leap aheads**
Backward chaining with leap aheads is helpful when the client already has the prerequisite steps for a final behavior in their behavior chain. In this example, Clive only needs to learn the final step in the behavior chain: how to strap the Velcro on his shoes. Since he already knows how to sit down (prior step), put his foot in the shoe (prior step), and take hold of the Velcro with his hand (prior step), these steps do not require teaching. The behavior analyst can "leap ahead" to teaching the final step in the chain.

168. **A) Applied Behavior Analysis (ABA)**
ABA is the science in which behavior analysts apply techniques derived from the principles of behavior to change behavior (e.g., increase behavior, teach and maintain behavior, reduce problem behavior) and positively enhance socially significant areas (e.g., communication, classroom management, generalization and maintenance of learning). ABA utilizes experimentation to clearly identify the variables driving changes in behavior. ABA applies principles derived from the EAB to change behavior.

169. **C) Betty, a first-year college student with autism spectrum disorder (ASD), takes a ballroom dancing class with a Board Certified Behavior Analyst (BCBA) during which she learns and practices how to ask people to dance and make small talk. In her second year of college, Betty regularly asks questions in class and responds to professors' questions**
Betty is demonstrating response generalization. During intervention with the BCBA, she learned and practiced how to ask people to dance and make small talk. Then, without training, she used those skills in an alternative but functionally equivalent manner when asking questions in class and responding to her professors' questions.

170. **B) Latency**
Julian is following the steps to responding to in-class questions, but he is not providing his answer to questions at an appropriate volume. This is an issue of magnitude, which refers to the strength or force of the behavior. The behavior analyst should aim to reduce the magnitude of the behavior, which in this case is the volume of Julian's vocal responses to questions, to a socially acceptable level.

171. **C) Click the clicker, then give the dog a treat. Repeat several times**
To create a conditioned response using a clicker, Pat should instruct her students to repeatedly first click the clicker, then give their dog a treat. Pat is teaching her students to use classical conditioning to link the clicker (a neutral stimulus) and the treat (an unconditioned stimulus) to transform the clicker into a conditioned stimulus that produces a conditioned response. For this to be effective, the conditioned stimulus (CS; the clicker) should occur before the unconditioned stimulus (US; the treat)—not simultaneously or after it. In this way, the clicker (CS) serves as a signal or cue to the dog that they are about to get a treat (US).

172. **D) Functional assessment**
Behavior analysts use functional assessment (e.g., performance diagnostics) to identify variables affecting personnel performance. Performance diagnostics (also known as performance analysis) uses a functional assessment approach to identifying variables affecting personnel performance. The primary model used for performance diagnostics at the individual level is the Antecedent-Behavior-Consequence (ABC) analysis.

173. **A) Access to social reinforcement**
When examining the antecedent column, we can see that each instance of the problem behavior is preceded by the teacher engaging in some activity that restricts Arya's access to the teacher's attention. When examining the consequence column, the narrative data show that the problem behavior is then followed by the teacher attending to Arya. Although limited, the data suggest that Arya engages in the crying behavior to obtain access to social reinforcement (i.e., teacher attention).

174. **A) Stimulus fading**
Stimulus fading involves making some feature of a target stimulus more salient, and then gradually fading it. In the scenario presented, J.E. makes the size of the target stimulus (i.e., number 7) bigger (i.e., more salient) and then proceeds to make it smaller in subsequent trials (i.e., fading the target stimulus) until its size matches that of the other numbers in the array. Thus, J.E. employed stimulus fading to teach the client to discriminate the number 7.

175. **D) Task analysis**
Before behaviors can be linked in a chain, behavior analysts must develop a task analysis (TA) that breaks down a complex task into a series of smaller, teachable steps. Develop and validate a TA using one of the following methods: Observe someone competently performing the task, perform the task yourself, ask for input from an expert, or use a systematic trial-and-error procedure. When determining the number of steps, consider the complexity of each step on the basis of what is manageable for the client. A treatment plan and an action plan are synonymous; both define the problem or diagnosis, prescribed treatment, treatment goals, planned actions to achieve treatment goals, a timeline for treatment progress, measurable objectives, and progress monitoring. Skinner's analysis offers a framework for language assessment and intervention.

176. **B) Extinction**
Implementation of an extinction procedure involves withholding reinforcers that maintain undesirable behavior. In the scenario presented, Alvin's vocal refusal behavior was reinforced by removal of the cereal and/or delivery of his favorite potato chip snack. By ignoring his refusal behavior, reinforcement was effectively withheld as a consequence for the behavior and, as a result, the frequency of its occurrence was reduced.

177. **D) Multiple stimulus without replacement**
Liam presented multiple stimuli to Gus. When Gus selects an item, it is removed (i.e., not replaced in the array) which reduces the number of stimuli remaining in the array. This type of preference

assessment, known as multiple stimulus without replacement, functions as a process that can be used to establish a preference hierarchy that indicates which stimuli are most preferred, which stimuli are moderately preferred, and which stimuli are least preferred.

178. **A) They conduct assessments that prioritize reinforcement procedures**
Behavior analysts should prioritize reinforcement procedures when designing interventions, but this is a question about their responsibility in assessment. Behavior analysts are to select and design assessments that are consistent with behavioral principles; based on scientific evidence; meet the needs, context, and resources of clients and stakeholders; and focus on maximizing benefits and minimizing risk of harm to clients and stakeholders.

179. **B) Function-based; contingency-independent; contingency-dependent**
Antecedent interventions based on MOs and S^Ds are considered function-based. Those based on MOs are contingency-independent (i.e., do not rely on differential consequences for the target behavior), whereas those based on stimulus control are contingency-dependent (i.e., rely on differential consequences for the target behavior).

180. **B) Records review**
When conducting a records review, historical data about an organizational setting are gathered and analyzed to inform a consultant's understanding of how the organization operates and the environmental variables affecting human behavior. These historical data are in the form of organizational artifacts, such as its strategic plan, organizational structure, job descriptions, products and services, culture, employee expectations, performance over time, and personnel.

181. **C) Avoid these social events and end the potential relationship before it starts. If Toby wants to pursue a relationship, he should wait at least 2 years after services have been discontinued**
Engaging in romantic relationships with current clients is not permitted because such relationships can result in conflicts of interest and impaired judgment. Behavior analysts cannot engage in romantic relationships with former clients for at least 2 years from the date the professional relationship ended.

182. **B) Describe the problem**
The first step in conducting performance diagnostics with an ABC analysis is to describe the problem (undesirable behavior). The remaining steps are to describe what the person should be doing instead (desirable behavior), determine how severe the problem is, complete an ABC analysis for the problem behavior, complete an ABC analysis for the desirable behavior, determine the diagnosis (i.e., summarize the antecedent and consequences), and determine the solution (i.e., add positive/immediate/certain consequences and antecedents for desirable behavior).

183. **A) Aziz neglected to incorporate a skill training component to help Malcolm acquire a functionally equivalent replacement behavior**
Aziz's implementation of a noncontingent schedule of reinforcement is appropriate as an antecedent-based strategy to reduce Malcolm's motivation to engage in exhibitionistic behavior. However, Aziz's intervention plan would have been more effective if he had not neglected to incorporate a skill training component to help Malcolm acquire a functionally equivalent replacement behavior (i.e., a response to garner attention from his fellow retirees without engaging in exhibitionistic behavior that made most members of the community feel uncomfortable).

184. **A) Behavioral skills training**
Behavior analysts utilize behavioral skills training (BST), which include both performance and competency-based training elements, to teach trainees to competently perform intervention procedures with fidelity. BST involves a process of describing the target skill, providing a written description, demonstrating the target skill, requiring the trainee to practice the target skill, and

providing feedback during practice. The last two steps (requiring a trainee to practice the target skill and providing feedback during practice) are repeated until mastery is achieved.

185. **B) "It may be helpful to try sensory integration therapy for addressing the motor skills problems. For the tantrums, however, I would suggest that we begin with a functional assessment."** It's important that behavior analysts respectfully collaborate with other professionals on treatment teams. This includes acknowledging the utility of other professionals' recommendations. However, there is no robust evidence to support sensory integration therapy as a sufficient standalone intervention for problem behaviors. As a behavior analyst, it is necessary to conduct a functional assessment to identify controlling variables and then proceed to design a function-based intervention plan for decreasing the tantrum behavior.

REFERENCE

Baer, D. M., Wolf, M. M., & Risley, T. R. (1968). Some current dimensions of applied behavior analysis. *Journal of Applied Behavior Analysis, 1*(1), 91.

After the Exam

Whether you passed the exam or not, we have some recommendations for you. Read on.

▶ AFTER PASSING THE EXAM: SOME RECOMMENDATIONS

Congratulations! Your hard work has paid off! Passing the Board Certified Behavior Analyst® (BCBA®) exam is a significant accomplishment and major milestone in your career as a behavior analyst.

There's a natural tendency when passing an exam like this to celebrate and then move on without taking a little time to process the experience. However, this can be a missed opportunity. Research suggests that acknowledging and savoring our positive experiences and successes is good for our well-being and resilience in the face of challenges. It took a lot of discipline, hard work, and intelligence to pass this exam. Let that sink in. Recognize and appreciate these positive qualities in yourself. Literally take a minute to reflect on and savor this positive experience. Imagine yourself installing it in your mind and body. Internalize your accomplishment. Life is often challenging; it's not every day that you experience a great success and sense of accomplishment. Enjoy it!

This can also be a good time for reflection. Fortunately, you'll never have to take this exam again; however, there may be other exams or tasks in your future that will require the same level of perseverance and focused effort to be successful. What can you learn from this experience? Consider the factors that fostered your success. Take note of the activities and practices that worked well for you as well as those that did not. What can you take from this experience to improve your performance and productivity in other aspects of your life?

As you move forward in your career as a behavior analyst, it's important to consider how you will continue to develop as a professional. Many behavior analysts find that membership activities through professional associations, attendance at behavior analysis conferences, reading relevant books and materials, and participating in training events function to enhance their skills and continually reinvigorate their passion for the profession.

PROFESSIONAL ASSOCIATIONS

There are many professional associations that offer helpful resources for BCBAs. These include the Behavior Analyst Certification Board® (BACB®), Association for Behavior Analysis International (ABAI), and the Association of Professional Behavior Analysts (APBA), to name a few.

Behavior Analyst Certification Board

The BACB is more than just a website to visit to learn about certification/supervision requirements, apply for your credential, and make reports of ethical violations. The BACB also regularly publishes a newsletter available at www.bacb.com/newsletters containing important information about changes and resources related to obtaining/maintaining certification, conducting supervision, and adhering to Ethics Code requirements. The organization also now offers a podcast available at www.bacb.com/bacb-podcasts that discusses items that are presented in the newsletters, such as:

- Episode 7: The ASD Practice Guidelines
- Episode 10: Addressing Potential Ethics Violations With Others
- Episode 22: Helpful Ethics Resources

Association for Behavior Analysis International

The ABAI has been around for nearly half a century as a membership organization for those interested in the science, application, and teaching of behavior analysis. The organization hosts multiple conferences each year in locations inside and outside of the United States. The ABAI also offers jobs placement services; access to special interest groups; many continuing education (CE) events; and six behavior analysis journals, including:

- *Behavior Analysis in Practice*
- *Behavior and Social Issues*
- *Education and Treatment of Children*
- *Perspectives on Behavior Science*
- *The Analysis of Verbal Behavior*
- *The Psychological Record*

Association of Professional Behavior Analysts

The APBA hosts an annual convention that takes place in a different city each year. Members are given access to several helpful resources including the organization's newsletter, bibliographies of applied research, and materials on professional credentialing and health insurance coverage. The APBA also offers its members discounted subscription rates to several publications, including *Child & Family Behavior Therapy, Journal of Organizational Behavior Management*, and *Journal of Mental Health Research in Intellectual Disabilities*.

Beyond organizations with "behavior analysis" (or a functional equivalent) in the title, there are trade associations that focus on industries that may be relevant to you as a behavior analyst. For the many behavior analysts who work with clients with autism spectrum disorder (ASD), outfits such as the Council of Autism Service Providers (CASP) or the Association for Science in Autism Treatment (ASAT) hold professional conferences and offer resources that may be of interest to you.

PROFESSIONAL CONFERENCES

Attending professional behavior analysis conferences can be a great way to connect with colleagues, grow as a behavior analyst, and obtain mandatory CE for recertification. In addition to the ABAI and APBA, there are numerous behavior analysis organizations that hold professional conferences every year. Many state and regional associations are out there, including affiliated chapters of the ABAI and APBA. In California, we currently have the California Association for Behavior Analysis (CalABA). In Massachusetts, we have the Massachusetts Association for Behavior Analysis (MassABA) and Massachusetts Professionals in Behavior Analysis (BABAT). To start, conduct a web search of behavior analysis association(s) in your area and consider what they can offer you if you elect to become a member.

For behavior analysts who reside outside of the United States or perhaps have a desire to engage in professional association activities in other countries, behavior analysis knows no borders. There are numerous behavior analysis associations present in many parts of the world!

BOOKS

For BCBAs interested in translating their applied behavior analysis (ABA) skills into professional consulting work, Bailey and Burch's *25 Essential Skills & Strategies for the Professional Behavior Analyst: Expert Tips for Maximizing Consulting Effectiveness* is essential reading. In it, the authors teach the essential skills and strategies that foster success when consulting with leadership of human-service organizations and major corporations. The book is organized into five sections, covering essential business skills, basic consulting repertoire, applying your behavioral knowledge, vital work habits, and advanced consulting strategies. Within these sections, a wide range of essential skills is covered, from business etiquette and negotiation to using power effectively and becoming a trusted professional. It's a book BCBAs find themselves returning to again and again.

BCBAs new to the profession often seek resources related to supervision. Kazemi, Rice, and Adzhyan's *Fieldwork and Supervision for Behavior Analysts: A Handbook* serves as a helpful guide to fieldwork and supervision activities. This handbook couples core competencies with case scenarios and offers structured supervision guidelines for facilitating skill acquisition. Britton and Cicoria's *Remote Fieldwork Supervision for BCBA Trainees* is another offering that aims to help prepare behavior analysts to provide high quality supervision and mentoring to trainees, whether it takes place in-person or remotely. In it, the authors offer a clear framework and comprehensive guidance for the BCBA supervisor.

PODCASTS

Inside the BACB Podcast

These days, everyone has a podcast . . . even the BACB! You can find the podcast at www.bacb.com/bacb-podcasts. Episodes typically feature Drs. Melissa Nosik and Jim Carr along with other experts from the field discussing issues of relevance for the BACB and its members. For example, you'll find episodes focused on the role of subject matter experts (SMEs) at the BACB, the history of ethics at the BACB, the ASD Practice Guidelines, myths and misconceptions about examination development, and the Ethics Code for Behavior Analysts.

ABA Inside Track Podcast

This is a weekly podcast hosted by behavior analysts Robert Parry-Cruwys, Diana Parry-Cruwys, and Jackie MacDonald that discusses the latest articles in the field of behavior analysis. Episode guests include leading researchers and practitioners. The organization's aim is to serve as a professional community that helps to keep behavior analysts up-to-date through engaging, informative, and entertaining conversations about everything ABA. There are more than 200 episodes conveniently organized by topic (e.g., ethics, supervision, assessment, treatment, skill building) on their website at www.abainsidetrack.com. Many episodes are centered around discussions of journal articles you'll likely want to read in advance of listening. *ABA Inside Track* is also a source for CE hours, some of which are free. Just listen to the episode (each of which is worth 1 CE credit), note the two secret code words shared during the episode, and then purchase credit for it on their website under the "Get CEUs" tab.

The Behavioral Observations Podcast

This is a popular podcast for behavior analysts hosted by behavior analyst Matt Cicoria who conducts interviews with luminaries in the field. In each episode, an expert guest is invited to discuss a topic of interest, ranging from teaching functional communication and public policy to classroom management and advice on starting a private practice. You can access the podcast through the website at https://behavioralobservations.com or common podcast hosting platforms such as iTunes and Spotify. You can also earn CE credits; listen to certain podcast episodes, take the accompanying quiz to demonstrate that you were listening, and earn a CE certificate. You can also sign up for *The Behavioral Observations Podcast* mailing list, connect with the hosts on Twitter @behaviorpodcast, and participate in their Facebook group at www.facebook.com/behavioralobservations.

Other Podcasts, Including #dobettermovement Podcast, ABA on Call, and Beautiful Humans

There are several other podcasts available that focus on behavior analysis, including *#dobettermovement Podcast* at https://collective.dobettermovement.us that is operated by "a community of like-minded, forward-thinking behavior analysts and professionals, all dedicated and passionate about improving and doing better in the field of ABA therapy." Their episodes cover a wide range of topics that address both practice as well as the critical sociopolitical dimensions of behavior analysis. The *ABA on Call* podcast hosted by behavior analysts Rick Kubina Jr. and Doug Kostewicz is another option that started in 2019 and explores topics in behavior analysis not often found in other podcasts, including the science of behavior and free will, ABA and creativity, future tech and ABA, and debunking ABA myths. And last, but not least, there is *Beautiful Humans: The Social ChangeCast* podcast hosted by behavior analysts Denisha Gingles and Arin Donovan who focus on bridging behavioral science and social justice to address critical social issues, current events, and all forms of oppression. Episodes have addressed topics such as privilege, power, and parenting; discussing systemic racism with children with autism; colonial research practices; and the ABA reform movement.

OPTIONS FOR CONTINUING EDUCATION

There have never been more ways for BCBAs to earn CE credits. Over the course of your career, you'll be presented with myriad opportunities for professional development. Given the ever-expanding proliferation of CE offerings, we recommend that you take time to carefully identify content that is (a) of interest and (b) will further develop your knowledge skills in relevant ways. The BACB's Authorized Continuing Education (ACE) Provider Directory at www.bacb.com/authorized-continuing-education-providers is a great place to search for potential CE providers for behavior analysts.

JOB HUNTING

After years of preparation, you're now a BCBA and ready to apply your knowledge and skills in support of clients. It's time to find a job and launch your career! The good news is that there has never been a better time to be a BCBA. Behavior analysis is used extensively in education, healthcare, animal training, and business management and has been shown to be effective in a wide variety of areas (e.g., parent training, substance abuse treatment, dementia management, brain injury rehabilitation, occupational safety intervention). Over the past two decades, the United States has witnessed significant growth. Between 2010 and 2020, the number of online job postings across a variety of fields and specialties requiring a BCBA, based on 50,000 sources, increased by 4,209 percent! Yowza!

When searching for a job, we recommend that you consider the type of setting, position type, and employer that will be the best fit for you. First, BCBAs work in a variety of settings and learning about the different options (e.g., clinics, schools) and associated advantages/disadvantages can be hugely beneficial. There are also BCBAs who are moving into the growing number of positions in the field of digital behavioral health that offer a combination of in-person and remote support to clients. What setting is best for you? Second, there are many position types. For instance, some BCBAs spend much of their time engaged in clinical work, whereas others are engaged in administration, teaching, research, and so on. There are also BCBAs that do salaried work and BCBAs that do contractual work and understanding how these forms of compensation differ can affect the consistency of your work as well as your bottom line, taxes, and benefits. What type of position is best for you? Third, it's important to look at employer characteristics. When doing this, consider any signs of the organization's commitment to quality and excellence in the field. Given the rapidly changing nature of the field, does the employer support professional development for staff? This can take a variety of forms, such as offering CE credits, giving CE stipends, providing high quality supervision, and enabling participation in professional conferences, training events, research, and other opportunities to enhance and further one's skills and knowledge. Engaging in ongoing professional development will ensure you're implementing best practices and facilitate career advancement. Also keep in mind that professionals these days tend to work for more than one agency and in more than one type of position over the course of their lives. While you may absolutely love one type of work today, it's sometimes difficult to predict what you'll enjoy or the level of compensation or responsibility you'll desire in the future. Put yourself in a position to grow your career, whether that means expanding your role, taking on additional responsibilities, moving into leadership, opening your own practice, or consulting with other organizations.

In addition to the extent to which an employer supports CE for staff, consider whether they (a) take active steps to support ethics and professionalism among staff; (b) have established policies related to health, safety, and emergency preparedness; and (c) support and take steps to promote diversity, equity, and inclusion. If the organization is accredited by the Behavioral Health Center of Excellence (BHCOE), the organization has demonstrated to an accrediting body that it meets standards for clinical and operational quality.

Throughout the job search process, be patient with yourself. It can take time, and everyone's experience is unique. While it may only take a week or less, it could take up to a month or two.

The time it takes to land a job can vary greatly based on how flexible you are on the type of position, whether you're willing to move or commute, how consistently you engage in searching, and your particular location, specialty area, and industry. It's important to remember that factors beyond your control, such as overall economic conditions and the job market, can also impinge on the time it takes to find a job. With optimism, patience, and consistent effort, you're sure to find a job that suits you well!

If you're not getting interviews or you're getting interviews but not the job, this should prompt reflection. Critically evaluate what's working for you and what is not. For instance, if you're getting interviews but not landing the job, it could be helpful to do some mock interviews with a friend or reach out for professional coaching. Perhaps you need to have a closer look at your résumé and to further refine it. Is everything you've shared accurate? Is it free of spelling and grammatical errors? Have you highlighted your achievements and distinguishing qualities?

You may also want to touch base with the people you've asked to serve as a reference to ensure they are able to provide a positive referral. You should contact each reference in advance to let them know that you are applying for jobs and ask if they're able to serve as a supportive reference that will provide positive commentary on your abilities, work ethic, and character. If they're not or seem hesitant, it's best to ask someone else. It's optimal to provide a variety of references that can offer observations of your work in different positions and roles and comment on different aspects of your character. Finally, it can be helpful to give your references a little guidance on the information it will be helpful for them to share.

Fortunately, BCBAs are in great demand, so you have every reason to be optimistic that you will find a position that's a good fit!

WHERE TO LOOK FOR JOBS

Reaching out to your professional network to alert them that you're looking for a job can be one of the most effective ways to find a position. A warm introduction by a colleague to an employer affords a significant advantage for job seekers. There are also a number of online job boards where BCBA job hunters can search for positions, post résumés, and apply for jobs. Recruiters often rely on job boards to source talent. Here are some suggestions to consider.

Association of Professional Behavior Analysts

APBA has an online Career Center filled with helpful resources for job seekers available at https://jobs .apbahome.net/career-resources. In addition to its regularly updated job board, it features guidance on developing a winning resume, preparing for job interviews, negotiating salary, working with recruiters, advancing your career, managing your online presence, and career planning. APBA even provides personalized career coaching (for a fee).

Association for Behavior Analysis International

The ABAI hosts a Career Center at https://careers.abainternational.org where you can search for jobs by position type, location, company, experience, job title, job category, salary, and education. They also offer solid career advice resources, such as articles on conducting a job search, preparing for a job interview, and exploring nontraditional jobs for BCBAs.

State Associations for Behavior Analysis

Numerous state associations for behavior analysis feature job boards on their websites where recruiters can post open positions. For instance, the CalABA hosts a job board at https://calaba.org/career-center/employment-opportunities with daily job postings for employment and internships. Consider taking a look at the website for the state association for behavior analysis where you would consider applying and see if they might be able to provide additional leads for you.

Jobs in Education

If you're interested in pursuing a position in the field of education, EDJOIN is a leading education job site available at www.edjoin.org where you can search for jobs by region, state, and organization. While there are job posts from locations all over the United States, there is a disproportionately large number of them coming from California. If you're more interested in positions in higher education, consider checking out HigherEdJobs at www.higheredjobs.com where you can search for administrative, faculty, and executive positions in colleges and universities across the country.

If you're interested in working in schools around the world, connect with one of the reputable recruiting agencies matching educators with international schools abroad. These agencies hold job fairs and connect job seekers with openings in international schools. Check out International School Services at www.iss.edu, The International Educator at www.tieonline.com, Search Associates at www.searchassociates.com, Educators Overseas at www.educatorsoverseas.com, and Council of International Schools at www.cois.org. Regional school associations also hold job fairs and post job openings in their member schools. Here are a few to look into: Association of International Schools in Africa at https://aisa.or.ke, American International Schools in the Americas at www.amisa.us, and The Association of American Schools of Central America, Colombia, the Caribbean, and Mexico at www.tri-association.org.

Job Boards

There is also a plethora of general job boards used by employers and job hunters alike. Indeed.com is arguably the most well-known and popular job board; however, there are numerous others worth exploring. Google for Jobs at https://jobs.google.com combs the internet to assemble job postings from general job boards as well as websites overseen by small businesses. Employers share open positions on www.ziprecruiter.com, which in turn posts those jobs on myriad other job boards. www.careerbuilder.com is a well-trusted platform for job hunting nationally, while https://craigslist.org is a good place to look for positions in your local area. Other job boards to consider utilizing include https://lensa.com, which leverages artificial intelligence to match job seekers with the most relevant positions, and www.theladders.com, which only features positions with salaries of $100k or more. If you're based in Canada, have a look at https://ca.talent.com/; it began in Canada, so is a good source for positions there, but the platform has a global reach and a robust presence in the United States.

LinkedIn

LinkedIn, available at linkedin.com, is a networking tool for professionals that can serve as a good place to search for jobs and inform others in your professional community that you're looking for a job. You can search for positions and elect to receive notices about openings. Your profile on LinkedIn can also serve as an excellent online résumé; in fact, professionals are increasingly sharing their LinkedIn profile on physical résumés and CVs. You can even use LinkedIn to research potential employers and explore how you or a colleague may already have a connection with the company you could leverage for a warm introduction. If you have a profile on LinkedIn, ensure it is up-to-date and professional. LinkedIn has become an important place to define your professional brand and market your skills. Posting periodically on LinkedIn and responding in a professional manner to relevant posts can be a great way to raise potential employers' awareness. Expect that potential employers will check out your profile on LinkedIn and, perhaps, other social media platforms when considering whether or not to invite you for an interview or hire you.

MyABAJobs

MyABAJobs is a job site for behavior analysis professionals available at https://myabajobs.com where you can search by keywords and location, post a résumé, and subscribe to a weekly job email blast.

The organization also has an active presence on Twitter and Facebook, regularly posting jobs for qualified behavior analysts.

Therapists in Tech

Although primarily focused on psychologists and therapists, *Therapists in Tech* (TNT) is a good resource for behavioral health professionals interested in careers in digital behavioral health (www.therapistsintech .com). TNT also hosts a community for posting jobs, networking, and information-sharing on the *Slack* communication platform.

Many Other Agencies

There are many agencies seeking BCBAs that may only post opportunities on their own website. Consider searching for agencies in the area in which you would like to work using an online search engine or directory listing and visiting the "careers" section of their websites.

PREPARING FOR INTERVIEWS

You've narrowed down the kind of position you would like and the type of setting in which you would like to work, updated your résumé, applied for jobs, and landed some job interviews. Now it's time to put your best foot forward in the interview. A little preparation can go a long way toward facilitating your success.

Take time to study the job description, think about the position, and research the company in advance of the interview. Consider why you think it's a good fit for you and make a list of your reasons. This will facilitate your ability to demonstrate that you are familiar with the position and clearly explain how your skill set and experience align with its requirements. Consider writing out responses to the most likely questions and practice providing answers that are clear and concise. As a rule of thumb, aim to answer questions in under a few minutes. It can also help to have a friend conduct a mock interview so you can practice saying your answers and receive constructive feedback.

Your ability to articulate how your previous work experiences exemplify your skills and prepare you to be successful in the position can set you apart from other applicants. When answering such questions, employ the acronym STAR.

- Situation: Provide a detailed description of a specific situation or task.
- Task: Explain what role you played and the goal of the task or project.
- Action: Describe the actions you performed to successfully address the situation, solve the problem, or complete the task. Focus on the contributions you specifically made to achieve the outcome.
- Result: Describe the result of your actions and how they made a critical contribution to achieving success or a positive outcome.

It's common for potential employers to ask applicants about their résumé, so be familiar with yours. Since you're used to writing SMART goals, use the same approach to provide **S**pecific, **M**easurable, **A**ttainable, **R**elevant, and **T**ime-bound descriptions of your achievements and accomplishments detailed in your résumé. For example, avoid giving a general comment on a previous position you held; instead, articulate how your specific actions in the job drove particular positive results, such as how an intervention you created and delivered enabled a client's improved behavior at school and how this, in turn, generated additional positive outcomes for the student.

Since job interviews often begin with an open invitation for the applicant to introduce themself, you'll want to prepare for this in advance. Remember, the interviewer isn't looking to hear your life story. They just really want you to share a little bit about who you are and why you're interested in and a good fit for the position. So, take this opportunity to briefly introduce yourself and share some background on your training, credentials, and relevant experience. If you wrote a cover letter when applying for the position, you can likely revisit some of the highlights you shared there. Your goal is to share experiences and information about yourself that will transform the interview into a conversation and persuade the interviewer that you're a promising candidate for the position.

It's also rather common for employers to ask applicants to comment on their strengths and weaknesses, so it helps to have an answer ready for this question as well. Aim to craft a response that shares how your specific strengths will facilitate your success in the position's requirements. Turn this into an opportunity to share additional details about how your skills and related experience prepare you to be successful at performing your duties in the role. In terms of skills, consider commenting on your writing, leadership, communication, technological, or organizational abilities. In terms of character, consider emphasizing your initiative, flexibility, honesty, empathy, patience, or ability to build rapport with others. Refrain from describing weaknesses that dissuade the interviewer from hiring you, such as your misanthropy or difficulty meeting deadlines, paying attention, or arriving at work on time. Share a weakness related to a strength, such as how your commitment to doing things well can occasionally impact your work–life balance, or a weakness related to the duties of the position that you're endeavoring to improve, such as practicing managing anxiety when delivering hard news to parents or learning a software program you'll use on the job.

Remember, job interviews are also a time for you to learn more about the position, setting, and company. Employers typically invite applicants to ask questions during the interview, so use this as an opportunity to not only gather the information you need to make an informed decision but also impress the employer by demonstrating you've done your homework and are well prepared for the interview. Come prepared with the questions you have about the job, such as those related to (a) caseload, (b) working hours, (c) workplace culture, and (d) other things that matter to you.

Caseload

Given the high demand for services, it is important for BCBAs to ensure that their caseloads are feasible and, therefore, ethical. If your caseload is too high, it can negatively impact your ability to provide high quality services and potentially result in burnout. To determine appropriate caseload size, consider the complexity and needs of the cases as well as your skill level and availability of support staff.

Possible questions to ask include:

- How many clients can I expect to have on my caseload?
- How many client hours will I be responsible for?
- What is the expected amount of case supervision to be provided?

In addition to asking about how many clients you may carry on your caseload, asking about client hours and amount of case supervision needed is necessary for understanding what your workload will really look like if you take the job. Service delivery hours vary by client; one client may require only a couple hours per week while another requires 40 hours per week. The greater the number of treatment hours needed for a particular case, the more time you will need to dedicate to it. Exactly how much? Well, that depends on the amount of case supervision (i.e., what you do as a BCBA to support the case, including direct and indirect supervision activities) that is to be provided. If you have a client that is receiving 40 hours of treatment per week and your expected case supervision activities is 2 hours for every 10 hours of treatment (i.e., 20% of treatment hours), that equates to 8 hours of work each week for you on that case. And when you do the math, don't forget to consider other time-consuming work-related activities you may need to engage in, such as attending agency meetings, driving, and so on.

For those BCBAs engaged in the treatment of clients with ASD, you can refer to the CASPs' Practice Guidelines for Healthcare Funders and Managers at https://casproviders.org/asd-guidelines for some general recommendations under section 6 on caseload supervision.

Working Hours

BCBAs can provide services to a wide variety of clients. As a result, companies that employ BCBAs are often open as much as possible to be available for their clients. This can mean companies open early in the morning, close late at night, and are open on the weekends. Consequently, it is important to be clear upfront about the company's expectations for working hours, limits on daily working hours, scheduling flexibility, and overtime compensation.

Workplace Culture

We recommend that you ask questions that will help you to assess your goodness-of-fit with the organization. Learn what you can about their values and what they care about, and how all of that translates to how you will operate within and for the organization. Possible questions to ask include:

■ How would you describe the organization's culture?
■ What are the organization's core values?
■ How do you ensure that clients receive high quality care?
■ How do you support the growth and professional development of staff?
■ How do you ensure the quality of care for the clients you serve?
■ Is your organization accredited by the BHCOE?

Other Things That Matter to You

This is about you—finding a job that is a good fit for you. Are there considerations we have not covered that are important to you and will weigh heavily in your assessment of a job's fit for you? What other questions might you have?

Also consider bringing a professional portfolio or binder with your questions written down on a notepad so as not to forget any in the moment.

Get a good night's sleep the day before the interview. On the day of the interview, take time to get yourself centered in a manner that works for you (e.g., exercise, meditation, positive affirmations). Have a nutritious breakfast. Put on professional attire and groom with care. Avoid wearing a fragrance that is too strong. Give yourself ample time to get to the interview on time. While you wait for the interview to begin, focus on taking long, deep breaths and relaxing your shoulders and jaw. Think to yourself: I've got this!

Remember: Sending a tailored thank you note to every interviewer within 24 hours of the interview can go a long way. You can also use the thank you note as an opportunity to briefly reiterate your enthusiasm for the position and your qualifications and share something you learned about the position or the company during the interview. Take time to carefully proofread your note and consider asking someone with strong editing skills to do so as well.

▶ AFTER NOT PASSING THE EXAM: WHAT NOW?

It's disappointing. You immersed yourself in the material and prepared for the exam but didn't pass. It may help to know that you're not alone. Remember, a lot of people *don't* pass it on their first try. According to the most recent testing data published by the BACB, just over one third of first-time examinees need to retake the exam.

But facts and figures can only do so much to soften the hit of a failed attempt at the exam. Failing the exam is failing the exam, and you're likely to experience a range of challenging emotions, ranging from disappointment and sadness to frustration and embarrassment—all of which are completely normal and to be expected. Instead of denying what's going on in your inner world, give yourself permission to feel your feelings and notice your thoughts. Breathe and give yourself time to process the situation.

This is a good time for self-care, and honestly recognizing how you're feeling is the first step. We all cope with challenges differently. Reflect on the strategies you've used in the past to cope with stress and difficulties successfully. What works well for you?

Take a comprehensive approach to self-care that addresses your thoughts, feelings, and behavior.

Bring your attention to the present moment. Deep breathing exercises and tuning into your five senses can be helpful. Focus on what you can control. You can't change the results of the exam, but you can control how you react. It's painful enough that you didn't pass the exam. Don't make it worse by punishing yourself.

BE KIND TO YOURSELF

Our own inner voice can be our harshest critic. Instead of beating yourself up or judging yourself, give yourself grace and support. Practice self-compassion. Think about what you would say to a friend, loved one, or child if they were in your shoes and feeling how you're feeling. Say those kind and comforting words to yourself. Recognize and accept how you're feeling. Instead of criticizing yourself and worrying unnecessarily, tell yourself that you're okay and that it's going to be okay. Think about the things in your life that are going well, that bring you joy, and for which you're grateful. Dr. Kristin Neff, an authority on self-compassion, offers free guided practices and exercises you might like to try on her website https://self-compassion.org/category/exercises/.

PUT THINGS INTO PERSPECTIVE

Remind yourself that it is only an exam. While it may feel like a big deal right now, in the grand scheme of things it's a minor setback that you can overcome. Now is a good time to critically evaluate how you approached preparing for the exam so you don't make the same mistakes twice. What did you do that worked? What didn't work? Which content areas did you know well? Which content areas were you weaker in? Which approaches to studying worked well and which didn't? Which study skills did you not try? Which test-taking strategies did you practice and use? Did they work? Are there test-taking strategies you didn't use?

GIVE YOURSELF PERMISSION TO START AGAIN

Perhaps you found it difficult to put in the time studying that's really required to pass the BCBA Exam. If that's the case, you'll want to consider steps you can take to bring more structure to your exam prep. Using a strategic planner like the one included in Chapter 2 of this book can help you maintain consistency. Consider working with a study buddy or a study group at set times to help hold you accountable to studying. Building in ways to reward yourself for studying consistently can enhance your motivation.

Instead of worrying or engaging in self-blame, take what you can learn from this experience and allow the emotions you're feeling to motivate you. Your best bet is to accept the situation, use problem-solving to devise solutions, build these solutions into your strategic plan, and start moving forward. Believe in yourself! You can do this!

▶ CONCLUSION

In this final chapter, we offered some recommendations on what to do after the exam. For those who passed the exam, we encourage taking time to process the experience, savoring the success and accompanying positive emotions, internalizing the accomplishment, and reflecting on the factors that fostered success. We also encouraged making a professional development plan and shared a number of different options for CE. This chapter also provided sound guidance on job hunting and preparing for job interviews. For those who did not pass the exam, we reminded them that a lot of people don't pass it on their first try, shared some tips on coping with the disappointment and regrouping, encouraged reflection on what to do differently and then to put those solutions into a strategic plan and move forward.

 BIBLIOGRAPHY

Bailey, J. S., & Burch, M. R. (2010). *25 essential skills & strategies for the professional behavior analyst: Expert tips for maximizing consulting effectiveness.* Taylor & Francis.

Behavior Analyst Certification Board. (2020). *Professional and ethical compliance code for behavior analysts.* http://bacb.com/wp-content/uploads/2016/03/160321-compliance-code-english.pdf

Behavior Analyst Certification Board. (2021). *US employment demand for behavior analysts: 2010-2020.* Author.

Britton, L. N., & Cicoria, M. J. (2019). *Remote fieldwork supervision for BCBA® trainees.* Academic Press.

The Council of Autism Service Providers. (2020). *Applied behavior analysis treatment of autism spectrum disorder: Practice guidelines for healthcare funders and managers* (2nd ed.). Author.

Kazemi, E., Rice, B., & Adzhyan, P. (2018). *Fieldwork and supervision for behavior analysts: A handbook.* Springer Publishing Company.

Plantiveau, C., Dounavi, K., & Virués-Ortega, J. (2018). *High levels of burnout among early-career board-certified behavior analysts with low collegial support in the work environment.* European Journal of Behavior Analysis, *19*(2), 195–207. https://doi.org/10.1080/15021149.2018.1438339

Appendix: Glossary of Terms

A

AB design. Experimental design that involves repeated measures taken during a preintervention baseline condition (A) and then again during an intervention condition (B).

ABA design. Reversal design that involves repeated measures taken during an initial baseline condition (A), then an intervention condition (B), and again after returning to the baseline condition (A).

ABAB design. Reversal design that involves an initial baseline phase (A), followed by an intervention phase (B), followed by a withdrawal phase (A), followed by a final intervention phase (B).

ABC design. Experimental design that involves repeated measures taken during a preintervention baseline condition (A), intervention condition (B), and second intervention condition (C).

ABC recording. A type of descriptive assessment in which behavior is viewed as a function of the antecedents that precede it and the consequences that follow it. Continuous ABC recording involves recording occurrences of the target behavior and specified environmental events as they occur. Narrative ABC recording, on the other hand, does not specify environmental events and involves recording only when the target behavior occurs.

Accuracy. The degree to which the observed value approximates the true value.

Analytic. Core dimension of behavior analysis that means control over a target behavior can be demonstrated (i.e., can be turned on and off), evidencing the existence of a functional relationship between the manipulated event and occurrence/nonoccurrence of the target behavior.

Applied. Core dimension of behavior analysis that means the variable of interest is important to an individual and/or society; that is, changes that improve an individual's quality of life (i.e., socially significant behaviors) are targeted.

Applied behavior analysis. A science in which behavior analysts apply techniques derived from the principles of behavior to change behavior (e.g., increase behavior, teach and maintain behavior, reduce problem behavior) and positively enhance socially significant areas (e.g., classroom management, generalization and maintenance of learning, communication). It utilizes experimentation to clearly identify the variables driving changes in behavior, and applies principles derived from the experimental analysis of behavior to change behavior.

Automatic contingencies. Environmental contingencies that can affect behavior without the mediation or deliberate actions of another person.

Automatic negative reinforcement. Termination or postponement (i.e., escape) of aversive stimulation that results directly from the behavior.

Automatic reinforcement. Reinforcement produced by a behavior or physical environment resulting from a behavior.

B

Backward chaining. A method of chaining that starts with the training of the last behavior in the chain before moving to the second to last and so forth, until all the links of the chain are joined and emitted as a single interconnected performance.

Bar graph. A graph that is used to display discrete sets of data (e.g., performance of an individual or group of subjects during different conditions).

Baseline logic. A form of experimental reasoning that calls for prediction (anticipated outcome of an unknown/future measurement), verification (demonstration of a functional relationship between the intervention and target behavior), and replication (repeating of independent variable manipulations and obtaining outcomes similar to that of a previous study).

Behavior. An organism's activity that results in a measurable change in its environment.

Behavioral skills training. An instructional method that involves describing the target skill, providing a written description, demonstrating the target skill, requiring the supervisee to practice the target skill, and providing feedback during practice. The last two steps (requiring the supervisee to practice the target skill and providing feedback during practice) are repeated until mastery is achieved.

Behavior-altering effect. A momentary increase or decrease in the frequency of a behavior that has been reinforced or punished by the stimulus whose value has been changed by the motivating operation.

Behavioral. Core dimension of behavior analysis that means that a study or intervention analyzes observable and measurable behavior in a precise and objective manner.

Behavior-change goals. The product of goal-setting, which involves establishing criteria for behavior change after identification of a socially significant target behavior.

Behaviorism. A philosophy of the science of behavior and its various forms. It assumes that a science of behavior is possible, and that behavior can be studied and changed in a manner similar to other sciences (e.g., biology). Behaviorism primarily looks to causes in the external environment for explanations of behavior. As an intervention, behaviorism holds that it is often most effective to organize the environment in such a way that certain behaviors are more or less likely.

C

Chaining. A process of linking specific sequences of stimuli and behaviors. Chaining is used to teach more complex behaviors that are to occur as a single interconnected performance. There are several methods, including forward chaining, total-task chaining, backward chaining, and backward chaining with lead aheads.

Changing criterion design. Experimental design in which the initial baseline phase is followed by a series of intervention phases with successive/gradual criteria for change.

Checklist. An indirect measure that lists specific behaviors with a description of the conditions under which each behavior will occur.

Codic. Verbal operant that is under the control of a verbal stimulus without point-to-point correspondence but with formal similarity, and has a history of generalized reinforcement. Codics include textual and dictation types.

Collaborative teaming. A process for collaborating with others to serve clients. Collaborative teaming strategies include developing and using a shared language, employing the same data collection process, displaying results in an understandable way, and working together to develop and implement a behavior-change program.

Comparative analysis. A type of analysis that compares two or more distinct interventions (e.g., multielement experimental designs).

Component analysis. A type of analysis that evaluates the relative contributions of the parts of an intervention. A drop-out component analysis involves implementing an intervention and then systematically removing parts of it, whereas an add-in component analysis involves systematically assessing parts individually or together before implementing the intervention.

Compound schedules of reinforcement. Schedules used for investigating a single response in which two or more schedules of reinforcement alternate, appear in succession, or occur at the same time. As such, a compound schedule consists of two or more types of schedules of reinforcement. Compound schedules include concurrent schedules, discriminative schedules, nondiscriminative schedules, and schedules combining the number of responses and time.

Conceptually systematic. Core dimension of behavior analysis that means all the interventions or procedures are grounded in the basic behavioral principles of behavior analysis in a manner that fosters integration and systematic expansion of the procedures.

Conditional discrimination. Emission of a differential response that is controlled by a single stimulus when it is in the presence of another stimulus.

Conditioned motivating operation. Motivating operation that requires learning to produce value-altering and behavior-altering effects. Conditioned motivating operations include surrogate, reflexive, and transitive types.

Conditioned motivating operation reflexive. Stimulus that has acquired its effects as a motivating operation as a result of it preceding the onset of unpleasant/painful stimulation.

Conditioned motivating operation surrogate. Stimulus that has acquired its effects as a motivating operation as a result of being paired with an unconditioned motivating operation.

Conditioned motivating operation transitive. Stimulus that establishes or abolishes the reinforcing or punishing value of another stimulus.

Conditioned punisher. Stimulus change that decreases the future frequency of the behavior that it immediately follows as a result of its previous pairing with one or more other punishers. It is the product of ontogeny.

Conditioned reinforcer. Stimulus change that increases the future frequency of the behavior that it immediately follows as a result of its previous pairing with one or more other reinforcers. It is the product of ontogeny, varies across individuals, and changes throughout the individual's lifespan.

Contingency contracting. A procedure involving the establishment of a document that specifies a contingent relationship between the completion of a specific task and access to a specified reinforcer. The contingency contract should provide a detailed description of the task and all relevant rules and describe the reward to be provided upon completion of the specific behavior.

Contingency-shaped behavior. Behavior that is learned through experience with contingencies.

Continuous reinforcement schedule. Schedule of reinforcement that requires the delivery of reinforcement after every occurrence of a target behavior.

Control. Level of scientific understanding derived from the discovery of functional relations in controlled experiments that demonstrate that a specific change to one event (independent variable) reliably produces a specific change in another event (dependent variable).

Criterion-referenced measure. A direct measure that evaluates a client's performance against some predetermined standard.

Cumulative record. A graph that is used to display the running total of responses over time. The cumulative total is represented on the vertical axis.

Curriculum-based measure. A direct, criterion-referenced measure that is used to evaluate performance on tasks that a client performs as part of planned instruction.

D

Dependent variable. The target behavior that an intervention is designed to change.

Derived stimulus relations. Emergence of untrained responses indicating a relation (e.g., the same as, opposite of, different from, better than) between two or more stimuli following a history of related instruction or experience. The properties of equivalence are derived from the logical relations of reflexivity, symmetry, and transitivity.

Description. Level of scientific understanding derived from systematic observations which enable us to describe events in quantifiable terms that can be examined for possible interactions with other known facts.

Descriptive assessment. A method of assessment involving direct observation of the target behavior in relation to other events under naturally occurring conditions. Descriptive assessments include continuous ABC recording, narrative ABC recording, and scatterplot recording.

Determinism. Attitude of science that assumes the universe is rational, governed by discoverable laws, and that events are completely determined by previously existing causes. As a result, all behavior possesses an identifiable cause and is thus predictable and to some degree determinable.

Differential reinforcement. Reinforcing specific responses and placing all others on extinction.

Differential reinforcement of alternative behavior. A differential reinforcement procedure that involves reinforcing a targeted alternative behavior for the problem behavior and withholding reinforcement for the problem behavior.

Differential reinforcement of incompatible behavior. A differential reinforcement procedure that involves reinforcing behaviors that are incompatible with the problem behavior and withholding reinforcement for the problem behavior.

Differential reinforcement of low rate behavior. A differential reinforcement procedure that involves providing reinforcement when the targeted behavior occurs below a predetermined criterion.

Differential reinforcement of other behavior. A differential reinforcement procedure that involves providing reinforcement when the problem behavior is absent for a predetermined amount of time and withholding reinforcement for the problem behavior.

Dimensions of applied behavior analysis. The core dimensions of behavior analysis, including applied, behavioral, analytic, technological, conceptually systematic, effective, and generality.

Dimensional quantities. Features of behavior that can be measured. Dimensional quantities include repeatability, temporal extent, and temporal locus.

Direct assessment. A method of assessment to discover the skill strengths and deficits of a client. Direct assessment involves the use of direct measures.

Direct measure. A measure that involves an observer recording the target behavior as it occurs. Direct measures include standardized tests, criterion-referenced measures, curriculum-based measures, and direct observation.

Discrete-trial teaching arrangement. An instructional procedure that breaks down behavior into discrete steps (i.e., learning trials) with a clear beginning, middle, and end. Trials are repeated with the client receiving reinforcement for correct responding.

Discrimination. Emission of a differential response when presented with two or more stimuli.

Discriminative stimulus. A stimulus that, when present, signals that a particular behavior is likely (or not) to be reinforced.

Duplic. Verbal operant that is under the control of a verbal stimulus with point-to-point correspondence (i.e., stimulus parts correspond with response parts), formal similarity (i.e., stimulus and response physically resemble each other), and has a history of generalized reinforcement. Duplics include echoics, mimetics, and copying text.

Duration. The length of time that behavior occupies; time elapsed between the onset and offset of the behavior.

E

Educational records. Data related to the client's education (e.g., transcripts, academic program, and disciplinary file). Educational records may contain documents that evidence the use of behavioral interventions and include functional assessment reports, behavior intervention plans, and progress monitoring data.

Effective. Core dimension of behavior analysis that means the intervention has altered the target behavior to a significant degree, is meaningful or socially important, and promotes long-term positive changes in the client.

Empiricism. Attitude of science that requires the practice of objective observation of an event of interest. Systematic measurement and accurate quantification are empirical methods used to develop scientific knowledge.

Equal-interval graph. A graph with both the vertical and horizontal axes divided into equal distances between marks to indicate the addition or subtraction of constant amounts. Equal-interval graphs include line graphs, bar graphs, cumulative records, and scatterplots.

Equivalence-based instruction. The process of forming equivalence classes (i.e., interchangeability between stimuli), which can be taught using matching-to-sample procedures with a minimum of two interrelated conditional discriminations.

Event recording. Recording the number of times that a behavior occurs.

Experimental analysis of behavior. A natural science approach to research that defines and clarifies the basic processes and principles of behavior. It was founded by B. F. Skinner with the publication of *The Behavior of Organisms* in 1938, which identified two types of behavior (operant and respondent). The operant three-term contingency is the primary unit of analysis. It is primarily a laboratory-based experimental approach that established the foundational principles of operant behavior.

Experimentation. Attitude of science that requires investigation to determine whether a functional relation exists between events. In an experiment, the independent variable is systematically controlled and manipulated to clarify its effects on the dependent variable.

External validity. The degree to which the results of the intervention (i.e., functional relationship demonstrated in an experiment) can be generalized to other behaviors, environments, and individuals/ populations.

Extinction. Removal of reinforcement for a behavior.

F

Free-operant observation. A type of stimulus preference assessment that involves observing and recording the length of time (i.e., duration) that a client approaches, contacts, or engages with the stimuli when they are "free" to emit any responses. Free-operant observations can be contrived (with prearrangement of the environment to include items/activities the client may like) or naturalistic (without an prearrangement of the environment prior to observing).

Free-operant teaching arrangement. An instructional arrangement that allows for the client to freely emit one or more responses. A discriminative stimulus is sometimes present but not required. Reinforcement is not specifically programmed but the client may engage in responses that produce reinforcement continuously or intermittently.

Frequency. Count of a behavior or behavior class. Frequency is calculated by adding up the number of occurrences.

Fixed interval. Schedule that specifies the duration that must pass before the first occurrence of a target response will be reinforced.

Fixed ratio. Schedule that specifies the number of times a target behavior must occur to receive reinforcement.

Forward chaining. A method of chaining that starts with the training of the first behavior in the chain before moving to the second and so forth, until all the links of the chain are joined and emitted as a single interconnected performance.

Functional analysis. A type of functional assessment that involves the manipulation of antecedents and/ or consequences to observe and measure their separate effects on problem behavior. There are multiple types, including the basic functional analysis, brief functional analysis (BFA), trial-based functional analysis (TBFA), interview-informed synthesized contingency analysis (IISCA), latency-based functional analysis (LBFA), and functional analysis of precursor behavior.

Functional assessment. A variety of methods used to gather data related to the cause (i.e., function) of a problem behavior. Functional assessments can include functional analyses, descriptive assessments, and indirect assessments.

Functional communication training. A contingency-independent antecedent intervention that involves the use of differential reinforcement of alternative behavior to teach communicative responses that compete with problem behaviors evoked by a motivating operation.

Functional response class. Group of responses defined by their function (i.e., the outcome they produce in the environment).

G

Generality. Core dimension of behavior analysis that means a change in behavior holds over time, across different settings, and/or spreads to other relevant and related behaviors.

Generalization. Spreading of the effects of some operation (e.g., reinforcement, punishment, or extinction) on one stimulus to other, different stimuli.

Generalized punisher. Conditioned punisher that has been paired with many other punishers.

Generalized reinforcer. Conditioned reinforcer that has been paired with many other reinforcers.

Group contingency. A contingency in which reinforcement for the entire group is dependent on an individual (dependent group contingency), a set of members drawn from the larger group (independent group contingency), or each member of the whole group (interdependent group contingency) achieving a performance criterion.

Group experimental design. Research design in which the analysis is conducted at the level of the group, not the individual.

H

High-probability request sequence. A contingency-independent antecedent intervention that involves presenting a series of simple requests followed by a target request.

Historical records. Data related to the client's history that may be learned through the review of many different possible types of records available.

I

Imitation training. Process for teaching imitative responses. Imitation training includes preassessment, training, postassessment, and probes for imitative behavior.

Independent variable. The intervention that is used to intervene on the dependent variable (i.e., target behavior). In an experiment, this is systematically manipulated to determine if alterations to it will produce reliable alterations in the dependent variable.

Indirect assessment. A method of assessment to discover the skill strengths and deficits of a client. Indirect assessment involves the use of indirect measures.

Indirect measure. A measure that does not involve direct observation but requires the client or others to recall and report information about the target behavior. Indirect measures include interviews, checklists, and rating scales.

Instruction. A verbal discriminative stimulus that specifies the response and contingency in a rule statement. It is often viewed as an instance of a rule.

Intermittent schedule of reinforcement. Schedule of reinforcement that does not involve reinforcing every occurrence of a target behavior. Intermittent schedules of reinforcement include fixed ratio schedules (with the exception of FR1), fixed interval schedules, variable ratio schedules, and variable interval schedules.

Internal validity. The degree to which the changes in the dependent variable (i.e., target behavior) can be attributed to the manipulation of the independent variable (i.e., intervention) and not the result of uncontrolled/extraneous factors.

Interresponse time. The length of time between two responses; time elapsed between the onset of one response to the onset of the next response.

Interval recording (or time sampling). Collection of procedures for observing and recording behavior, including whole interval recording, partial interval recording, and momentary time sampling.

Intraverbal. Verbal operant that is under the control of a verbal stimulus without point-to-point correspondence and has a history of generalized reinforcement.

Interview. An indirect measure that involves meeting with significant others to obtain relevant information about a behavior of interest.

L

Latency. The length of time from the onset of a stimulus (e.g., verbal instruction, cue) to the initiation of a behavior.

Level. Position along the vertical axis where a series of data points converge.

Line graph. A graph based on the Cartesian plane (i.e., two perpendicular number lines) that is used to display change over time as a series of connected data points. Each data point represents a relationship between some dimensional quantity of behavior (i.e., dependent variable) and time and/or environmental condition (i.e., independent variable).

M

Magnitude. Intensity of the behavior.

Maintenance. The degree to which a client continues to perform a behavior when some or all of an intervention that evokes it has been removed.

Mand. Verbal operant that is under the control of a motivating operation and has a history of specific reinforcement.

Matching-to-sample. A discrete-trial procedure that starts with the client making a response to the sample stimulus (i.e., conditional sample). The sample stimulus may or may not be removed before presenting the comparison stimuli, one of which matches with the conditional sample. When the client selects the comparison stimulus that matches with the sample stimulus, reinforcement is delivered.

Medical records. Data related to the client's health (e.g., clinical findings, diagnostic test results, care plans, medication).

Model. An antecedent stimulus presented to evoke an imitative response. Models can be planned (i.e., prearranged) or unplanned (i.e., antecedent stimuli that occur in everyday social interactions).

Momentary time sampling. Recording procedure in which, at the end of each interval, the target behavior is recorded as having occurred if it occurred at only at the end of the interval. Momentary time sampling may over- or underestimate the occurrence of the behavior when intervals exceed 2 minutes.

Monitoring client progress. Process for tracking and evaluating responsiveness to intervention as evidenced by behavior change over time. Steps to monitoring client progress include operationalizing the behavior, developing a progress monitoring plan, selecting a measurement system, collecting baseline data and defining goals, setting intervention goals, collecting progress monitoring data, analyzing/summarizing/visually presenting the data, and evaluating/utilizing data for decision-making.

Motivating operation. An environmental variable that produces value-altering and behavior-altering effects.

Multielement design. Experimental design that involves delivering and measuring effects of two or more interventions in a rapid, alternating fashion. The design can be used to compare the effects of different interventions or the effects of an intervention with no intervention (i.e., baseline).

Multiple baseline design. Experimental design that involves establishing two or more independent baselines and introducing the intervention in a staggered fashion for each baseline. This design can be used to compare responding across different behaviors for a client, a behavior across different clients, or a behavior across different settings.

Multiple stimulus preference assessment. A type of stimulus preference assessment involving the presentation of an array of three or more stimuli at a time. Multiple stimulus preference assessments include multiple stimulus without replacement (MSWO) and multiple stimulus with replacement (MSW).

N

Naturalistic teaching arrangement. An instructional approach that uses procedures recommended for programming of generalization to promote the development of verbal behaviors. There are a variety of naturalistic teaching approaches available which tend to be described as loosely structured with no planned order of instruction. Activities are chosen and paced by the client, and loose shaping contingencies are used to reinforce desirable behaviors.

Negative punishment. Removal (or reduction in intensity) of a stimulus immediately following a behavior, which decreases the future frequency of the behavior.

Negative reinforcement. Removal (or reduction in intensity) of a stimulus immediately following a behavior that serves to increase the future frequency of the behavior.

Noncontingent reinforcement. A contingency-independent antecedent intervention that involves delivering reinforcement on a fixed or variable interval schedule.

O

Ontogeny. How an individual's behavior develops over its lifetime based on their experiences with the environment.

Operant extinction. Reduction in behavior resulting from the discontinuation of reinforcement for it.

Operant conditioning. Type of learning that occurs as a result of rewards and punishments. This concerns operant behavior, which is behavior we have control over. Operant behavior is modified by its history of consequences, which can be reinforcing (thereby increasing the frequency of a behavior) or punishing (thereby decreasing the frequency of a behavior).

Operational definition. Objective, clear, and complete description of an observable and measurable target behavior.

P

Paired stimulus preference assessment. A type of stimulus preference assessment involving the presentation of two target stimuli at a time. Each stimulus is randomly paired with all other stimuli, but every possible pair must be presented. The client's selection between the two target stimuli presented at each trial is recorded.

Parametric analysis. A type of analysis that compares different levels of an intervention. It involves examining the effects generated by manipulating one or more dimensions/levels of the intervention.

Parsimony. Attitude of science that suggests that an explanation of a thing or event ought to be based on the fewest possible assumptions or unobservable constructs. It encourages scientists to prefer the simplest, logical explanation supported by experiments or reason.

Partial interval recording. Recording procedure in which, at the end of each interval, the target behavior is recorded as having occurred if it occurred at any time during the interval. Partial interval recording usually overestimates the total duration of the behavior but may underestimate the rate of high-frequency behaviors.

Percentage. A ratio expressed as a fraction of 100. This is calculated by multiplying the numeric value (e.g., count of a response divided by the total number of responses or opportunities/intervals in which it could have occurred) by 100.

Philosophic doubt. Attitude of science that assumes scientific knowledge is tentative and continually developing. Consequently, scientists remain skeptical about the validity and truthfulness of all scientific knowledge and open to modifying their beliefs based on new knowledge and discoveries.

Phylogeny. How a species' behavior has evolved over evolutionary time as it slowly makes changes necessary for survival.

Positive punishment. Presentation (or increase in intensity) of a stimulus immediately following a behavior, which decreases the future frequency of the behavior.

Positive reinforcement. Presentation (or increase in intensity) of a stimulus immediately subsequent to a behavior that serves to increase the future frequency of the behavior.

Prediction. Level of scientific understanding derived from repeated observations that demonstrate that two events systematically covary (i.e., correlate).

Product measure. A measure of behavior through examination of its effects produced on the environment. Measurement takes place after the occurrence of the behavior.

Professional practice. A domain of behavior analysis that is guided by the science of behavior analysis and involves delivering behavior analytic services to human subjects grounded in the principles of behaviorism, research from the EAB, and ABA. It is a hybrid discipline informed by various mental health fields, education, communication disorders, physical therapy and criminal justice.

Progressive schedules of reinforcement. Schedules in which each successive reinforcement opportunity is thinned regardless of a person's behavior.

Punisher. Stimulus change that decreases the future frequency of the behavior that it immediately follows.

Punishment. Basic principle that describes a functional relationship in which a behavior immediately followed by a stimulus change (i.e., consequence) decreases the future frequency of the behavior.

R

Radical behaviorism. Conceptual system developed by B. F. Skinner that seeks to understand behavior in all its forms and collapses the distinction between private events (i.e., thoughts and feelings) and public events (i.e., behavior that is observable and measurable). It assumes all behaviors are influenced by the same kinds of variables and result from an individual's experiences and environments.

Rate. Count of behavior or behavior class per unit of time (e.g., per minute/hour/day). Rate is calculated by dividing the number of occurrences by the unit of time in which observations were conducted.

Rating scale. An indirect measure that lists items that a respondent can rate on a numerical or ordinal scale.

Reflexivity. Stimulus–stimulus relation is indicated in the selection of a comparison stimulus that matches the sample stimulus (e.g., A = A) without training to do so.

Reinforcement. Basic principle that describes a functional relationship in which a behavior immediately followed by a stimulus change (i.e., consequence) increases the future frequency of the behavior.

Reinforcer. Stimulus change that increases the future frequency of the behavior that it immediately follows.

Reliability. The degree to which the measure will produce consistent results.

Repeatability. The concept that behavior can be counted as it repeats across time. Measures based on repeatability include count, rate, and celeration.

Replication. Attitude of science that requires that experiments be repeated to determine the reliability of results. The validity, reliability, and usefulness of scientific findings are increased when experiments are reproduced, and the basic pattern of results is replicated numerous times.

Respondent conditioning. Type of learning whereby new stimuli develop the capacity to elicit responses through the pairing process. Respondent conditioning focuses on responses that are inborn, automatic, and involuntary. Pavlov, with whom this type of learning is most associated, focused on the connections between stimuli and responses (i.e., reflexes).

Response. A specific instance (i.e., occurrence) of behavior.

Response class. Group of responses defined by its form or function.

Response generalization. The degree to which a client emits an untrained response that serves the same function as the trained target behavior.

Response prompt. Antecedent stimulus that operates directly on the response (e.g., modeling, physical guidance, and verbal instructions) to assist the client in the emission of a target response. Response prompts include prompt delay (constant and progressive), system of least-to-most, system of most-to-least, and graduated guidance.

Reversal design. Experimental design that demonstrates the effect of an intervention by alternating its presentation and removal over time. ABA and ABAB designs are reversal designs.

Rule. Verbal antecedent that is in the form of a simple request or instruction, or describes a behavioral contingency.

Rule-governed behavior. Behavior that is under the control of verbal antecedents that are considered rules.

S

Scatterplot. A graph that is used to display the relationship between the variables depicted by the horizontal x and vertical y axes. The data points do not form a data path, but they can form patterns on the plane that suggest certain relationships.

Scatterplot recording. A type of descriptive assessment that involves recording when the target behavior occurs. Time is divided into shorter intervals and different marks are made on the observation form to indicate the extent to which the behavior occurred for each time interval.

Schedule of differential reinforcement. Schedules in which reinforcement is made contingent upon responses occurring at a predetermined rate of responding.

Schedule of reinforcement. Rule or protocol that specifies the requirements for reinforcement.

Selectionism. Attitude of science that assumes behavior is selected to continue or to be extinguished based on an individual's experiences and the consequences of their behavior. The environment affects living things through selectionism at the individual level (ontogeny) and the species level (phylogeny).

Self-instruction. Overt or covert prompting of desired behaviors and guiding oneself through a behavior chain or sequence of tasks.

Self-management. This refers to the personal application of behavior change tactics to produce a desired change in behavior. There are a variety of approaches to self-management that differ in the degree to which they emphasize antecedents or consequences for the behavior targeted for change.

Self-monitoring. This involves observing and recording one's own behavior. Self-monitoring is often taught in conjunction with self-management strategies.

Semilogarithmic chart. A graph that has a horizontal x axis that is divided into equal distances between marks, but the vertical y axis uses a logarithmic scale.

Setting/situation generalization. The degree to which a client emits a trained response in a setting that is different from where it was trained.

Shaping. A process of establishing a target response that involves the use of differential reinforcement for a progression of responses that are more like the target response (i.e., successive approximations of a terminal behavior).

Simple discrimination. Emission of a differential response that is controlled by a single stimulus.

Single stimulus preference assessment. A type of stimulus preference assessment involving the presentation of target stimuli one at a time in random order. Each item is presented several times, and the client's response to each item is recorded.

Single-subject experimental design. Research design used to determine whether changes in the independent variable are driving changes in the dependent variable. In single-subject experimental designs, the subject is the unity of intervention and data analysis, the subject provides its own control for comparison, and the target behavior is measured repeatedly across different levels or conditions of the intervention.

Social positive reinforcement. Reinforcing reactions from others (i.e., attention).

Socially mediated contingencies. Environmental contingencies that can affect behavior with the mediation or deliberate actions of another person. Behavior analysts have primarily focused on socially mediated reinforcement.

Socially mediated reinforcement. Reinforcement produced by the actions of another person resulting from a behavior.

Social negative reinforcement. Termination or postponement (i.e., escape) of unwanted interactions with others as well as unpleasant tasks/activities.

Social validity. This refers to the degree to which targeted behaviors are appropriate, procedures are acceptable, and behavioral outcomes are meaningful.

Standard celeration chart. A graph that is primarily used to display the fluency and accuracy of a target behavior. The vertical y axis uses a logarithmic scale that allows us to record data points representing .001 to 1,000 times per minute.

Standardized test. A direct assessment measure with specific procedures that must be followed for its administration.

Stimulus. An event that affects the behavior of an individual. It involves a change in energy that affects a living organism through one or more of its sense organs.

Stimulus class. Cluster of stimuli with shared formal, temporal, and/or functional elements (i.e., physical features, timing of occurrence in relation to a behavior of interest, and/or effect on behavior).

Stimulus control. Alteration of the frequency, duration, latency, or magnitude of behavior by the presence or absence of an antecedent stimulus. This is established when a response is only reinforced when a specific stimulus is present, and not reinforced when other stimuli are present.

Stimulus generalization. The degree to which a client emits a trained response in the presence of a stimulus that is physically similar to the stimulus that was used to train it.

Stimulus prompt. An antecedent stimulus that operates directly on the antecedent task stimulus (e.g., movement, positioning, redundancy) to assist the client in the emission of a target response. Stimulus prompts include stimulus shaping (gradually altering the form/topography of a stimulus until it eventually resembles the target criterion) and stimulus fading (making some feature of a target stimulus more salient, and then gradually fading it).

Symmetry. Stimulus–stimulus relation is indicated in the demonstration of reversibility of a sample stimulus and comparison stimulus (e.g., if A = B, then B = A) without training to do so.

T

Tact. Verbal operant that is under the control of a nonverbal stimulus and has a history of specific reinforcement.

Tangible reinforcement. Reinforcing materials or other stimuli.

Task analysis. Systematic process of breaking down a complex behavior into smaller, more manageable components in order to better understand and target the behavior for change. It facilitates clear and measurable goals, effective interventions, and identification of barriers to treatment.

Technological. Core dimension of behavior analysis that means all procedures of an intervention are clearly detailed and described and that data and results of an experiment or study are clearly presented in an understandable and replicable manner.

Temporal extent. The concept that behavior can be timed as it occurs during some amount of time. The measure of duration is based on temporal extent.

Temporal locus. The concept that the timing of behavior can be measured as it occurs at a certain point in time with respect to other events. Measures based on temporal locus include latency and interresponse time.

Time sampling (or interval recording). Collection of procedures for observing and recording behavior, including whole interval recording, partial interval recording, and momentary time sampling.

Timing. Recording the passage of time with the use of a timing device (e.g., stopwatch).

Token economy. A behavior change system characterized by a set of contingencies that specify how tokens are earned/distributed and exchanged for reinforcers. It has three core components, including a list of target behaviors to be reinforced, a generalized conditioned reinforcer, and a menu of backup reinforcers.

Topography. Physical form of the behavior.

Topographical response class. Group of responses defined by their form (i.e., what they look like).

Total-task chaining. A method of chaining that calls for the provision of training on each behavior in the chain during every training session until the client performs it competently.

Transitivity. Stimulus–stimulus relation is indicated in the demonstration of a derived stimulus–stimulus relation following the training of two other stimulus–stimulus relations (e.g., if A = B and B = C, then A = C and C = A).

Treatment integrity. The degree to which an intervention is implemented as designed.

Trend. Direction of a series of data points.

Trials to criterion. A measure of the number of response opportunities (i.e., trials) required to achieve a predetermined level of performance (i.e., mastery criterion). Trials to criterion data can be reported in terms of count, rate, duration, or latency.

U

Unconditioned motivating operation. A motivating operation that does not require learning to produce value-altering and behavior-altering effects.

Unconditioned punisher. Stimulus change that decreases the future frequency of any behavior that it immediately follows independent of the individual's learning history. It is the product of phylogeny and is naturally undesirable.

Unconditioned reinforcer. Stimulus change that increases the future frequency of the behavior that it immediately follows independent of the individual's learning history. It is the product of phylogeny and satisfies the basic life needs of an organism.

V

Validity. The degree which we are measuring what we intend to measure. Valid measurement requires that a socially significant behavior is directly measured, its relevant dimension for answering the question is measured, and the data represent its occurrence under relevant conditions for answering the question.

Value-altering effect. A momentary increase or decrease in the reinforcing effects of a stimulus.

Variability. The amount of discrepancy between the values of a series of data points.

Variable interval. Schedule that specifies the average duration that must pass before the first occurrence of a target response will be reinforced.

Variable ratio. Schedule that specifies the average number of times a target behavior must occur to receive reinforcement.

Verbal operants. Types of expressive language (i.e., verbal behavior), which include duplics, mands, tacts, intraverbals, and codics.

W

Whole interval recording. Recording procedure in which, at the end of each interval, the target behavior is recorded as having occurred if it occurred throughout the entire interval. Whole interval recording usually underestimates the occurrence of the behavior.

Index